People and Stories in Ancient History:
A HISTORICAL ANTHOLOGY

Ballard & Tighe

Brea, California

AUTHORS

Gregory Blanch, Ph.D., received a bachelor of arts degree in history from The Ohio State University and a master's degree in education from California State Polytechnic University. He earned his doctorate from the Claremont Graduate University. He is the co-author of *Explore World History*, 2nd ed.

Roberta Stathis, Ph.D., received a bachelor of arts degree in anthropology and social sciences and a master's degree in education from California State University, San Bernardino. She earned her doctorate from the Claremont Graduate University. She is the co-author of *Explore World History*, 2nd ed.

CONTRIBUTING WRITERS

Christopher Fish, M.A.
Kevin Adkins, M.F.A.
Patrice Gotsch, M.A.T.

GENERAL HISTORICAL EDITOR

Cheryl A. Riggs, Ph.D., is professor and chair of the history department at California State University, San Bernardino.

*For our nieces and nephews old and young,
our godsons and goddaughters near and far,
and especially for Ethan.*

People and Stories in Ancient History:
A HISTORICAL ANTHOLOGY

An IDEA® Content Resource from Ballard & Tighe
MANAGING EDITOR: Patrice Gotsch
EDITOR: Rebecca Ratnam
ART DIRECTOR: Philip Malcolm
EDITORIAL STAFF: Kristin Belsher, Linda Mammano, Nina Chun
PRINTING COORDINATORS: Danielle Arreola and Cathy Sanchez

2005 Printing
ISBN 1-55501-651-0   Catalog #2-862

Brea, California • (800) 321-4332 • www.ballard-tighe.com

Table of CONTENTS

ABOUT THE BOOK

People and Stories in Ancient History: A Historical Anthology chronicles events and people involved in ancient history from prehistoric times to the fall of the Roman Empire. You will read about real people—archaeologists, rulers, pharaohs, kings, emperors, philosophers, poets, and religious leaders—who shaped the world we live in today. You will learn about these people by reading excerpts from letters, stone monuments, books, literature, and speeches. Here are some of the people you will meet:

Hammurabi, the first ruler in history to produce a code of written laws

Julius Caesar, perhaps one of the greatest leaders of ancient Rome

Hatshepsut, the first female to call herself pharaoh

Cleopatra, the Egyptian queen who dreamed of ruling the world

Buddha, the founder of Buddhism

Alexander the Great, the Macedonian king who conquered Persia

You also will read about compelling events in ancient history, including:
- How early humans transitioned from hunter-gatherers to farmers
- The building of the Great Wall of China
- The rise of democracy in ancient Greece
- The founding of the Roman Republic

Most readings will have the following features:

Key dates you will learn about in the reading

A picture of the person, place, or event you are reading about

A map that shows you where the events you are reading about took place

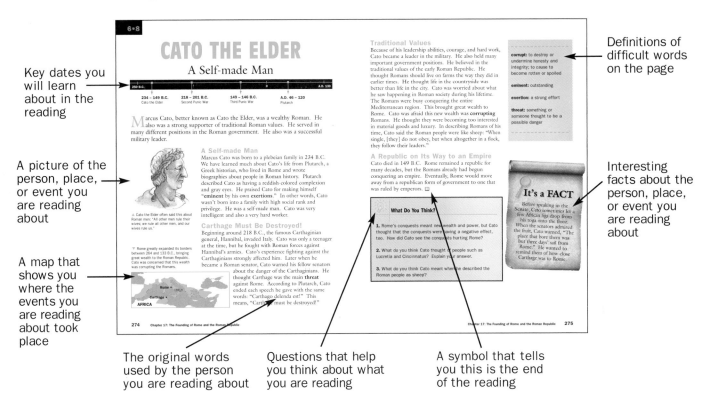

The original words used by the person you are reading about

Questions that help you think about what you are reading

A symbol that tells you this is the end of the reading

Definitions of difficult words on the page

Interesting facts about the person, place, or event you are reading about

Some readings are designed to help you analyze excerpts of historical writings. Here is an example of one primary source reading:

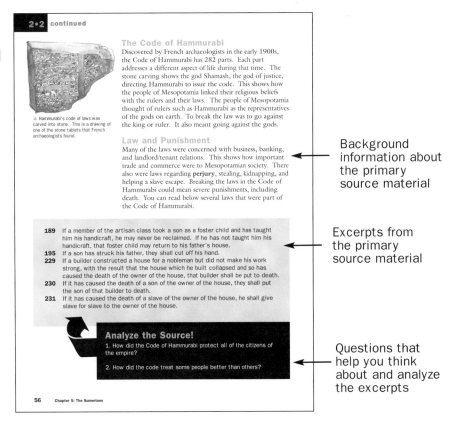

Background information about the primary source material

Excerpts from the primary source material

Questions that help you think about and analyze the excerpts

THE QUEST FOR ANCIENT TREASURE

The Beginnings of Archaeology

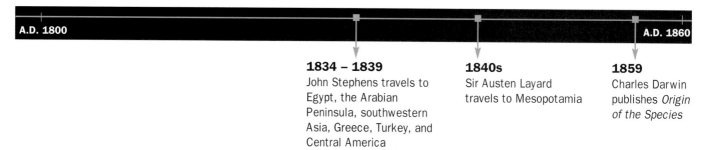

A.D. 1800 | | | **A.D. 1860**

1834 – 1839
John Stephens travels to Egypt, the Arabian Peninsula, southwestern Asia, Greece, Turkey, and Central America

1840s
Sir Austen Layard travels to Mesopotamia

1859
Charles Darwin publishes *Origin of the Species*

We know that people lived in prehistoric times—the time before writing was invented. The clues ancient people left behind are all around us. They left us clues in their buildings, tools, weapons, cave paintings and sculptures, and even in their footprints and handprints.

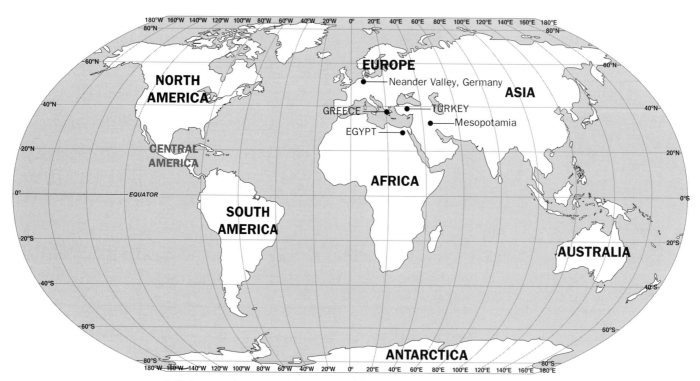

▲ This map shows some locations of famous archaeological finds.

An Interest in the Past

Our interest in the past is not new. In the 1500s, a man named William Camden wrote about human beings' "back-looking curiositie." Camden thought curiosity about the past was one of the qualities that set humans apart from other animals. During the 1500s and 1600s, a scientific revolution swept across Europe. Scientists working during this time invented new tools to help them with experiments and observations. Science became highly competitive. Scholars across Europe began to organize scientific societies. They published their ideas in scientific journals. During the 1700s in Europe—a period known as the Enlightenment—great thinkers discussed new ideas about how people could create better societies. It was in this context of the scientific revolution and the Enlightenment that archaeology was born.

Archaeology's Early Beginnings

In the early 1800s, some people began to focus their time, attention, and resources on trying to solve mysteries of the past. By this time, a great deal was known about **stratigraphy**. People knew that the oldest materials in a stratified site were in the bottom layer. They knew that more recent materials were in the top layer. However, archaeology was not really a science. Most of the "archaeologists" during this time were lawyers, doctors, and men in other professional fields who were interested in travel, adventure, fame, and fortune. These **pioneers** of archaeology played an important role in showing that history could be found in the **artifacts** left behind by ancient peoples.

Ancient Mesopotamia

Some of these pioneers in archaeology wanted to learn more about ancient cultures. Sir Austen Henry Layard, for example, became very interested in ancient Mesopotamia. In the 1840s, he traveled to the region of southwestern Asia—the region that covers the present-day countries of Turkey, Iran, Iraq, Israel, and Syria. He hired many local people and they began digging up sites where the ancient Assyrians had established their civilization. Layard wanted quick results. His workers uncovered two Assyrian palaces in a month!

artifact: an object made and used by humans or early humanlike creatures

pioneer: a person who is one of the first to do something or go somewhere; an innovator

stratigraphy: the study of layers of material in the earth, especially their distribution and age

▼ This photograph shows a stratified site, a place in the earth where layers of materials can be exposed by archaeologists.

The Ancient Maya

John Lloyd Stephens also wanted to find out about cultures of the past. In 1834, he traveled to Egypt, the Arabian Peninsula, southwestern Asia, Greece, and Turkey. In 1839, he left for Central America to search for the remains of the ancient Maya. Neither Stephens nor his partner Frederick Catherwood, an English artist, had any formal training in archaeology. Still, they left an excellent firsthand account and detailed illustrations of Maya buildings and monuments.

Uncovering the Origins of Humans

Early pioneers in archaeology also wanted to learn more about the ancestors of modern humans. In the early 1800s, Jacques Boucher de Perthes found stone tools in the same layer of ground as extinct animals such as woolly mammoths. This suggested to Perthes that early humans had killed these animals. This meant that humans lived at a much earlier time than previously thought. When workers found pieces of a skull in the Neander Valley in Germany in 1856, people wondered to whom the bones might have belonged. Were they the bones of a modern man who had been sick? Were they the bones of an early apelike man?

▲ Perthes found stone tools in the same layer of ground as extinct woolly mammoths.

The Missing Link

Charles Darwin, a British scientist, published a book called *Origin of the Species* in 1859. In his book, Darwin suggested a **theory** of evolution—an idea of how living things developed and changed over time. Some scientists believed Darwin's ideas meant that human beings were related to apes. Some experts thought the bones from the Neander Valley might be that "missing link." Archaeologists began to look for **fossil** bones of early humans and relatives of early humans. Some looked specifically for a so-called "missing link"—fossil bones that showed the creature that linked apes with modern humans. 📖

▲ Charles Darwin suggested a theory of evolution.

What Do You Think?

1. Where would you expect to find the oldest objects in a pit—in the top layer, middle layer, or bottom layer?

2. Who are some of the pioneers in archaeology?

THE QUEST FOR ANCIENT TREASURE

Archaeology from the 1800s to Today

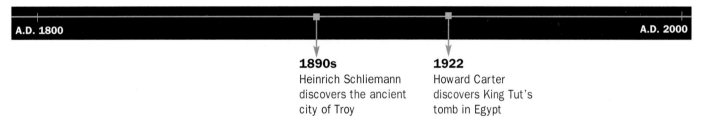

A.D. 1800   A.D. 2000

1890s
Heinrich Schliemann
discovers the ancient
city of Troy

1922
Howard Carter
discovers King Tut's
tomb in Egypt

By the mid-1800s, a few universities began to offer programs in archaeology. Students started learning archaeological vocabulary and methods. Greater importance was placed on establishing **chronologies** and keeping careful track of where artifacts were found. A few universities, especially American and European universities, began "schools of archaeology" in other countries. Museums were established during this time. These museums sponsored research and also displayed artifacts from archaeological expeditions. However, most of the archaeological expeditions of this time consisted of an archaeologist and perhaps a student or two. Workers in the local area supplied most of the hard labor.

Archaeology during the 1800s

By the late 1800s, the field of archaeology was growing and developing. New scientific advances and achievements gave archaeologists new tools and strategies to use in their search for information about the past. Heinrich Schliemann is a good example of this new approach to archaeology. Schliemann was a successful German businessman who became very interested in Homer's story of Troy and the Trojan War. Schliemann decided that he would search for the ancient city of Troy. However, he was more methodical and scientific in his approach than earlier archaeologists. In Greece, Schliemann hired experienced engineers and other experts to help with the **excavation**. He hired many people to work at a large site in Greece.

chronology: the order in which things occur

excavation: a hole made by digging

▲ Heinrich Schliemann was the first person to uncover the ancient city of Troy.

Schliemann's Treasures

Surveyors measured the site, workers dug huge **trenches** so artifacts could be uncovered, photographers took pictures of the artifacts that were dug up, and architects rebuilt structures. Schliemann placed some of the items he found in museums. However, Schliemann and others at this time thought they were entitled to keep the items they wanted. Because they found them, they thought of the items as their own treasures. Schliemann's wife even wore jewelry that had been excavated at these ancient sites.

▲ This drawing shows an archaeologist making drawings of Schliemann's excavations of Troy in the 1890s.

Uncovering the Tomb of a King

Howard Carter is another famous archaeologist. Carter, the Englishman who discovered King Tut's tomb, first traveled to Egypt in 1891. He started out as a "tracer"— someone who copied drawings and inscriptions on paper for further study. Working at dig sites was hard work, but Carter loved it. Later a wealthy supporter agreed to pay for Carter's search for an unopened pharaoh's tomb. Carter's discovery in 1922 of King Tut's tomb was one of the most amazing finds in archaeology. The treasures inside had not been stolen, damaged, or destroyed. It took more than a decade to make a list of all the artifacts!

▲ This is a drawing of one of the artifacts found in King Tut's tomb. It is an ornament worn on the chest.

Archaeology in the 20th Century and Beyond

After World War II (1939–1945), the field of archaeology took a great leap forward. There were three major reasons for this advancement. First, scientists had developed new technologies, especially **radiocarbon dating**, that allowed archaeologists to date artifacts much more accurately than ever before.

Using stratigraphy, for example, all an archaeologist could conclude is that material on the bottom layer was older than material on the top layer. It was not possible to say how material in any of the layers compared with material found in layers at other locations. However, with radiocarbon dating, archaeologists could state with some certainty the **absolute date** of an object. This meant that archaeologists working in different parts of the world could compare their findings with one another.

A second reason why archaeology advanced in the mid-20th century is that countries throughout South America, Africa, and Asia took great national pride in the archaeological finds uncovered on their lands. These finds were part of their history.

A third important development occurred during this same time. Universities all over the world began offering programs in archaeology. Archaeology was no longer considered a pastime for wealthy gentlemen. It developed into a scientific discipline, requiring serious study and training. Today's archaeologists work in teams in the field and in laboratories. The treasure they seek is information that will help us understand more about human history.

◀ Carter and other archaeologists of his time often wore a particular kind of hat—a **pith helmet**—to keep the sun off their faces during the heat of the day. The image of a slightly chubby older man with a pith helmet became a **stereotype** of an archaeologist.

---

absolute date: exact or precise date based on a common measurement scale (such as a year)

pith helmet: a sun hat made from dried pith, which is a substance found in the center of branches, stems, or plants

radiocarbon dating: a scientific way to date plants and animals

stereotype: a person, group, event, or issue considered to be typical; lacking any individuality

trench: a long, deep hole dug in the ground, usually with steep vertical sides

---

 What Do You Think?

1. The author suggests that the idea of "treasure" was different for early archaeologists and modern archaeologists. Explain this difference.

2. If you were an archaeologist, what information about human history would you be interested in exploring?

HOMINID HUNTERS
The Leakeys

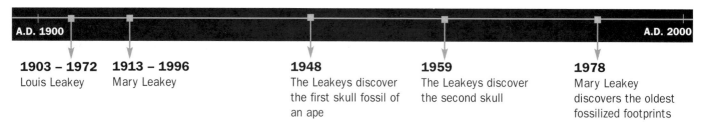

A.D. 1900				A.D. 2000

1903 – 1972
Louis Leakey

1913 – 1996
Mary Leakey

1948
The Leakeys discover the first skull fossil of an ape

1959
The Leakeys discover the second skull

1978
Mary Leakey discovers the oldest fossilized footprints

What do we know about the early physical and cultural development of human beings? The people who provide answers to this question are paleoanthropologists. They are hominid hunters!

Organizing Living Things into Groups

Scientists organize all living things into groups. This helps scientists study living things within categories. For example, scientists would place dogs in a category with animals such as wolves and coyotes because they all have similar **characteristics**. In the same way, scientists place humans in a category with other living things that have similar characteristics. The grouping—or family—that includes human beings and primates (e.g., apes and monkeys) is called the **hominid family**.

THE HOMINID FAMILY

MONKEY	APE	HUMAN

The Work of Paleoanthropologists

The scientists who study early human beings and their ancestors are known as paleoanthropologists. This comes from the Greek words *palaio*, which means "ancient," *anthropos*, which means "man," and *ology*, which refers to "study." So, the word *paleoanthropology* means "study of ancient man." Most paleoanthropologists have attended school to learn about archaeology, biology, geology, and other academic subjects.

Paleoanthropologists have uncovered much information about the early physical and cultural development of human beings. Perhaps the most famous paleoanthropologists are the members of the Leakey family.

Louis Leakey

Louis Leakey was one of the most important men in the field of paleoanthropology. He was born in 1903 near Nairobi. His parents were British citizens who had traveled to Africa as **missionaries**. When he was a young man, he left Africa to go to college in Great Britain. He studied anthropology at Cambridge University and graduated in 1926. Then he joined an archaeological expedition in eastern Africa. While most experts at that time believed that human beings first developed in Asia or Europe, Leakey had the idea that human beings first developed in Africa. He wanted to find evidence to support his theory.

Leakey excavated various sites in Africa, including Olduvai Gorge. On these expeditions, he found tools, bones, and other evidence of early humans. This experience convinced him that he wanted to make this field his life's work. He returned to study in Cambridge and gained support to return to Olduvai Gorge. Donald Johanson, a noted paleoanthropologist working today, observed that Leakey wanted to prove "that Africa was humankind's homeland—and to discover evidence for his own belief that [human beings] ... had a very ancient **origin**."

characteristic: feature; attribute; quality

hominid family: includes mammals that walk upright and have comparatively large brains

missionary: someone sent to another country to do religious work

origin: beginning

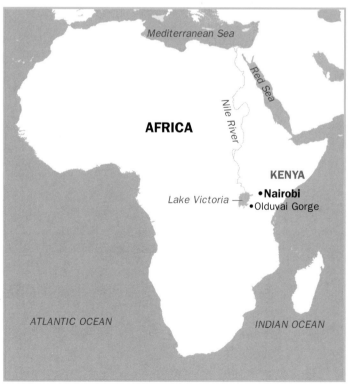

▼ Leakey was born near Nairobi, the capital of the East African country of Kenya.

implication: an indirect indication; suggestion; inference

launch: to begin; to start

paleontology: the study of life forms from the past, especially prehistoric life forms, through the study of fossils

Discoveries at Olduvai Gorge

Olduvai Gorge proved to be a very good location to search for early human beings. While he was there, Leakey found fossil evidence of the oldest member of the hominid family discovered up to that time. He also fell in love with and married a young woman named Mary Nicol. The couple worked together and made many important discoveries about the hominid family and how it developed. In 1959, Mary found a skeleton—which Louis called "Zinj"—that created huge excitement in the scientific world. According to Donald Johanson, it was this find that "**launched** the modern science of paleoanthropology, the study of human origins."

Over time, Louis and Mary began to follow different interests. While he traveled and worked all over the world, Mary stayed at Olduvai Gorge. Louis Leakey died in 1972 and was buried in Kenya. He was a pioneer in paleoanthropology, and his fossil discoveries changed our ideas about the development of early humans. Louis Leakey also inspired a generation of scientists interested in the field of paleoanthropology, including Donald Johanson and Tim White.

Mary Leakey

"Given the choice, I'd rather be in a tent than in a house." This is what Mary Leakey told a reporter in the early 1990s. She loved to be in the field hunting for fossils and was very successful in finding them! Mary Leakey made a name for herself in archaeology and **paleontology** at a time when most people working in these fields were men.

Mary Nicol was born in 1913. Her father was a landscape painter. He also had a great interest in archaeology. He took his family with him on many trips to Europe. During one of his trips to France, Mary saw cave paintings for the first time. She was amazed by this ancient artwork and wanted to know more about the people who had painted these pictures. Even though she was a girl, she got to go along on some archaeological excavations and was allowed to keep any of the finds she made. She described the experience as "powerfully and magically exciting." From that time on, she wanted to be an archaeologist.

▲ Mary Nicol was amazed by the ancient cave paintings she saw.

As a young woman, Mary enrolled at a college in London and began to take classes in anthropology. She also worked at an excavation in England. She became an expert on ancient stone tools and developed a great talent for drawing these items. In fact, her ability to draw was the reason she met her future husband, Louis Leakey. Louis Leakey was already a famous archaeologist. He needed someone to illustrate his new book.

In 1935, Louis Leakey invited Mary Nicol to go on a dig in Africa. She joined him there in 1936. Later that year, Louis and Mary were married. Donald Johanson described her as "shy, reserved, socially uncomfortable and, in her own words, not very fond of other people." He said that she "preferred to carefully evaluate scientific evidence before reaching any conclusions."

Mary Leakey's Most Important Discoveries

After many years of work in Africa, Mary Leakey made three very important discoveries. In 1948, she uncovered the first fossilized skull of an ape. It has been dated at about 20 million years old. In 1959, Mary Leakey discovered another skull. This one was about two million years old. In 1978, Mary Leakey made her most important discovery. She found the earliest fossilized footprints known. She called this discovery "immensely exciting—something so extraordinary that I could hardly take it in or comprehend its **implications** for some while."

In 1994, Mary Leakey wrote the story of her life in a book, *Disclosing the Past*. Although she never finished college, universities such as Yale, Oxford, and the University of Chicago gave her honorary degrees to recognize her achievements. Mary Leakey died at her home in Africa in 1996.

A Family Tradition—Richard Leakey

Louis and Mary Leakeys' second son, Richard, shared his parents' interest in the past. He made important new discoveries about early humans, including a complete 1.6 million-year-old skeleton of an African *Homo erectus*. Richard's wife, Maeve, and their daughter, Louise, also were attracted to the field of paleoanthropology. Recently, Maeve and Louise discovered hominid fossils in northern Kenya that are more than four million years old. 📖

What Do You Think?

1. Why do scientists organize living things into groups?

2. What is the name of the family into which scientists place human beings?

3. How are the paleoanthropologists you read about in this article alike? How are they different?

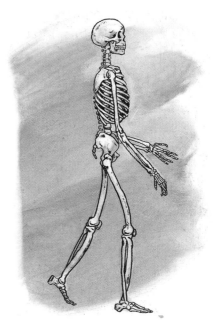

▲ The footprints Mary Leakey found were the first records of human beings walking upright on two legs.

HOMINID HUNTERS
Donald Johanson and Tim White

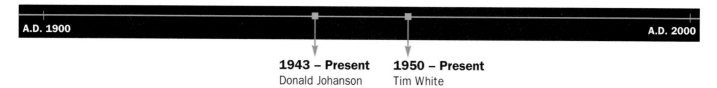

A.D. 1900   A.D. 2000

1943 – Present   **1950 – Present**
Donald Johanson   Tim White

Archaeologists and paleoanthropologists are "**academic** detectives." They are interested in solving the mysteries of the past. Archaeologists study the life and culture of people who lived in prehistoric times. Paleoanthropologists study the humanlike creatures that came before modern human beings. Archaeologists and paleoanthropologists examine **primary sources** such as fossils and artifacts. They look at **secondary sources** such as writings and studies done by other archaeologists and paleoanthropologists. They also work with people in other academic fields to help them understand the past.

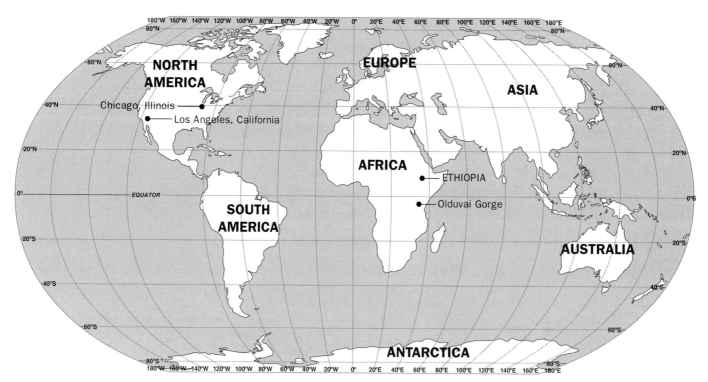

▲ Donald Johanson was born in Chicago, Illinois. Tim White was born in Los Angeles, California. Both men traveled to Africa to work on archaeological projects there.

Looking for Clues

If you are interested in learning about the people who lived in prehistoric times, an archaeologist can help. Prehistoric people did not write about their lives, but this is not a problem for archaeologists. They learn about the people of the past by studying what these earlier people left behind. Archaeologists look for clues in fossils such as bones and artifacts such as pottery, tools, jewelry, weapons, clothing, and art. They look for clues in the structures people built and the places where they buried their dead. They also look for clues in the land where they hunted animals, and gathered and grew food. These things give archaeologists clues about people who lived in prehistoric times.

▲ These archaeologists are looking for clues to the past.

Donald Johanson

If you want to know about early humanlike creatures, you will need the help of a paleoanthropologist. Donald Johanson is one of the most famous American paleoanthropologists today. He is part of the generation of people who were inspired by the Leakeys' work. Johanson was born in Chicago, Illinois in 1943. His parents had come to America from Sweden to make better lives for themselves.

Like Mary Leakey, Donald Johanson became interested in anthropology at a very early age. In an interview, Johanson recalled that a neighbor was an anthropologist who often traveled to Africa. He said, "I was thrilled as a young boy to sit with him, surrounded by his library of knowledge, and to talk to him about his adventures in Africa. And I became very interested in Africa. I became very intrigued by the idea of going to a place as foreign and remote as Africa." Johanson also was interested in biology. He liked to collect butterflies, and he identified different plants and insects.

academic: having to do with school subjects such as history, literature, geography, and so forth

primary source: artifacts, fossils; writings or pictures created by people who were involved in or saw the events they described

secondary source: writings or pictures created later by people who were not involved in or who did not see the events they described

▲ As a young boy, Donald Johanson enjoyed collecting and identifying insects.

alter: to change

irreversible: permanent; unable to be changed

It's a FACT

Johanson nicknamed the skeleton "Lucy" because after the team found the skeleton, they heard "Lucy in the Sky with Diamonds," a song by the Beatles, playing on the radio.

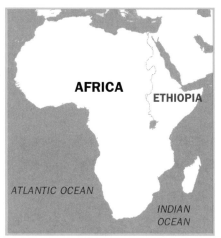

▲ Johanson and his team made exciting finds in Ethiopia.

From Student to Teacher

At first, Johanson didn't study very hard in high school. His school counselor told him that he wasn't "college material" and suggested that he go to a trade school. Luckily, however, Johanson did not take that counselor's suggestion. Instead, he went to college and took science and anthropology courses, eventually earning a doctorate from the University of Chicago. During the summers, he worked on various archaeological excavations. In the early 1970s, he also traveled to Africa several times to do fieldwork and began teaching at a university in Ohio.

Lucy—The Most Complete Skeleton

Donald Johanson made his most famous find in Africa in 1974. During that year, he discovered a skeleton of a female hominid. Officially, this skeleton is identified as AL 288-1. Johanson called the skeleton "Lucy." Lucy has been described as "the oldest, most complete specimen of an extinct species which was not human, but from which the human race may be descended."

Other Exciting Discoveries

Johanson and his team made other exciting finds in eastern Africa, including a collection of fossil hominid bones at one site and some hominid bones with stone tools. The bones and tools were 2.5 million years old, which made them the oldest found so far. After finding these fossils, however, Johanson could no longer do fieldwork in the region. The political situation in Ethiopia was too dangerous.

Australopithecus Afarensis

Johanson decided to begin analyzing all the fossils he and his team had found. They concluded that the bones all belonged to a species of hominids, which they named *Australopithecus afarensis.* In 1981, Johanson started a nonprofit research center focusing on prehistory that he called The Institute of Human Origins. For the next several years, Johanson and his colleagues led several more expeditions.

Not everyone agrees with Johanson's conclusions about the age of the fossils or what they mean, but Johanson's ideas have encouraged a great deal of new discussion about the origin of human beings.

Tim White—Footprints and Bones

Tim White was one of the very bright, young paleoanthropologists who assisted Donald Johanson in analyzing the finds from excavations in Ethiopia and Olduvai Gorge. White was born in 1950 in Los Angeles, California. As a young boy, he roamed the San Bernardino Mountains in search of obsidian flakes and pieces of pottery that were made by American Indians who lived in the area a long time ago. White collected lizards and snakes and dreamed of studying dinosaurs.

▲ As a boy, White searched for pieces of American Indian pottery. These are some examples of pottery made by American Indians.

Early Work

As a young man, White went to college at the University of California, Riverside, where he studied biology and anthropology. Later, he went to the University of Michigan and earned a doctorate in anthropology. During this period, he also had a chance to travel to Kenya to work for three summers on a project with Richard Leakey. Richard Leakey was so impressed with White's work that he recommended that White assist Mary Leakey on her project. White helped Mary Leakey excavate the hominid footprints she discovered in 1978.

This experience led White to begin working with Donald Johanson. Together, they came up with new ideas about the physical and cultural development of early humans. Their analysis of the evidence—4.4-million-year old hominid bones and teeth—led them to believe that hominids first began to walk upright in the forests of Africa.

An Irreversible Task

When asked how he would like to be remembered, Tim White said, "One of the things I'm most proud of is the high-level involvement of Africans in our project because they will carry the knowledge to the next generation." He also wants people to understand that excavating a site is **irreversible**: "The fact is, you get only one shot to do this right. When you work at a site, you **alter** it forever." 📖

What Do You Think?

1. According to this article, who is interested in solving the mysteries of the past?

2. How are the Leakeys, Donald Johanson, and Tim White alike? How are they different?

3. Tim White made the point that excavating a site is irreversible and suggested that this is a very serious responsibility. How is his attitude different from the way in which earlier archaeologists such as Heinrich Schliemann approached excavations? Explain your answer.

EVALUATING
Archaeological Evidence

Sometimes archaeologists and paleoanthropologists find clues about prehistoric times by accident. Children playing might discover a prehistoric site completely by chance. That is how the cave paintings in Altamira, Spain were discovered. Oftentimes, however, academic detectives have information to help them decide where they should look. Before they start digging, these academic experts find out everything they can about an area. Often they look closely at the land area using **technology** to help them decide where to look for clues. For example, they might take pictures of the area from an airplane to get a broad overview of the land.

Methods and Tools

After they have chosen a site, archaeologists and paleoanthropologists are ready to begin excavation of the site. They are looking for **evidence**! First, they carefully mark out the site. They measure the area into small sections. Then they begin digging, but they work very slowly and carefully. They use tools such as small trowels, pick axes, and brushes. They make drawings or take photographs as they work. They also make notes. They want to be certain they have a permanent record of how everything was found.

Once they have uncovered the clues, archaeologists and paleoanthropologists must decide what the information means. They take the fossils and artifacts to a laboratory where the evidence is studied very carefully. How old are the bones or artifacts? What are the bones and artifacts made of? How were the artifacts made?

◄ This archaeologist is examining and organizing fossils found at an excavation site.

Determining the Date of a Fossil or an Artifact

Academic detectives use many different modern scientific tools, including the following:

- **Stratigraphy:** a method to decide if one object is older than another. The idea is that the oldest things are in the bottom layer of a site and more recent objects are in the top layer.
- **Radiocarbon dating:** a scientific way to date plants and animals. Carbon dating can give academic detectives a very good idea of when something lived in years. However, it can only be used if the material being tested is between 1,000 and 50,000 years old.
- **Tree-ring dating:** a way to date an object by comparing a piece of wood found with the object to an established tree calendar, which experts have created by studying tree rings.

evidence: information that supports a judgment or decision

technology: the application of science for practical uses

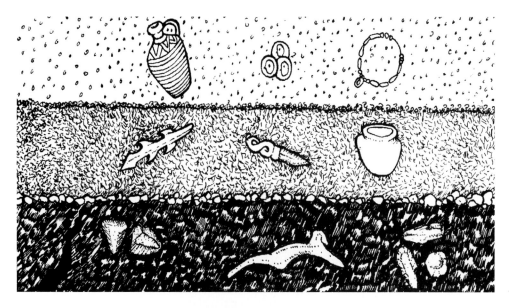

◄ Stratigraphy is the study of layers of rock and soil.

◄ Studying tree rings can help scientists date a fossil.

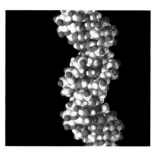

▲ This shows a computer picture of DNA. Scientists can look at DNA to tell whether people are related to each other.

Determining the Composition of a Bone or an Artifact

- **CAT (Computerized Axial Tomography) scan:** a scientific test that combines many different x-ray pictures with the aid of a computer to get a three-dimensional view of bones and organs.
- **DNA (Deoxyribonucleic Acid) test:** a scientific test that allows experts to identify the basic make-up of living things.

These methods and tools help archaeologists and paleoanthropologists identify the **facts**. They then use their **judgment** to make conclusions about these facts. However, even with all the modern scientific tools available, archaeologists and paleoanthropologists still face many problems in deciding what the evidence means.

Problems with Evidence

Oftentimes, archaeologists and paleoanthropologists have *incomplete evidence*. There may not be enough evidence to give a clear understanding. For example, they may find only a few small fossil pieces that do not give them enough information to make a strong conclusion. Sometimes, archaeologists and paleoanthropologists have *conflicting evidence*. In other words, they have two pieces of information that are inconsistent with one another. A paleoanthropologist can look at a fossil bone from a hominid's hand and know that the hominid would not have been able to grip objects. However, what if the paleoanthropologist found stone tools with this hominid hand bone? This would present puzzling and conflicting evidence. When faced with conflicting evidence, academic detectives search for more clues. Until they find more information, they must be careful about making strong conclusions.

Sometimes the problem that archaeologists and paleoanthropologists must face is *incorrect*, ***biased***, or even *false information*. If incorrect, biased, or false information is used to tell about the past, people can have an incorrect understanding of history. The case of the Piltdown man is a good example.

PROBLEMS WITH EVIDENCE	
INCOMPLETE EVIDENCE	CONFLICTING EVIDENCE

The king was cruel.

The king was kind.

▲ This chart shows two kinds of problems academic detectives can have with the evidence they find.

Piltdown Man

In 1912, a man in Piltdown, England announced that he had discovered "apelike" fossils. Archaeologists and paleoanthropologists were very excited about this discovery. They called the fossils "Piltdown man." They thought they had found an early ancestor of modern human beings. More than 40 years later, however, they found out that this discovery was a trick. Someone had buried the skull of a human being and the jawbone of an ape to make it look as if this was the "missing link" that scientists thought existed.

Academic detectives must look at the evidence very carefully to decide if it is accurate and fair. Usually this means they must look at the source of information to decide if it is credible. In other words, is the information believable? Is it information they can trust? They also must look at the evidence with an open mind and be ready to consider new information. They must be careful not to let their personal **opinions** affect their judgment about the facts. For example, in the case of the Piltdown man, the scientists had a strong opinion that there was a creature that was a "missing link" between apes and modern humans. Their opinion got in the way of their judgment. ▯

What Do You Think?

1. Of the problems academic detectives face, which one do you think is the most serious? Why?

2. What is the difference between an opinion and a judgment? Give an example of each.

skull of a human being

jawbone of an ape

▲ The "Piltdown man" is an example of false evidence. Scientists were tricked into believing that this "fossil" was the missing link between man and ape.

Prehistoric Times and the
STONE AGE

| 3 MYA | | | | B.C. 0 A.D. |

c. 2.5 MYA
Paleolithic Stone
Age begins

c. 15,000 – 10,000 years ago
Mesolithic Stone
Age begins

c. 10,000 – 8,000 years ago
Neolithic Stone
Age begins

To make the study of history a bit less complicated, archaeologists and historians divide the past into blocks of time called periods. When time is divided in this way, it makes it easier to understand a particular period of time and the changes that took place from one period to the next.

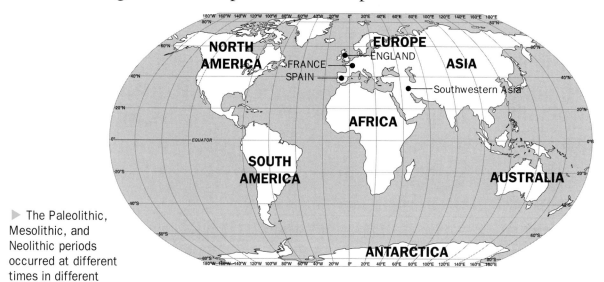

▶ The Paleolithic, Mesolithic, and Neolithic periods occurred at different times in different parts of the world.

How Long is a Period?

Some periods in history are very long, from tens of thousands of years up to millions of years. Other periods such as the "Renaissance" are very short. Some historical periods are named after a particular person. For example, the "Elizabethan" period is named after the English Queen Elizabeth I who ruled England from 1558 to 1603. Usually major trends or ideas characterize a period of time. For example, during the agricultural revolution, which began about 10,000 years ago, people learned how to **domesticate** plants. They still hunted and gathered food, but increasingly they depended on the crops they grew as their major food supply. This meant that they began to live in one place all year round.

Stages of Human Development

Regardless of the name of the period, its characteristics, or the span of time it covers, almost all periods overlap. In other words, stages of human development usually don't start and stop at particular, well-defined dates. Instead, there are **transitions** between periods because different groups of people in different parts of the world move in new directions at different times. For example, farming first appeared in southwestern Asia about 10,000 years ago, but it did not appear in other areas until much later.

Prehistoric Times and the Stone Age

Archaeologists and historians organize prehistoric times—the time before written history—into a period of time called the Stone Age. It is generally agreed that the Stone Age covers the period from about 2.5 million years ago to about 5,000 years ago. During the Stone Age, our ancient human ancestors began making tools. The Stone Age is often divided into three parts: the Old Stone Age, Middle Stone Age, and New Stone Age.

The Paleolithic or Old Stone Age

The oldest tools discovered so far date back to about 2.5 million years ago. At this "beginning point" of the Old Stone Age, early humans made their first tools out of small rocks. These tools were about the size of a baseball and were made by striking **flakes** of stone from each side. Other types of Old Stone Age tools were discovered at Olduvai Gorge. These tools, known as "choppers" or "chopping tools," were made from flint or quartz. This type of toolmaking continued until about 15,000 years ago. As humans learned how to make better tools, they were able to expand the area in which they lived and hunted.

domesticate: to train to live with and be of best use to humans

flake: a small, flat piece or layer that is broken off from a larger object

transition: changing from one form, state, activity, place, or time to another

▼ Early humans made their first tools out of small rocks.

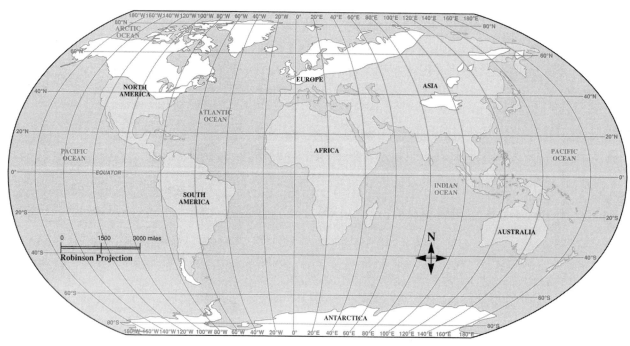

▲ The areas shaded white show parts of the earth that were covered by ice.

moderate: about in the middle; not too hot or cold; temperate

retreating: going backward or withdrawing

Humans Spread throughout the World

Toward the end of the Old Stone Age, about 10,000 years ago, our human ancestors and modern humans spread throughout the world. This occurred primarily because the ice sheet covering northern Europe began to melt. As the **retreating** ice created more grazing land, herds of animals moved north. People followed these animals because that was their source of food. They also used the animal hides for clothing. They used the animal bones to make tools. Some of the most well-known evidence we have from this period of time are the cave paintings found in southern France and northeastern Spain. As the glacial ice retreated, humans began to depend on a greater variety of animals, fish, and plants.

◄ Early humans used animal hides for clothing.

The Mesolithic or Middle Stone Age

The Middle Stone Age began about 15,000–10,000 years ago, at the end of the last Ice Age. Because archaeologists have studied Europe so extensively, we know a lot about the Mesolithic in Europe. During this time, people continued to hunt, gather, and fish, but they were able to do these activities in a more **moderate** climate. People also began to use a new stone tool that was good for cutting and slicing. This tool allowed Mesolithic people to use new hunting and fishing techniques along many of the lakes and rivers. Archaeologists have found a great deal of evidence about many groups of people who lived in central and northern Europe during this period. These Mesolithic cultures continued to exist in Europe until approximately 5,000 years ago. The Mesolithic cultures of southwestern Asia transitioned to the New Stone Age sooner. The Mesolithic cultures of Africa transitioned to the New Stone Age later.

The Neolithic or New Stone Age

As described by archaeologists, the Neolithic period began about 10,000–8,000 years ago. During this period, people first began to make and use polished stone tools. While this new type of tool was important, it was not the only significant development. Much more important was that people living in southwestern Asia—the region that covers the present-day countries of Turkey, Iran, Iraq, Israel, and Syria—became the world's first farmers. They learned to domesticate plants such as wheat and barley. These grains became a part of their diets. They also domesticated animals such as sheep and goats. By about 5,500 years ago, agriculture had become a regular activity on the flood plain of the Tigris and Euphrates rivers in present-day Iraq.

▲ During the Neolithic period, people began to make and use polished stone tools.

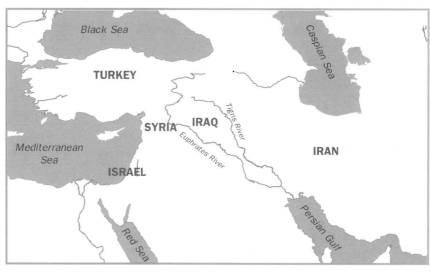

▲ People living in southwestern Asia became the world's first farmers.

economy: the production, development, and management of materials and goods

season: one of the four natural divisions of the year—spring, summer, fall, winter

Change in Economy

The real significance of the New Stone Age was not just the new toolmaking techniques. It was the total change in the **economy** due to agriculture and its effect on people's lives. They no longer had to live as nomadic hunters and gatherers who had to move with the **seasons** in order to feed themselves. During the Neolithic, people could build permanent homes because they had learned to grow a food source that they could count on. They could store extra grain. They could live together in larger groups. Some people could perform more specialized jobs. Human communities—villages and towns—developed. This was a dramatic change in human history. 📖

What Do You Think?

1. Why do archaeologists and historians divide the past into blocks of time? Do you organize your own history into periods (e.g., when you were in elementary school)? Explain your answer.

2. What is the Stone Age? What are the three parts of the Stone Age called?

3. Which is the oldest part of the Stone Age? Which is the most recent?

4. How did the domestication of plants and animals change human history?

▲ During the Neolithic period, people started living in permanent homes such as the ones shown in the drawing above.

OUR HUMAN ANCESTORS

A.D. 1900		A.D. 2000

1924
Discovery of
*Australopithecus
africanus*

1974
Discovery of "Lucy"

1990s
Discovery of
ardipithecines

Archaeologists and paleoanthropologists have discovered evidence of our earliest human ancestors in Africa, particularly in East Africa. The region of East Africa contains the Rift Valley. This valley has provided a rich source of information about human history because the remains of many early hominids have been preserved in volcanic deposits there. When a volcano blows up or erupts, it produces lava (melted rock) and other material that can cover things such as bones, tools, and other items in a layer. As the lava cools, it preserves the items in a layer of hardened lava or rock. Finding fossil evidence in volcanic material gives scientists an important advantage. It means they can use modern dating techniques to determine the exact age of the fossils. By attaching dates to fossils, scientists can understand more clearly when various hominids lived. This, in turn, helps them create a hominid "family tree."

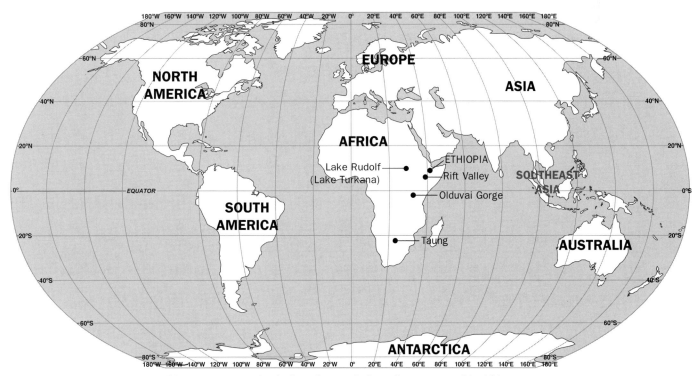

▲ Most experts today believe human beings first appeared in Africa.

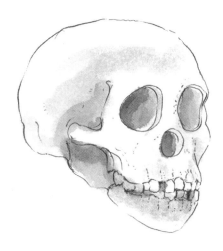

▲ This is a drawing of the fossil skull of *Australopithecus africanus.*

The Earliest Hominids— The Australopithecines?

In 1924, in Taung, South Africa, a man named Raymond Dart found a fossil skull that he identified as evidence of early humans. He called this human ancestor *Australopithecus africanus.* This name means "southern ape of Africa." The name *Australopithecus* or australopithecine is used to describe a group of some of the earliest hominids. Other archaeologists and paleoanthropologists, like Louis and Mary Leakey, found additional fossil evidence of the australopithecines. More experts began to focus their attention on East Africa in the search for the earliest hominids. One of the most exciting finds occurred in 1974. In that year, the paleoanthropologist Donald Johanson and his team uncovered the skeleton of a female australopithecine that they named "Lucy." Laboratory tests revealed that Lucy was 3.18 million years old!

But Wait ... What about the Ardipithecines?

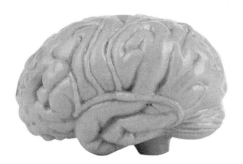

▲ This is a diagram of the human brain. Scientists believe that the ardipithecines and australopithecines had smaller brains than modern humans.

In the mid-1990s, Tim White pushed back the date of the earliest hominids even further. He analyzed a collection of bones, including a skeleton, which he and his team found in Ethiopia. White found that these bones were from a group of hominids who lived about 4.4 million years ago. This group of hominids is named *Ardipithecus.* We still are not sure whether these hominids could walk upright on two feet. Researchers are continuing to study these hominid bones. Currently, however, many scientists think this is the oldest hominid related to modern humans.

Every day it seems that more information is revealed about early hominids. As more bones are found, scientists are able to make stronger conclusions about what the evidence means. They believe that the ardipithecines lived before the australopithecines. Both groups lived over a large region in East Africa. Both had smaller brains than modern humans. They probably had dark skin and more hair than modern humans. They ate many different kinds of foods, including plants, insects, and animals. Scientists have found that some australopithecines were smaller and lighter, while others were larger and more heavily built.

The australopithecines (and perhaps the ardipithecines) walked upright, but they did not walk in the same way as modern humans. No evidence suggests that these early hominids made art or used fire or that they built shelters or buried their dead.

hearth: fireplace

The Dawn of Modern Human Beings

So, we think our oldest hominid relatives were the ardipithecines, who were followed by the australopithecines. What hominid relatives came next? Experts do not have enough evidence to answer that question completely. However, some experts believe the current evidence suggests that other hominids appeared in this order:

- *Homo rudolfensis* (named after the location where the first bones were found—Lake Rudolf, which is now called Lake Turkana): first discovered by Richard Leakey in 1972; dated at older than 1.9 million years, but younger than 2.5 million years.
- *Homo habilis* (called "handy man" or "handy human" because the bones were found with stone tools): first discovered by the Leakeys at Olduvai Gorge; later examples discovered by Tim White; dated at 1.8 million years.
- *Homo ergaster* (*ergaster* is a Greek word that means "work man"): the almost complete skeleton of an 11-year-old boy was found in 1984-1988; dated at 1.5 million years; many experts believe that *Homo ergaster* is the most direct ancestor of modern humans; *Homo ergaster* made and used stone tools.
- *Homo erectus:* fossils of *Homo erectus* were first found in Southeast Asia; *Homo erectus* has been dated to about 1.2 million years ago; some experts believe *Homo erectus* was the first hominid to use fire, but there is much debate about this idea because **hearths** are not commonly found with hominids until the last 100,000 years.

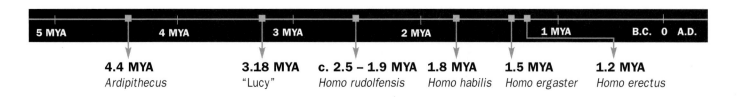

| 5 MYA | 4 MYA | 3 MYA | 2 MYA | 1 MYA | B.C. 0 A.D. |

4.4 MYA
Ardipithecus

3.18 MYA
"Lucy"

c. 2.5 – 1.9 MYA
Homo rudolfensis

1.8 MYA
Homo habilis

1.5 MYA
Homo ergaster

1.2 MYA
Homo erectus

▲ This is one artist's idea of what Neanderthals looked like.

Neanderthals

The Neanderthals, who lived from about 100,000 to 30,000 years ago, are part of the same family as modern humans. However, recent evidence confirms that they are not direct ancestors of modern human beings. As new finds are made and analyzed, scientists will learn more about human origins. Until then, discussion and debate about the ancestors of modern human beings will continue.

Modern Humans

What does this all mean? When did modern human beings begin to appear? Here's one way to think about it. About two million years ago, hominids that shared some of the characteristics of modern human beings—such as walking upright and using tools—lived on the African grasslands. Then, about one million years ago, some of these hominids moved away from Africa. We have evidence of their stone tools at sites in southwestern Asia, southern Asia, and, by 500,000 years ago, in Europe. By about 125,000 years ago, hominids we would recognize as early humans had spread throughout Europe and beyond. However, other than the tools that they made and used, we don't know very much about what life was like for these early humans.

Advanced Technology and Language

Today, most experts accept the idea that the ancestors of modern human beings came from Africa. However, there is a great deal of discussion and debate about how populations of modern human beings spread across the world.

Many think that early modern human beings replaced other hominid groups, who became extinct. The spread of early modern human beings probably took place between 60,000 and 50,000 years ago. Many experts believe that during this period these early modern human beings developed more advanced technology. They also developed advanced language and the ability to make and use symbols. Their advanced technology and language abilities helped them adapt to many different environments. Experts have found evidence of these early modern human beings throughout Europe, including the Cro-Magnon site in France. These early modern human beings created colorful art. There also is evidence that they buried their dead.

▲ Early modern human beings created art on the walls of caves.

Adapting to Different Environments

Throughout history, there have been times when ice covered large parts of the earth's surface. People refer to these periods of time as ice ages. Humans learned to adapt their way of living in response to the changing climate and the environment in which they lived. The most recent Ice Age ended about 10,000 years ago. By this time, groups of modern humans lived in many different parts of the world—deserts, forests, grasslands, and mountain regions. These people adapted to their different environments, but all lived as nomadic hunters and gatherers. They built temporary shelters and moved regularly in search of the animals and plants that made up their diets. They made clothing for themselves. They used fire to keep warm and to cook. They painted vivid pictures of animals and other figures in caves and on rocks. They created specialized tools that helped them survive in the environment in which they lived. As the earth became warmer and the ice retreated, they followed herds of animals to new areas, including the continents of North and South America. 📖

What Do You Think?

1. On what continent do most scientists believe that the ancestors of modern human beings developed?

2. What group of hominids do scientists think is the most direct ancestor of modern human beings?

3. Why is there so much discussion and debate about the origins of modern human beings?

4. How did geography affect the spread of modern human beings throughout the world?

◄ These early human beings are getting ready for the long, cold winter.

THE CULTURE
of Early Humans

| 3 MYA | | | B.C. 0 A.D. |

c. 2.5 MYA
Paleolithic Stone
Age begins

**c. 15,000 – 10,000
years ago**
Mesolithic Stone
Age begins

**c. 10,000 – 8,000
years ago**
Neolithic Stone
Age begins

The word *anthropology* comes from two Greek words that mean "the study of man." Anthropologists are interested in studying human societies all over the world. Anthropologists are especially interested in learning about people's cultures. What anthropologists mean by the word *culture* is all the knowledge, beliefs, art, laws, customs, traditions, and habits of a group of people. Anthropologists want to understand the patterns of behavior, thoughts, and feelings that people learn in order to be part of the group.

The Study of Human Societies

Many anthropologists study the cultures of groups of people living today. Anthropologists might come to your school to study the culture of American students. They would observe your behavior. They also would ask questions: What values are important to you? Being part of the group? Being independent? Displaying honesty? Physical strength? Wisdom? What are your customs? Do men open doors for women? Do you eat lunch with the same group of people every day? What foods do you eat? What are your laws? What are your ideas about art, music, religion, and technology? What is your idea of beauty? The anthropologists' observations of your group's behavior and the answers you and your classmates give to their questions reveal your group's culture.

Anthropologists also are interested in learning about groups of people who lived in prehistoric times. They can't observe these groups or ask them questions. Instead, they look for clues that these prehistoric people left behind. Early humans left many pieces of evidence that anthropologists examine in order to understand what the lives and cultures of these groups were like.

Culture of Early Humans

During the Paleolithic or Old Stone Age, people lived as nomadic hunters and gatherers. They did not stay in the same place all year. They moved according to the seasons and the availability of food. In the winter, they moved to areas that were warmer and sheltered them from cold weather. In the spring, summer, and fall, they moved to areas where they could gather nuts, wild berries, roots, and other plant materials to eat. They set up camps in areas where they could hunt animals or catch fish and other seafood.

Hunters and Gatherers

Groups of people who lived as hunters and gatherers did not **accumulate** very many **material goods**. They did not create pottery or build permanent homes. Why? Because they moved often. It wouldn't have made sense for them to spend time making things that would break easily. It also wouldn't have made sense for them to build sturdy, permanent homes. It was more important for them to make lightweight, **portable** structures they could carry with them when they moved to a new camp. However, these hunters and gatherers did create things to make their lives better. Anthropologists have found fish hooks and fish spears, as well as stone tools and weapons that have geometric designs and symbols carved on them. These artifacts help us understand how they lived, what they ate, and how they spent their time. The most dramatic evidence of the culture of early humans is the art they left behind.

accumulate: to collect; to pile up or gather

material goods: physical things such as clothing, supplies, dishes, cookware, tools, furniture, and so forth

portable: capable of being carried; easily moved or carried

▼ Prehistoric people worked together to fish for food.

burst of creativity: a sudden occurrence of imagination, originality, or expressiveness

exaggerated: physically enlarged; emphasized; abnormally developed

sculpture: a figure or design that is carved in wood, chiseled out of stone, made out of clay, or cast in metal

Jewelry, Sculptures, and Paintings

About 30,000 years ago, early humans throughout the world began to create artwork. No one knows why there was this **burst of creativity**. Some groups made simple jewelry such as shell necklaces. Others carved small **sculptures** out of ivory, bone, or antler. Some painted small pictures on pebbles or small rocks. They could carry these pictures with them from place to place. Other people painted huge paintings on the walls of caves.

What did these early artists show in their artwork? Most of the artists painted animals—bison, horses, bulls, deer, and other animals they hunted. Anthropologists think they wanted to "capture" the spirit of these animals in the hope that they would be successful in hunting them. The idea is similar to a person today wanting something very much—say, a new bicycle. That person might cut out a picture of the bicycle he or she wants, tape it to a wall, and look at it every day.

Sometimes artists showed a very **exaggerated** female form, usually without any clothes. Anthropologists think they wanted to show how important it was to the group for women to give birth. These Stone Age artists usually did not create art showing the male form.

Cave Paintings

By far, the Stone Age artists' most beautiful works are the cave paintings found in southern France and northern Spain. One of the first cave paintings was found by a little girl, Maria de Sautuola, who was exploring a cave in Altamira, Spain in 1879 with her father. Maria saw paintings of brightly colored bulls and pointed them out to her father. Her father was interested in archaeology and knew something about prehistoric times. He thought the paintings must be very, very old. However, experts at that time disagreed. Many years later, however, other caves with similar paintings were discovered. Experts began to accept that these cave paintings were indeed very, very old. In fact, Stone Age artists probably painted them 13,000 to 14,000 years ago.

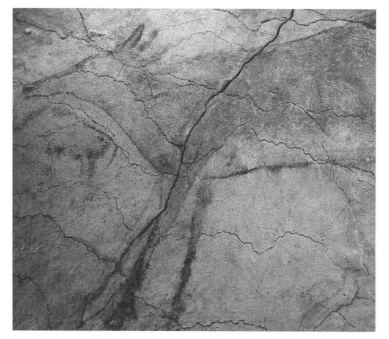

▲ Maria de Sautuola was the first modern person to see this cave painting in Altamira, Spain.

Hall of the Bulls

Today, we have located more than 200 cave painting sites. Some people think that the Hall of the Bulls at Lascaux in France is the most magnificent cave painting of all time. Many of the paintings are hundreds of feet from the cave entrance and high above the cave floor. How did Stone Age artists paint these pictures?

The oldest cave paintings found so far are the paintings in the Chauvet Cave at Vallon Pont d'Arc in France. This cave was named after the man, Jean-Marie Chauvet, who headed the team that explored the cave. One person described what it was like when Chauvet and his team entered the cave: "There was a moment of ecstasy. ... [They] rushed over, they overflowed with joy and emotion. ... These were minutes of indescribable madness."

Telling a Story

One of the paintings in the cave appears to tell a story. It shows a rhinoceros, a dying bison, and a man wearing a mask. It's not clear if the man is hurt or dead. This painting is far back in the cave. At the time it was created, very few people could have seen it and only if they had a lighted torch. Why did the artist paint it? Who would have seen it? No one knows for sure. Using radiocarbon dating techniques, Chauvet and his team determined that these paintings were created between 30,000 to 32,000 years ago.

Questions Remain

As new evidence is uncovered, we may learn more about Stone Age art. For now, many questions remain. Who created these works of art? Did they sign their artwork? Why did they create them? Who would have seen them? Were they trying to tell stories with their pictures? 📖

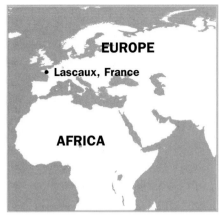

▲ The most famous cave paintings are those at Lascaux, France.

What Do You Think?

1. What is culture? How do anthropologists learn about the culture of prehistoric peoples?

2. Describe the hunter-gatherer societies. Why were they nomadic? What evidence do we have of their beliefs? What does their art tell us about them?

3. Why do you think Stone Age people created artwork? Why do people today create artwork?

Reader's Theater
Presents

THE STORY OF THE CAVE PAINTINGS

Practice reading the script. When the script says, "SCIENTISTS," everyone in the class joins in the reading. Read with expression!

→

ROLES

★ **NARRATOR 1**
★ **NARRATOR 2**
★ **MARCELINO**
★ **MARIA**
★ **JUAN**
★ **SCIENTISTS (ALL)**

Maria: What are bison?

Marcelino: Bison are animals that lived in this land long ago.

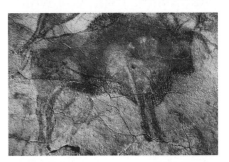

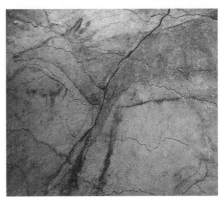

▲ These are photographs of some of the cave paintings in Altamira, Spain.

Narrator 1: One day, in the year 1879, a little girl named Maria was walking with her father, Marcelino.

Narrator 2: Maria's family lived in a place called Altamira.

Narrator 1: Altamira is in northern Spain.

Narrator 2: Marcelino wanted to explore a cave near their house.

Marcelino: Stay close, Maria. The cave is very dark, and you might get lost.

Narrator 1: Maria took her father's hand, and they went into the cave. It was dark and a little scary.

Marcelino: I'll light a torch so we can see.

Narrator 1: Marcelino lit the torch. The cave went on for hundreds of feet. He started to walk farther into it.

Narrator 2: But Maria noticed something.

Maria: Father, look up at the ceiling. There are pictures painted everywhere!

Marcelino: You're right! There are pictures of goats, horses, and bison!

▲ One of the first cave paintings was found in Altamira, Spain.

Maria: Who painted these pictures?

Marcelino: Maybe people who used to live here long ago. Maybe they painted these pictures.

Narrator 1: After they left the cave, Marcelino talked to his friend Juan.

Marcelino: Juan, you won't believe what Maria and I found in some nearby caves!

Narrator 2: Juan was a teacher at the University of Madrid. He knew all about ancient people.

Juan: Take me there! I'd like to see these paintings for myself.

Narrator 1: So Marcelino took Juan to the caves and showed him the paintings.

Juan: Oh! I think these are very, very old.

Marcelino: How old?

Juan: They may have been painted more than 10,000 years ago!

Narrator 2: Juan and Marcelino told everyone what they had found.

Narrator 1: But many scientists did not believe them.

Scientists: You're lying. Those paintings are too nice to be thousands of years old.

Juan: That's because they've been hidden for so long, and no one has touched them.

Scientists: We don't believe you. You're making it up so you can become famous.

Narrator 2: Even though the scientists thought they were lying, Juan and Marcelino never gave up.

Narrator 1: After a while, some scientists started believing them.

Narrator 2: And then in 1902, the same scientists who called them liars wrote a letter and said they were sorry.

Narrator 1: By that time, everyone knew that the paintings were made by people who lived in the Ice Age, at least 11,000 years ago!

Narrator 2: And scientists are still studying the paintings today. 📖

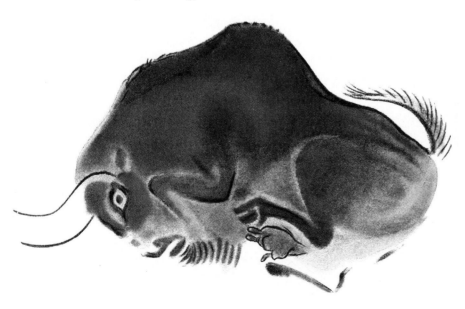

▲ This is an artist's reproduction of cave art showing a charging buffalo.

Early Human Communities
PALEOLITHIC AGE

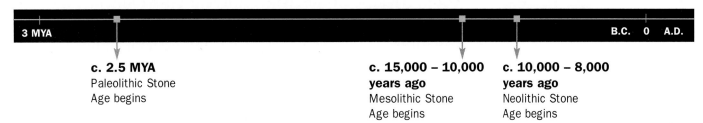

3 MYA   B.C. 0 A.D.

c. 2.5 MYA
Paleolithic Stone
Age begins

**c. 15,000 – 10,000
years ago**
Mesolithic Stone
Age begins

**c. 10,000 – 8,000
years ago**
Neolithic Stone
Age begins

Archaeologists have divided the time we call "prehistory" into three ages: the Paleolithic (Old Stone Age), Mesolithic (Middle Stone Age), and Neolithic (New Stone Age). During each of these ages, people used increasingly advanced tools and weapons. They also learned new ways to make tools and weapons, and they organized themselves in specific ways. Looking at the earliest human communities can help us understand how people have adapted to changing environments and new information.

Adapting to Their Environment

The Paleolithic or Old Stone Age is the longest part of prehistory. Generally, archaeologists refer to the Paleolithic as the period from about 2.5 million to 10,000 years ago. Archaeologists have identified Paleolithic human communities in Europe, Africa, Asia, Australia, and North and South America. In each of these locations, people adapted to their natural environment. This adaptation is reflected in the tools they made, the shelter they used or built, the clothes they wore, and the food they ate. For example, Paleolithic people who lived in cold climates near an ocean made tools to hunt sea animals and catch seafood.

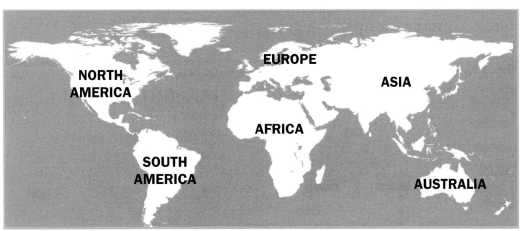

◀ Archaeologists have identified Paleolithic human communities in Europe, Africa, Asia, Australia, and North and South America.

Chapter 4: The People of Çatal Hüyük 41

Paleolithic Communities

Paleolithic people made and wore clothes to keep them warm and protect them from the cold. Those who lived in hot, dry deserts made tools and used weapons to catch animals of the desert. They wore clothing that kept them cool. Because of the many different environments, the Paleolithic sites archaeologists have found show many local variations. However, there are some general things we know about all these Paleolithic communities. For example, during the Paleolithic, people lived in small groups and they did not have much contact with other groups. In fact, it was unusual for groups to come into contact with one another.

▶ These Neanderthals used fire to keep warm and cook meat.

Hunters and Gatherers

All Paleolithic groups lived as hunters and gatherers. Groups ranged over large territories. They probably settled in a campsite or shelter for a couple of weeks or months. Then they moved to another campsite or shelter in another part of their territory. Archaeologists know that Paleolithic people used fire for warmth. Archaeologists have found evidence of burnt animal bones, which leads them to conclude that these early people also used fire for cooking.

Tools and Weapons

In the early part of the Paleolithic, people made and used pebble tools. They also made flake "points" for spears. In some places, Paleolithic people made and used more advanced flake tools and hand axes. In other places, people developed chopper tools or blade tools. Depending on the location, Paleolithic people used ivory, bone, and other materials to make the tools and weapons they needed in their environment.

Paleolithic Art

Paleolithic people also created art. It was during this period that artists made small sculptures out of stone, ivory, antlers, and other materials they found in their environment. They also created beautiful, brightly colored cave paintings. Most of these paintings showed the animals who lived in their environment. Sometimes they included handprints with their paintings. Archaeologists do not know the significance of these handprints. Perhaps they were the artists' signatures. 📖

What Do You Think?

1. What are the three periods of prehistory? Which is the oldest? Which is the most recent?

2. After reading this article, what evidence would lead you to conclude that Paleolithic people used fire? Explain your answer.

◀ Paleolithic people left handprints, perhaps as a form of signature.

Early Human Communities

MESOLITHIC AGE

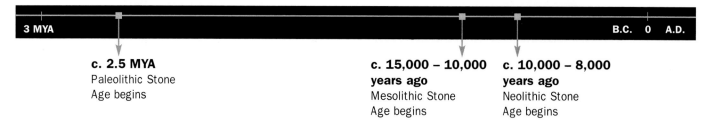

| 3 MYA | | B.C. 0 A.D. |

c. 2.5 MYA
Paleolithic Stone
Age begins

**c. 15,000 – 10,000
years ago**
Mesolithic Stone
Age begins

**c. 10,000 – 8,000
years ago**
Neolithic Stone
Age begins

The Mesolithic or Middle Stone Age occurred at different times in different places. For example, the Mesolithic period lasted from about 15,000 to 10,000 years ago in southwestern Asia and from about 10,000 to 5,000 years ago in Europe. The Mesolithic was a transitional period between the Old Stone Age and the New Stone Age.

Improvements in Tools and Weapons

During this period, some things stayed the same. For example, people used many of the same kinds of tools and weapons that were developed during the Paleolithic. Often, they improved these tools and weapons.

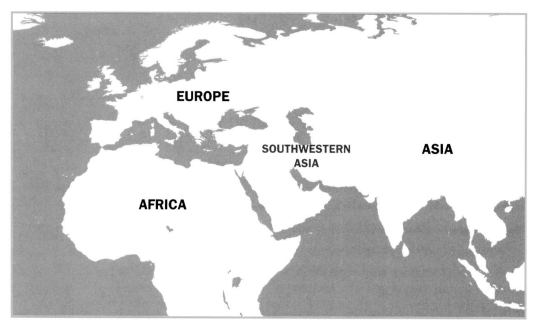

EUROPE

SOUTHWESTERN
ASIA

ASIA

AFRICA

▲ The Mesolithic period lasted from about 15,000 to 10,000 years ago in southwestern Asia and from about 10,000 to 5,000 years ago in Europe.

Changes in Art

Some things changed during the Mesolithic. For example, people no longer created cave paintings. However, they decorated their tools and weapons by carving designs and symbols on them.

Spread of Forests

During the Mesolithic, forests spread across many areas of the world. For example, in Europe, many birch and pine forests spread across the continent. In response, Mesolithic people used new techniques to make tools that helped them live in forested areas. They made woodworking tools and created axes by grinding rather than chipping or flaking processes. They made better fish hooks, spears, and harpoons, as well as fish nets, boats, sleds, and skis. Also during this period, humans began to domesticate dogs. Mesolithic people probably used dogs to help them track and hunt animals.

▲ During the Mesolithic, forests spread across many areas of the world.

▲ Mesolithic people were the first people to domesticate dogs.

What Do You Think?

1. Compare Paleolithic and Mesolithic people. How were they alike? How were they different?

2. How did geography change the lives of Mesolithic people?

Early Human Communities
NEOLITHIC AGE

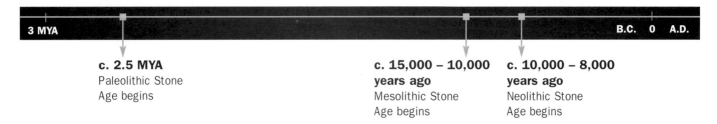

| 3 MYA | | | | B.C. | 0 | A.D. |

c. 2.5 MYA
Paleolithic Stone
Age begins

**c. 15,000 – 10,000
years ago**
Mesolithic Stone
Age begins

**c. 10,000 – 8,000
years ago**
Neolithic Stone
Age begins

During the Neolithic, or New Stone Age, dramatic changes occurred in human communities throughout the world. What changed dramatically was that Neolithic people figured out a new way to produce food.

The Rise of Permanent Settlements

Neolithic people still hunted, fished, and gathered wild berries and roots. However, increasingly they learned how to plant seeds, care for the young plants, **harvest** the fully grown crops, and then grind the grain into flour. At about the same time, they began to domesticate animals such as goats and sheep for their milk, meat, wool, and skin. By domesticating plants and animals, Neolithic people developed a way to ensure a **predictable** supply of food. Having a predictable supply of food meant they could stay in the same place all year round. They could build permanent homes and settlements. This changed their way of life forever.

▲ Neolithic people began to domesticate animals such as goats and sheep.

Neolithic Settlements Spread

Around 10,000 years ago, in the region of southwestern Asia, Neolithic people learned how to grow crops such as wheat and barley. Planting, **tending**, and harvesting these crops required groups of people to work together. And in order to grind these grains into flour, people needed heavy grinding stones and places to bake the flat bread they made out of flour. It was no longer **practical** for such groups to live nomadic lives. People in this region began to settle in permanent villages. They built houses, places to tend their animals, storage areas for grain, and places to worship their gods. They settled close to sources of water—lakes, streams, and rivers.

harvest: to gather a crop from the field where it is grown

practical: useful

predictable: something that is possible to know in advance

tend: to take care of or serve the needs of

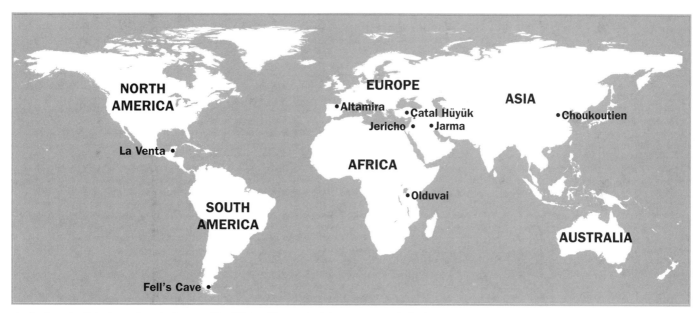

▲ Archaeologists have located many Neolithic villages and towns, especially in southwestern Asia. These settlements include Çatal Hüyük, Jericho, and Jarma. However, archaeologists have found Neolithic settlements all around the world. These sites include Choukoutien (Asia), Altamira (Europe), La Venta (North America), Olduvai (Africa), and Fell's Cave (South America).

What Do You Think?

1. What did Neolithic people have in common all over the world? What are some regional differences?

2. This article suggests that the development of agriculture changed people's lives forever. Do you agree or disagree with this statement? Explain your answer.

People Adapted to Their Environments

Humans adapted to the wide variety of environments in similar ways. For example, people in the Americas learned to grow maize (or corn), black beans, potatoes, chilies, tobacco, and other plants that were native to those continents. People in southern Asia domesticated cattle. People in southeastern Asia grew rice and sugar cane, and raised pigs, chickens, and water buffalo.

Similarly, Neolithic people in each of these areas developed new varieties of clothing and shelter, depending on the resources they had available to them. In areas where people had lots of trees and wood, they built homes and used forest resources. They used furs from animals in their environment to make their clothing. They also used plants, clay, stone, and other resources to make the things they needed—mats, baskets, pots, grinders, tools, and weapons. They even used these resources to make art and jewelry. ▢

▲ People in the Americas learned to grow chilies (left) and maize (right).

The People of
ÇATAL HÜYÜK

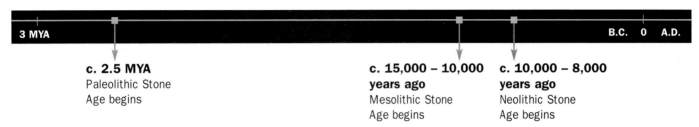

| 3 MYA | | | B.C. 0 A.D. |

c. 2.5 MYA
Paleolithic Stone
Age begins

**c. 15,000 – 10,000
years ago**
Mesolithic Stone
Age begins

**c. 10,000 – 8,000
years ago**
Neolithic Stone
Age begins

During the Neolithic, or New Stone Age, people in the region of southwestern Asia learned how to domesticate animals such as goats and sheep. They developed new tools, including barbed harpoons, bone needles, and fish hooks. Most importantly, they learned how to grow crops such as wheat and barley. Planting, tending, and harvesting of these crops required groups of people to work together. And, in order to grind these grains into flour, people needed heavy grinding stones and places to bake the flat bread they made out of flour. It was no longer practical for such groups to live nomadic lives. Around 10,000 years ago, people in this region began to settle in permanent villages. They built houses, places to tend their animals, storage areas for grain, and **shrines** to worship their gods. One of these Neolithic villages developed in present-day southern Turkey in a place called Çatal Hüyük.

The Architecture of Çatal Hüyük

The British archaeologist James Mellaart is credited with discovering and excavating Çatal Hüyük in the early 1960s. He and his team came upon two large, grassy mounds. However, on one side of the mound they could see a brick structure. They were excited about what they might find and eagerly began their excavation. Eventually, they uncovered 12 levels of the town of Çatal Hüyük. They found more than 150 rooms and buildings. Some of the rooms were decorated with murals, carved **reliefs**, and sculptures.

relief: artwork that is created by projecting figures of forms from a flat surface

shrine: an altar, chapel, or other place where people express their religious beliefs

▲ This is a drawing of the ruins of a shrine found at Çatal Hüyük.

erupt: to explode or blow up

mud brick: a brick made out of mud and dried in the hot sun

plaster: to apply a mixture of clay, sand, and water, usually to a wall

It's a FACT

All the houses appear to be about the same. This has led archaeologists to conclude that the people of Çatal Hüyük did not have different social classes.

Houses without Doors

The town of Çatal Hüyük had no streets. The people built their houses right next to one another. The houses had no doors, and they were built right next to each other. People moved from one part of the town to another by climbing through an opening on the roof of their house and then walking across the roofs. The hole in the roof also served as a chimney.

The architecture of Çatal Hüyük provided benefits to the people of the town. For one thing, enemies could not easily attack them and wild animals could not enter the town. Also, because the houses shared common walls, the structures were sturdy and new houses could be added easily. In addition to the houses, many of the rooms in Çatal Hüyük were used as religious shrines.

The houses and shrines were built of **mud bricks**. The people of Çatal Hüyük also used strong wood frames to make the brick structure stronger. They **plastered** and painted the floors and walls. Each house had a raised area or platform along one of the walls where people could sleep, eat, and work. The people of Çatal Hüyük buried their dead under these platforms.

The Art of Çatal Hüyük

We can learn about the people of Çatal Hüyük and their lives by looking at the art they created, including the paintings they created. Artists of Çatal Hüyük painted hunting scenes on some of the walls in their houses. These paintings are similar to the pictures that Paleolithic and Mesolithic people created. However, around 5700 B.C., something very different appeared in a painting at Çatal Hüyük. This painting showed a group of humans hunting deer. This was different from earlier paintings in which human figures almost never appeared. An art historian said the humans in the painting were "an organized hunting party, not a series of individual figures." The art historian observed that the artist "took care to distinguish important descriptive details—for example, bows, arrows, and garments—and the heads have clearly defined noses, mouths, chins, and hair."

The World's First Landscape Painting

Archaeologists also noted another exciting change in art at Çatal Hüyük. A painting in one of the religious areas of the town showed a picture of a landscape. This has been called the world's first landscape painting. A landscape painting is a picture of a natural setting such as a mountain, valley, or forest. The painting at Çatal Hüyük shows a town at the front of the painting and two mountain peaks in the background. There are lines and dots coming out of the taller mountain peak. Art historians think the artist was trying to show a volcano that was **erupting**.

In addition to paintings, archaeologists also found relief sculptures and a wide variety of wooden containers, baskets, and pottery. They found clay seals, jewelry made from stone beads, small religious statues, and bowls made of stone. They found rings and other decorative items made of copper. They also found polished obsidian—a shiny, black, natural glass—that had been made into mirrors.

▲ The people of Çatal Hüyük made jewelry like the ones shown in the drawing above.

The Religion of Çatal Hüyük

Religion must have been very important to the people of Çatal Hüyük. Çatal Hüyük was filled with shrines where people worshipped their gods. These shrines were decorated with wall paintings and carved reliefs of animal heads, cow skulls, and the horns of bulls. Archaeologists believe the bulls' horns were a sign of men's strength and their ability to have children. Archaeologists usually found a goddess figure near the bulls' horns. This goddess figure has a human form. The shrines also included symbols of women's ability to have children. To date, archaeologists have not found any evidence to suggest there were priests or kings.

The people of Çatal Hüyük buried their dead under the floors of their houses. A dead body was wrapped in cloth and buried with items that might have been important to the person when he or she was alive. For example, archaeologists have found things like necklaces, knives, and belts buried with bodies. Archaeologists have not found any evidence that the dead were buried with religious figures or food or containers for water. As a result, archaeologists have concluded that the people of Çatal Hüyük did not believe in an afterlife. New excavations may reveal new information that could change our ideas about Çatal Hüyük. 📖

What Do You Think?

1. Describe the architecture of Çatal Hüyük. What were the advantages and disadvantages of the architecture?

2. What new developments in art occurred at Çatal Hüyük?

3. Archaeologists have concluded that there were no kings or priests in Çatal Hüyük. What evidence did they use to come to this conclusion? Do you agree or disagree? Explain your answer.

MESOPOTAMIA
The Land between Two Rivers

| 8000 B.C. | | 0 |

6000 – 3000 B.C.
Rise of civilization in
Mesopotamia

The first civilizations developed in an area called Mesopotamia. This Greek word means "the land between two rivers." The two rivers are called the Tigris River and the Euphrates River. Both of these rivers and the area of Mesopotamia are now part of modern-day Iraq.

▶ Mesopotamia is part of an area that is sometimes called the Fertile Crescent (shaded area). The Fertile Crescent stretches from modern-day Jordan on the west, north toward Turkey, and then south to the border of modern-day Iran and Iraq.

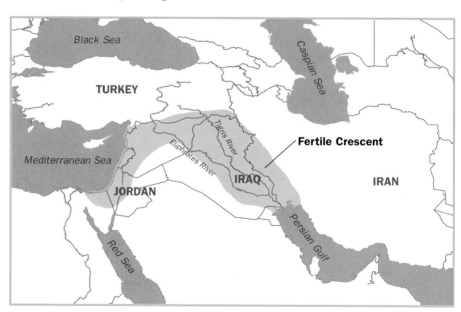

Fertile Crescent

The river valleys of the Tigris and Euphrates created an area of land that was well suited for farming. The **silt** from the rivers created land that was rich in minerals and nutrients needed to grow crops. The first people to settle this area and take advantage of the farm-friendly land were the Sumerians.

Irrigation and Transportation

The Sumerians turned the marshy areas by the rivers into farmland. At first, they grew date trees and barley grain, which is similar to wheat.

It's a FACT
The Tigris and Euphrates rivers did not flood on a regular schedule.

The Sumerians built **dikes**, canals, and reservoirs to collect and save water during the dry seasons. Without these **innovations**, the hot sun would have dried out the fields and ruined the crops. The Sumerians also used the rivers for transportation.

The land of Mesopotamia did not have the right type of stones to make the tools that farmers and artisans needed. That did not stop the Sumerians. They simply traveled by boat to other lands where they collected, bought, and traded for rocks and other **raw materials**. In this way, the Sumerians communicated and traded with other groups of people. As a result, new ideas spread throughout the region and beyond.

City-States

The success of Sumerian farming and trade helped **transform** their villages into small cities, and eventually into larger city-states. In all, there were 12 major Sumerian city-states. Two of the largest city-states were Ur and Lagash. Some city-states existed independently. Some city-states were grouped together under one ruler. In the city-states, people worked together to build an organized society.

dike: a raised portion of land used to stop or control the flow of water; commonly used in irrigation systems

innovation: a new way of doing things; a new process

raw material: a resource from which something else can be made

silt: fine dirt left behind by running water; typically rich in minerals necessary for farming

transform: to make a great change in the appearance or character of something

▲ Without people working cooperatively, the irrigation systems needed for farming could not have been built.

commerce: business

cuneiform: a series of wedge-shaped symbols used in the first forms of writing; these symbols were etched into clay tablets

▲ The Sumerians built great cities. This is one artist's idea of how a Sumerian city might have looked.

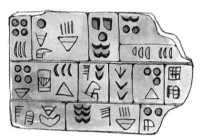

▲ Sumerians wrote on clay tablets.

What Do You Think?

1. What does the word *Mesopotamia* mean?

2. Who were the first people to grow crops in Mesopotamia?

3. What are some reasons why a civilization developed between the Tigris and Euphrates rivers?

4. How did trade and writing affect the spread of ideas and culture?

Organized Societies

With better farming, trade, and communication, the Sumerians could spend more time on other things. For example, they had time to devote to religion, politics and law, crafts, and **commerce**. Soon new groups and specialized roles appeared in Mesopotamian society. For example, no longer did everyone farm the land. Some people began to work as priests, artisans, and merchants. The Sumerians developed the first written language using symbols known as **cuneiform**. They also were the first civilization to use written records.

Contributions of Sumerians

The development of farming, irrigation, trade, communication, city-states, law, and religion are only some of the contributions the Sumerian people made to the development of all future civilizations. These contributions were all made possible by the fertile land created in between the Tigris and Euphrates rivers. ◻

HAMMURABI
and His Code of Laws

6000 – 3000 B.C.
Rise of civilization in
Mesopotamia

1792 – 1750 B.C.
Hammurabi of Babylon takes
control of Sumer and develops a
code of laws

Mesopotamia did not have natural barriers such as mountains, deserts, or seas. This meant that the people living in the area did not have any natural protection. As a result, one empire after another in the Fertile Crescent rose and fell. The invasions and the empires helped unify the region between the Tigris and Euphrates rivers. The invasions and empires also aided in the rapid spread of ideas first developed by the Sumerians. However, by 1800 B.C., the Sumerians as a distinct people no longer existed.

Hammurabi of Babylon

Babylonia was one of the most important Mesopotamian empires. Hammurabi was Babylonia's most important ruler. The Mesopotamians were the first people to produce written laws. These laws were posted in public places where all could see them. The laws provided some protection for everyone. One of Hammurabi's most important actions as ruler was to order the collection of all the laws of the land. This comprehensive list of laws was carved into stone. It has become known as the Code of Hammurabi.

▲ This is a drawing of a stone carving showing Hammurabi.

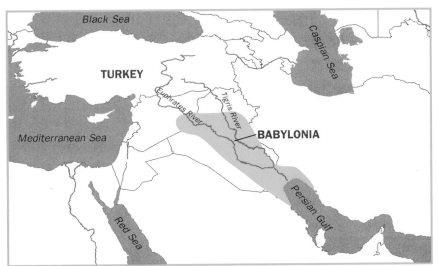

◄ The shaded area shows the extent of Hammurabi's empire.

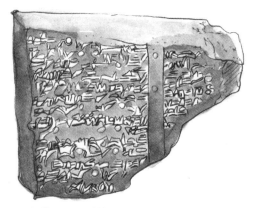

▲ Hammurabi's code of laws was carved into stone. This is a drawing of one of the stone tablets that French archaeologists found.

The Code of Hammurabi

Discovered by French archaeologists in the early 1900s, the Code of Hammurabi has 282 parts. Each part addresses a different aspect of life during that time. The stone carving shows the god Shamash, the god of justice, directing Hammurabi to issue the code. This shows how the people of Mesopotamia linked their religious beliefs with the rulers and their laws. The people of Mesopotamia thought of rulers such as Hammurabi as the representatives of the gods on earth. To break the law was to go against the king or ruler. It also meant going against the gods.

Law and Punishment

Many of the laws were concerned with business, banking, and landlord/tenant relations. This shows how important trade and commerce were to Mesopotamian society. There also were laws regarding **perjury**, stealing, kidnapping, and helping a slave escape. Breaking the laws in the Code of Hammurabi could mean severe punishments, including death. You can read below several laws that were part of the Code of Hammurabi.

189 If a member of the artisan class took a son as a foster child and has taught him his handicraft, he may never be reclaimed. If he has not taught him his handicraft, that foster child may return to his father's house.

195 If a son has struck his father, they shall cut off his hand.

229 If a builder constructed a house for a nobleman but did not make his work strong, with the result that the house which he built collapsed and so has caused the death of the owner of the house, that builder shall be put to death.

230 If it has caused the death of a son of the owner of the house, they shall put the son of that builder to death.

231 If it has caused the death of a slave of the owner of the house, he shall give slave for slave to the owner of the house.

Analyze the Source!

1. How did the Code of Hammurabi protect all of the citizens of the empire?

2. How did the code treat some people better than others?

Not All People Were Equal

Not all people in Mesopotamian society were equal. Slaves had very limited rights or no rights at all. As you can read in the excerpt from the Code of Hammurabi, punishment for harming a **noble** was more severe than for harming a slave. Also, men were given more freedom and rights than women. However, the code of laws also protected women and children from being taken advantage of or harmed. One law says, "If a woman so hated her husband that she has declared, 'You may not have me,' … that woman … may … go off to her father's house."

The Basis for Other Legal Systems

The Code of Hammurabi is considered the basis for many systems of laws developed throughout the history of **Western civilization**. Many of the laws in the Code of Hammurabi were reflected in later Hebrew law. For example, Hebrew law included the idea of "an eye for an eye and a tooth for a tooth." The Code of Hammurabi also has been linked to the legal systems of ancient Greece and Rome, and to English Common Law, which is the basis of the legal system in the United States.

noble: a member of the highest rank in a society; nobles were usually wealthy landowners

perjury: the act of lying under oath, usually in a court of law

Western civilization: having to do with the culture and beliefs of people in Europe and areas settled by Europeans

What Do You Think?

1. What is an example of a natural barrier?

2. Who discovered the Code of Hammurabi?

3. How did the Code of Hammurabi affect later civilizations?

◀ Hammurabi collected all the laws of Mesopotamia and had them carved into stone.

THE EMPIRE BUILDERS

The Hittites, Phoenicians, and Aramaeans

1500 B.C.   500 B.C.

1300 B.C.
Hittite Empire
at its peak

1200 B.C.
Fall of Hittite Empire

After the reign of Hammurabi and the rule of the Babylonians, other invaders conquered Mesopotamia. These new groups absorbed the rich culture left behind by previous empires and added their own contributions.

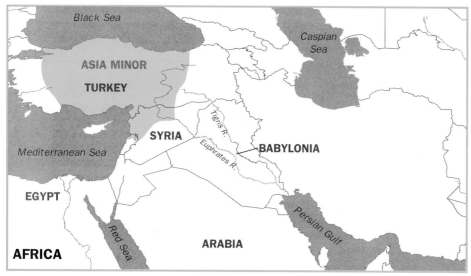

▲ The shaded area shows the extent of the Hittite Empire from c. 1350–1300 B.C. The Hittites were at their peak around 1300 B.C.

The Hittites

The Hittites were the first of these groups. The Hittites came from the area called Asia Minor, which is modern-day Turkey. The Hittites were attracted to Mesopotamia because they wanted to control the trade routes along the Euphrates River. The Hittites were at their peak around 1300 B.C.

The Hittites controlled a large area, including Mesopotamia and northern Syria, as well as their homeland of Asia Minor.

Using Iron

The Hittites adopted many features of Mesopotamian culture such as cuneiform writing, a code of laws, art, and religious beliefs. They also added something new to Mesopotamian culture—the use of iron. Iron was much more common than tin and copper, the elements needed to make bronze. The Hittites used iron to make tools, religious objects, and weapons. Invasions of other peoples from the north led to the fall of the Hittites around 1200 B.C.

Smaller Groups Build Nations

After the end of the Hittite Empire, there was a pause in the constant flow of invaders to Mesopotamia. This allowed smaller groups, such as the **Semitic** peoples, to build small nations of their own. The Semitic peoples were nomadic. Gradually, however, they settled in southwestern Asia in an area that today is commonly called the Middle East. These Semitic groups included the Phoenicians and Aramaeans.

caravan: a group of people traveling together

Semitic: refers to the language of nomadic groups of people, including the Hebrews, who traveled across the deserts of Mesopotamia

The Phoenicians

The Phoenicians settled in cities such as Beirut (in modern-day Lebanon) along the coast of the Mediterranean Sea. The Phoenicians became excellent sailors and sea traders. They sailed around the entire Mediterranean Sea, including to North Africa and places as far away as present-day Spain.

The Phoenicians developed the first alphabet. Their alphabet replaced the old cuneiform way of writing. By combining letters to make words instead of using thousands of symbols, writing became much easier. The Phoenicians helped spread Mesopotamian culture and ideas to new and faraway places.

The Aramaeans

The Aramaeans settled in Syria, Palestine, and parts of Mesopotamia. The Aramaeans were great land travelers, sending large **caravans** across long stretches of land for the purpose of trade. Like the Phoenicians, the Aramaeans helped spread the culture of Mesopotamia to different areas and peoples. 🕮

▼ The Phoenicians developed the first alphabet.

Phoenician Alphabet	𐤀	𐤁	𐤂	𐤃	𐤄	𐤅	𐤇	𐤉	𐤊	𐤋
Modern Alphabet	A	B	C, G	D	E	F	H	I, J	K	L

Phoenician Alphabet	𐤌	𐤍	O	7	𐤒	𐤓	W	†	Y	𐤎	Z
Modern Alphabet	M	N	O	P	Q	R	S	T	U, V, W	X	Z

THE EMPIRE BUILDERS
The Assyrians and the Chaldeans

1500 B.C.   500 B.C.

1200 B.C.
Fall of Hittite Empire

612 B.C.
Fall of Assyrian Empire

604 – 562 B.C.
Reign of Nebuchadnezzar
of the Chaldeans

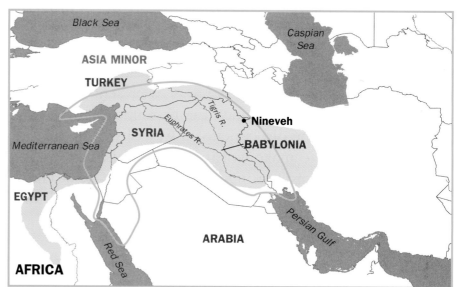

Assyrian Empire
c. 680 B.C.

Chaldean Empire
c. 604–562 B.C.

The Assyrian Empire

In the 900s B.C., the next great Mesopotamian empire, Assyria, began to rise. The Assyrians also were a Semitic and nomadic people. Originally, they came from the area around the upper Tigris River. Over the next 200 years, the Assyrians developed into fierce fighters. They improved the use of iron-tipped bows, **cavalry**, and horse-drawn chariots. They conquered large areas of land, including Mesopotamia, Syria, Palestine, and Egypt.

Harsh Rulers

The Assyrians were very harsh to people who did not want to be ruled by them. They were known for uprooting entire nations of people and forcing them to relocate to strange lands far from their homes. They also forced conquered people to help them build their cities. On the next page, you will read an excerpt from an account of how one Assyrian rebuilt his home.

cavalry: soldiers trained to fight while riding horses

The kings of Arabia, who had violated the oaths sworn to me, whom I had taken alive in the midst of battle with my own hands, I made to carry the basket and ... to do the taskwork, for the building. ... Molding its bricks, performing labor upon it, they passed their days to the accompaniment of music. Amidst gladness and rejoicing I completed [the house] from its foundation to its top ... [and] filled it with splendid furnishings.

What Do You Think?

1. Why do you think the Assyrians uprooted entire groups of people and forced them to move to faraway lands? What would this action achieve?

2. How did each of the groups you read about absorb the rich culture left behind by previous empires? What new contributions did they make?

Controlling a Large Empire

The Assyrians improved roads, created messenger routes similar to our postal service, and built great irrigation systems. These improvements helped them keep control over their large empire.

The Assyrians adopted the religion, literature, and art of Mesopotamia as their own. They introduced this culture to new people they conquered. Despite their attempts to keep control of their empire, rebellions and invasions slowly weakened the Assyrians. Nineveh, the capital of Assyria, was destroyed in 612 B.C. This marked the end of the Assyrian Empire.

The Chaldeans Take Over

Several groups, led by the Chaldeans, were responsible for destroying the Assyrian capital. The fall of the Assyrian Empire led to the founding of the Chaldean Empire in 604 B.C. The Chaldeans, another Semitic people, are sometimes called the New Babylonians because they were from an area bordering Babylonia to the north and the Arabian desert to the south. In addition to Babylonia, their empire included Assyria, Syria, and Palestine.

The Chaldeans were ruled by a very strong leader, King Nebuchadnezzar. Like the Assyrians, the Chaldeans continued the spread of Mesopotamian culture. After the death of Nebuchadnezzar in 562 B.C., the Chaldean Empire broke apart because his successors were weak and could not work together. The pieces of the Chaldean Empire were quickly conquered by the next great empire, the Persians. 📖

▲ This is a drawing of Nebuchadnezzar, king of Babylonia.

RELIGION IN MESOPOTAMIA

Religion was at the heart of Sumerian society. Religion connected politics, literature, and art. It also played an important role in the development of laws such as the Code of Hammurabi. Sumerians believed in many different gods. This type of religion is called polytheism, which is the belief in more than one god.

MESOPOTAMIAN GODS AND GODDESSES

| ANU | NINHURSAG | EA | ENLIL |

century: a period of 100 years

Christianity: the religion of Christians

Islam: the religion of Muslims

Judaism: the religion of Jews

The Gods Rule the Universe

The people of Mesopotamia believed that they did not have any control over their own lives. The Sumerians believed that their gods controlled everything in the universe, including the sun, moon, weather, crops, rivers, fire, successes, and failures. If a Sumerian had a healthy child or a good crop, or won a battle, it was because of the goodness or favor of a god. If there were disease or drought, or if a battle were lost, it was because of an angry god or an evil god.

Temples and Priests

Mesopotamian cities often identified with a particular god. The people and rulers of these cities dedicated their lives to carrying out the wishes of their gods. They built temples, called ziggurats, to honor their gods. These temples became the center of city life. Sumerian priests supervised the temples and collected rent. They usually controlled most of the land in and around the Mesopotamian cities. They also ran businesses and collected offerings from the city people. Most of the common people worked for the priests to support the temple. These jobs included farming and crafts. Some people also worked as servants. In addition to supervising the worship of their gods, the priests made sure farmers had enough land to farm and that the irrigation systems were working. The priests also made sure the city's economy stayed strong. They even planned for emergencies by making sure the city stored enough food and other supplies.

▲ This is a ziggurat in the Sumerian city of Uruk.

The Importance of Religion

The importance of religion in Mesopotamian culture was passed on through the **centuries** to other cultures and peoples who came into contact with the great Mesopotamian civilizations. This is part of the reason why this region of southwestern Asia is so important to many religions today, including **Judaism**, **Christianity**, and **Islam**. 📖

What Do You Think?

1. The Sumerians believed in many gods. What is this kind of religion called?

2. Who did the Sumerians think controlled their lives?

3. Why were the priests important to Mesopotamian society?

4. How important was religion in Sumerian society? How does this compare with other societies you have learned about?

▲ The ziggurat was the largest building in the city.

CONTRIBUTIONS
of the Sumerians

The people of Mesopotamia made great contributions to the world in the areas of writing, mathematics, science, and medicine.

▲ Sumerians created a system of writing.

epic: a long story or poem of particular importance to a specific culture or people

▲ Sumerians developed the concept that there are 60 minutes in an hour.

Writing

The early Sumerians developed a system of symbols called cuneiform. These symbols were etched on clay tablets. These symbols served them much like our alphabet works for us today. Each symbol represented an idea. Eventually, the Sumerians created thousands of symbols in their cuneiform system. Cuneiform allowed the Sumerians to keep business and historical records. They also used cuneiform symbols to write some of civilization's first great literary works, including the *Epic of Gilgamesh.*

Mathematics

The Sumerians developed multiplication and division tables. In the area of geometry, they figured out how angles and degrees made up shapes such as triangles and circles. Sumerians developed the idea that a circle is made up of 360 degrees and an hour is made up of 60 minutes.

▶ Sumerians made advancements in geometry.

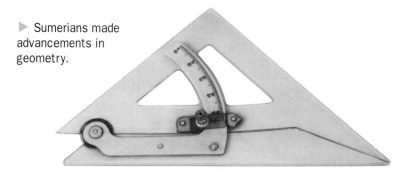

Science and Medicine

Sumerians learned much from observing the sky. They recorded how the sun, moon, stars, and planets moved and related to one another. Using this knowledge, they developed one of the first calendars—a lunar calendar—based on the cycles of the moon.

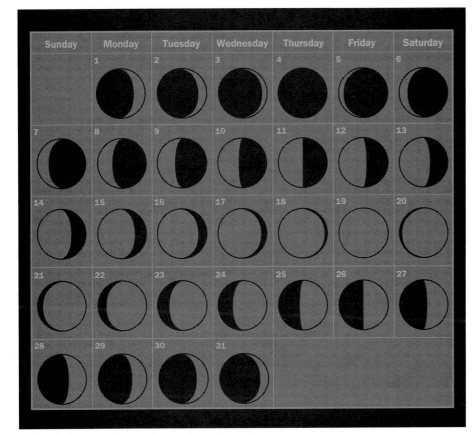

Sunday	Monday	Tuesday	Wednesday	Thursday	Friday	Saturday
	1	2	3	4	5	6
7	8	9	10	11	12	13
14	15	16	17	18	19	20
21	22	23	24	25	26	27
28	29	30	31			

▲ Sumerians invented the first calendar based on the cycles of the moon.

What Do You Think?

1. Name one advancement the Sumerians made in the area of mathematics.

2. How did the people of Mesopotamia apply their knowledge of science to practical problems? How do people apply scientific ideas today to practical problems?

3. Why does the author suggest that much of our knowledge today is rooted in the work of the people of Mesopotamia? Do you agree or disagree with this position? Explain your answer.

While Sumerians believed that all illness and disease was caused by the gods, their priests were trained in medicine. The priests could identify many different diseases. They also developed treatments using herbs and other substances to help people get well.

What the Sumerians Taught Us

The Sumerians planted the seeds for some of the great scientific and mathematic discoveries of later civilizations, such as those made by Greeks and Romans. Much of our knowledge about algebra, geometry, astronomy, and other concepts might not have been possible without the contributions of the Sumerians. 📖

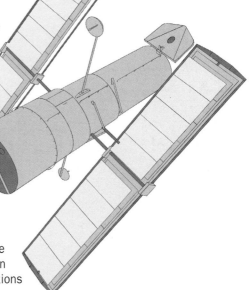

▶ The invention of the Hubble telescope might not have been possible without the contributions of the Sumerians.

THE EPIC OF GILGAMESH

Mesopotamian Literature

One of the best known stories in Mesopotamian literature is the *Epic of Gilgamesh.* It tells the story of a Mesopotamian king and his search for answers to life's questions.

Friendship and Death

According to the story, Gilgamesh, the hero, was the king of the city of Erech. A great warrior and leader, he and his companion Enkidu went on many adventures. Then, suddenly, Enkidu died of an illness. This took Gilgamesh by surprise. At first, he did not believe Enkidu was dead. You can read below an excerpt from the *Epic of Gilgamesh* that tells what happened:

'O Enkidu, my younger friend, ...
We,
We two,
Have conquered all, climbed all ...
What is this sleep that has now come over you?
You have gone dark and cannot hear me!'
But Enkidu does not raise his head.
Gilgamesh felt for his heartbeat
But there was none.

Enkidu's death was very hard on Gilgamesh. He decided to take a journey to find the secret of everlasting life.

▲ Gilgamesh was the king of the city of Erech.

The Search for Answers

Gilgamesh was very stubborn. He kept searching for answers even though he experienced one disappointment after another. His story did not end happily. Gilgamesh did not find a solution to the problem of death, and he did not find the secret of eternal life. In fact, he learned that "only gods live forever … but as for us men, our days are numbered, our occupations are a breath of wind." Gilgamesh learned what most Mesopotamians believed, that heaven was not a place for humans, but only for the gods.

A Glimpse into Mesopotamian Life

Stories such as the *Epic of Gilgamesh* reveal how harsh life was for the people of Mesopotamia. Floods, droughts, wars, and invasions made Mesopotamians very **pessimistic** about their lives and the future.

pessimistic: filled with negative thoughts

▲ Gilgamesh and Enkidu were the best of friends.

What Do You Think?

1. Who was Gilgamesh? What did Gilgamesh decide to do after his friend Enkidu died?

2. Why were the Mesopotamians so pessimistic about life?

3. How does the *Epic of Gilgamesh* help us understand life in Mesopotamia thousands of years ago? What story do you think will reveal life today to future generations? What will they learn about us from that story?

EGYPT
The Mighty Nile River

At about the same time that the Sumerians were developing their culture and cities in Mesopotamia, the Egyptians were building their own great civilization. The Egyptian civilization developed in the Nile Valley.

▲ The Nile River is the longest river in the world. It is over 4,000 miles long.

▲ The Egyptian civilization developed along the Nile River.

Fertile Land in the Nile Valley

The Egyptian civilization developed along the Nile River in northeastern Africa. The Nile River system flows north into the Mediterranean Sea. Without the Nile River, Egypt would be mostly desert. Because of the Nile, one of the world's great civilizations flourished. Every year, the Nile River would flood. This flooding almost always happened at the same time every year. When this happened, the land would be covered with soil that was rich in minerals. This made good farmland. Because cities needed to be close to drinking water and to food, Egyptian cities developed along the banks of the Nile River.

▲ The Egyptians used a shadoof to lift water for irrigation. In the background you can see Egyptian houses made of reeds.

▲ This photograph shows an example of hieroglyphics.

Irrigation and Farming

The ancient Egyptians learned how to control the flooding of the Nile River with irrigation systems. Farmers in the Nile Valley produced more than enough food for the Egyptian people. The surplus meant the Egyptians did not have to worry about growing enough food. It also meant that they could spend time on other activities. For example, they learned how to **smelt** metal. They also developed their own written language called **hieroglyphics**.

Egyptian pharaohs were very powerful.

Safety and Security

Unlike the Mesopotamians who constantly had to worry about invading armies, the land around the Egyptians protected them. The Egyptians were surrounded by natural barriers, including deserts, mountains, and the sea. These natural barriers kept most invaders out. The Egyptians could focus on building a great civilization. They achieved great things in the areas of engineering, government administration, and religion. Because the Egyptians had a wealth of resources, they could build incredible structures such as the pyramids.

Egyptian Pharaohs

Another result of the security and isolation of Egypt was the powerful presence of the pharaohs. Since invading armies did not conquer Egypt and set up new rulers and governments, as was the case in Mesopotamia, the Egyptian government became very rich, strong, and centralized. The Egyptian kings, or pharaohs, became very powerful because they were at the center of the government. Unlike the Mesopotamian kings who were considered messengers of the gods, the pharaohs were considered to be actual gods living on earth. Also, the pharaohs owned all the land and received all the taxes collected from people living on those lands. In contrast, in Mesopotamia, citizens were allowed to own their land.

Different Circumstances

While both the Egyptians and Sumerians developed their civilizations at about the same time, there are many differences in the character and history of their societies. The abundance of food and water allowed the Egyptian people to concentrate on the arts and sciences. The natural barriers surrounding Egypt gave Egyptians a sense of security and led to a strong government and strong rulers. 📖

EGYPTIAN HISTORY
The Old, Middle, and New Kingdoms

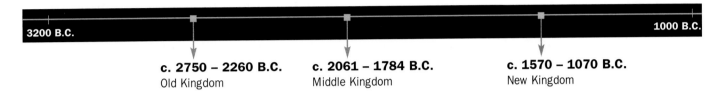

3200 B.C.			1000 B.C.

c. 2750 – 2260 B.C.
Old Kingdom

c. 2061 – 1784 B.C.
Middle Kingdom

c. 1570 – 1070 B.C.
New Kingdom

Historians divide Egyptian history into three major periods: the Old Kingdom, the Middle Kingdom, and the New Kingdom. They call the times between these major eras **intermediate** periods.

The Old Kingdom

Around the year 3000 B.C., Menes, the legendary ruler of the Upper Kingdom in Egypt, led his army into Lower Egypt. He united the entire Nile Valley under one king. As Egyptian society became more unified and centralized, Egyptian culture began to flourish. This is the period in Egyptian history called the Old Kingdom. The Old Kingdom lasted from about 2750 to 2260 B.C. During this era, Egyptians began to build tombs for the rulers, including the great pyramids.

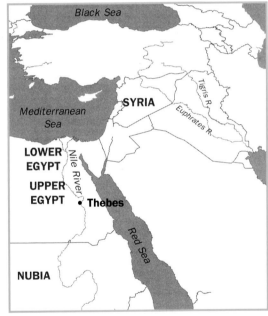

A Strong Central Government

During the Old Kingdom, a strong central government began to develop in Egypt. There were no independent city-states like those in Mesopotamia. The Egyptians owed all their **allegiance** to the pharaohs. Men were required to work on big government projects such as building the pyramids.

Pharaohs had great power. They also had great responsibilities. They were responsible for overseeing the river irrigation systems and maintaining justice and order within the kingdom. They also were expected to communicate the will of the gods to the people on earth.

allegiance: loyalty

intermediate: in the middle; in between

civil war: fighting between different groups in a country

corruption: dishonesty

dynasty: a series of rulers linked by a family relationship or by geographic location

tribute: gifts or payments to show loyalty, respect, or gratitude

The Rise of Nobles

As time went by, local leaders slowly became very powerful. These leaders became nobles in Egyptian society. Their most important duty was to collect taxes for the pharaohs. For most people in Egypt, the nobles were the only authority that the local people knew and feared. The nobles became rich by collecting taxes. They began to fight each other in a series of **civil wars**.

Eventually, the central government collapsed. There was confusion and chaos throughout Egypt. This chaotic time was known as the First Intermediate Period. Without a strong pharaoh and central government, society started to break down. Egyptians no longer repaired the irrigation system, which greatly affected their food supplies. People wanted strong rulers to govern Egypt again.

The Middle Kingdom

Eventually, a new **dynasty** of pharaohs was established. This was the beginning of the Middle Kingdom. The Middle Kingdom lasted from 2061 to 1784 B.C. The new and improved government of the Middle Kingdom showed its strength by invading the land called Nubia. Nubia (modern-day Sudan) was an area of Africa, south of the Egyptian kingdom, rich in minerals and gold. This gold brought great wealth to the Egyptian people and their pharaohs.

However, the pharaohs could not keep their power because of poor leadership and **corruption**. Eventually, the nobles rebelled against the pharaohs. Egypt became weak from fighting more civil wars. For the first time in its history, a foreign group took control of Egypt. This group was known as the Hyksos. This period of time is called the Second Intermediate Period.

◀ This is a drawing of a Hyksos hunting chariot. The Hyksos introduced new technology to the Egyptians.

Hyksos Take Control

The Hyksos easily took over Egypt. They adopted many aspects of Egyptian culture. The Hyksos rulers even called themselves pharaohs. The Hyksos introduced new weapons to the Egyptians, including the two-wheeled horse-drawn chariot and a new kind of bow. After ruling Egypt for only 100 years, an Egyptian army from the city of Thebes forced the Hyksos out of Egypt. The Egyptians were united and became powerful once again. They used their new power and the new weapons the Hyksos had introduced to build one last great ancient kingdom. This is known as the New Kingdom (1570–1070 B.C.).

The New Kingdom

During the New Kingdom, the pharaohs were determined to protect Egypt from further invasions. They decided to expand outward and create a new empire. The Egyptians conquered land as far north as Syria and Palestine. They also conquered areas to the south of Nubia. The people in the lands they conquered paid large amounts of **tribute** to the Egyptians. Once again Egypt had become a rich and powerful kingdom. With the new wealth, Egyptians built new temples to honor their gods. They also restored old temples that had fallen into disrepair. The capital city of Thebes became one of the richest cities of the age. Many different pharaohs ruled during the New Kingdom. However, one New Kingdom pharaoh stands out because he caused much trouble. His name was Akhenaton and he tried to change the Egyptian religion. He wanted everyone to worship Aton, a god of the sun. He closed most temples where people worshiped other gods. This caused many problems. Egypt briefly lost much of its conquered land.

▲ Pharaoh Akhenaton and his queen Nefertiti are playing a game called *senet.* Senet was a very popular game among all classes of Egyptians during the New Kingdom.

treaty: an agreement or settlement

What Do You Think?

1. What are the three major periods in ancient Egyptian history?

2. How are the three major periods similar? How are they different? Which period would you have wanted to live in? Why?

3. During what period in ancient Egyptian history did the rulers begin to build pyramids?

4. What were the advantages and disadvantages of Egypt's isolation?

Battles with the Hittites

The New Kingdom returned to greatness under a new dynasty of rulers who conquered many new lands. However, another group of people—the Hittites—was becoming very powerful. The Hittites, who had conquered Mesopotamia, would not let Egypt expand without a fight. The Egyptians and Hittites fought many long wars and fierce battles. The fighting ended with a famous peace **treaty** under the Pharaoh Ramses II. This was the first written peace treaty in history. However, the constant fighting had weakened the Egyptian empire. It began its long, final decline.

The New Kingdom Fades

Following the death of Ramses's son, Ramses III, Egyptian religious leaders, nobles, and even the military began to fight one another. Already weakened by war with the Hittites, Egypt never regained the strength and power it had achieved during the New Kingdom. 📖

▶ The Egyptians fought many wars.

KHUFU

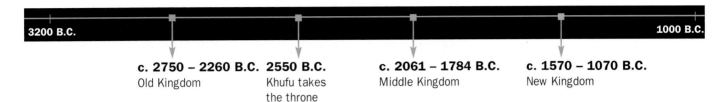

c. 2750 – 2260 B.C.
Old Kingdom

2550 B.C.
Khufu takes
the throne

c. 2061 – 1784 B.C.
Middle Kingdom

c. 1570 – 1070 B.C.
New Kingdom

The Pharaoh Khufu ruled ancient Egypt during the Old Kingdom period. During this time, pharaohs began to build temples in honor of the gods. They also built tombs to honor themselves and help them in the afterlife. Khufu is remembered for building what became known as the Great Pyramid of Giza.

Khufu—Man and God

Khufu became pharaoh in 2550 B.C. and ruled Egypt for 23 years. Like the pharaohs before him, Khufu was considered both a god and a man. Khufu set himself apart from past rulers by claiming to be connected to two powerful Egyptian gods. This made the position of pharaoh even more powerful.

Life under Khufu

Khufu used his power to organize a better, stronger government. He divided the kingdom into 42 districts and chose governors to represent him in each district. These governors collected taxes to support Khufu's government. They also enforced Khufu's laws. Since money had not yet been invented during Khufu's reign, taxes were usually paid with cows and crops.

Khufu was known as a great traveler. He visited different areas of the kingdom to lead religious ceremonies at the many temples. Priests and members of his court often joined him on his journeys. While on these journeys, Khufu and his traveling partners enjoyed sailing, hunting, and fishing.

▲ Giza is on a high **plateau** overlooking the Nile River.

plateau: a flat, elevated area of land

▲ Artisans created carvings such as these on the walls of palaces, tombs, and temples.

When Khufu was not traveling, he enjoyed life at his court. Thanks to his excellent organization and tax collection system, his court could buy gold, jewelry, and fine food and drink. The arts also flourished under Khufu. He hired artisans to create elaborate stone carvings. He also hosted large parties with dancing and musical performances.

Building the Great Pyramid

Khufu wanted to build a great monument to himself that would show future generations how great and powerful he was. He chose the Giza Plateau as the place to build this great pyramid. The plateau is located high above the Nile Valley, making it an impressive place for the impressive pharaoh. The plateau consisted mainly of limestone. The limestone provided most of the building material needed for construction.

Khufu used his well-organized government to manage the building of the pyramid. The construction of his tomb became a national project. Khufu demanded that the governors of Egypt's 42 districts provide him with thousands and thousands of workers. Once these workers arrived at Giza, they were divided into well-organized work groups. Each group was assigned a special job. It was considered an honor to work on the construction of Khufu's pyramid. Many of these workers took the skills they learned and made new careers for themselves in stonecutting, boat building, and art.

▼ The Great Pyramid of Giza is surrounded by smaller pyramids and temples.

Khufu's Legacy

Following Khufu's death, his body was mummified. The Egyptians believed that by preserving a person's body through mummification, that person's spirit would better recognize his body in the afterlife. After many religious ceremonies, Khufu's mummy was placed in a sealed tomb in the Great Pyramid. Khufu also left behind strict orders about how priests should honor his spirit and protect his tomb. And, while the greatness of the Old Kingdom did not last forever, Khufu's wish to be remembered survived through the centuries to the present day—4,500 years later. The Great Pyramid, along with its two smaller neighboring pyramids, remains one of the great wonders of the world. 📖

It's a FACT

Five large boats were buried in the Great Pyramid to help Khufu sail across the sky in the afterlife.

Over 35,000 people lived in workers' villages around the pyramid construction site.

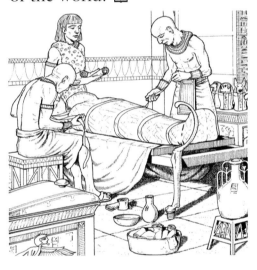

◀ To prepare a body for mummification, the internal organs were removed, and the body was cleansed and specially treated and then tightly wrapped.

What Do You Think?

1. What did Khufu do to make the position of pharaoh more powerful?

2. Name three things that Khufu did to make the Egyptian government run better. Which do you think was most important? Why?

3. Why did Khufu want to build such a large pyramid? Why do people build large monuments today?

4. How did the building of the Great Pyramid change Egyptian society?

Under Khufu's rule, Egypt developed:

- A stronger, better-organized government

- A better way for the government to collect taxes and pay for government programs

- A sense of national pride with the building of the Great Pyramid

- A large group of skilled workers who would pass on their knowledge to future generations

- A more complex religious organization

- A large group of priests who would pass on their knowledge to future religious leaders

THUTMOSE I, THUTMOSE II, HATSHEPSUT, AND THUTMOSE III

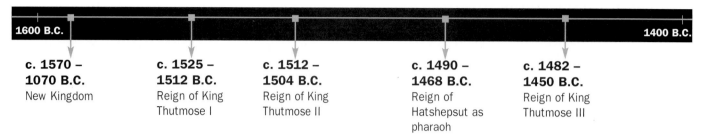

| 1600 B.C. | | | | | 1400 B.C. |

c. 1570 – 1070 B.C.
New Kingdom

c. 1525 – 1512 B.C.
Reign of King Thutmose I

c. 1512 – 1504 B.C.
Reign of King Thutmose II

c. 1490 – 1468 B.C.
Reign of Hatshepsut as pharaoh

c. 1482 – 1450 B.C.
Reign of King Thutmose III

▲ During the New Kingdom, Egypt conquered Nubia in the south and territory as far north as Syria.

Thutmose I, Thutmose II, Hatshepsut, and Thutmose III all ruled during Egypt's New Kingdom. The New Kingdom was established when the Egyptians forced the Hyksos out of Egypt. These rulers helped build and expand Egypt's New Kingdom by conquering Nubia in the south and territory as far north as Syria.

Thutmose I

Thutmose I was a commoner. He served first as a soldier and later as a general under the Pharaoh Amenhotep I. Thutmose married the princess Ahmose. When Amenhotep I died without an **heir**, Thutmose seemed to be the logical choice to become pharaoh. Thutmose used his military skills to conquer lands from Nubia in the south all the way to Syria and the Euphrates River in the north. His victories brought wealth and stability to the new empire.

Thutmose I was known as a great builder. While he was pharaoh, he had monuments built in honor of his military victories. One monument, now known as the **Obelisk** of Thutmose I at Karnak Temple, still stands today. It is 64 feet in height.

◀ This is the Washington Monument in Washington, D.C. The Obelisk of Thutmose may have been an inspiration to the designers of this monument, who were seeking to capture the mystery and greatness of the ancient Egyptian monuments.

Thutmose II

Thutmose II, like his father Thutmose I, was not fully of noble blood. To strengthen his position as pharaoh, he married his half-sister Hatshepsut, whose mother was the princess Ahmose. Thutmose II also enjoyed military successes in Nubia against the people of Kush and against the **Bedouin** tribes in the area around Palestine. These victories strengthened the new Egyptian empire. However, historians believe that Thutmose II was rarely in good health. He died after a short reign. When he died, his son Thutmose III was too young to rule Egypt on his own.

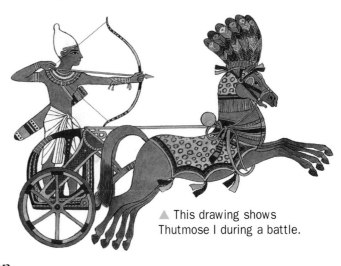

▲ This drawing shows Thutmose I during a battle.

Hatshepsut—A Woman Pharaoh

Hatshepsut, who was older than her husband Thutmose II, declared herself pharaoh within a year of his death. While Egyptian women enjoyed certain rights in their society, and there had been queens of Egypt in the past, Hatshepsut was the first woman to declare herself a pharaoh. This shocked many Egyptians. As a result, Hatshepsut may have spent a lot of time and energy defending herself. She tried to take full credit for forcing the Hyksos to leave Egypt. She also claimed that her father, Thutmose I, had wanted her to be his heir and not Thutmose II.

Hatshepsut proved her strength as a ruler by sending a trading expedition to the mysterious land of Punt, which was probably located in modern-day Somalia. This expedition established trade with the people of Punt. It brought Egypt into contact with other peoples of Africa. Egyptians learned about new spices, ivory, ebony, and even animals and trees never before seen in Egypt.

Thutmose III

After Thutmose III became an adult, he led a successful rebellion against Hatshepsut. Then he became pharaoh in his own right. Little is known of what happened to Hatshepsut. Thutmose III tried to erase Hatshepsut from history. He made sure that monuments and carvings that mentioned or honored Hatshepsut were destroyed. The ancient remains from this time show how someone tried to scratch out any mention or picture of Hatshepsut.

▲ This is a drawing of Hatshepsut, the first woman in Egypt to call herself pharaoh.

Bedouin: a member of a group of nomadic peoples who traveled through and settled in the deserts of southwestern Asia

heir: a person who is next in line to assume a title or office

obelisk: a tall, slim stone pillar with a pyramid on the top

alliance: a formal agreement, partnership, or connection between people or groups

▲ This is a drawing of Thutmose III.

◄ Thutmose III had carvings of Hatshepsut erased. You can see a small portion of the carving that was not erased.

What Do You Think?

1. What did Hatshepsut do that no Egyptian woman had done before?

2. How did marrying noble women help both Thutmose I and Thutmose II? Can marrying well help people advance in society today? Explain your answer.

3. Why do you think Thutmose III wanted to erase Hatshepsut from history?

Thutmose III went on to become a great pharaoh and strong military leader. In Palestine, Thutmose III defeated an **alliance** led by the king of Kadesh and peoples who wanted to be independent from Egypt. Thutmose III led his chariots and army along a narrow and dangerous path to fight the Kadesh alliance at the fortress called Meggido. By taking the most dangerous route instead of the easier routes, Thutmose III surprised the Kadesh alliance and became known as a great military leader. Thutmose made sure that the rulers of all of Egypt's territories paid tribute to him. This made Egypt wealthier and more secure.

Expanding Egypt

All four of these rulers—Thutmose I, Thutmose II, Hatshepsut, and Thutmose III—played an important role in the development of Egypt's New Kingdom and the Egyptian empire. Through military victories and trade with new peoples, Egypt grew both culturally and economically. ▢

Reader's Theater
Presents

THE STORY OF PHARAOH HATSHEPSUT

Practice reading the script. When the script says, "PEOPLE OF EGYPT," everyone in the class joins in the reading. Read with expression! ➝

ROLES

★ NARRATOR 1
★ NARRATOR 2
★ SENMUT
★ HATSHEPSUT
★ NEFERURA
★ PEOPLE OF EGYPT (ALL)

Narrator 1: Long ago, in the land of Egypt, a little girl named Neferura was crying quietly in her room.

Narrator 2: Neferura's teacher, Senmut, found her there and tried to comfort her.

Senmut: Why are you crying, little Neferura?

Neferura: The other kids were making fun of me. They say my mother can't be a real pharaoh because she is a woman.

Senmut: Don't cry, Neferura. Those kids don't know how special your mother is.

Narrator 1: Neferura's mother was no ordinary Egyptian woman.

Narrator 2: Her mother was Hatshepsut, the pharaoh of Egypt.

Neferura: I still don't see why she can't be like all the other mothers.

Senmut: Well, why don't I tell you the story of your mother? When I'm done, you won't be sad anymore. You will be very proud of her.

Neferura: I don't know about that. But tell me the story anyway.

Senmut: Do you know that when you were very little, your father was the pharaoh?

Neferura: Yes, everyone knows that.

Senmut: Well, after your father died, the people were very worried.

People of Egypt: Our pharaoh is gone! Who will lead us now?

Senmut: Normally, your little brother would have become the pharaoh. But he was too young. So your mother went to see the priests of Re, the sun god.

Hatshepsut: The people have no pharaoh, and my son is not old enough. What should I do?

Senmut: The priests said that Re wanted Hatshepsut to be the pharaoh.

People of Egypt: But Hatshepsut is a woman! Only a man can be pharaoh!

Senmut: Your mother thought about it for a long time. Then she had an idea.

Hatshepsut: I know what I'll do. I will dress like a man, and wear the beard of a man. Then the people will see me as the pharaoh, and Re will be happy.

Neferura: What happened then?

Senmut: After your mother became the pharaoh, she decided to do many great things.

Hatshepsut: I will send ships to faraway lands and bring back wonderful things for my people.

Neferura: Where did they go?

Senmut: To the land of Punt, a very long distance from here. They brought back gold, spices, and many new animals.

People of Egypt: What great things you've brought us!

Hatshepsut: I will build great temples and statues.

Senmut: She built the largest statues in the entire world.

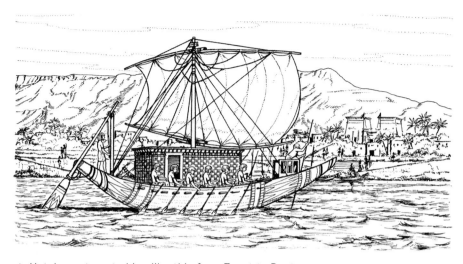

▲ Hatshepsut sent ships like this from Egypt to Punt.

Narrator 1: Some of these statues can be seen even today, more than three thousand years later.

Narrator 2: Of course, you have to go to Egypt to see them in person.

Senmut: So you see, that's why your mother is so special. Do you feel better now?

Neferura: Yes I do! I'm going to go tell the other children. They won't think it's so funny anymore.

Senmut: Well, go and tell them. But be nice!

Neferura: I will. Thanks! 📖

▲ This is Hatshepsut's tomb and temple on the Nile River.

TUTANKHAMEN

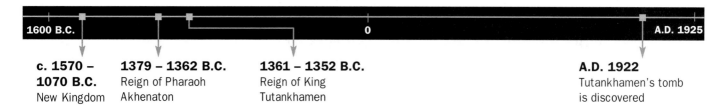

c. 1570 – 1070 B.C.
New Kingdom

1379 – 1362 B.C.
Reign of Pharaoh
Akhenaton

1361 – 1352 B.C.
Reign of King
Tutankhamen

A.D. 1922
Tutankhamen's tomb
is discovered

The Pharaoh Tutankhamen, also called King Tut, is probably the most famous pharaoh in history. Tutankhamen is not remembered for what he did in life, but for the spectacular tomb in which he was buried. This tomb was discovered in 1922. English archaeologists discovered a room filled with gold, statues, chariots, and furniture. They then discovered a back room where they found Tut's body. It had been well preserved in tightly wrapped cloth. His body had been placed inside a golden **sarcophagus**.

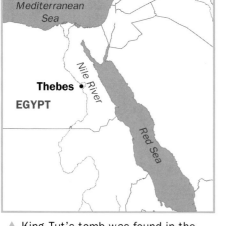

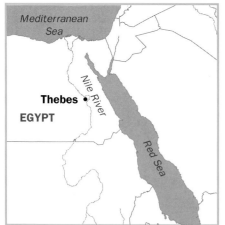

▲ King Tut's tomb was found in the Valley of the Kings in Thebes.

The Afterlife

The ancient Egyptians believed that after people died, their bodies and spirits went to the afterlife. They believed that in this next world they would need things from their everyday life on earth. The richer and more powerful the person, the more things that person would need in the afterlife. That is why the pharaohs had great tombs such as the pyramids built for themselves.

The Boy King

Tutankhamen was born into a very **turbulent** time during the New Kingdom. Pharaoh Akhenaton, also known as King Amenhotep IV, had forced a new religion upon his people. Instead of allowing people to worship many different gods, Akhenaton ordered everyone to worship the god Aton. This angered many people, including the priests of the many different temples who had to give up much of their wealth to the pharaoh. When both Akhenaton and his son died within months of each other, Tutankhamen was made pharaoh. He was only nine years old at the time. It is not clear whether Tut was a nephew or other relative of Akhenaton.

▲ Tutankhamen became pharaoh when he was only nine years old.

A Popular Leader

Because Tutankhamen was so young when he became pharaoh, a priest named Ay advised him. Ay convinced Tut to restore the old religion. He persuaded Tut to allow people to worship whichever gods they wanted. Tut also restored all the old religious temples, which had fallen into disrepair under Akhenaton. These actions made Tut very popular. They also made Ay very powerful.

Tutankhamen died at the age of 18 under mysterious circumstances. Some historians think he died of a rare disease. Others believe he may have been poisoned or murdered by Ay. Tut was young but was starting to act more independently. Perhaps Ay thought Tut would no longer need his guidance. Perhaps Ay thought he would be a better king. In fact, after Tut died, Ay married Tut's wife and became the pharaoh himself.

King Tut's Legacy

Tutankhamen's greatest legacy is found in the material goods that he left behind. His remains and his untouched tomb have given archaeologists and historians a clearer understanding of what life was like for ancient Egyptians. 📖

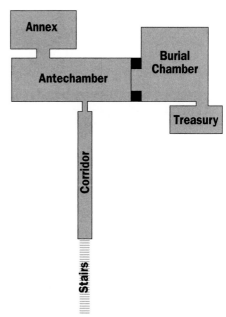

▲ This diagram shows the layout of Tutankhamen's tomb chambers that archaeologists found in 1922.

sarcophagus: a container (or coffin) carved or decorated with sculpture in which a dead body is placed

turbulent: chaotic; unstable; confused

 What Do You Think?

1. Why did Egyptian pharaohs fill their tombs with so much wealth and so many everyday objects?

2. Who helped the young boy Tut rule Egypt?

3. For what reasons might some ancient Egyptians want to see a boy become pharaoh?

4. Ancient Egyptians did not have the same kind of freedom of religion that we have in America today. Still, they valued the ability to worship their own gods. Why do you think freedom of religion was important to the ancient Egyptians? Why is it important today?

RAMSES THE GREAT

| 1600 B.C. | | | 0 | A.D. 1900 |

c. 1570 – 1070 B.C.
New Kingdom

c. 1289 – 1224 B.C.
Ramses the Great is pharaoh

1270 B.C.
Ramses signs peace treaty with the Hittites

A.D. 1881
Archaeologists discover the tomb of Ramses the Great

▲ Ramses the Great had monuments built all over Egypt.

Ramses the Great, also called Ramses II, was the third ruler of Egypt's 19th dynasty. Ramses the Great was known as a great warrior and builder. He ruled Egypt for 66 years.

A Great Warrior and Builder

While still a prince, Ramses was sent by his father, Pharaoh Seti I, to stop a rebellion in the southern kingdom of Nubia. Ramses used his skill with horse-drawn chariots—something the Egyptians had learned from the Hyksos—to win the battle and make a name for himself. A few years later, Seti I died. As a result, Ramses became pharaoh. He was only 24 years old.

After Ramses became pharaoh, he used his time and energy to build great temples that honored the Egyptian gods. He also built monuments for both his father and himself. Ramses had many wives during his long life, but his most famous was Queen Nefertari. Nefertari was known for her beauty and for the support she gave Ramses.

A Glimpse into Ancient Egypt

Ramses the Great is very popular with archaeologists. Because he built so many temples and monuments, archaeologists have been able to learn a lot about Ramses and what life was like during his lifetime. Ramses ordered that the stories of great events of his life be carved on the walls of these buildings. Archaeologists have learned a great deal from these carvings. Some of the most impressive monuments in all of Egypt were built under Ramses the Great, including the Luxor temples and a statue of Ramses seated at a grand throne. This is one of the largest statues ever made.

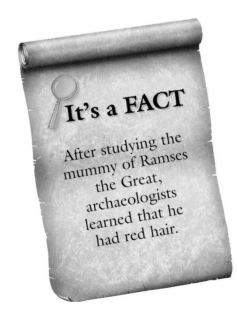

It's a FACT

After studying the mummy of Ramses the Great, archaeologists learned that he had red hair.

In 1881, archaeologists discovered the mummy of Ramses the Great in a secret tomb, hidden from grave robbers. After studying the mummy, archaeologists learned that Ramses had died of natural causes.

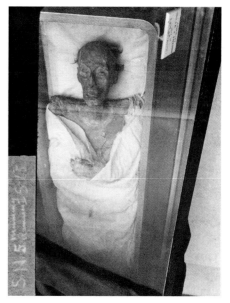

▲ Ramses the Great's mummy is at the Egyptian Museum in Cairo, Egypt.

▲ These statues are at the entrance of the Great Temple at Abu Simbel. All four statues represent Ramses the Great.

War and Peace with the Hittites

Ramses the Great spent much of his **reign** fighting the Hittites. The Hittites had their own empire and controlled the lands of present-day Turkey, Mesopotamia, and northern Syria. While Ramses was still a young man, the Egyptians and the Hittites fought a four-day battle at the walled city of **Kadesh**. Ramses led 20,000 Egyptian soldiers into battle against almost 40,000 Hittites.

Kadesh: the fortress-like, walled Egyptian city where a great battle was fought between Ramses the Great's army and the Hittites

reign: rule

◄ Ramses II fought the Hittites at the battle of Kadesh.

compromise: a settlement in which both sides give up some of the things they want

What Do You Think?

1. Why did Ramses fight with the Hittites?

2. Why did Ramses make peace with the Hittites?

3. In what ways were the many temples and monuments built by Ramses important to archaeologists?

4. What were the advantages of Ramses's long rule as pharaoh?

While the battle seemed to end in a tie, Ramses claimed victory because his soldiers had been outnumbered almost two to one. In some accounts of the battle, it is said that Ramses fought off the Hittites all by himself.

The war with the Hittites went on for many more years with many battles. Eventually, both sides realized that a peace treaty would be the best **compromise** for both kingdoms. This treaty, signed in 1270 B.C., was the first peace treaty in recorded history. The remainder of Ramses's reign was a peaceful one. Without the expense of war, Ramses was able to use his wealth to improve the lives of his subjects, and to continue to build great monuments.

▲ This photograph shows a relief of Ramses on the temple wall.

The Legacy of Ramses the Great

Ramses the Great died around 1224 B.C. He was 96 years old. Ramses is considered one of Egypt's greatest pharaohs. He was a great warrior and a great peacemaker. We have learned a great deal about ancient Egypt by studying the buildings and monuments he left behind. 📖

▲ This is the Temple of Ramses II in Abydos, Egypt.

RELIGION IN ANCIENT EGYPT

Religion was a very important part of life in ancient Egypt. Religion shaped Egyptian culture. Ancient Egypt's government, medicine, arts, and sciences all were influenced by the Egyptians' religious beliefs.

Worship of Many Gods

The religion of ancient Egypt was polytheistic. This means the Egyptians worshiped many gods. Their gods took different forms, including human, animal, and spirit forms. Some gods had both human and animal features. The Egyptians believed in gods of the sky, sun, earth, and even the Nile River itself.

The Egyptians also believed that all of creation was tied together, or interconnected, including humans and nature. They felt that people's lives were affected by the changing of the seasons, the changing of the tides, the movement of the stars, the sun, and the phases of the moon. There were gods that controlled these things, and in turn controlled the lives of the people.

It's a FACT

The ancient Egyptians worshiped a goddess of cats named Basteet.

EGYPTIAN GODS AND GODDESSES

NUT	GEB	HATHOR	OSIRIS
Goddess of the Sky	God of the Earth	God of Music	God of the Dead

▲ Over the thousands of years of ancient Egyptian history, gods rose and fell in importance. These pictures and the ones on the next page show some of the Egyptian gods and goddesses.

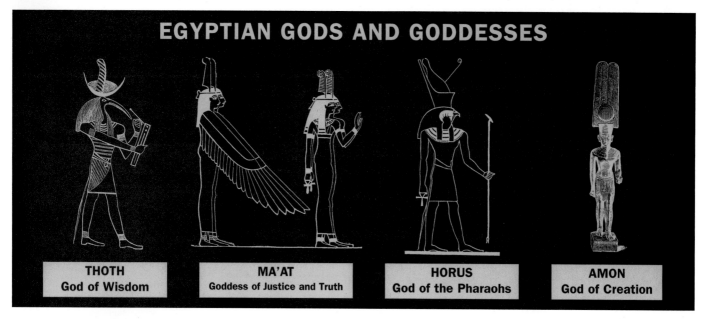

EGYPTIAN GODS AND GODDESSES

| **THOTH** God of Wisdom | **MA'AT** Goddess of Justice and Truth | **HORUS** God of the Pharaohs | **AMON** God of Creation |

▲ This is an illustration of a column with masks of Hathor, god of music, carved into it.

The Afterlife

The ancient Egyptians were very concerned with the afterlife—the world a person entered after death. They did not believe that death was the end, but rather the beginning of eternal life. The Egyptians believed it was very important how a person entered the afterlife. Egyptians buried their dead with many possessions important to everyday life. They believed these things would be needed in the next life. Mummification was also a common practice in ancient Egypt. Egyptians believed it was important for the body to be protected during the long journey to the afterlife when the body would come back to life.

Pyramids

In the early part of ancient Egyptian civilization, only the pharaoh and the very wealthy had the resources to pay for all the religious ceremonies that prepared a person for the afterlife. The great pyramids and tombs of the pharaohs were all built to ensure the safe passage of the pharaoh to the afterlife. Some pharaohs even had great sailing ships buried with them. However, as time passed, all people were able to participate in these special ceremonies to prepare for the afterlife. Soon rules and codes were developed to help people properly carry out the afterlife preparations. People wrote manuals to record these rules. The best example of one of these manuals is *The Book of the Dead*. Not only did people have to worry about making the journey to the afterlife, but they also had to worry about being judged by the gods for their actions on earth.

The Book of the Dead

The Book of the Dead is a collection of hymns, prayers, and instructions on how people could succeed in the afterlife journey and please the gods. One part of *The Book of the Dead* contains a prayer that must be read in front of the gods. This prayer was intended to prove that the individual had lived a good life. The person being judged had to make many promises, including that he or she has not:

- committed evil or murder
- done violence to the poor or mistreated slaves
- allowed anyone to suffer or go hungry
- caused pain to the Egyptian people
- stolen offerings in the temples
- cheated in business dealings
- stolen land or water, or damaged a canal
- harmed children or animals

This prayer shows that even the weakest and poorest in society had some protection. The protection of land, animals, and the water supply also were very important issues to the Egyptians.

The Pharaohs as God-Kings

The ancient Egyptians believed that their kings, or pharaohs, had special powers given to them by the gods. Upon becoming a pharaoh, a person was no longer a mere human being. Pharaohs were joined with Horus, the god of the pharaohs. Horus gave the pharaohs strength, wisdom, and special knowledge of the gods. The pharaohs played a critical role because everything was connected to and controlled by them.

The pharaohs owned all the land, controlled the entire government, and demanded the people's complete loyalty. The pharaohs could force people to work on special projects such as irrigation systems, temples, and pyramids. In return, the pharaohs promised to rule according to Ma'at. This meant that they would act with justice, law, and truth as their guide. The pharaohs made sure that people had enough food and water, and that the government was prepared to help people in times of emergency. People believed that as long as the pharaoh lived according to Ma'at, no evil would happen to the kingdom. However, if a pharaoh failed in these duties, Egypt would face great problems. 📖

▲ This is an illustration of a statue of Osiris, god of the dead.

What Do You Think?

1. Who did the people of ancient Egypt believe controlled their lives?

2. What is *The Book of the Dead*?

3. Ancient Egyptians believed that the pharaohs were god-kings. How did this belief help explain why good and bad things happened?

4. Egyptian pharaohs were both religious and political leaders. What are the advantages and disadvantages of a system where there is no separation between church and state?

DAILY LIVES
of Ordinary People

Egyptians were usually expected to follow in the footsteps of their parents. If a boy's father was a farmer, he was expected to become a farmer. There were many kinds of craftsmen and artisans, including stonecutters, carpenters, boat builders, carvers, blacksmiths, and even barbers. Fathers would pass their knowledge and skills on to their sons. While women and girls usually were not allowed to participate in the same kinds of activities as the men and boys, they still had busy lives. Women played an important role in the temples. They weaved, danced, and played instruments. The flute and harp were the most common instruments in ancient Egypt.

▲ Scribes were very important members of Egyptian society. They were always in demand because many people did not know how to read and write.

Scribes: Writing for the People

One of the most desirable jobs in ancient Egypt was that of a scribe. Why? Scribes were very important members of Egyptian society, and the job of a scribe required very little hard physical labor. Scribes were taught to read and write using the hieroglyphs. It was not easy learning how to write the thousands of picture-words. Scribes spent years of study in special schools. Scribes kept records for the government, the temples, and large households. They wrote letters for people and businesses, agreements for merchants, and private prayers for people. They also were responsible for writing the stories and histories that were carved on the stone walls of the temples and tombs. These accounts have given archaeologists and historians important information about the ancient Egyptians.

▲ This drawing shows Egyptian women playing the harp.

Traders: Bringing Goods around the World

Because Egypt was surrounded by desert, travel by boat became very important. Water transportation was the primary way Egyptians traded with each other and with other cultures. Cargo boats carried Egyptian goods to other areas. These goods included baskets, pottery, blocks of granite and bricks, cattle, and food. Since wood was scarce along the Nile, it was common for Egyptians to trade with the people of present-day Lebanon, who had a surplus of trees.

◀ Animals such as oxen and donkeys helped farmers plow the fields.

mine: a hole in the earth where people dig out metals, salt, and other minerals

Farming: Providing Food

The Nile River regularly flooded during the summer. The Egyptians welcomed this flooding. It provided rich nutrients for the soil. As a result, Egyptians had excellent farmland and farming was a common occupation. When the Nile flooded, farmers could not work in the fields, but they still had lots to do. They kept busy making tools to plow the land, jugs to transport water to the crops, and cloth sacks to hold grain. During the flooding, farmers also were called upon to work on building projects sponsored by the pharaohs.

When the Nile River flooding stopped, farmers immediately began to repair the canals and irrigation systems. Then they plowed and seeded the fields. While farming could be extremely difficult, farmers usually were rewarded for their labor with large crops. The Egyptian diet included many different kinds of breads made with wheat and barley. Honey, milk, and eggs also were common. Figs and grapes grew well in the Egyptian climate and were popular fruits and desserts.

Slaves: Supporting Egypt

Slavery became an accepted and important part of life in ancient Egypt. Slaves were usually people from foreign lands defeated by Egypt's great armies. Egyptian citizens could become slaves if they were unable to pay their bills or taxes. Slaves were usually put to work at temples, construction sites, or in **mines** to support Egypt's many building projects.

Slaves in ancient Egypt could be bought, sold, and even rented. However, slaves were allowed to save money, marry free people, and could even buy their freedom. Slaves could even hire servants of their own. Slaves who had a special skill could lead comfortable lives and gain their freedom. Freed slaves enjoyed the same rights as other Egyptian citizens. 📖

 What Do You Think?

1. Boys and girls in ancient Egypt had different job opportunities. What were they?

2. Why were scribes so important in ancient Egypt? Are writers as important today? Explain your answer.

3. Which job do you think was most important in ancient Egypt? Which job would you have wanted to have? Why?

▲ This drawing shows a slave girl (on the left) helping an Egyptian woman.

EGYPTIAN
Architecture and Art

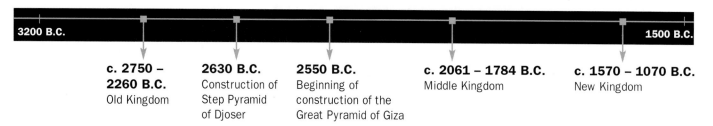

3200 B.C.

**c. 2750 –
2260 B.C.**
Old Kingdom

2630 B.C.
Construction of
Step Pyramid
of Djoser

2550 B.C.
Beginning of
construction of the
Great Pyramid of Giza

c. 2061 – 1784 B.C.
Middle Kingdom

c. 1570 – 1070 B.C.
New Kingdom

1500 B.C.

Egyptian architecture and art were greatly influenced by the Egyptians' religious beliefs. Because Egyptian religion was so focused on the importance of the afterlife, tombs became the main focus of architecture. Ancient Egyptians believed that a person's spirit would enter the afterlife, and that the spirit would continue to use the person's body. Because of this, mummification and the practice of burying food, furniture, pets, and even boats with the dead person became very common. The tomb to hold the mummies and all the things for the afterlife was very important.

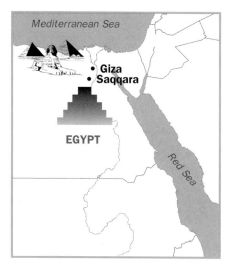

▲ Pharaoh Djoser had a step pyramid built in Saqqara. The most famous Egyptian pyramids are in Giza.

Early Tombs in Ancient Egypt

In the early years of the ancient Egyptian civilization, tombs were very simple. Most were rectangular, flat, and made of mud bricks. This design was meant to best protect the interior from the wear and tear of time and weather. Over the years, Egyptians built larger tombs as more and more possessions were buried with mummies. Soon the tombs were built with rounded roofs. These roofs reminded Egyptians of their belief about how life began. They believed that life began when land first popped out of a water-covered world. The rounded roof of the tomb looked like a small island of land popping out of the water. Tombs for wealthy and powerful Egyptians could be very large and complex. Some were the size of palaces.

The Step Pyramid of Djoser

During the Old Kingdom, in 2630 B.C., Pharaoh Djoser wanted to make a tomb for himself that was bigger than anything that had been built before. He hired Imhotep, the best architect in Egypt, to design his tomb.

The base of Djoser's tomb was a flat, rectangular shape. Then Imhotep decided to build upward. He built layer on top of layer. The design looked much like a layered cake. When it was finished, Djoser was very pleased with the "step pyramid," which was over 200-feet high. No one had ever built anything like it before. Imhotep also developed the process of covering over the mud bricks with stone blocks. The stone blocks formed a long-lasting, protective outer shell around the pyramid. Djoser believed this tomb would serve him well in the afterlife.

▲ This is the Step Pyramid of Djoser. The Step Pyramid is like a giant layer cake. It is in Saqqara, Egypt.

The Pyramids of Giza

Following the building of Djoser's pyramid, pharaohs began constructing larger and grander pyramid tombs. Around 2550 B.C., Pharaoh Khufu decided that he would outdo Djoser and built the Great Pyramid of Giza. Khufu's pyramid, built high above the Nile River on the Giza Plateau, was 481-feet high. This was more than twice the height of Djoser's pyramid. Khufu's son, Pharaoh Khafre, built his own pyramid at Giza. Khufu's grandson, Pharaoh Menkaure, also built his own pyramid at Giza. While the pyramids by Khafre and Menkaure were not as big as Khufu's pyramid, all three are examples of Egyptian organization and engineering.

▶ This photograph shows the most famous Egyptian pyramids, which are located in Giza.

▲ Some historians believe that the nose of the Sphinx was shot off by Turkish soldiers who were using the monument for target practice.

▲ In recent years, Egyptians have tried to restore parts of the Sphinx.

It's a FACT

Egyptian gods were always drawn or carved with human bodies and the heads of special animals.

---

posture: the way a person stands, sits, or walks

The Sphinx

Also located at Giza is the mysterious Sphinx. The Sphinx, which has the head of a pharaoh and the body of a lion, is 66-feet high and 187-feet long. While no one is sure exactly when the Sphinx was made or who built it, some experts believe the head is of Khufu's son, Pharaoh Khafre. It is also believed that the Sphinx was meant to guard all the pyramids and tombs at Giza. Carved out of limestone, the Sphinx has suffered much damage over the centuries. Khafre's nose and beard have fallen off, and there is damage to parts of the lion body including the feet and tail. Despite the damage to the Sphinx, it stands as a reminder of the artistic skill and vision of the ancient Egyptians.

Artistic Rules

Egyptian artists had to work within very strict artistic rules, which changed very little over the centuries. One of the artistic rules they followed is called Frontalism. According to the rule of Frontalism, people and gods were drawn with their heads facing to the side and their bodies facing forward. The **posture** of people in the paintings and sculptures was very stiff. The faces were always drawn to show the person calm and at peace.

Gods in Art

Today, creativity is often the most important factor in judging great artists. In ancient Egypt, the best artists were the people who closely followed the strict rules of art. To put it another way, the best artists of ancient Egypt were the ones who could copy the best!

The Egyptians did not believe that gods had animal heads and human bodies. However, this is how they were shown in Egyptian art. The animal heads represented the gods' powers and the human bodies showed that the gods were more than just animals.

▲ This is an example of Egyptian art.

The Use of Color and Size

Egyptian artists used a great deal of color in their jewelry, statues, and paintings. Color had very important symbolic meaning to the Egyptians. Red usually represented the desert and power. Blue represented the Nile and life. Yellow represented the sun. Because the climate of Egypt is so dry, much of the color of the ancient art has survived to modern times. Even some of the original paint on the Sphinx has survived.

Size also played a role in Egyptian art. The more important a figure in a particular drawing or carving, the larger it was. Certain kings and gods were drawn much larger than the persons and things around them. Their large size showed their importance. This is also seen in the pyramids. Later pharaohs would try to outdo earlier pharaohs of the past by building bigger and bigger monuments, temples, and tombs. 📖

What Do You Think?

1. What did the first Egyptian tombs look like? How did they change over time?

2. Why do you think size was important in ancient Egyptian art? Is size important in art today? Explain your answer.

3. What do you think the Sphinx represents? What evidence supports your answer?

4. Why do you think that Egyptian art changed so little throughout the history of ancient Egypt?

EGYPTIAN LANGUAGE AND WRITING

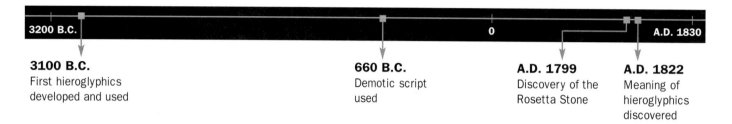

| 3200 B.C. | | 0 | | A.D. 1830 |

3100 B.C.
First hieroglyphics
developed and used

660 B.C.
Demotic script
used

A.D. 1799
Discovery of the
Rosetta Stone

A.D. 1822
Meaning of
hieroglyphics
discovered

Like the Sumerians in Mesopotamia who created cuneiform writing, the Egyptians developed their own written language called hieroglyphics. Unlike English, where words are formed by combining some of the 26 letters in the English alphabet, Egyptian hieroglyphs were pictures meaning different words, actions, or ideas. During the Middle Kingdom period in Egyptian history, there were over 750 hieroglyphic pictures. Toward the end of the New Kingdom, there were thousands of pictures in the hieroglyphic alphabet!

Reading Hieroglyphics: A Difficult Task!

In the hieroglyphic alphabet, some pictures represented sounds like the "th" sound. Other pictures stood for whole words. For example, squiggly lines represented "water." A picture of a cow meant "cow." There were no symbols for vowels (A, E, I, O, U). The Egyptians knew what vowel sounds to make depending on how the pictures were arranged. They did not use any punctuation—things such as commas, periods, and question marks.

| **Hieroglyphs** | | | | |

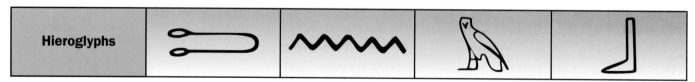

▲ These are some examples of hieroglyphs.

Hieroglyphs were usually written in columns or rows, but could be read in any direction. Columns could be read from top to bottom or bottom to top, and rows could be read left to right (like English), or right to left. It often depended on how the pictures were drawn. For instance, a picture of a bird facing toward the right would mean that the text should be read from left to right. If the animal picture faced toward the left, the text should be read from right to left. There were many clues like this that made hieroglyphs very complicated. Only the smartest students in school were able to learn how to read and write hieroglyphs.

Hieratics: An Easier System of Writing

Because hieroglyphs were so difficult to write and read, the Egyptians developed an easier system of writing called hieratics. The hieratic alphabet took the picture forms of hieroglyphs and made them look less like pictures and more like cursive writing. Lines and squiggles replaced the pictures. This simpler form of writing allowed more people to read and write. It also made writing on papyrus, Egyptian paper, easier and more common. Hieratic writing was used to keep tax and business records. Hieroglyphic writing was used mostly on tombs and temples to tell the stories of the gods and pharaohs.

Demotic Writing: Even Simpler!

Around 660 B.C., an even more simplified writing system began to be used. This was called demotic writing. Demotic writing looked more like the script writing of today. The symbols flowed together, making it much easier to write. Demotic writing soon was used for record keeping and for writing literature.

▲ Hieroglyphics used pictures to represent different words, actions, or ideas.

▼ Here is an example of how Egyptian writing was simplified.

Hieroglyphs	⟜	⋀⋀⋀	🦅	𓃀
Simplified to	⌇	⌐	∿	∟

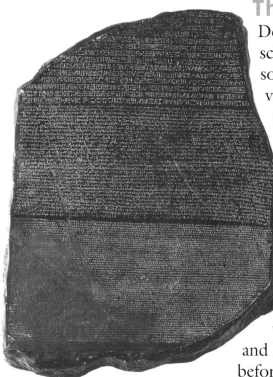

▲ The Rosetta Stone helped historians learn to read hieroglyphs.

The Rosetta Stone

Demotic writing was the key that allowed modern scholars to translate hieroglyphs. In 1799, French soldiers discovered a stone tablet in the Nile River village of Rosetta. This tablet, called the Rosetta Stone, told the story of a pharaoh in three different languages: Greek; demotic; and hieroglyphic. It took over 20 years to figure out the translation. A French scholar, Jean Champollion, broke the code in 1822. Before this time, the hieroglyphic alphabet was a mystery. People had stopped using it after the end of the Egyptian empire when Greeks and later Romans controlled Egypt. Since Champollion knew ancient Greek, he was able to translate the demotic writing from the Greek writing. Since demotic symbols came from hieratic and hieroglyphic symbols, it was only a matter of time before Champollion was able to translate the hieroglyphs. Thanks to the luck of some French soldiers and the skill of a scholar, the rich history of the ancient Egyptians was revealed to the modern world. 📖

 What Do You Think?

1. What is the first written language the ancient Egyptians developed?

2. Compare the three writing systems of ancient Egypt. How are they alike? How are they different?

3. How did the Rosetta Stone help us understand ancient Egypt?

4. Which do you think was more important—luck or skill—in Jean Champollion's translation of the Rosetta Stone? Explain your answer.

RELIGION
in Ancient Kush

| 2000 B.C. | | | 0 | A.D. 400 |

1950 – 1100 B.C.
Egyptian rule over Kush

750 B.C.
Kush conquers
Egypt

200 B.C. – A.D. 300
Meroitic Age

A.D. 350
Fall of Meroë

The Egyptians greatly influenced the religious beliefs of the people Kush. Like the Egyptians, the people of Kush were polytheistic. They worshiped and believed in many gods.

The God Amon

At first, the most important god of the people of Kush was the Egyptian god Amon. During Egypt's New Kingdom, Pharaoh Ramses II built a great temple to the god Amon in Nubia. The god Amon was known as "The Hidden One" who gave people and the world the breath of life. Amon often was shown as a ram (a male sheep). Amon became so important to the people of Kush that Kush chiefs and kings began to use the word *Amon* in their names.

Thebes and Memphis

During the period when Kush ruled Egypt, one of the kings of Kush moved his capital to Thebes. Thebes was one of the most important religious cities in Egypt. It also was the center of worship of Amon. During this same period, the kings of Kush also began to be interested in the religious ideas followed in the Egyptian city of Memphis. In Memphis, the priests taught the story of the god Ptah. According to the priests of Memphis, Ptah created the universe. Ptah would imagine the creation of the world in his heart, say aloud what was in his heart, and then that part of life in the world would be created. Both the Egyptians and the people of Kush believed that a person's intelligence was in the heart, not the brain.

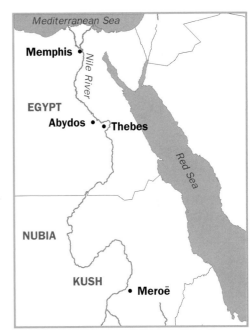

▲ Thebes was one of the most important religious cities in Egypt.

◄ This is a drawing of the god Ptah.

fertility: the ability to grow and develop; highly productive

What Do You Think?

1. What is the difference between a polytheistic religion and a monotheistic religion? **Hint:** *Monos* is a Greek word that means "single" or "one." Name a monotheistic religion.

2. How did geography affect the religious beliefs of the people of Kush? **HINT:** Think about the symbols of Amon and Apedemek.

3. How did the Egyptians influence the religious ideas of the people of Kush? Who influences the religious ideas of the people of the United States today?

Isis and Osiris

The Egyptian gods Isis and Osiris were very important in Kush. Isis and Osiris were sister and brother. Isis was considered the mother of all pharaohs, both Egyptian and Kushite. The people of Egypt and Kush believed that Isis brought her brother Osiris, a king, back to life after he had been killed. The people of Kush believed that Isis and Osiris provided strength and wisdom to their rulers.

New Influences

Over time, as the Kingdom of Kush developed independently from Egypt. From 200 B.C. to A.D. 300, known as the Meroitic Age, Amon and the other Egyptian gods became less important. King Nastasen, who ruled the Kingdom of Kush from 328 to 308 B.C., was not very interested in the old beliefs of Egypt. By 225 B.C, the Nubian god Apedemek, who represented **fertility** and life, had become the most important god in the Kingdom of Kush. The Kingdom of Kush became more and more influenced by African cultures to the south, and the animals they found there. For example, Apedemek was represented by a lion.

▲ This is a drawing of Apedemek, the god of fertility.

Developing an Independent Culture and Belief System

The history of the religious beliefs of the Kingdom of Kush shows how the people of Kush went from being very influenced by the advanced culture of the ancient Egyptians, to developing their own independent culture and beliefs. We do not yet understand the language of the people of Kush, so their ideas are revealed only through the temples and drawings of the gods and goddesses they left behind. ▯

LANGUAGE AND WRITING
in the Kingdom of Kush

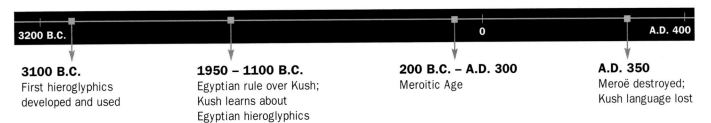

3200 B.C.			0	A.D. 400

3100 B.C.
First hieroglyphics developed and used

1950 – 1100 B.C.
Egyptian rule over Kush; Kush learns about Egyptian hieroglyphics

200 B.C. – A.D. 300
Meroitic Age

A.D. 350
Meroë destroyed; Kush language lost

The Kush language is the second oldest known form of written communication in Africa. The oldest is Egyptian hieroglyphs. However, some language experts argue that over time the Kush, or **Meroitic**, system became better than the Egyptian language. These language experts point to the fact that the people of Kush simplified the complex system of pictures down to about 20 basic signs. The Kush alphabet included symbols for vowel sounds. The Kush language also had a symbol showing the division between two words. The Egyptian system of writing did not have these features.

From Egyptian Hieroglyphics to Kush Cursive

The Kush developed two forms of writing. One they borrowed from Egyptian hieroglyphics. The other—a script or cursive writing—they created themselves. The script was originally based on the picture form of hieroglyphs. Over time, this Kush script came to look more like letters and words. And, as time went on, writing became more common in Kush society. The early, or hieroglyphic, forms of Kush writing were known only by the nobility and a select group of scribes. However, as Kush writing became more like script, it was easier for more people to read and write. Literacy became more common in Kush society.

Meroitic: the language of the people of Kush

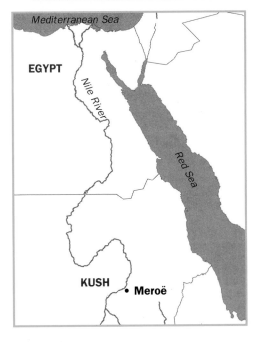

▶ The word *Meroitic* comes from the name of the capital city of the Kingdom of Kush— Meroë.

THE MEROITIC ALPHABET

Hieroglyph	Cursive Letter	Phonetic Value	Hieroglyph	Cursive Letter	Phonetic Value
	ς2	a		3	l
	ς or ∣	e		⌐	kh
	+	i		3	kh
	|||	y		VII	s
	𝔅	w		3	sh
	μ	b		⋛	k
	⋛	p		ß	q
	3	m		∤	t(i)
	ℛ	n		⼁⼓	te
	∧	ñ(i)		⌐	te
	ω	r		∇	z

The Mysterious Kush Language

Over the centuries, the Kingdom of Kush was invaded and overrun by nomadic tribes. Slowly, the Kush culture began to decline. Once again, the Kush language was used by only the nobility. The common people of Kush began to use the languages introduced by the conquering tribes. By A.D. 350, the city of Meroë had been invaded and destroyed. When this happened, the royalty and noble class of the Kingdom of Kush were wiped out. Since these were the last people to use Meroitic, the meaning of the language of Kush was lost with them.

To this day, modern language experts have not been able to understand the Meroitic language, in either the hieroglyph or script forms. Archaeologists hope someday to find a Kush version of the Rosetta Stone. This could help them figure out the meanings of the Kush symbols and script. If experts are ever able to crack the code of the Meroitic alphabet, we will be able to learn much more about a culture that is still relatively unknown. 📖

▲ The Rosetta Stone is a tablet that contains three languages. Language experts used their knowledge of the Greek language to decipher the Egyptian hieroglyphs.

What Do You Think?

1. What is the oldest known form of written communication in Africa? What is the second oldest known form of written communication in Africa?

2. In what ways was the Kush system of writing better than the Egyptian system?

3. Why did the Kush language disappear? Do languages disappear today? Why?

4. Why do you think language experts hope to discover a Meroitic version of the Rosetta Stone? What could we learn about the Kingdom of Kush if we understood their writing system?

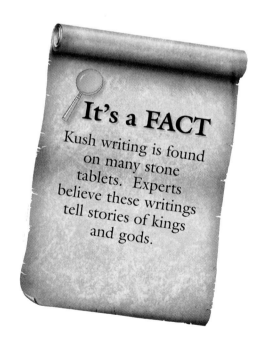

It's a FACT
Kush writing is found on many stone tablets. Experts believe these writings tell stories of kings and gods.

The Rise of the
INDUS VALLEY CIVILIZATION

3600 B.C.		2000 B.C.

3500 B.C.
Nomadic herders arrive
in the Indus Valley

2500 B.C.
The Indus Valley
civilization begins to
rise in importance

The Indus Valley civilization developed in a large river valley that is located in modern-day Pakistan. People came to the area because of the Indus River. It provided life-giving water, rich fish and animal life, and fertile soil for farming.

▲ The Indus Valley civilization (shaded area) developed in a large river valley.

The Indus River

The Indus River is about 1,800-miles long. It begins in the high mountains of southwestern Tibet and flows northwest for about 680 miles. Then it turns and flows southwest through Pakistan to the Arabian Sea. The Indus River is the major river in this region, but a number of **tributaries** and rivers make up the river system where the Indus Valley civilization developed. The **river basin** covers about 3,000 square miles.

The Indus Valley Civilization

Historians think that the people who settled in the Indus Valley came from the mountains of present-day Iran. This area is to the west of the Indus Valley. At first, the people who arrived in the Indus Valley lived as hunters and gatherers. They probably moved to the valley during the wintertime to get away from the extreme cold temperatures in the mountains. Over time, they learned how to grow food in the rich soil of the river valley. This gave them a dependable food supply.

▲ This is what the Indus Valley looks like today.

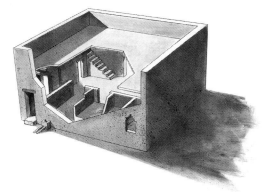

▲ The houses of Mohenjo-Daro and Harappa were made of brick.

Permanent Settlements

With a dependable food supply, the people could stay in one place year round and build permanent homes. Soon, the population increased. Settlements grew in size and number. The people in these settlements traded with other people in the region.

By 2500 B.C., many towns and cities had developed in the Indus Valley. Two of the most important cities were Harappa and Mohenjo-Daro. Each city covered hundreds of acres of land. Harappa was in the Indus River **delta**. Mohenjo-Daro developed on a level, flood **plain** southwest of Harappa. In ancient times, Mohenjo-Daro was a busy **seaport**. Trade was very important to its economy. The Indus River provided a transportation route that connected cities and towns in the Indus Valley. Land routes also linked cities and towns.

delta: a deposit of sand and soil at the mouth of a river; usually shaped like a triangle

plain: a large area of flat land

river basin: an area of land that contains a river and all the streams that flow into it

seaport: a harbor or town that has facilities for seagoing ships

tributary: a small river (or stream) that flows into a larger river

◀ The ruins of Mohenjo-Daro were discovered in 1925.

▲ This figurine of a woman was found at Mohenjo-Daro.

What Do You Think?

1. Who do historians think first settled in the Indus Valley? Where did they come from?

2. Explain how agriculture in the Indus Valley led to the rise of cities and towns.

3. In ancient times, why did people settle near rivers? Do people settle near rivers today? Explain your answer.

Climate Change in the Indus Valley

Today, the climate in the Indus Valley is hot and dry. However, two key pieces of evidence suggest that the region was much wetter in ancient times. The clues to support this conclusion come from bricks and seals.

Archaeologists discovered that the people of the Indus Valley built their cities with fired bricks rather than sun-dried bricks. This was a puzzling discovery. Why would people bake bricks in ovens instead of just letting the bricks dry in the sun? Experts have concluded that there may have been too much rain or humidity to allow the people of the Indus Valley to dry their bricks in the sun.

The second piece of evidence comes from the many seals that have been found in the Indus Valley. These seals, which the people may have used to identify property, are decorated with pictures of elephants, tigers, water buffaloes, and rhinoceroses. The seals also show smaller animals such as bears, deer, monkeys, and wolves. These kinds of animals only live in wet environments.

Scientists think the climate in the region today is hotter and drier as a result of two factors. First, there were changes in the course of the Indus River. Second, human activities such as cutting down trees and allowing animals to graze on the grasslands affected the environment. ▢

▲ Archaeologists have found many seals carved with pictures of animals such as the ones above.

THE ARYAN INVASION

3600 B.C.			1200 B.C.

3500 B.C.
Nomadic herders arrive in the Indus Valley

2500 B.C.
The Indus Valley civilization begins to rise in importance

c. 1900 B.C.
The Indus Valley civilization becomes less important; the Aryans begin to arrive in the Indus Valley

1500 B.C.
The Aryans dominate the Indus Valley

The people of the Indus Valley developed a remarkable civilization. One historian described the city of Mohenjo-Daro as "the very first city" in which people living today could find their way around without a guide. Like other cities in the Indus Valley, Mohenjo-Daro had straight streets that were laid out in a grid pattern. Along the streets, people could find shops to buy goods and places to eat. Homes were well-built. Many houses had running water and bathrooms connected to city sewer systems. There were buildings to store grain, places for people to worship, and a great bath with large and small pools.

▲ This photograph shows a bath in Mohenjo-Daro.

The Decline of the Indus Valley Civilization

However, around 1900 B.C., Harappa and Mohenjo-Daro began to decline. By around 1500 B.C., the Aryans, a warlike group of people from **Eurasia**, dominated the Indus Valley. What happened to the people of the Indus Valley civilization? Did floods destroy their crops and force people to abandon their cities? Did an earthquake cause a change in the course of the Indus River? Did the Aryans invade and force them to leave?

Questions remain as to why the Indus Valley civilization declined. However, in recent years, many experts have concluded that an important reason why people began to abandon their cities has to do with **tectonic** activity.

Eurasia: the continents of Europe and Asia

tectonic: having to do with a large piece of the earth's crust

paradise: any place of ideal loveliness and plenty

steppe: a plain with few or no trees

The Tectonic Explanation

The earth's crust is made up of large pieces called tectonic plates. When these tectonic plates shift, they can create volcanoes and earthquakes. Many scientists now believe that a large section of coastline along the Arabian Sea was forced upward by a tectonic shift. This had consequences for the Indus Valley. A land barrier was created that stopped the Indus River from flowing into the sea. Over many years, the water backed up and flooded the cities.

The Aryans Arrive in the Indus Valley

Whatever the reason for the decline of the Indus Valley civilization, by 1500 B.C., the Aryans had become the dominant group. The Aryans were fierce warriors who came from the steppe region of Eurasia. Their life in that region was very difficult. Over time, the Aryans spread over Persia and then across the northern plains of India. When they first arrived in India, they settled in the Indus Valley. At the time, this area was covered with forests and had an abundant supply of water. This must have seemed like a paradise to the Aryans who had come from an environment where there were few trees and finding food was difficult. The Aryans called themselves the "noble ones" or "superior ones."

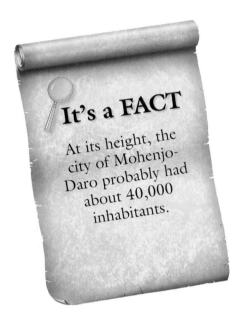

It's a FACT

At its height, the city of Mohenjo-Daro probably had about 40,000 inhabitants.

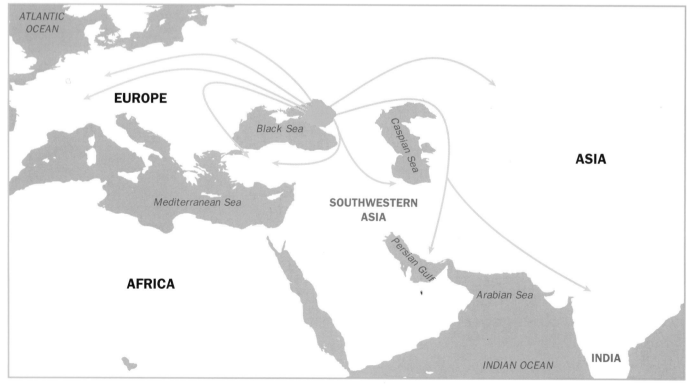

▲ The Aryans migrated to India, southwestern Asia, and Europe.

Aryan Society—
Organized into Classes and Castes

The Aryans lived in family groups that were organized into tribes. Over time, tribes in different areas came together and formed larger organizations. These larger organizations were based more on geography than on family ties. At first, the Aryans had two main classes of people—the nobles and the commoners. Over time, they added two other classes. Priests, called Brahmans, were at the top. The second class was made up of warriors and nobles. The artisans and merchants were in the third class, and the servants were at the bottom. Over time, each of these four classes was divided into sub-classes. We call these classes and sub-classes "castes." Later, the Aryans added another group to their society—the "untouchables." Untouchables were people outside the caste system.

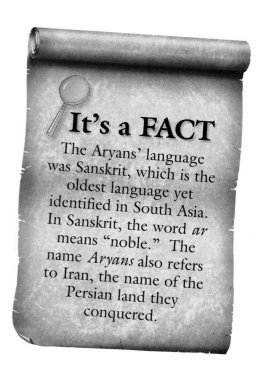

It's a FACT

The Aryans' language was Sanskrit, which is the oldest language yet identified in South Asia. In Sanskrit, the word *ar* means "noble." The name *Aryans* also refers to Iran, the name of the Persian land they conquered.

▲ Warriors were part of the second class.

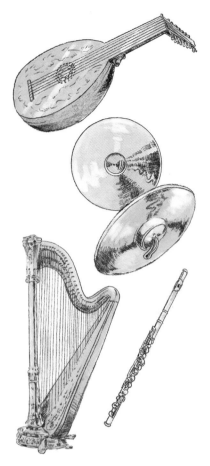

▲ The Aryans played instruments like these modern ones.

What Do You Think?

1. Where did the Aryans come from?

2. What did the Aryans think of the Indus Valley when they first arrived?

3. Describe the Aryans' religion. How is it similar to and different from other religions you know about?

4. What is the significance of the Aryan invasion?

Aryan Culture

The Aryans did not build cities. They did not appear to be interested in creating artwork such as paintings or sculpture. They did not even create pictures of their gods or make beautiful pottery. However, music, dance, and song were an important part of Aryan life. At first, they did not have a writing system. Their priests memorized the poems and chanted them during religious rituals. The Aryans appeared to have enjoyed gambling and chariot racing.

Aryan Religion Blends with Native Beliefs

The Aryans worshiped nature gods. Their gods represented such things as rain, the ocean, and the sun. Indra, one of their most important gods, was both the god of war and the storm god. The religious ideas of the Aryans blended with the ideas of the people already living in the area. Over hundreds of years, these religious ideas formed a set of beliefs and practices known as Hinduism.

The Significance of the Aryan Invasions

As the Aryans spread over the Indian subcontinent, they had a significant effect on the people already living in the area. The Aryans' ideas and culture brought changes to society and religion on the Indian subcontinent. For example, the Aryans introduced stricter rules for social classes. They also emphasized the importance of conducting rituals correctly in order to keep the gods happy. However, the Aryans did not force their ideas and culture on the people of the region. It is more accurate to say that the Aryans' ideas and culture mixed with the ideas and culture of the people who had been living in the region. According to historians, by about 200 B.C., the cultural blending in this region formed what today we call "Indian culture." 📖

ARYAN SOCIETY
The Caste System

The Aryans lived in family groups that were organized into tribes. A chief ruled over each tribe. Over time, tribes in different areas came together to form larger organizations. These larger organizations were based more on geography than on family ties. At first, the Aryans had two main classes of people—the nobles and the commoners. Over time, they added two other classes.

Aryan Society—Classes and Castes

Aryan society was organized with the priests, called Brahmans, at the top. The second class was made up of warriors and nobles. Farmers, artisans, and merchants were in the third class, and the servants were at the bottom. Most people in Aryan society were servants. Over time, each of these four classes was divided into sub-classes. We call these classes and sub-classes "castes." People were born into a caste and they died in that same caste. A person could not become a member of another caste.

A New Group—The Outcasts

Later, the Aryans added another group to their society—the "untouchables." Untouchables were people outside the caste system. Sometimes people in this group are known as "outcasts." Outcasts performed jobs that were considered "unclean" or that involved ending a life. Outcasts included butchers, tanners, and people who fished.

People who were outcasts had almost no rights. They lived in settlements away from people in the other castes. They could not go to the temples or schools where people in other castes went. They could not even get their water from the same wells as people in other castes.

▲ This shows a spice vendor, part of the third class which included farmers, artisans, and merchants.

Nobles and Warriors

Servants

Brahmans (Priests)

Merchants and Traders

▲ According to legend, the four main classes emerged from a creature who lived long, long ago. The Brahmans—the priests—are thought to come from the mouth of this creature. The nobles and warriors come from its arms. The merchants and traders come from its legs. And the servants come from its feet.

unequal: not the same as another in social position

What Do You Think?

1. What were the four main classes in ancient India?

2. What fifth group was added?

3. What are the advantages of a caste system? What are the disadvantages?

3. The caste system is based on the idea that people are created unequal. America's founders disagreed with this idea. How did these two ideas result in different kinds of societies?

The Life of Outcasts

In some areas, Brahmans would not let an untouchable's shadow fall upon them. They would not step in the same spot where an untouchable stepped. Some Brahmans had servants whose role was to walk ahead of them and clear the way of any untouchables. In some parts of the Indian subcontinent, outcasts had to work at night and sleep during the day so that people in other castes did not have to look at them. Outcasts could be treated harshly for coming into contact with people in other castes. They could even be killed for touching someone in one of the castes.

The Caste System Today

The basic idea of the caste system is that everyone has a place in society and that this place can never change. It also is based on the idea that people are created **unequal**. The caste system is no longer legal in India. The government of India has even passed laws to help people who were outcasts go to school and get better jobs. However, the ideas and attitudes about the caste system still influence people's lives. 📖

ARYAN SOCIETY
Castes and Religion

The Aryans worshiped nature gods. Their most important gods were Shiva, Indra, Varuna, and Surya. These gods represented such things as rain, the ocean, and the sun. Indra was both the god of war and the storm god. Sacrifice to the gods was an important part of the Aryan religion.

The Brahmans

In Aryan society, there were four major groups. The priests or Brahmans were at the top. Knowing how to conduct sacrifices correctly to the gods was very important. That's why the Brahmans became the most important and powerful class.

Rituals and Sacrifices

It was up to the Brahmans to conduct the religious rituals correctly. If they failed to do so, the Aryans believed their gods would not answer their prayers. Then there might be floods, famine, disease, or other natural disasters. People paid the Brahmans to make these sacrifices and to conduct the rituals. Over time, the Brahmans came up with more and more rules about the sacrifices and rituals. Brahmans also taught the idea of an afterlife.

▲ This is a statue of the god Shiva.

Brahmanism Evolves into Hinduism

Over hundreds of years, the religious ideas of the Aryans blended with the ideas of the people already living in the area. These ideas formed into a set of beliefs and practices known as Hinduism. People who follow the ideas of Hinduism are known as Hindus. Like the Aryans in earlier times, Hindus believed that people were born into a particular class. They also believed in an afterlife.

▶ This picture shows carvings of Hindu gods on the walls of a Hindu temple.

▲ This Hindu priest is performing a ritual.

reincarnation: the idea that a person's soul is reborn in another body—either animal or human

What Do You Think?

1. What Aryan idea had a strong influence on Hinduism?

2. What is reincarnation?

3. How could a belief in reincarnation give stability to a society?

4. How is the Hindu belief in the cycle of life similar to or different from other religious beliefs you know about?

Reincarnation

Unlike Aryans, Hindus believed in **reincarnation**. Hindus believed that people in lower castes were being punished for sins they had committed in earlier lives. Hindus believed that if people calmly accepted their position in life and lived correctly, then they would be reborn in a higher caste in their next life.

Hinduism differed from the Aryan religion in another way. Hindus believe it is important to show images of their gods. They worship the image as the actual god. For this reason, Hindus dress images, bring them refreshments, place sweet-smelling flowers around them, and light lamps to provide them with light.

Create, Preserve, and Destroy

There are many different gods in Hinduism, but the chief god is Brahman. Hindus believe that other gods are the different faces of Brahman. For example, Brahma is the face of Brahman the creator, Vishnu is the face of Brahman the preserver, and Shiva is the face of Brahman the destroyer. Hindus believe Brahman's major powers are to create, preserve, and destroy.

Cycle of Life

Hindus believe in a cycle of life that begins with birth, ends with death, and then begins again with rebirth. They believe a soul continues in this cycle until it is perfect. Then the cycle ends and the soul becomes part of Brahman.

Because Hindus believe that each person and animal has a soul, they do not kill animals or eat meat. Hindus especially consider cows as sacred.

The Vedas

We have learned a great deal about religious ideas in ancient India from the Vedas. The Vedas are a written record of knowledge. In Sanskrit, the word *veda* means "knowledge." The *Rig-Veda* is the oldest of the Vedas. It is a collection of religious poems organized into four major sections or texts. The *Rig-Veda* was composed sometime between 1700 to 1000 B.C. The *Rig-Veda* was intended for and used by the Brahmans. 📖

Siddhartha Gautama
THE BUDDHA

2000 B.C.   0

1500 B.C.
The Aryans dominate
the Indus Valley

c. 563 – 483 B.C.
The Buddha

The Aryans had a strong influence on the religious ideas of the people of the Indian subcontinent. However, over time, the people of this region began to question the power of the priests, the Brahmans. Even after the priests had made many sacrifices to the gods, there were still droughts and floods and other natural disasters. Some people began to look for other answers to questions about the meaning and purpose of life. A man named Siddhartha Gautama was one of these people.

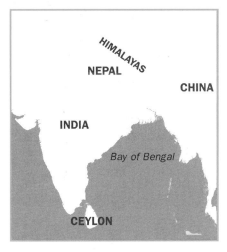

▲ As a boy, Siddhartha and his family lived in the foothills of the Himalayas.

A Privileged, Royal Child

Siddhartha Gautama, the man we call the Buddha and the founder of Buddhism, was born about 563 B.C. Most people agree that Siddhartha was born into a royal family. His family lived in an area that is now the southern edge of Nepal, just north of India, in the foothills of the Himalayas. As the child of a royal family, Siddhartha led a very safe, secure, and privileged life. His parents did not want him to see or experience any ugliness and unhappiness. As a young boy, he never left the palace. He never met everyday people or saw how they lived their lives. His parents did everything they could to keep him happy and amused. They did not want him to become bored or lonely or want for any material things. However, as Siddhartha grew older, he became curious about what life was like beyond the palace.

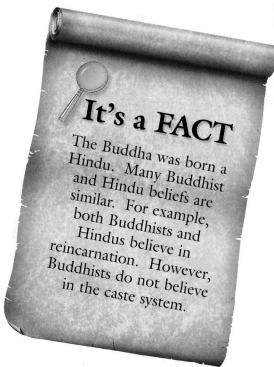

It's a FACT
The Buddha was born a Hindu. Many Buddhist and Hindu beliefs are similar. For example, both Buddhists and Hindus believe in reincarnation. However, Buddhists do not believe in the caste system.

▲ His followers say the Buddha gained enlightenment near this tree.

poverty: the condition of being poor

Silk Road: a land route that connected China with Europe

Seeing Life for Himself

As the traditional story is told, Siddhartha finally decided he had to see for himself what life was like outside his palace walls. For several nights in a row, Siddhartha left the palace. As he walked on the nearby streets, he saw things he had never seen or heard of before. He saw people who were sick, people who were old, people who were poor, and even people who had died. Never before had Siddhartha seen illness, old age, **poverty**, or death. This experience changed him forever. He could not understand how he could live such a wonderful life in the palace, and at the same time there was sickness, old age, poverty, and death. He decided on a course of action. He would give up all of his worldly pleasures and spend his time looking for answers to his questions about the world. He wanted to understand how the beauty of his palace life existed at the same time as all of the suffering he saw in the world.

A Blinding Flash and Enlightenment

One night Siddhartha left the palace on horseback. He rode to a place that was far away from everyone and everything. For days, he sat under a tree and tried to understand what life and suffering meant. After many days, the "answer" came to him in a blinding flash. In that moment, his followers say that he became enlightened—free from wanting material things or power. In that moment, his followers say that he became the Buddha, a name that means "enlightened one." Another name for enlightenment is "nirvana."

Different Representations of the Buddha from around the World

The Buddha's Teachings

Over time, the Buddha developed a way of talking about his enlightenment. He also began to talk about how others could reach enlightenment. The Buddha said that the first thing a person must do is to accept what he called the "Four Noble Truths." His first noble truth is that life is full of suffering and sorrow. His second truth is that people's desire for things and their desire to gain power causes suffering. His third truth is that people can overcome suffering and sorrow when they give up their desire for things and their desire for power. His fourth truth is that people can learn to give up these desires by following the "Eightfold Path."

The Eightfold Path is the Buddha's guide to help people stop wanting things. The Eightfold Path calls upon people to have right views, right intentions, right speech, right action, right livelihood, right effort, right mindfulness, and right concentration. The Buddha's followers believed they would find enlightenment if they followed the standards of behavior set forth in the Eightfold Path.

What Do You Think?

1. Who is the founder of Buddhism? Where did he live? When did he live?

2. The Buddha taught that the more people want material things, the unhappier they become. Do you agree or disagree with this idea? Why?

3. How did Buddhist ideas spread throughout India, Ceylon, Central Asia, and China? How do religious ideas spread today?

Buddhism Spreads

More and more people in India began following the Buddha's teachings. Buddhism appealed to many people because it promised an end to pain and suffering. According to Buddhist teachings, if people follow the Four Noble Truths and the Eightfold Path, they can achieve enlightenment, which frees them from suffering and want.

Buddhist ideas spread throughout India and south to the island of Ceylon, which is present-day Sri Lanka. Buddhism also spread to Central Asia and even as far as China. As Buddhist travelers and missionaries traveled the **Silk Road**, they brought their ideas about Buddhism. The earliest written references to Buddhism in China appear around A.D. 65. By A.D. 220, there were Buddhist statues, paintings, and other art in China.

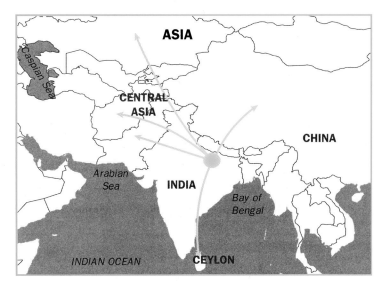

▲ Buddhist ideas spread throughout India, Ceylon (present-day Sri Lanka), Central Asia, and China.

CHANDRAGUPTA MAURYA
The Beginning of the Mauryan Empire

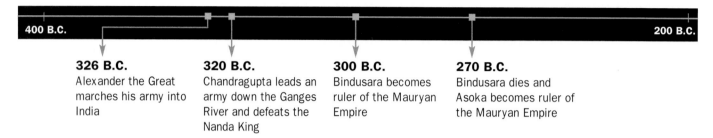

326 B.C.	**320 B.C.**	**300 B.C.**	**270 B.C.**
Alexander the Great marches his army into India	Chandragupta leads an army down the Ganges River and defeats the Nanda King	Bindusara becomes ruler of the Mauryan Empire	Bindusara dies and Asoka becomes ruler of the Mauryan Empire

Chandragupta Maurya was an ambitious young man. He took advantage of an opportunity and became the most powerful leader in ancient India. He established the Mauryan Empire. After he died, his son expanded and ruled the empire. When Chandragupta's grandson, Asoka, became ruler, the Mauryan Empire covered almost the entire Indian subcontinent.

▲ The shaded region shows the extent of the Mauryan Empire around 232 B.C.

The Beginning of the Mauryan Empire

In 326 B.C., Alexander the Great, one of the greatest generals in history, marched his armies into India. At the time, a man who was a member of the Nanda family was the most powerful Indian leader. Alexander intended to conquer India, including the Nanda king's territory.

According to a traditional story, a young and ambitious man named Chandragupta, who was a member of the Maurya family, joined Alexander's forces. However, Alexander left India before he could conquer the region. The withdrawal of Alexander's armies created political **instability** in India. Chandragupta took advantage of this instability. Around 320 B.C., he led an army down the Ganges River and defeated the Nanda king. As a result of this conquest, Chandragupta became the most powerful ruler in India. This was the beginning of the Mauryan Empire.

The Mauryan Empire Expands

Around 300 B.C., a famine swept across India. Because of his Hindu beliefs, Chandragupta saw the famine as a sign from the gods. He thought the gods were punishing him for his mistakes and weaknesses as a ruler. Chandragupta decided to give up power and become a follower of **Jainism**. Bindusara, Chandragupta's son, became the next ruler of the Mauryan Empire.

Like his father, Bindusara led armies to conquer new territories. He kept the lands in the north under strong control. He gained new territories as he expanded the empire southward. During his reign, Indian farmers grew more crops and merchants became more important in Indian society. People in the Mediterranean area and in western Asia knew about the Mauryan Empire. When Bindusara died around 270 B.C., his sons fought over who would become the next Mauryan leader. Asoka won this fight.

Asoka became known as one of ancient India's greatest rulers. He is sometimes known as the "emperor of peace." He was born a Hindu, but a dramatic event convinced him to become a Buddhist. This decision changed India forever. 📖

It's a FACT

According to a traditional story, Chandragupta slept in a different bedroom of his palace every night because he was afraid someone would kill him.

---

instability: not steady; lacking permanence; likely to change

Jainism: a religion of India that teaches that the soul never dies and that there is no perfect or supreme god

---

What Do You Think?

1. Why is it easier to seize power during times of political instability?

2. How was Bindusara like his father?

3. How do you think people in the Mediterranean area and in western Asia knew about the Mauryan Empire?

▲ This drawing shows an Indian army using elephants trained for war. Chandragupta and his son led armies like this to conquer new territories.

ASOKA
Emperor of Peace

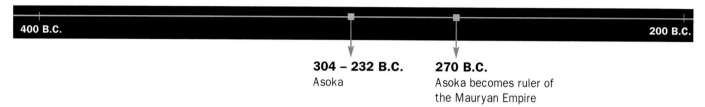

400 B.C.		200 B.C.

304 – 232 B.C.
Asoka

270 B.C.
Asoka becomes ruler of
the Mauryan Empire

Chandragupta was a young, ambitious man. He took advantage of an opportunity to create and rule an empire—the Mauryan Empire. When his grandson, Asoka, became ruler, the Mauryan Empire covered almost the entire Indian subcontinent. Then, an event dramatically changed Asoka's life. This change affected all of India.

▲ When Asoka became ruler, the Mauryan Empire (shaded area) covered almost the entire Indian subcontinent.

Asoka's Political Achievements

At first, Asoka ruled the same way his father and grandfather had ruled. He strengthened Mauryan control in the northern lands and expanded the empire farther south. His empire included many groups of people with different languages, customs, and traditions. During his rule, the Mauryan Empire covered almost all of present-day India and Pakistan. The only part the Mauryans did not rule was the southernmost part of the subcontinent.

A Fierce Warrior

Asoka was known as a fierce warrior. He led his armies into battle. He conquered one kingdom after another and added these new territories to his empire. When the kingdom of Kalinga revolted against his rule, he led his armies to stop the rebellion. He was successful in stopping the rebellion, but the cost in human life was very high. Approximately 100,000 people died and 150,000 were taken prisoner. It was a bloody and awful battle that changed Asoka forever.

A Crisis of Conscience

After the battle with Kalinga, Asoka became extremely upset. He began to think about all the suffering he had caused. Asoka had been born a Hindu. However, this recent battle caused him to have a **crisis of conscience**.

According to the traditional story, Asoka became a **devout** Buddhist after the bloodshed at Kalinga. As a Buddhist, he began to think about the world in a different way. This change in thinking led him to rule his empire in a very different way, too.

Asoka's Moral Laws

Asoka created a government for his empire that was based on different **moral** laws. These moral laws were based on Buddhist teachings. They emphasized respect for life and nonviolence. Even though Asoka was a devout Buddhist, the moral laws also emphasized the importance of accepting people with different religious beliefs. We have learned about the moral laws Asoka used to govern his empire from his writings. He had his ideas carved onto large rocks. Later, his ideas were carved on **pillars**. Some carvings or inscriptions reveal his ideas about how he saw his role as ruler. One inscription says:

> There is no better work than promoting the welfare of the whole world. Whatever may be my great deeds, I have done them in order to discharge my debt to all beings.

His inscriptions also provided the people of his empire with guidance on how to live good and ethical lives. One inscription says:

> To do good is difficult. One who does good first does something hard to do. I have done many good deeds, and, if my sons, grandsons, and their descendants up to the end of the world act in like manner, they too will do much good. But whoever amongst them neglects this, they will do evil. Truly, it is easy to do evil.

crisis of conscience: a time of extreme personal reflection in which a person thinks about and questions his/her beliefs, ideas, and/or actions

devout: faithful; devoted

moral: designed to teach good and evil in terms of human behavior

pillar: a column

Analyze the Source!

Choose one of the moral laws and explain it in your own words. Then give reasons why you agree or disagree with the law. Compare this law with a law today.

▶ After his crisis of conscience, Asoka dedicated himself to improving the lives of the people in his kingdom. For example, he had rest stops built for travelers.

It's a FACT

The top of a column or pillar is called the capital. Asoka had figures of lions carved on the capitals of his pillars. The lion capital of Sarnath is the most famous capital. Sarnath is the place where the Buddha is said to have given his first religious speech.

Improving People's Lives

Asoka's inscriptions reveal how he felt about the people of his empire. He described the people of his empire as "my children." He said he wanted them to have "every kind of welfare and happiness in this world and the next." Importantly, he did not simply talk about these ideas, he actually put his ideas into action. To improve people's lives, he had wells dug, rest stops built, and trees planted to provide shade. He even created places where animals could get water. He appointed government officials who were Buddhists. He ordered these government officials to make sure that his policies were carried out. These government officials reported directly to him.

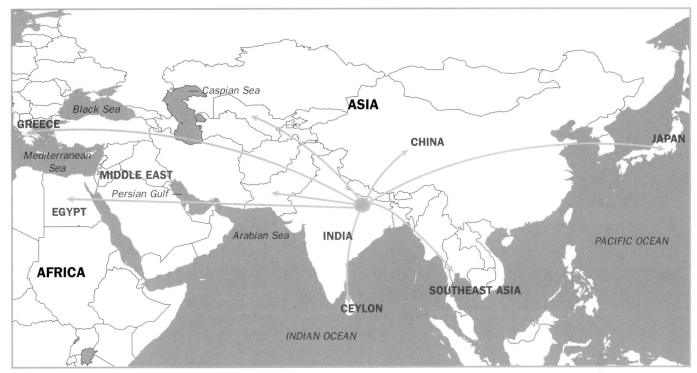

▲ Asoka sent missionaries along trade routes to spread Buddhist ideas.

Spreading Buddhist Beliefs

Asoka sent monks throughout India and beyond to share Buddhist ideas. These monks traveled south to Ceylon, as well as east and west along the trade routes. They visited lands such as Greece, Egypt, and Persia. Eventually, Buddhism spread to Southeast Asia, China, and Japan.

Asoka's Legacy

Under Asoka's rule, the people of the Mauryan Empire enjoyed safety and prosperity. After his death around 232 B.C., the Mauryan Empire quickly began to fall apart. The Brahman priests were a politically powerful group and Asoka's shift to Buddhism removed them from power. After Asoka's death, the Brahman priests regained power and Buddhism eventually faded.

Today, Asoka is remembered as one of ancient India's greatest rulers. He is sometimes known as the "emperor of peace." He played an important role in the spread of Buddhism. People in modern times admire his ideas about respect for life, nonviolence, and religious tolerance. 📖

What Do You Think?

1. How large was the Mauryan Empire during Asoka's rule?

2. What event changed Asoka's life and his way of thinking?

3. How did becoming a Buddhist change the way Asoka ruled? How are rulers today influenced by their religious ideas?

Reader's Theater
Presents

THE STORY OF EMPEROR ASOKA

Practice reading the script. When the script says, "PEOPLE OF KALINGA," everyone in the class joins in the reading. Read with expression! ➡

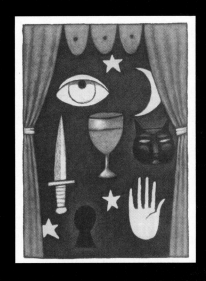

ROLES

★ NARRATOR
★ DEMETRIUS
★ MONK
★ ASOKA
★ ASOKA'S SOLDIERS
★ PEOPLE OF KALINGA (ALL)
★ SOUND EFFECTS

Narrator: One hot day in the year 245 B.C., a Greek trader named Demetrius sat down under a tree by the side of the road.

Demetrius: It is so nice to sit under the shade on such a hot day!

Narrator: Demetrius had been traveling for many weeks and was a stranger in this land. He saw a monk walking up the road and called out to him.

Demetrius: Excuse me! Could you tell me what kingdom this is?

Monk: This is the kingdom of Maurya, ruled by the great Emperor Asoka.

Demetrius: What sort of emperor is he? I'm new here, and I don't want to get myself in any trouble.

Monk: Emperor Asoka treats all people with kindness.

Demetrius: Really? That doesn't sound like most emperors I've heard of.

Monk: Emperor Asoka is not like most rulers. He follows the teachings of the Buddha.

Demetrius: Who is the Buddha? Is he a god?

Monk: No. He was a wise man who showed us the "Universal Law."

Demetrius: What law is that?

Monk: I will show you.

Narrator: The monk led Demetrius down the road to a large stone pillar. There were words carved into the pillar.

Demetrius: Oh my! Some of these words are in Greek!

Monk: Emperor Asoka has written about the Buddha in many languages.

Narrator: Demetrius read some of the writings aloud.

Demetrius: "The Universal Law is the path to happiness. It includes much good, little evil, and kindness to all living things." What a strange thing for an emperor to say! Most emperors I've heard of are more interested in fighting wars.

Monk: Emperor Asoka was like that once.

Demetrius: What happened?

▲ This is a stone sculpture of Asoka.

Monk: About 15 years ago, Emperor Asoka made war on the kingdom of Kalinga.

Asoka: Go to the land of Kalinga, my soldiers, and conquer it!

Asoka's Soldiers: We will go, my lord!

Monk: There was a great battle.

Sound Effects: (Make a sound like many soldiers fighting.)

Monk: Asoka's soldiers won the battle, but there was much suffering on both sides.

People of Kalinga: Our houses have been destroyed, and many of our friends have died!

Asoka's Soldiers: Many of our friends are dead, too!

Monk: The emperor saw how terrible war was and became very sad.

Asoka: This suffering is awful! There must be a better way to rule.

Monk: The emperor read the teachings of the Buddha for ideas.

Asoka: From now on, I will stop fighting and follow the way of the Buddha. I will do things to make life better for all people.

Monk: Ever since then, the emperor has done many great things.

Demetrius: Like what?

Monk: He has given the doctors money to grow plants that cure diseases. He has dug many wells to give the people water. He even planted the trees you were resting under so travelers would have shade when it is hot.

Demetrius: Well, I have to say he does sound like a great ruler. When I go home, I must tell my friends about him. 📖

▲ Asoka built many shrines like this in honor of the Buddha.

THE GUPTA EMPERORS

A Golden Age in India

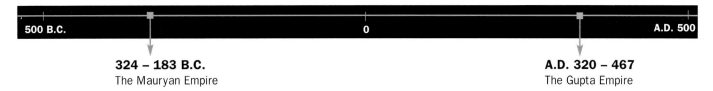

500 B.C.   0   A.D. 500

324 – 183 B.C.
The Mauryan Empire

A.D. 320 – 467
The Gupta Empire

Hundreds of years after the Mauryan Empire lost power, rulers from a new family brought order and unity to India. These rulers were the Guptas. During their reign, India enjoyed a golden age. Literature, medicine, and science flourished.

The Beginning of the Gupta Dynasty

Shortly after Asoka's death in c. 232 B.C., the Mauryan Empire fell apart. For the next several hundred years, India experienced a time of political chaos. Kingdoms fought one another. Invaders came into northern India. Life was no longer safe or prosperous for the people of India. Then in A.D. 320, a leader came to power in the same region where the Mauryan Empire had begun. This new leader began to conquer one small kingdom after another. His name was Chandra Gupta I. He established a new Indian dynasty—the Gupta Dynasty.

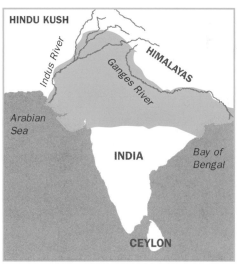

▲ The shaded region shows the extent of the Gupta Empire around A.D. 375.

India's Golden Age

In A.D. 375, Chandra Gupta II became emperor. Like his grandfather, Chandra Gupta I, Chandra Gupta II hoped to conquer and unify the Indian subcontinent. He wanted to bring unity and stability to India. He did many things to try to achieve this goal. For example, he gave more support to the ideas of Hinduism, which emphasized a caste system. Chandra Gupta II also promoted learning and supported the development of universities. He encouraged writers, scientists, artists, dancers, singers, and others to visit his court. These talented and educated visitors were known as the "jewels" of his court. During the reign of Chandra Gupta II, India was the most advanced country in the world. It was during this period that India enjoyed a golden age.

Sanskrit Literature

About 1750 B.C., the Aryans crossed the Hindu Kush mountains and began to spread across the Indian subcontinent. Their arrival in the area that is now India and Pakistan brought many new ideas, beliefs, and cultural traditions to this region. One of the most important changes that resulted was the change in their language. Sanskrit became the language of the upper classes in India. The earliest written accounts of Hindu beliefs, including the *Rig-Veda*, were written in Sanskrit. Below is an excerpt from the *Rig-Veda* in Sanskrit and English. It has been translated and discussed by many scholars. Many books have been dedicated to just this one hymn.

नासदासीत्रोसदासीत्तदानीं नासीद्रजो नो व्योमापरो यत् ।
किमावरीवः कुहकस्यशर्मंत्रंभः किमासीद्गहनं गभीरं ॥ १ ॥

Translation:
Then even nothingness was not, nor existence,
There was no air then, nor the heavens beyond it.
What covered it? Where was it? In whose keeping
Was there then cosmic water, in depths unfathomed.

न मृत्युरासीदमृतं न तर्हि न राञ्याऽअहऽऽआसीत्रकेतः ।
आनीदवातं स्वधया तदेकं तस्माद्धान्यन्नपरः किञ्चनास ॥ २ ॥

Translation:
Then there was neither death or immortality
nor was there then the torch of night and day.
The One breathed windlessly and self-sustaining.
There was One then, and there was no other.

Epic Poems

During India's golden age, two of India's greatest epic poems were written down. Up until this time, they had been passed along orally. The *Mahabharata* (muh-HAH-bah-ruh-tuh) tells the story of five brothers who try to conquer an Indian kingdom. One of the most famous parts of the *Mahabharata* is the *Bhagavad Gita* (BAG-uh-vad GEE-tah). In this section, the Indian god Krishna encourages one of the brothers before he leaves for a battle. Krishna talks about important Hindu beliefs. The *Bhagavad Gita* is considered one of the most important Hindu writings.

The *Ramayana* (RAH-mah-yuh-nuh) tells the story of Rama and his wife Sita. It is a love story filled with action and adventure. In one part, Rama and an army of monkeys fight a battle with an evil king to rescue Sita. Like the *Mahabharata*, the *Ramayana* includes many different stories that were told orally for generations.

It's a FACT

Sanskrit is an Indo-European language. It is related to Latin, German, and English.

Ancient Stories

The *Puranas* (pu-RAH-nuhs) are other stories that were brought together during India's golden age. The word *Puranas* means "ancient stories." The *Puranas* include stories where animals talk and act like people. The *Puranas* reveal Hindu ideas. These stories helped teach everyone in society, including people in the lower classes, about Hindu beliefs.

◄ This carving on the wall of a Hindu temple shows one of the scenes from the *Ramayana*.

ore: a mineral or group of minerals from which a valuable element, such as metal, can be taken out

plumage: a bird's feathers

purify: to clean; to get rid of impurities

startled: frightened

"The Cloud Messenger"

In the Gupta royal court, poets recited their poems for the enjoyment of all. Sometimes competitions were held to see who could write the most beautiful poems. One of the most celebrated poets of this age was a man named Kalidasa. He wrote beautiful poems, including his most famous one, "The Cloud Messenger." This poem tells the story of a god who was forced to leave his home in the Himalayas for a year. He became very homesick and began to tell his thoughts to a cloud overhead. He asked the cloud to tell his wife that he loves her and misses her. Below is an excerpt of this poem.

> I see your ... gaze in the **startled** eyes of deer, your cheek in the moon, your hair in the **plumage** of peacocks, and in the tiny ripples of the river I see your sidelong glances, but alas, my dearest, nowhere do I find your whole likeness.

Kalidasa also wrote plays. These plays were enjoyed by the members of the Gupta royal court, as well as by ordinary people. One of Kalidasa's plays, *Shakuntala* (shak-UN-tuh-luh), is considered one of the best examples of Sanskrit drama. This play tells of a love story that is complicated by many twists and turns. In the end, however, everyone lives happily.

Medicine

During India's golden age, Indian doctors gained advanced knowledge about medicine. They learned how to use plants to make various kinds of medicines. They understood that cleanliness was important to people's health. They knew how to fix broken bones and heal wounds. They even had a general understanding of the importance of the spinal cord in the human body. During this time, an Indian doctor wrote a medical textbook. This textbook brought together all the medical knowledge of ancient India. Many of the ideas about medicine that developed during this period are still important in India today.

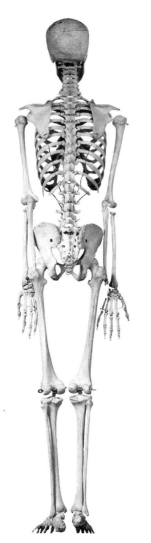

▲ Indian doctors had an understanding of the importance of the spinal cord in the human body.

Advances in Mathematics

During this same period, Indians made new discoveries in mathematics. For example, they developed the idea and symbol for zero. They also worked with negative numbers. An Indian mathematician, we do not know who, began using a number system that consisted of zero and nine digits. Arabs learned about these advances in mathematics. They called this "Indian science" and over time passed this knowledge to the Europeans. Today, we call these Indian numbers Arabic numerals. We call the Indian number system the decimal system. Indians also developed advanced mathematics, including algebra and geometry.

New Discoveries

Knowledge in the field of science also increased during the Guptas' reign. Scientists made great advances in metallurgy. Metallurgy is the science of getting metals out of **ore**, **purifying** the metals, and combining them. Scientists described how to combine metals to make new metals that were very strong and resisted rusting. Indians used their knowledge of metallurgy to build columns, strong swords and tools, and even to make parts in rockets.

During this period, Indian scientists also became very interested in astronomy. They studied the heavens and observed the movements of the stars. Using the advancements made in mathematics, Indian scientists made many new discoveries. 📖

What Do You Think?

1. Which Indian ruler is most associated with India's golden age?

2. Why were the talented and educated visitors known as the "jewels" of Chandra Gupta II's court? What does this mean?

3. Name two examples of Sanskrit literature that were written during India's golden age.

4. What do you think was the most important accomplishment of India's golden age? Explain your answer.

◀ In the 400s, an Indian scientist and mathematician named Aryabhata (AR-yuh-buh-tuh) wrote that the earth was round and that it rotated around the sun. It would be hundreds of years before scientists in Europe made these same discoveries.

Origins of
CHINESE CIVILIZATION

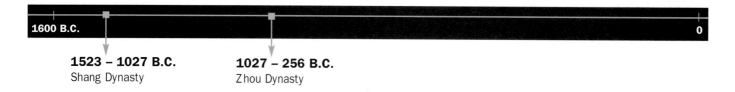

1600 B.C.		0

1523 – 1027 B.C.
Shang Dynasty

1027 – 256 B.C.
Zhou Dynasty

The Chinese think of the Huang He (hwahng hay) or Yellow River in two ways. On the one hand, the river is a source of life and prosperity. It provides the people with water, fish and animal life, and rich soil for farming. It also gives people a natural transportation route.

An Old Chinese Saying

The people have four sorrows. The first is flood, the second drought. The third is locusts, the final warlords.

River of Sorrows

The Huang He is also called the River of Sorrows. Like other rivers, each year the water level in the river rises and falls, depending on the amount of rainfall and the amount of snowfall at the river's source. Like other river valley civilizations, the ancient Chinese sometimes had to face the problem of too much water, which resulted in flooding. When flooding occurred, many people who lived in the Huang He valley were killed. Their homes and fields were destroyed. Later, even more people died because the crops were ruined and there was not enough food.

A Source of Archaeological Information

The Huang He valley is a rich source of information about early human beings. Archaeologists have found fossil evidence of early humanlike creatures that lived along the Huang He almost a million years ago. Fossils also show that about 5,000 years ago, modern human beings settled in the area. These people lived in groups. They grew crops and caught fish from the river. They created beautiful pottery and developed stable and successful settlements. From these settlements along the Huang He came one of the world's greatest civilizations—the Chinese civilization.

Origins of Chinese Civilization

As people in the Huang He settlements grew more food, they were able to support an increasingly larger population. Archaeologists believe that the first people to rule in this region were the Xia (shee-UH). The leader of the Xia, Yu the Great, is said to have stated: "Who controls the Yellow River controls China." Yu is considered the first person to control flooding of the Huang He. However, until new archaeological evidence is uncovered, information about the Xia remains unclear. In contrast, archaeologists have found a great deal of evidence about the Shang (shawng), the next group to rule in this region.

It's a FACT

For hundreds of years, Chinese farmers believed that a dragon lived in the Huang He and controlled the waters. Look at the Huang He on a map. Some people believe it shows the outline of an angry dragon with its back arched.

▲ This is a photograph of the Yellow River today.

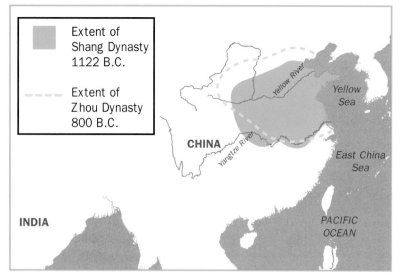

▲ The Shang and Zhou built great dynasties in ancient China.

The Shang Dynasty

Around 1500 B.C., a man named Tang came to power. He was the first ruler of the Shang Dynasty. He and the Shang rulers who followed after him had an important advantage over other groups in China at this time. They had bronze weapons. In their written records, the Shang wrote notes about what was happening in their kingdom. They saw their own fortunes rise and fall in the same way the waters of the Huang He rose and fell. In 1490 B.C., for example, they wrote, "confusion in the empire." In 1293 B.C., they wrote, "Then there was peace and prosperity."

Shang Nobles

Over time, two classes of people developed in the Huang He valley—nobles and peasants. The nobles saw themselves as the "Middle Kingdom." The gods were above them and the peasants were below them. The nobles lived lives of luxury. They spent most of their time hunting, conducting religious ceremonies, and waging war. The Shang nobles ordered the building of temples. They also were interested in supporting and enjoying art, culture, and fine foods. The Shang moved their capital from one place to another, depending on the wishes of the king. However, the Shang capital was always close to the Huang He.

▶ Shang nobles enjoyed hunting.

▲ Shang nobles used bronze weapons to control the peasants.

Shang Peasants

During the Shang Dynasty, most peasants worked as farmers for the nobles. Some also worked as artisans. Peasant women raised silkworms from which they made silk for the nobles. Peasants also provided the labor to build the temples, palaces, and tombs. Some peasants worked as servants for the nobles. In general, peasants lived in very poor conditions. They often did not have enough to eat and lived short, hard lives.

The Zhou Dynasty

After about 500 years of rule, the Shang Dynasty came to an end. The rulers had become **corrupt**. They were cruel to the people they ruled. The nobles seemed only interested in enjoying themselves and living lives of luxury and pleasure. Over time, the Shang nobles began to lose control over their territories. A group of people from the west highlands, the Zhou (joh), conquered the Shang, ending the Shang Dynasty's rule. The Zhou established their own capital along the Huang He. They also built their own cities and ruled the region. However, in time, the Zhou also lost power. After the Zhou Dynasty, China experienced many changes and a time of great upheaval, constant warfare, and chaos. 📖

---

corrupt: dishonest; unfair

 What Do You Think?

1. When do archaeologists think the first modern people settled along the Huang He?

2. Yu the Great said that whoever controls the Yellow River controls what? What did he mean?

3. Why did the Shang compare themselves to the Huang He? What evidence did they provide to support this comparison?

4. How did the Shang rulers contribute to the downfall of the Shang Dynasty? What lesson can leaders learn from the example of the Shang rulers?

GEOGRAPHY AND GOVERNANCE

In some ways, it seems unlikely that ancient China would develop into a strong and unified empire. Unlike other civilizations, the Chinese did not have a natural basis for unity. Ancient China was made up of people with different traditions, beliefs, and languages. And, as important, China's geographic features seemed like barriers that kept the people of ancient China from being unified.

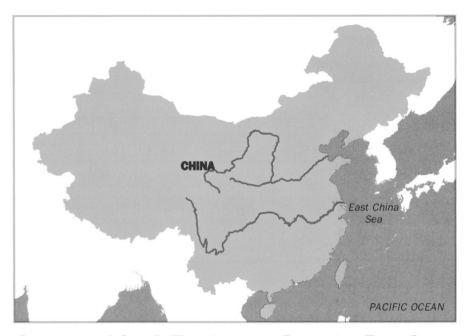

CHINA

East China Sea

PACIFIC OCEAN

▶ This map shows the area that China covers today.

Geographical Features Create Barriers

The ancient Chinese empire covered a huge area. It was about 3,400 miles from north to south and about 3,200 miles from west to east. The Pacific Ocean formed its eastern and southern boundary. Deserts and mountains formed its borders to the north and west. Within this huge area also are some of the world's longest rivers. China's geographical features made ruling of the Chinese empire difficult. These geographical features also stood in the way—**literally**—of the spread of ideas and goods. And, for a very long time, the geographical features of China served as natural boundaries that isolated China from the rest of the world.

Geography, Government, and the Spread of Ideas and Goods

What does geography have to do with governing and the spread of ideas and goods? The answer to this question, especially in ancient times, was that geography had a huge effect! Without modern transportation or communication systems, it took a long time for news to travel to outlying areas. An emperor might make a decision that would take years to be known throughout the empire. This made it very difficult for rulers to come to power, govern, and stay in power. Ideas and goods spread to different parts of the empire, but that took a long time. Communication was slow and travel was dangerous. It took strong emperors and a huge amount of resources to build communication and trade **networks**. As merchants and other people traveled along these trade networks, they brought more than goods. They also exchanged religious and philosophical ideas as well as their cultural beliefs and attitudes.

intensive agriculture: a kind of farming that is very concentrated in an area

literally: really; actually

network: anything that looks like or functions like a net; a group of systems that is connected

Intensive Agriculture

The Chinese empire developed in areas that supported **intensive agriculture**. The most important geographical feature in northern China was the Huang He (or Yellow River). The land in the Huang He valley was perfect for growing wheat, a grain called millet, and beans. The most important geographical feature in southern China was the Yangtze River. Over time, Chinese farmers learned how to drain the land in this region. It became a perfect place for them to grow rice.

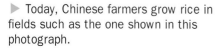
▶ Today, Chinese farmers grow rice in fields such as the one shown in this photograph.

▲ The steppe region of Mongolia has few or no trees.

isolation: a condition of being set apart from others; not to have any outside influences or contact

The Chinese did not spread out into areas that they considered unsuitable for farming. As a result, the Chinese did not expand north into the steppe of Mongolia or into the dry western region. They also did not expand into the jungles and mountains of the southwest.

Isolation from the Rest of the World

China's geographical features had another effect. During ancient times, China's geographical features served to isolate it from the rest of the world. The Pacific Ocean protected China's eastern and southern borders. The Himalayas formed the southwestern boundary. These geographical features were barriers to communication with other civilizations. They allowed China to develop its civilization in **isolation**. This isolation continued until people began to domesticate camels and use them for travel in the late 300s B.C. ▢

What Do You Think?

1. Did the Chinese have a natural basis for unity? Why or why not?

2. What body of water forms China's eastern and southern boundary?

3. What did geography have to do with government and the spread of ideas and goods in ancient China? Is geography still an important factor today? Why or why not?

4. What are the benefits and disadvantages of isolation?

Reader's Theater
Presents

THE EMPEROR AND THE SIGNAL FIRES

Practice reading the script. When the script says, "ALL THE EMPEROR'S SOLDIERS," everyone in the class joins in the reading. Read with expression!

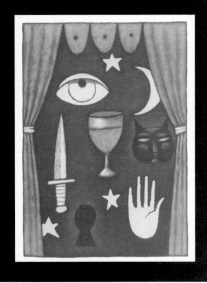

ROLES

★ **NARRATOR**
★ **TRAVELER**
★ **SOLDIER**
★ **EMPEROR**
★ **BAO SHI**
★ **ALL THE EMPEROR'S SOLDIERS (ALL)**
★ **SOUND EFFECTS**

Narrator: Long ago, in the kingdom of Zhou, a traveler met a soldier on a mountaintop. The soldier was living in a hole dug into a great mound of earth.

Traveler: Excuse me, but what are you doing here, so far from the city? And why are you living in this mound of dirt?

Soldier: This is one of the emperor's beacon towers. Do you see that pile of wood on top of this mound?

Traveler: Yes.

Soldier: If invaders come from the north, it is my job to light that wood on fire.

Traveler: Why?

Soldier: When I light the fire, another soldier on the next mountaintop will see it and light his own fire. Then the soldiers on other mountains will light their fires, until all the fires on all the mountaintops are lit. When the emperor's generals see the fires, they will send men to defend the kingdom.

Traveler: That must be quite a sight. Why don't you light your fire now so I can see for myself?

Soldier: If I do that, when no invaders are coming, it would endanger the kingdom.

Traveler: How? Surely there's no harm in having a little fun.

Soldier: Let me tell you a story. Many years ago, there was a great emperor of the kingdom of Zhou. This emperor conquered many lands. In one of the lands, he met a princess named Bao Shi.

▼ Whenever the kingdom was in danger, mountain fires were lit as a signal to the emperor's armies.

▲ Bao Shi was not impressed with any of the jewelry the emperor gave her.

Emperor: Bao Shi, you are the most beautiful woman I have ever seen. I will bring you back to my kingdom and make you my empress.

Soldier: Bao Shi was indeed beautiful, but she never smiled. The emperor tried many things to make her smile. He gave her precious jewels, fine clothes, and exotic foods.

Emperor: See all the wonderful things I have given you? Don't they make you happy?

Soldier: But still Bao Shi did not smile.

Bao Shi: I have seen many beautiful things in my life.

Soldier: Eager to impress Bao Shi, the emperor lit the signal fires. From all across the land, the emperor's soldiers came to defend the kingdom.

Sound Effects: (Make a sound like thousands of men running across the countryside.)

Soldier: The soldiers had traveled many miles. When they arrived, they were tired and covered with dirt. When Bao Shi saw the men, she began to giggle and then she laughed out loud.

Bao Shi: How silly you all look, with your armor covered with mud and your faces dripping with sweat!

▼ Bao Shi laughed at the emperor's soldiers who came to defend the kingdom.

Soldier: The emperor was so pleased to see Bao Shi smile, he forgot all about the men.

All the Emperor's Soldiers: My lord, why have you called us here?

Emperor: Oh, it was nothing. You can all go home.

Soldier: The emperor's soldiers were angry that the emperor had fooled them. But a few months later, the emperor lit the signal fires again to impress Bao Shi.

▼ Invaders attacked and destroyed the kingdom.

Sound Effects: (Make a sound like thousands of men running across the countryside.)

All the Emperor's Soldiers: We have come again to defend you, my lord! Where are the invaders?

Emperor: There are no invaders. Go back home.

Soldier: Again, the soldiers were angry as they made the long walk home. Then one day, an army of invaders came down from the north to attack the kingdom. The emperor lit the signal fires. But nobody came.

All the Emperor's Soldiers: We know this trick. The emperor is only calling us to impress his empress.

Soldier: When the invaders arrived, they found the kingdom undefended. They destroyed the palace and took over the land.

Traveler: How terrible!

Soldier: Yes. It was a terrible tragedy.

Narrator: And that is why the signal fires must only be lit in emergencies. 📖

CONFUCIUS
and the Age of Philosophers

700 B.C.   400 B.C.

c. 601 – 531 B.C.
Laozi

c. 563 – 483 B.C.
The Buddha

551 – 479 B.C.
Confucius

The world Confucius was born into was marked by social and political disorder. He was upset by the constant warfare between the various Chinese rulers. Confucius did not like what he saw happening in China. He encouraged people to look back to a time in history when China was unified and orderly.

▲ Confucius was born in the state of Lu.

Confucius's Early Life

Confucius was born in 551 B.C. in the state of Lu, in present-day northeastern China. Modern historians are not certain about some of the details of his life. For example, they are not sure exactly where he worked, the particular job that he held, or when he lived in certain places. Despite these questions, however, they have pieced together some general information about Confucius's life.

A Government Worker

Confucius was from a poor family, but his family may have once been part of the noble class. His father died when he was very young. While still a boy, he traveled widely and studied in the city of Zhou. For most of his early life, he wanted an appointment to an important government position. However, he was only partly successful in achieving this goal. Generally, he was able to get only minor government positions. And he usually only held these positions for short periods of time.

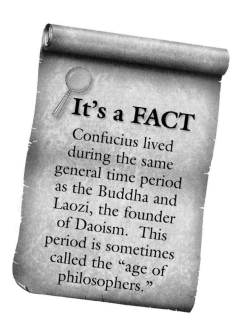

It's a FACT
Confucius lived during the same general time period as the Buddha and Laozi, the founder of Daoism. This period is sometimes called the "age of philosophers."

It's a FACT

Confucius's full Chinese name was K'ung Ch'iu or K'ung Chung-ni. He also was known as K'ung Fu-tzu, which became known to us as "Confucius."

An Outspoken Teacher

During the years he was a government worker, Confucius was an outspoken teacher. Many students (or "disciples") gathered around him to hear his ideas. On at least two occasions, he wandered the Chinese countryside with his disciples going from one royal court to another. Eventually, he gave up on ever finding a permanent government position. He decided to return to his home to teach and write.

Traditional Values

During his lifetime, Confucius was not a famous or powerful man. In many ways he was like other men of his time. What made him stand out from others was his concern for the way people lived their everyday lives. During his lifetime, Confucius taught people how important it was to live life according to the traditional values of virtue. For Confucius, these traditional values included qualities such as kindness, goodness, respect, and "proper conduct." Proper conduct referred to the way people should act in their relationships with others in society. The message that Confucius taught was simple: To have peace and order in the world, people must return to the traditional values of virtue. Confucius believed society would be stable and orderly if people understood and performed their roles.

Confucianism—A Belief System

Confucius was not a religious leader. He did not teach about God or heaven. He was more concerned with practical and earthly subjects such as treating people fairly, good manners, and improving family relations. The ideas Confucius taught are considered a belief system that we call Confucianism. Confucianism is concerned with how to live in this world. Confucius felt that each person must have five qualities: integrity, righteousness, loyalty, selflessness, and goodness. Confucius believed that the world becomes a better place when all people, both men and women, strive toward these ideals.

Order in the Family and Society

Confucius believed that the family, not the individual, is the basic unit of society. As a result, he emphasized order in the relationships among family members. Confucius described five social relationships that must always be honored: father and son; ruler and subject; husband and wife; older brother and younger brother; and older friend and younger friend. Confucius taught that the people in these relationships had a responsibility to each other. For example, a father, who is always superior to his son, has a responsibility to care for the well-being of the son. The son, in turn, is always inferior or subordinate to his father and must give the father his unquestioned loyalty. These same, well-defined roles between people in superior and subordinate positions held for each of the social relationships. This meant that a ruler was responsible for caring for his subjects and subjects owed the ruler their loyalty. Confucius believed that if each person performed his or her role in society with sincerity and understanding, there would be no need for laws and punishments. Society would be orderly.

> **Confucius shared many ideas with his students, including the following:**
>
> Silence is a friend who never betrays.
>
> Don't do unto others what you yourself would not like.
>
> In education, there are no class distinctions.

PLAN FOR RIGHT LIVING

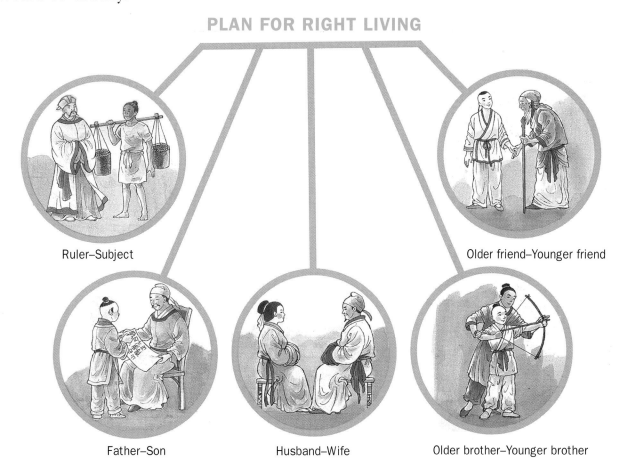

Ruler–Subject

Older friend–Younger friend

Father–Son

Husband–Wife

Older brother–Younger brother

▲ These are the five social relationships that Confucius said must always be honored.

What Do You Think?

1. Confucius taught that the most important unit in society is the family, not the individual. He believed that the family had a responsibility to help its members be successful. Do you agree or disagree with this idea? Explain your answer.

2. What are the advantages of a Confucian system where relationships in society are clearly defined? What are the disadvantages?

From the *Analects*
Book Four, V:
He said: Riches and honor are what men desire; if not obtained in the right way, they do not last. Poverty and penny-pinching are what men hate, but are only to be avoided in the right way.

Book Seventeen, II:
He said: Men are born pretty much alike; it's practicing something that puts distance between them.

Education and Bureaucracy

As people learned more about Confucius's ideas, they began to place a higher value on education. Through education, people could learn how to perform their role in society. Schools were established to teach Confucian ideas. Men attended these schools to prepare themselves for government jobs. Previously, the emperor had appointed nobles to these government jobs. Over time, however, men who were educated in these schools became important government officials. They began to form a group we sometimes refer to as the Confucian bureaucracy—men educated in Confucian thinking who served as officials in the government. This created a significant change in Chinese society.

Confucius's Ideas Today

Throughout his life, Confucius traveled from place to place with people who strongly believed in his teachings. When Confucius died in 479 B.C., he did not leave books or writings to explain his ideas. Instead, the information we have about his teachings comes from books his disciples wrote. One of the most famous of these books is called the *Analects* or *Conversations*. This book consists of many statements by Confucius. You can read on the left two excerpts from the *Analects*.

Not everyone agrees that all the information in the *Analects* reflects Confucius's ideas accurately, but it provides a reference that tells us about Confucius and his ideas. Today, Confucius is known as one of China's most influential and important teachers. Confucius developed a way of thinking about the world that has been followed by more people, for a longer period of time, than any other person in the history of the world. In addition to China, almost every other Asian country uses some parts of Confucius's teachings as a guide. 📖

Analyze the Source!

Choose one excerpt. Tell what it means in your own words.

LAOZI AND DAOISM
The Way and Its Power

700 B.C. | 400 B.C.

c. 601 – 531 B.C.
Laozi

c. 563 – 483 B.C.
The Buddha

551 – 479 B.C.
Confucius

▲ This is one artist's idea of what Laozi looked like.

A scholar who studied religion in China once wrote that a Chinese religion has as many viewpoints as it has people who believe in it. This is another way of saying that Chinese religion is interpreted and understood in different ways by different people. A good example of this is the Chinese belief system we call Daoism. In China, the ideas of Daoism were adaptable and flexible. This flexibility is one of the reasons that Daoism has lasted so long.

Laozi—The Founder of Daoism

Scholars know very little about Laozi, the person credited with founding Daoism. Historians think Laozi was born around 601 B.C. He may have lived about the same time as Confucius, but he was probably a little older. Our ideas about Laozi are shaped by a book he is credited with writing. The name of this book is *Dao Te Ching*, which means "the way and its power." Dao (pronounced dow) is translated into English as "the way" or "the path." One thing we do know is that Laozi lived during a time of great social disorder. Many people were distrustful of religion. However, because life in China had become so unpredictable, many were eager to escape from the everyday routine of life. They found this escape in a return to a simpler life.

◀ This is a well-known Daoist symbol—Yin and Yang. It represents the balance in the universe.

Chapter 12: The End of Feudalism 149

The History of Daoism

The early Chinese, like many other peoples, believed that rocks, mountains, the sun, stars, animals, and other things in nature had spirits. This is sometimes called nature worship. Laozi took the ancient Chinese tradition of nature worship and made it into a way of life. He developed the idea that the Dao was the beginning of all things. He also taught that the Dao was the force behind all changes in the natural world. According to Laozi, the Dao is a force that surrounds everything and everyone. However, while the Dao flowed through all living and non-living things, he said it was not possible to see it. The Dao could only be experienced by people who were living in harmony with nature.

▲ This photograph shows mountains, trees, the sky, and other things in nature. Laozi took the ancient Chinese tradition of nature worship and made it into a way of life.

Having a Healthy Lifestyle

Laozi's ideas about the importance of nature influenced the way people thought about their bodies. They believed there was a connection between living in harmony with nature and having a healthy lifestyle. Many people who believed in Daoism became interested in herbal medicine and a healthy diet. They also developed systems of physical exercise to keep their bodies strong and healthy.

▲ Daoism teaches that movement and exercise are important in order to stay balanced with nature.

Laozi's Legacy

Daoism became one of the three main belief systems of China. However, during his life, Laozi never preached to large groups of people or organized groups of followers. He really never did anything to promote his ideas. This is very different from the approach Confucius and the Buddha took. Both spent years teaching others about their beliefs.

Whether it is a historical fact or a myth, it is said that Laozi was so unconcerned with the success of his philosophy that he never even stayed to answer questions from those who came to find him. Perhaps his attitude is best understood by the Daoist saying: "Those who know do not speak; those who speak do not know."

Moral Virtue

There are many things about Daoism that are very different from other religions you may know about or have learned about. However, there are also many things in Daoism that are easily understood by all people. For example, Daoists believe that each person's most important responsibility is to develop moral virtue. Daoists believe the most important moral virtues are compassion (or kindness), **moderation**, and humility.

moderation: avoiding extremes

What Do You Think?

1. Why do you think Laozi might have been unconcerned with the success of his philosophy?

2. What does the Daoist saying, "Those who know do not speak; those who speak do not know" mean?

3. What are the advantages of a belief system that is flexible? What are the disadvantages?

4. How is Daoism like the belief systems of other civilizations you have read about? Did these civilizations also have a tradition of nature worship and a concern about being in harmony with nature?

THE FIRST EMPEROR
and His Clay Army

| 250 B.C. | 0 |

221 – 206 B.C.
Qin Dynasty

Shi Huangdi, the man known today as the First Emperor of China, was born in 259 B.C. At the time, various groups in China were at war with one another.

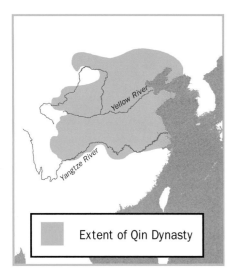

Extent of Qin Dynasty

▲ The First Emperor became the ruler of the Qin Dynasty when his father died in 246 B.C.

The First Emperor's Life

When his father died in 246 B.C., the First Emperor became ruler of the Qin Dynasty. The Qin were warlike and believed that people were basically evil. The Qin thought the only way to control people was through fear and harsh punishments. One advisor said, "In an orderly country, punishments are numerous and rewards are rare." This way of thinking is called legalism.

Very little is known about the First Emperor's early life. At first, his mother and one of his father's advisors ruled on his behalf. From 238 B.C., however, he ruled on his own. He had many children—some say more than 20. The First Emperor was known for how hard he worked and how much energy he had. He was very organized and very good at planning.

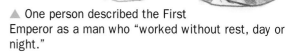
▲ One person described the First Emperor as a man who "worked without rest, day or night."

The First Emperor's Policies

The First Emperor's policies reflected his legalistic beliefs. He organized a powerful army that created fear in his enemies. The First Emperor's army was **infamous** for killing prisoners without mercy.

The First Emperor made the government more efficient. He divided the empire into 36 provinces and appointed officials to govern each province. The officials organized the people in the provinces into groups. The officials held each person in the group responsible for all the others in the group. In other words, if one person broke a law, everyone in the group was punished.

The First Emperor also made changes in the way land was distributed. He took land away from the nobles and gave it to the peasants to farm. He wanted to make sure that there would always be enough food for his armies.

Conquering Enemies

The First Emperor was very successful at conquering the Qin's enemies. It was said that he **devoured** his enemies "as a silkworm devours a mulberry leaf." By 221 B.C., he had unified China and declared himself Qin Shi Huangdi. He thought he was the first of what would be **endless** generations of Chinese emperors. He created a centralized government that future Chinese emperors would use as their model. He linked the provinces together by a network of more than 4,700 miles of roads. These roads were wide enough for three lanes of traffic. They also were lined with trees for shade.

Standardizing

The First Emperor made sure that many things in the empire were **standardized**. For example, he made sure that all **axles** had a standard width. He also standardized China's weights and measures. He gave China a standard **currency** and a standard way of writing. He marked all the boundaries of his empire and extended the Great Wall to defend China against the people who lived to the north. He also tried to make people think in a standard way. One traditional story says he did not want people to read the books written by earlier Chinese philosophers. As a result, he ordered the burning of many books. It is said that 460 scholars who would not follow his orders were sent to work on the Great Wall and were buried alive there.

It's a FACT

Legalism is the belief that a government should control people through rewards and punishment. It requires a strict following of laws. The First Emperor and his officials were great believers in legalism.

axle: the bar or rod on which a wheel turns

currency: money

devour: to eat up greedily; to destroy, consume, or swallow up

endless: being or seeming to be without an end; continuous

infamous: well known in a negative way; notorious

standardize: to make, cause, or adapt to fit a commonly used and accepted authority; to cause to be the same

▲ This is the Great Wall of China today. The First Emperor linked many small sections of the wall together to form one long continuous wall that protected China.

What Do You Think?

1. What is legalism?

2. How were the ideas of legalism reflected in the First Emperor's policies?

3. What do you think was the First Emperor's greatest accomplishment? Explain your answer.

Fame After Death

Shi Huangdi died on a trip to one of the eastern provinces. His closest advisor, Li Si, kept the First Emperor's death a secret until he made sure that his own son became the Second Emperor.

Shi Huangdi was buried with thousands of life-sized clay soldiers as well as many clay horses and chariots. Almost 40 years ago, some Chinese peasants digging a well accidentally discovered Shi Huangdi's tomb. In 1974, archaeologists began to excavate the tomb, which is about 25 miles from the modern city of Xian. We have learned a great deal about Chinese culture and warfare from this archaeological site. People all over the world marvel at the finds that have come from the First Emperor's tomb. He has become one of the most famous emperors in Chinese history. 📖

THE HAN DYNASTY

| 250 B.C. | 0 | A.D. 250 |

204 B.C. – A.D. 220
Han Dynasty

Liu Bang was a Chinese peasant whose courage and determination made him a heroic figure in Chinese history. When Liu Bang became ruler of the Han Dynasty, he took the name Emperor Gaodi. He was different from the Qin rulers and other leaders of the time. Rather than killing conquered peoples, he showed them mercy. He was a ruler who became known for moderation.

An Imperial Bureaucratic State

The Han emperors developed the Chinese **imperial** bureaucratic state. This bureaucracy was the foundation of China's government for almost 2,000 years. The Han emperors took several actions that resulted in the creation of this imperial bureaucracy.

First, the Han emperors introduced a law that formalized China's system of government. They said the government should consist of the emperor and three senior officials. Nine junior officials were appointed to help the senior officials.

Second, the Han emperors made sure that the powers of these government officials **overlapped**. They also made sure that the period of time the officials served in office overlapped. This meant that no one official could gain too much power.

Third, the Han Emperor Gaodi adopted strict ethical standards based on Confucian ideas. Out of this came the idea of a **civil service** system based on **merit**. Government officials were appointed based on their intelligence and other qualifications, not because of family connections. You can read below an order Emperor Gaodi gave in 196 B.C. regarding the importance of merit.

civil service: all of the people who work for the government (except people in the military, the people who make laws, and the judges)

imperial: belonging to an empire or emperor

merit: ability; deserving of reward or praise

overlap: to extend over and cover part of; to coincide partly

If any of the princes or governors discovers a man of talent and virtue ..., he should personally invite him to serve the government. ... An official who knows a virtuous man ... and chooses not to report it shall lose his position.

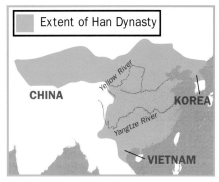

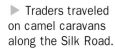
Han rulers conquered parts of present-day Vietnam and Korea.

The Expansion of the Empire

In addition to reforming the government, Emperor Gaodi and subsequent Han emperors took actions to bring peace and stability to China. They allowed rulers in the eastern and southern parts of China to continue in power as long as they pledged their loyalty to the Han emperor. Over time, the Han emperors replaced these rulers with members of their own family.

One Han ruler, Emperor Wudi, sent armies to expand China's territories. His armies fought tribes of nomads in the north. They conquered land to the south and east, including parts of present-day Vietnam and Korea.

Increasing Trade

With peace and stability in the empire, trade became much more important. An increasing number of traders followed the Silk Road south to India and west to Rome. People in Europe had learned about and wanted goods from China, India, and other parts of Asia. Wealthy Romans, in particular, were eager to buy silk—no matter how much gold and silver they had to pay. People in eastern Asia traded silk for goods they wanted from western Asia and Europe, including glassware, horses, cotton, linen, and metal items.

▶ Traders traveled on camel caravans along the Silk Road.

Connecting East and West

There were many roads along the general route between East and West. One route went from the Han city of Changan (modern-day Xian) across Asia, westward across the Iranian plateau, and then on to the Mediterranean Sea. Another began at Changan, but then went south and then west toward the Mediterranean. The routes connecting East and West were known generally as the Silk Road. The name "Silk Road" reflects the fact that silk was one of the most important trade items that traveled along these routes.

Many items were carried along the Silk Road besides silk, including jade, horses, ivory, glass, spices, cotton, and incense. The people who traveled the Silk Road also shared ideas about science, mathematics, astronomy, medicine, warfare, and other subjects. People in the West and in other parts of the world learned about the wonders of Han China. 📖

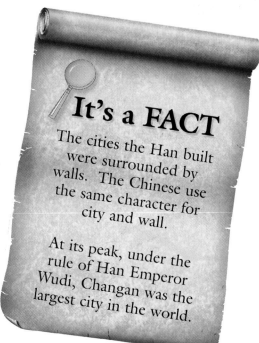

It's a FACT

The cities the Han built were surrounded by walls. The Chinese use the same character for city and wall.

At its peak, under the rule of Han Emperor Wudi, Changan was the largest city in the world.

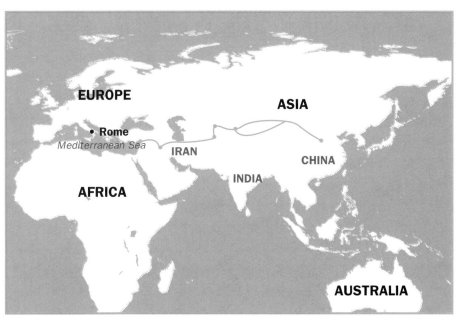

▲ There were many roads along the general route between East and West. The map above shows the major routes.

What Do You Think?

1. How was Emperor Gaodi different from other Chinese rulers?

2. What three actions did the Han emperors take to create an imperial bureaucratic state?

3. Did Emperor Gaodi support the idea that a poor peasant with outstanding abilities could rise in Chinese society? Explain your answer.

4. How did the Han emperors expand their empire through conquest? How did they expand it through trade? Which do you think was more important? Why?

THE SILK ROAD
The Internet of the Ancient World

250 B.C.	0	A.D. 250

204 B.C. – A.D. 220
Han Dynasty

Have you ever worn a piece of clothing made of silk or felt a piece of silk? It feels smooth, light, soft, and cool to the touch. It is also very strong and beautiful. Throughout history, people have considered silk **precious** and desirable. During the Han Dynasty, merchants traveled the long, hard, and dangerous route between China and Europe because their customers wanted silk goods and they were willing to pay a lot of money for them. The land route these merchants traveled became known as the "Silk Road."

Making Silk

The Chinese began making silk more than 3,000 years ago. Some people—we don't know who—noticed that a certain kind of caterpillar liked to eat mulberry leaves. They also saw that these caterpillars produced silk thread to form their cocoons. After the caterpillars turned into moths, the people placed the cocoons in hot water. This softened the thread. Then it was ready to be formed into **fine** thread. This thread was used to make silk cloth. The Chinese were very careful not to let anyone know how silk was made. Anyone who wanted silk had to get it from China.

▶ This drawing shows Chinese women making silk.

The Roman Empire and the Han Dynasty

Around 100 B.C., ancient Rome was becoming a powerful empire in western Europe. Romans controlled a huge amount of territory. They were rulers of the Mediterranean world. Around this same time, the Han Dynasty ruled over a strong empire in eastern Asia. People in Europe knew about and wanted goods from China, India, and other parts of Asia. Wealthy Romans, in particular, were eager to buy silk—no matter how much gold and silver they had to pay.

Silk was expensive even for wealthy Romans. It was so costly that even the richest Romans often could afford to buy only small pieces. They sewed these pieces onto their linen or woolen clothing. People in eastern Asia traded silk for goods they wanted from western Asia and Europe, including glassware, horses, cotton, linen, and metal items.

Connecting East and West

The Silk Road was not really one road. There were many roads along the general route between East and West. One route went from the Han city of Changan (modern-day Xian) across Asia, westward across the Iranian plateau, and then on to the Mediterranean Sea. Another began at Changan, but then went south and then west toward the Mediterranean.

Different Natural Environments

Regardless of which route they took between East and West, travelers saw many different lands and many different natural environments. They saw mountains covered with snow. They crossed dry, sandy deserts. They stopped for rest, water, food, and shade in **oasis** towns.

Caravans on the Silk Road

Depending on the **terrain**, merchants carried their goods on two-humped camels, donkeys, and ox- or horse-drawn carts. These merchants traveled together in groups called caravans. They always were on the lookout for robbers who wanted to steal their goods.

fine: thin; slender

oasis: a fertile area in the desert where underground water rises and travelers can get water and shade

precious: valuable; worth a great deal

terrain: the physical geography of an area or region; the characteristics of land (such as rocky, hilly, flat, mountainous)

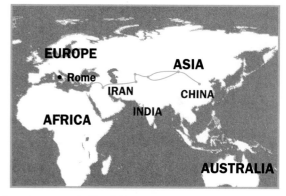

▲ The Silk Road connected China and the Western world.

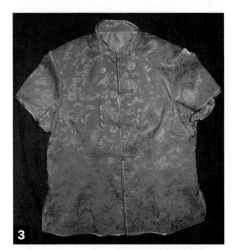

Missionaries on the Silk Road

During the Han period, almost no one made a round trip or even traveled the entire length of the Silk Road. However, there was one exception. Missionaries of various religions traveled the Silk Road sharing their ideas and beliefs. As they traveled along the Silk Road, Buddhists from India spread the news about Buddhism throughout Asia. Today, millions of people across the world believe in the teachings of Buddhism.

Sharing Ideas

The items that were carried along the Silk Road—silk, jade, horses, ivory, glass, spices, cotton, and incense—passed through the hands of many different traveling merchants. The people who traveled the Silk Road also shared ideas about science, mathematics, astronomy, medicine, warfare, and other subjects. They exchanged news and ideas about technology, fashion, crafts, and religion. The Silk Road connected people from the East and West. It was the Internet of the ancient world. 📖

What Do You Think?

1. Who were the first people to learn how to make silk? What was the Silk Road?

2. Do you agree that the Silk Road was the Internet of the ancient world? Why or why not?

3. What do you think was the most important item or idea that traveled along the Silk Road? Explain your answer.

▲ These were some of the items traded along the Silk Road: **1.** spices such as pepper and cardamon **2.** horses **3.** silk such as the silk used to make this blouse **4.** ivory from the tusks of elephants.

A Prince Becomes

700 B.C. — 400 B.C.

c. 601 – 531 B.C.
Laozi

c. 563 – 483 B.C.
The Buddha

551 – 479 B.C.
Confucius

Centuries after the Buddha's death, some faithful believers in the teachings of Buddhism wrote about the history of the Buddha's life. They described the Buddha in a very favorable way, but they did not portray him as a god. Instead, they presented him as a very kind and gentle man.

A Privileged, Royal Child

Siddhartha Gautama, the man we call the Buddha and the founder of Buddhism, was born about 563 B.C. Most people agree that Siddhartha was born into a royal family. They lived in an area that is now the southern edge of Nepal, just north of India, in the foothills of the Himalayas. As the child of a royal family, Siddhartha led a very safe, secure, and privileged life. His parents did not want him to see or experience any ugliness and unhappiness. As a young boy, he never left the palace. He never met everyday people or saw how they lived their lives. His parents did everything they could to keep him happy and amused. They did not want him to become bored or lonely or want for any material things. However, as Siddhartha grew older, he became curious about what life was like beyond the palace.

▲ As a boy, Siddhartha and his family lived in the foothills of the Himalayas.

Seeing Life for Himself

As the traditional story is told, Siddhartha finally decided he had to see for himself what life was like outside his palace walls. For several nights in a row, Siddhartha left the palace. As he walked on the nearby streets, he saw things he had never seen or heard of before. He saw people who were sick, people who were old, people who were poor, and even people who had died. Never before had Siddhartha seen illness, old age, poverty, or death. This experience changed him forever.

He could not understand how he could live such a wonderful life in the palace, and at the same time there was sickness, old age, poverty, and death. He decided on a course of action. He would give up all of his worldly pleasures and spend his time looking for answers to his questions about the world. He wanted to understand how the beauty of his palace life existed at the same time as all of the suffering he saw in the world.

A Blinding Flash and Enlightenment

One night Siddhartha left the palace on horseback. He rode to a place that was far away from everyone and everything. For days, he sat under a tree and tried to understand what life and suffering meant. After many days, the "answer" came to him in a blinding flash. In that moment, his followers say that he became enlightened—free from wanting material things or power. In that moment, his followers say that he became the Buddha, a name that means "enlightened one." Another name for enlightenment is "nirvana."

The Buddha's Teachings

Over time, the Buddha developed a way of talking about his enlightenment. He also began to talk about how others could reach enlightenment. The Buddha said that the first thing a person must do is to accept what he called the "Four Noble Truths."

▲ His followers say the Buddha gained enlightenment near this tree.

The Four Noble Truths

1. Life is filled with suffering.
2. Desire for material things and power causes suffering.
3. Suffering ends when people no longer desire material things and power.
4. People can learn to give up their desire for things and power by following the Eightfold Path.

What does this mean? Think about this idea. Suppose you want a new toy or game or pair of shoes. The more you want it, the unhappier you become. The Buddha's solution to this unhappiness is for people to learn to stop wanting things. This is not an easy thing to do. In fact, it is very difficult.

To help people stop wanting things, the Buddha came up with a guide for his followers. This guide is called the "Eightfold Path." It called upon people to have right views, right intentions, right speech, right action, right livelihood, right effort, right mindfulness, and right concentration. The Buddha's followers believed they would find enlightenment if they followed the standards of behavior set forth in the Eightfold Path.

The Eightfold Path

1. Right views means knowing the truth.
2. Right intentions means trying to resist evil.
3. Right speech means not saying things that will hurt others.
4. Right action means showing respect for other people and things.
5. Right livelihood means working at a job that does not hurt others.
6. Right effort means trying not to think evil thoughts.
7. Right mindfulness means trying to be aware of the world.
8. Right concentration means taking the time to meditate and think clearly.

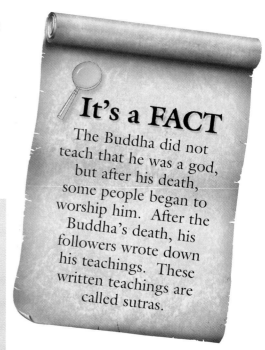

It's a FACT
The Buddha did not teach that he was a god, but after his death, some people began to worship him. After the Buddha's death, his followers wrote down his teachings. These written teachings are called sutras.

Buddhism Spreads to China

During the later part of the Han Dynasty's rule, Buddhism began to spread to China. As Buddhist travelers and missionaries traveled the Silk Road, they brought their ideas about Buddhism to China. The earliest written references to Buddhism in China appear around A.D. 65. By the end of the Han Dynasty, historians point to Buddhist statues, paintings, and other art as evidence of the northward spread of Buddhism into China.

Buddhism appealed to many Chinese because it promised an end to pain and suffering. According to Buddhist teachings, if people followed the Four Noble Truths and the Eightfold Path, they could achieve enlightenment, which freed them from suffering and want. Neither the teachings of Confucius or Laozi made the same connection between the individual person's ethical conduct and enlightenment. Buddhism offered them something that they did not find in Confucianism or Daoism.

▲ This is one representation of the Buddha in Southeast Asia.

principle: a basic truth, law, or assumption

ritual: a ceremony that takes place the same way every time

sect: a group of people forming a distinct unit or group within a larger group

People Follow Rituals and Sutras

As Buddhism became more popular in China, people began to follow **rituals** and Buddhist writings called sutras. Monks became leaders in an organized Buddhist religion. Buddhism also influenced language, literature, and architecture in China. Temples and shrines were designed to reflect Buddhist ideas of simplicity and freedom from the want of material goods.

Different Types of Buddhism

As with most belief systems, people interpreted Buddhism in different ways. Throughout Asia, different kinds of Buddhism began to be practiced by **sects** or groups of followers. Some of these sects are more likely to be found in China. Others are more likely to be found in India or Japan. While each major sect has a different method of teaching the **principles** of Buddhism, all have the same goal—for each person to reach enlightenment, what Buddhists think of as a state of "eternal bliss."

What Do You Think?

1. What experience changed Siddhartha Gautama forever?

2. What evidence do historians have that tells when Buddhism spread to China?

3. The Buddha taught that the more people want material things, the unhappier they become. Do you agree or disagree with this idea? Why?

4. How are the Buddha's ideas like other belief systems or religions you have learned about? How are they different?

SIMA QIAN
and China's First History

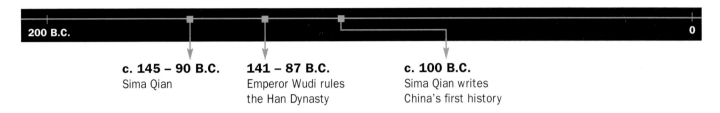

200 B.C.				0

c. 145 – 90 B.C.
Sima Qian

141 – 87 B.C.
Emperor Wudi rules
the Han Dynasty

c. 100 B.C.
Sima Qian writes
China's first history

Emperor Wudi of the Han Dynasty ruled China from 141 to 87 B.C. During his rule, Sima Tan was the Grand Historian in his court. It was the Grand Historian's job to supervise religious rituals, keep track of the **astrological** calendar, and oversee the Emperor's library and historical records. After Sima Tan died, his son Sima Qian took his place and became the new Grand Historian for Emperor Wudi. He took over all his father's duties. Most importantly, about 100 B.C., 10 years after his father's death, Sima Qian finished what his father had always wanted to do—he wrote the first history of China.

The *Shiji*—Records of the Scribes

The history book you are reading today is very different from Sima Qian's book about China's history. His book, called the *Shiji*, which means "Historical Records," was written with a brush and ink, not with a pen, typewriter, or computer. Sima Qian wrote the story of China's history on thousands of strips of bamboo. These bamboo strips were bound together with pieces of silk cord. The *Shiji* looked more like a bamboo roll-up shade than like our modern idea of a book. One historian said it would have taken a cart to move the *Shiji* around.

> **astrological:** having to do with the position of the stars and planets in the sky

The History of the World

Sima Qian set out to write a history of the world. He considered China and the people and states around China "the world." His work began with the earliest beginnings of China through the time in which he was living.

▶ Sima Qian wrote his book on strips of bamboo like the ones shown in this picture.

biography: a written account of a person's life

discard: to throw away

forebear: ancestor; family member who lived in earlier times

remiss: not pay attention to one's duty; negligent

sovereign: a king or queen; the ruler of an empire or country

weep: to cry

Five Major Sections

The *Shiji* is organized into five major sections. The book tells about the various rulers, discusses important topics such as the arts, and describes events. The *Shiji* also includes **biographies** of important figures in Chinese history. For example, Sima Qian wrote about the lives of Confucius and the First Emperor.

Sima Qian and His Father

Most of Sima Qian's book describes people, issues, and events. He does not say much about what he thought about these topics. He doesn't tell much about his personal life. We don't know if he had brothers and sisters or if he ever married. We do know that he was devoted to his parents. In his book, he wrote about his father, Sima Tan. You can read below an excerpt from his description of a conversation he had with his father as Sima Tan lay dying. This excerpt reveals how Confucian ideas influenced his thinking about relationships, duty, and honor.

Analyze the Source!

Tell what the excerpt means in your own words. How does this excerpt reflect Confucian ideas?

[His father, Sima Tan, said:] "I am dying. You must become the Grand [Historian], and as the Grand [Historian] do not forget that which I have desired to set in order and write. ... The feudal lords have joined together, but their ... records have been scattered and discontinued. Now the Han has arisen and all the world is united under one rule, yet as Grand [Historian] I have not set in order and recorded the glorious **sovereigns**, worthy rulers, loyal ministers, and gentlemen who died for righteousness. I am fearful that the historical writings of the world will be **discarded**. You must bear this in mind."

Sima Qian bowed his head, and said, **weeping**, "Your humble son is not very clever, but I would like to thoroughly set in order the old traditions that our **forebears** put together. I dare not be **remiss**."

Doing the Right Thing

Sima Qian was dedicated to fulfilling his duty and acting in what he thought was the proper way. At times, he suffered greatly when he did what he thought was right. For example, once he defended a man who was unpopular with the emperor. This man was not his friend, but Sima Qian thought the man was being treated unfairly. The emperor was not happy that Sima Qian stood up for this man. In fact, he decided to punish Sima Qian by forcing him to choose between death or never being able to have children. Sima Qian knew that he had to continue living in order to finish his book. As a result, he chose for his punishment never to be able to have children.

An Important Contribution to History

When did Sima Qian die? No one knows for sure, but historians commonly date his death around 90 B.C. His book became one of the most important books in China and the first in a long series of books about Chinese history. 📖

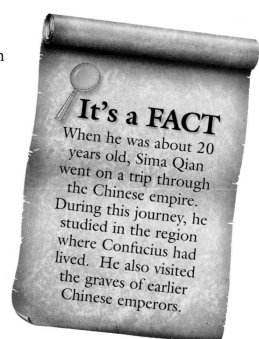

It's a FACT

When he was about 20 years old, Sima Qian went on a trip through the Chinese empire. During this journey, he studied in the region where Confucius had lived. He also visited the graves of earlier Chinese emperors.

▲ Here is one artist's idea of what Sima Qian looked like.

What Do You Think?

1. What were the duties of a Grand Historian in the court of Emperor Wudi?

2. What did Sima Qian do that no one had done before?

3. Sima Qian was willing to act according to his beliefs even if it meant he would suffer greatly. Would you be willing to stand up for someone even if it meant you might suffer? Would it make a difference if the person was your friend? Explain your answer.

Origins of
JUDAISM

2100 B.C.				1000 B.C.

c. 2061 – 1784 B.C.
Middle Kingdom of Egypt

1900 B.C.
God commands Abraham to first settle in Canaan

1290 B.C.
Moses leads the Israelites out of Egypt

1050 B.C.
The Philistines conquer Israel

By about 2000 B.C., in addition to the Nile River valley, the Egyptian Empire included the land around the eastern border of the Mediterranean Sea. Today, this region of southwestern Asia is commonly called the "Middle East." Some people in this area lived in towns and had permanent homes. Other people were nomads. Nomads stay in one area for a while, and then move on to a different area. Usually, nomadic groups included members of the same family. The **Semites** were one of the nomadic groups in this region. They moved from place to place looking for grazing land for their animals.

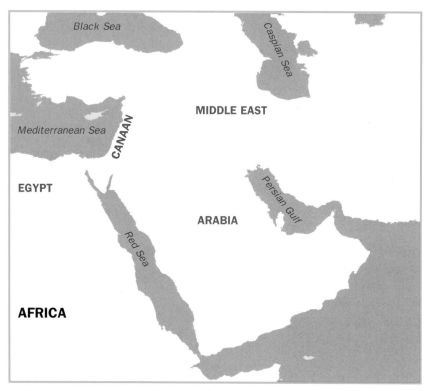

▲ Today, the region of southwestern Asia is commonly called the "Middle East."

Abraham—Patriarch of the Hebrews

Each nomadic group followed a male leader called a patriarch. Abraham was the patriarch of a group of Semitic people known as the Hebrews. The first book of the Bible, which is called Genesis, tells the story of Abraham and the Hebrews. The Hebrews believed they had a special relationship with the God they worshiped.

The Hebrews in Egypt

During the period known as the Middle Kingdom of Egypt, many people migrated from Canaan (later known as Palestine) to Egypt. It is thought that some of these people were descendants of Abraham. At first, the Hebrews were treated well. Over time, however, they became slaves in Egypt. Sometime around 1290 B.C., a man named Moses led a group of Hebrew slaves out of Egypt. According to the Bible, they started the long and difficult journey back, across the desert, to Canaan. They considered Canaan the "Promised Land" because it was the land that God promised to Abraham and his descendants. The Hebrews' escape from Egypt is described in **Exodus**.

Moses and the Ten Commandments

The Hebrews believed that their successful escape from Egypt was a powerful sign. They believed it showed that they had a special relationship with their God, who they called Yahweh, the Hebrew word for God. It was not an easy or quick journey to Canaan. In fact, it took Moses and his followers 40 years to cross the desert on their way to Canaan. During this journey, Moses stopped to pray on Mt. Sinai. The book of Exodus describes a covenant or promise God made with the Hebrews on Mt. Sinai. It was on Mt. Sinai that Exodus describes how God gave Moses a set of laws called the Ten Commandments. The Ten Commandments provided the Hebrews with a set of principles, or rules, to guide their daily lives. You can read the Ten Commandments on the right.

▶ The Ten Commandments provided the Hebrews with a set of principles, or rules, to guide their daily lives.

Exodus: the name of the second book of the Bible; the word *exodus* means "a departure from a place that involves large numbers of people"

Semite: one of the groups of people who lived in the eastern Mediterranean area; Semitic peoples include Jews and Arabs, and in ancient times, Babylonians, Assyrians, Phoenicians, and others

I
You shall have no other gods before me.

II
You shall not make for yourself an idol.

III
You shall not misuse the name of the Lord your God.

IV
Remember the Sabbath day by keeping it holy.

V
Honor your father and your mother.

VI
You shall not murder.

VII
You shall not commit adultery.

VIII
You shall not steal.

IX
You shall not give false testimony about your neighbor.

X
You shall not covet your neighbor's house; you shall not covet your neighbor's wife … nor anything that belongs to your neighbor.

captivity: the period in which someone or something is held as a prisoner

generation: all of the people who are born at approximately the same time

Israelite: a Hebrew; a member of any of the various groups who descended from Jacob, one of the Hebrew patriarchs

God's Chosen People

When the Hebrews finally returned to Canaan, they identified their traditions with those of Abraham, the man God had commanded to first settle there around 1900 B.C. The Hebrews believed there was only one God and that God had brought them out of slavery in Egypt. They also believed that God had given them 10 ethical rules by which they must live their lives. These laws stated very clearly standards of right and wrong. They believed that God said to Moses, "I will be your God and you will be my people." They began to think of themselves as God's chosen people. They believed it was the duty of each new **generation** to renew its promise to be God's chosen people. Over time, the Hebrews came to be known as **Israelites**.

The Israelites and the Philistines

The Israelites settled in the land of Canaan and grew increasingly powerful. However, they were organized very loosely into various groups or tribes. The groups did not have a strong central authority to unite them. This left the Israelites at a disadvantage when the Philistines, people from the surrounding area, wanted to expand their territory.

When under attack, the Israelites banded together to protect the Ark of the Covenant. This ark was a chest that contained the laws God had given to Moses. By 1050 B.C., the Philistines had conquered Israel and occupied most of their territory. Finally, the Israelites decided there was only one way to recapture their land. They decided to establish a king to lead them in battle against the Philistines. Their first king was Saul, but their next king and his son did the most to unify the Israelites.

David and Solomon—Kings of Israel

David is the boy described in the Bible who fought with only a slingshot against Goliath, the giant Philistine warrior. David later became king of the Israelites around 1000 B.C. Under David's rule, the Israelites defeated the Philistines. The Israelites captured the city of Jerusalem and established it as their capital. According to the Bible, David wanted to build a great temple that would house the Ark of the Covenant. He died in 962 B.C., before he could accomplish this goal. David's son, Solomon, became king. According to the Bible, he completed building this large temple in Jerusalem. Solomon ruled much like other kings during his time. He made alliances with neighboring kingdoms, demanded that his subjects pay taxes, and ordered the construction of many buildings. Solomon is considered a very wise ruler in Hebrew history.

After Solomon's death, the Israelites' kingdom was divided into two parts. The northern part was known as Israel. The southern part was known as Judah. The people who lived in Judah and who followed the traditions of David became known as Jews. Their religion became known as Judaism.

The Babylonian Captivity

The divided Hebrew kingdom was much weaker. Soon, the region became the target for a new power in the area, the Assyrians. By 772 B.C., the Assyrians had destroyed all of the kingdom of Israel. Later, in 586 B.C., Babylonia, an even newer empire, destroyed the kingdom of Judah. The Babylonian king, Nebuchadnezzar II, destroyed the temple of Solomon, burned Jerusalem, and captured and sent thousands of Jews to Babylon. This period of time is called the Babylonian **Captivity**. 📖

What Do You Think?

1. What name is commonly used today to refer to the region of southwestern Asia?

2. Who is considered the patriarch or father of the Hebrews?

3. Explain how the Ten Commandments provide a set of principles for people to guide their daily lives.

4. How did the division of the Israelites' kingdom into two parts hurt them?

▲ This modern-day illustration shows one artist's idea of how Nebuchadnezzar looked.

DAVID & GOLIATH

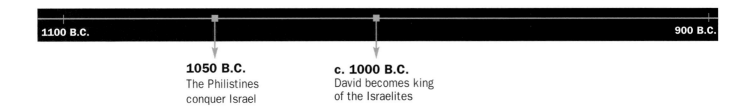

1100 B.C.		900 B.C.

1050 B.C.
The Philistines
conquer Israel

c. 1000 B.C.
David becomes king
of the Israelites

The Israelites who settled in the land of Canaan were organized very loosely into various groups or tribes. This loose organization among the tribes was a disadvantage when the Philistines, people from the surrounding area, began to expand their territory. By 1050 B.C., the Philistines conquered Israel and occupied most of their territory.

▲ In this drawing, the priest is conducting a ceremony to make David king of the Israelites.

An Israelite King

The Israelites decided there was only one way to recapture their land. They decided to establish a king to lead them in battle against the Philistines. Their first king was Saul. However, it was their next king, David, who defeated the Philistines when he was a young **shepherd**. The excerpt on the next page is taken from the Bible. It describes the battle between the young shepherd, David, and Goliath, the giant Philistine warrior. This is not just a historical account. It is also a story of faith. It is written from a particular point of view. This doesn't mean the story is inaccurate; however, it is not written in a critical or analytical way.

The Story of David and Goliath

Now the Philistines gathered their forces for war ... Saul and the Israelites ... drew up their battle line to meet the Philistines. The Philistines occupied one hill and the Israelites another, with the valley between them.

A champion named Goliath, ... came out of the Philistine camp. He was over nine feet tall. He had a bronze helmet on his head and wore a coat of ... armor ... and a bronze **javelin** was slung on his back.

Goliath stood and shouted to the **ranks** of Israel, "Why do you come out and line up for battle? ... Choose a man and have him come down to me. If he is able to fight and kill me, we will become your subjects; but if I overcome him and kill him, you will become our subjects and serve us. ...

For forty days the Philistine [Goliath] came forward every morning and evening and took his stand.

According to the Bible, David's father asked him to take some bread to his brothers who were serving in Saul's army. As he was talking with his brothers in the camp, Goliath came out and shouted his challenge. David could not believe that no Israelite was willing to fight Goliath. David finally convinced Saul that with God's help he could beat Goliath. David did not put on armor or a helmet. Instead, he picked up five smooth stones and put them inside the small bag he carried. With only his slingshot and the five smooth stones, David walked toward Goliath.

David said to the Philistine, "You come against me with sword and spear and javelin, but I come against you in the name of the Lord Almighty, the God of the armies of Israel. ... This day the Lord will hand you over to me, and I'll strike you down." ... As the Philistine moved closer to attack him, David ran quickly toward the battle line to meet him. Reaching into his bag and taking out a stone, he slung it and struck the Philistine on the forehead. The stone sank into his forehead, and he fell face down on the ground.

So David **triumphed** over the Philistine with a sling and a stone; without a sword in his hand he struck down the Philistine and killed him.

javelin: a light spear that is used as a weapon

rank: a group (of soldiers)

shepherd: a person who takes care of and watches over a flock of sheep

triumph: to be victorious; to win

What Do You Think?

1. Who was the Philistines' great warrior? Who fought on behalf of the Israelites?

2. What weapons did the two warriors have?

3. How can this account be viewed as a story of history for Hebrews and also a story of their faith?

4. What lesson can people learn from this story?

RUTH & NAOMI

The Bible includes many stories about the people who were part of **Jewish** history. One of the most interesting and important stories is contained in the book of Ruth. This story centers around two women, Ruth and Naomi.

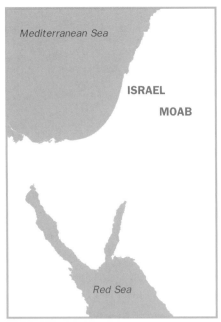

▲ Naomi and her family migrated from Israel to Moab. Later, Naomi and Ruth traveled back to Israel.

A New Life in Moab?

As the story is told, Naomi's family lived in Israel. Her husband was an important and rich man. During a time of great **famine**, he decided that he, Naomi, and their two sons should **migrate** to a neighboring country, Moab. Although Jewish law would have allowed Naomi to stay behind, she decided to follow her husband. After they arrived in Moab, Naomi was faced with many problems. First, her husband died. Then her two sons married non-Jewish women. Later, her two sons died.

Going Home to Israel

Although Naomi was an old and penniless woman, she was not ready to give up on her life. She decided to make her way back to Israel. Both of her daughters-in-law wanted to make the trip with her. Naomi tried to discourage them from making this journey with her. Neither of the young women were Jewish, and Naomi thought life would be too uncomfortable and hard for them in Israel. Naomi convinced one daughter-in-law to stay behind. The other daughter-in-law, Ruth, refused to change her mind. According to written accounts, Ruth said to Naomi:

▲ This drawing shows Ruth traveling with Naomi to Israel.

"Where you go I will go,
and where you stay I will stay.
Your people will be my people
and your God my God.
Where you die I will die,
and there I will be buried."

Ruth made it clear that she would always be loyal to Naomi. She said that only death would part them.

Life in Israel

After the two women reached Israel, Ruth had to find a way to support them. How would they eat? Where would they live? The only way Ruth could provide food for them was to work as a gleaner. After farmers had harvested their crops, gleaners were allowed to go on the fields and pick up any leftover grains. This was very hard work and produced very little food.

While working as a gleaner, the man who owned the field, Boaz, noticed Ruth. He was impressed by her modest manner. Ruth also noticed Boaz. She wanted to marry again. She thought a husband would care for her and also welcome Naomi into his family. Naomi saw that Ruth was interested in Boaz. Over time, she helped Ruth and Boaz marry. At the end of the story, Ruth and Boaz have a child, a boy. The child, Obed, becomes the father of Jesse and the grandfather of David—the second king of Israel.

▲ This drawing shows Ruth working as a gleaner in Boaz's fields.

Lessons from This Story

For some people, the story of Ruth and Naomi suggests that God works "behind the scenes" to help bring about a happy ending, regardless of how much suffering a person might have to endure. For other people, the story of Ruth and Naomi is a story of one woman's determination to overcome **adversity**. They see in Ruth a woman who overcame hardships, honored her mother-in-law, and created a better life for herself. The story of Ruth and Naomi held many lessons for people in ancient times. It continues to provide lessons for people today. 📖

adversity: hardship; troublesome time

famine: a time when food is very scarce and people do not have enough to eat

Jewish: relating to people of the Jewish religion; the ancient Hebrews were the ancestors of the Jews

migrate: to move from one place or region to another

What Do You Think?

1. Why did Naomi and her family migrate to Moab?

2. How would you describe Naomi's attitude toward life? How did she deal with adversity?

3. Why did Ruth want to marry again?

4. What do you think is the most important lesson from the story of Ruth and Naomi?

Yohanan ben Zaccai
A WISE LEADER

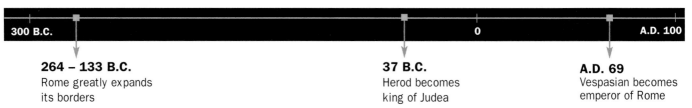

| 300 B.C. | | 0 | A.D. 100 |

264 – 133 B.C.
Rome greatly expands
its borders

37 B.C.
Herod becomes
king of Judea

A.D. 69
Vespasian becomes
emperor of Rome

By 133 B.C., the Roman army had conquered most of the lands along the Mediterranean Sea. Rome was the dominant power in the region. Judea, an area in the southern part of ancient Palestine, was in one of the provinces Rome ruled. In 37 B.C., Herod became king of Judea. It was in Judea that two Jewish groups fought a battle of ideas. Yohanan ben Zaccai was a hero in this battle.

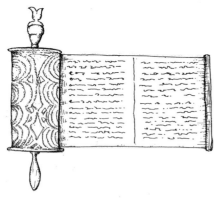

▲ Some people believed that the Torah was the final authority in all matters.

▼ Herod, a pro-Roman ruler, was king of Judea.

The Greatest Authority in Judaism

Herod was a pro-Roman ruler. This meant that he cooperated with the Romans. The Jews did not like or trust King Herod very much. During his rule of Judea, there were two different **schools of thought** about what was the most important **authority** in Judaism.

One school of thought believed that the written traditions of the Jewish faith were the most important authority of Judaism. This group insisted that the Torah was the final authority in all matters. They did not welcome any new religious ideas or new interpretations.

A second group of Jews believed that the oral tradition of law—the ideas handed down through each generation since Moses—was just as important as the written word. This group insisted that obedience to the laws was more important than rituals. Some of the people in this group were rabbis. Rabbis were educated men who read the Torah and commented about it. During this time, there were two important rabbis, Shammai and Hillel. Yohanan ben Zaccai was one of Rabbi Hillel's students.

Rebellion against Rome

During and after the reign of Herod, the Jews in Judea became increasingly unhappy with their Roman rulers. Over time, the Jews began to rebel openly against Rome. The first **rebellion** took place in Jerusalem in A.D. 66. Rome sent General Vespasian to stop this rebellion.

One group of Jews, called **Zealots**, was prepared to die rather than **submit** to Roman authority. Yohanan ben Zaccai disagreed with this position. He thought it would be better to surrender to the Romans. He did not think that it made sense to fight a hopeless battle in which all the Jews would be killed. He thought it was important that the study of Jewish texts and ideas continue no matter who was in charge. However, the Zealots refused to surrender. Yohanan ben Zaccai decided to think of a way to leave Jerusalem. He came up with a clever plan. He pretended that he had died. Then he had friends carry his "dead body" out of Jerusalem in a **coffin**.

authority: the rules giving one power

coffin: a box in which a dead body is placed before it is buried

rebellion: an organized attempt to openly resist authority; an uprising

school of thought: a group of people whose ideas have a common influence or unifying belief

submit: to give in; surrender

zealot: a person who is fanatically committed to something; a Zealot was a member of a Jewish group that resisted Roman rule

▲ In A.D. 73, the Zealots in the city of Masada killed themselves rather than surrender to the Romans. This is a photograph of Masada today.

Yohanan ben Zaccai and Vespasian

Yohanan ben Zaccai was not afraid of dying. He was not afraid of the Romans either. In fact, once outside of the city, he went directly to the headquarters of the Roman general, Vespasian. He wanted to make sure that the study of sacred Jewish texts would continue whether or not Romans were in charge. Yohanan ben Zaccai told Vespasian that he had a vision in which Vespasian had become emperor of Rome. He asked Vespasian to allow him to create a small school where he could study the Torah in peace. Vespasian told Yohanan ben Zaccai that if his vision came true, he could start his school.

A Center of Jewish Learning

Within the next 12 months, Vespasian became emperor of Rome. He kept his promise to allow Yohanan ben Zaccai to create a school where students could study the Torah. This school became the center of Jewish learning for hundreds of years. Yohanan ben Zaccai was a hero in the battle of ideas that was waged in Judea thousands of years ago. Today, he is known within the Jewish community as a person of great intelligence and wisdom. 📖

▲ Vespasian allowed Yohanan ben Zaccai to create a school where students could study the Torah.

What Do You Think?

1. Who was the dominant power in the Mediterranean world during the time that King Herod ruled Judea?

2. What is a rabbi?

3. Why did Yohanan ben Zaccai disagree with the Zealots?

4. Think about an issue that is important today. Can you identify two schools of thought about this issue? What do these different schools of thought disagree about?

THE JEWISH DIASPORA

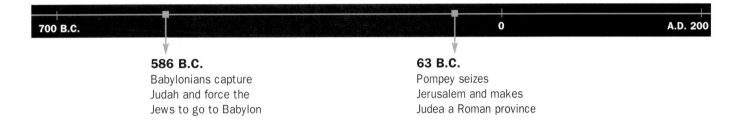

| 700 B.C. | | 0 | A.D. 200 |

586 B.C.
Babylonians capture
Judah and force the
Jews to go to Babylon

63 B.C.
Pompey seizes
Jerusalem and makes
Judea a Roman province

Throughout their history, the Jews have had to fight for the right to practice their religion and to live freely. As early as 722 B.C., Jews were forced to leave Palestine when the Assyrians conquered the area. Thousands of Jews were sent to work in the northern region of Mesopotamia. In 586 B.C., the Babylonians captured the kingdom of Judah and sent the Jews to Babylon for about 40 years. Later, the kingdom of Judah became known as Judea and its people known as Judeans. When the Persians destroyed the Babylonian empire in 539 B.C., the Jews were allowed to return to their homeland. For several centuries the Jews lived in relative peace as one powerful ruler and then another came into power and then faded away. However, by 63 B.C. the Roman general Pompey had seized Jerusalem and made Judea a Roman province. Roman officials now ruled Judea.

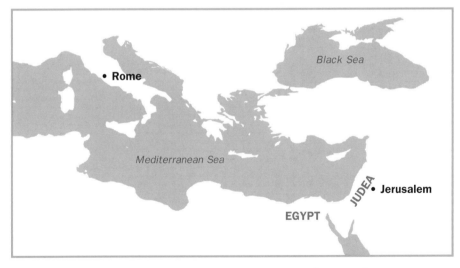

◀ By 63 B.C., the Roman general Pompey had seized Jerusalem and made Judea a Roman province.

Rebellions against Roman Leaders

Over many years, the Jews became increasingly angry at their Roman rulers. This anger led to several rebellions. The first rebellion began in A.D. 66 when a group of Jews known as Zealots fought the Romans. The Roman emperor, Nero, sent his general, Vespasian, to stop the rebellion. Vespasian's son, Titus, helped fight this battle.

Chapter 14: The Ancient Israelites **179**

Under Titus, the Romans destroyed the Jewish temple in Jerusalem and burned the city to the ground. You can read below how the Roman historian Tacitus (c. A.D. 56–120) described this event.

besieged: people who are under attack

frenzy: violent excitement; agitation

minority: a group of persons numbering less than half of the total

perseverance: resolve; determination

restrain: to hold back; contain

upper hand: a position of control or advantage

Titus pitched his camp before the walls of Jerusalem, and displayed his legions in battle order. The Jews formed their line close under the walls. ... The temple had its own walls. ... It is recorded that the **besieged**, of every age and both sexes, amounted to 600,000. All who could bore arms. ... Men and women showed equal **perseverance**: they feared life more than death if they should be forced to leave their country. ...

About the fifth hour of the following day the Jews were overpowered and shut up in the inner court of the temple, whereupon Titus withdrew. ... [Then] one of the soldiers, awaiting no order ... snatched a brand from the burning timbers and ... hurled the fire through a little golden door which gave access to the rooms around the sanctuary on the north. As the flames shot up the Jews raised a cry worthy of the disaster. ...

[Titus] was unable to **restrain** the **frenzy** of his soldiers, and the fire got the **upper hand**. ... And so ... the temple was burned down.

▼ This drawing shows the temple in Jerusalem before it was burned down.

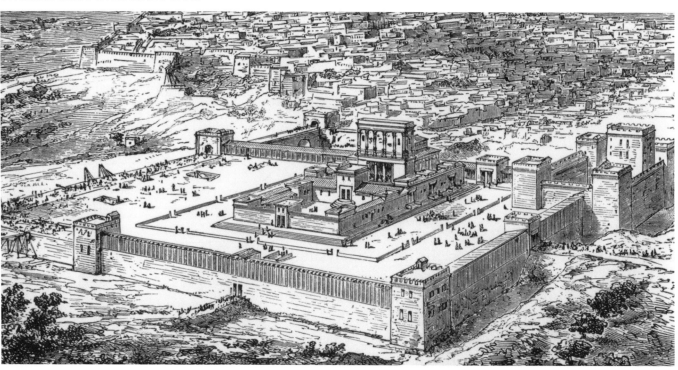

The Diaspora

Some Jews fled east into Mesopotamia. Some went north to Galilee. Others traveled south into Egypt. In A.D. 117, Jews living in Egypt rebelled against Roman authority. This time the Roman emperor, Trajan, stopped the rebellion. The next Roman emperor, Hadrian, took violent action against the Jews in Palestine when they refused to obey his command to become more "Roman." A man known as Bar Kokhba, which means "son of the star," led the rebellion against the Romans. In A.D. 135, he was executed along with other Jewish religious leaders. In all, the Romans killed more than half-a-million people. Jews became a **minority** in Palestine. From this time until the founding of the state of Israel in 1948, Jews lost all political authority in this region. This dispersion or spreading of Jews from Palestine to other places throughout the world is known as the Diaspora.

Scattered Jewish Communities

Jewish communities grew in many places. Many Jews remained in Babylon. Many migrated to Egypt and throughout the Arabian Peninsula. During the time of the Roman Empire, there were Jewish communities in Athens, Greece, and in Rome and other northern Italian cities. There were also Jewish communities in Córdoba, Spain, and in the city of Marseilles, France. Though scattered over much of the known world, the Jews were united by their belief in their God and in Hebrew scriptures and laws. ▭

What Do You Think?

1. What happened in 63 B.C.?

2. What happened after the Romans burned down the temple in Jerusalem and destroyed the city?

3. What do you think the Roman emperor Hadrian meant when he ordered the Jews to become more "Roman"?

4. What were the causes and effects of the Diaspora? What do you think is the most important consequence of the Diaspora?

Lessons from the
JEWS

The history of the Jews and their religion, Judaism, have had an important impact on our lives today. How did a small group of nomads in southwestern Asia come to **exert** such a significant influence on Western civilization?

▶ This drawing shows one artist's idea of Moses bringing the Ten Commandments to the ancient Israelites.

Ethical Standards for Behavior

The Bible reveals the most obvious ways that Jewish thinking has affected **modern** life. Perhaps the most well-known story is the account of Moses receiving the Ten Commandments from God on Mt. Sinai. Each commandment begins with the words, "thou shalt" or "thou shalt not." These commandments form a set of rules that continue to be the basis for our traditions and laws regarding human conduct. The Ten Commandments teach the importance of respect for family and neighbors. They also forbid murder, theft, lying, and other actions. The Jews were one of the first groups of people to declare these as **absolute** principles for ethical behavior. The Ten Commandments established standards of right and wrong.

Each Person Has Value

The Jews passed on another idea that is part of the basic foundation of Western civilization. This is the idea that each person has value. Before the time when the Jewish patriarch Abraham left for Canaan, people understood events to be cyclical. That is, they believed history was like a wheel. They thought that what had happened in the past would happen again in the future. People believed that they could only wait for events to come round and round again. In this sense, they thought that history repeated itself.

Over time, however, the Jews developed a very different view of the world. They began to think that each person had a **unique** future. This future was not simply a repeat of what had happened in the past. They developed the idea of a "better tomorrow." The Israelites believed that there was value in each individual because each person was made in "the image of God." This meant that each individual was different from every other individual. The idea that people are individuals and have value as individuals is one of the most important **legacies** passed down from the Jews.

absolute: not limited or restricted; total

exert: to put forth; to bring; to bear

legacy: something handed down or left behind after a person dies

modern: having to do with the present time; recent or current time

unique: being the only one of its kind

What Do You Think?

1. What set of rules gave the Jews standards of right and wrong?

2. Why did the Israelites believe that there was value in each person?

3. How did the Ten Commandments encourage good conduct and discourage bad conduct? Give an example of each.

4. How is the idea that each person has individual value reflected in American society today?

AESOP'S FABLES

Have you heard the story of the race between the rabbit and the turtle? "The Hare and the Tortoise" is one of the most famous fables in the world. It is recognized as the work of a man named Aesop who lived in ancient Greece thousands of years ago.

assent: to agree

assertion: claim; statement

fatigue: tiredness; exhaustion

ridicule: to laugh at; to mock

▼ "The Hare and the Tortoise" is one of the most famous fables in the world. The lesson in this fable is "slow but steady wins the race."

The Hare and the Tortoise

A Hare one day **ridiculed** the short feet and slow pace of the Tortoise, who replied, laughing, "Though you may be swift as the wind, I will beat you in a race." The Hare, believing her **assertion** to be simply impossible, **assented** to the proposal; and they agreed that the Fox should choose the course and fix the goal.

On the day appointed for the race the two started together. The Tortoise never for a moment stopped, but went on with a slow but steady pace straight to the end of the course. The Hare, lying down by the wayside, fell fast asleep. At last waking up, and moving as fast as he could, he saw the Tortoise had reached the goal, and was comfortably dozing after her **fatigue**.

Slow but steady wins the race.

A Story with a Lesson

A fable is a particular kind of story. The main characters in fables often are animals, birds, insects, or even trees. When you read a fable, you can understand it in two different ways. One way is as a simple story about some characters and an event in their lives. For example, in the story of "The Hare and the Tortoise," you followed a race between a rabbit and a turtle. However, there is always another meaning in a fable that is intended to instruct the reader. In the story of "The Hare and the Tortoise," the lesson is that even if you are not the fastest, you can still succeed if you keep working. You can read below another of Aesop's fables.

It's a FACT

In fables, certain animals represent human characteristics. For example, the fox represents cleverness, the lion represents courage, and the horse represents pride.

The Dogs and the Fox

Some dogs, finding the skin of a lion, began to tear it in pieces with their teeth. A Fox, seeing them, said, "If this lion were alive, you would soon find out that his claws were stronger than your teeth."

It is easy to kick a man that is down.

Again, there are two ways to understand this fable. It is a story about some dogs tearing apart a lion's skin, but it also contains a lesson that is intended to help human beings improve their behavior. The fox instructs the dogs that the lion is already dead. It is not very brave or strong to tear apart something that cannot defend itself.

Aesop—The Father of Greek Fables

We do not have much information about the Greek storyteller called Aesop who is credited with writing these fables and so many others. We know he was born a slave about 620 B.C. He was an extremely intelligent boy with a good sense of humor. Aesop had several masters, but was eventually given his freedom.

▲ This is a drawing of Aesop. Most of the information we have about Aesop and his fables is based on the work of a French scholar, M. Claude Gaspard Bachet de Mezeriac. He published a book called *Life of Aesop* in 1632.

What Do You Think?

1. What is a fable?

2. Who is considered the father of Greek fables?

3. The lesson in "The Hare and the Tortoise" is "slow but steady wins the race." Give an example to show what this means.

4. What obstacles did Aesop face in life? What advantages did he enjoy?

Sharing His Wisdom

As a freedman, Aesop traveled throughout ancient Greece. He shared his learning and wisdom with others through the fables he told. He also helped settle problems that occurred between some of the Greek city-states such as Corinth and Athens. Aesop was killed on one of these missions. He traveled to Delphi to deliver some gold for the citizens to divide among themselves. However, when he saw how greedy the people were, he decided to take the gold back to the Greek leader who had sent him to Delphi. The people of Delphi were furious at Aesop and sentenced him to death. They killed him as if he were a common criminal. Soon, however, the people of Delphi began to experience disasters and misfortune. These problems continued until they publicly apologized for their crime against Aesop. The saying, "the blood of Aesop," came to mean that "wrongs will be punished."

Aesop's Fables

Aesop did not write all the fables in the collection of stories known as *Aesop's Fables.* Some were stories people told long before Aesop lived. He also made up many of his own. These stories were passed down through generations of storytellers. Later these stories were written down. New fables also were added. However, because he created so many of the stories, the collection of fables bears his name. Aesop is considered the father of Greek fables. 📖

Reader's Theater
Presents

THE TROJAN WAR

Practice reading the script. When the script says, "TROJANS," everyone in the class joins in the reading. Read with expression!

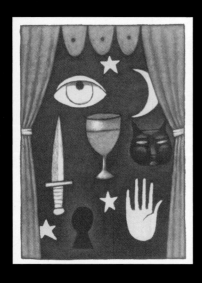

ROLES

★ **NARRATOR 1**
★ **NARRATOR 2**
★ **HOMER**
★ **MOTHER**
★ **GREEKS**
★ **ODYSSEUS**
★ **TROJANS (ALL)**
★ **SOUND EFFECTS**

Narrator 1: This story takes place in ancient Greece.

Narrator 2: One night long, long ago, a boy named Homer was having a hard time falling asleep.

Homer: I can't sleep, mother. Will you tell me a story?

Mother: What kind of story do you want to hear?

Homer: One with heroes and great battles.

Mother: Okay. Go upstairs and get into bed, and I'll tell you one of my favorite stories.

Narrator 1: So Homer went upstairs and got into bed.

Narrator 2: And his mother told him the story of the Trojan War.

Mother: Many years ago, there was a great war between the Greeks and the people of Troy.

Homer: What were they fighting about?

Mother: The Trojans had kidnaped a Greek woman named Helen. People said she was the most beautiful woman in the world. The Greeks were very angry that she was kidnaped.

Greeks: We will send 1,000 ships to Troy and rescue Helen!

Homer: One thousand ships! The Greeks must have won easily!

Mother: No, they did not win easily. You see, the walls of Troy were very strong. The Greeks fought hard against the Trojans, but they could not get into the city of Troy.

Sound Effects: (Make a sound like many men fighting.)

Mother: After nine years, the Greeks were ready to give up.

Greeks: Many of us have already died, and we still can't get into the city! We should just go home.

Mother: Then one of the Greek leaders, Odysseus, had an idea.

Odysseus: Maybe we can sneak inside the city.

Greeks: But how can we do that? The Trojans always keep the gates locked.

Odysseus: Here's what we're going to do. We'll pretend that we're giving up, and leave the Trojans a gift to give to their gods.

Greeks: How will that help us?

Odysseus: You'll see.

Mother: Odysseus and the Greeks built a huge wooden horse as their gift to the Trojans.

Sound Effects: (Make a sound like people sawing wood and hammering nails.)

Mother: The horse was hollow, so there was a lot of room inside.

Odysseus: One hundred of our best soldiers will hide inside this horse. The rest of you, get on your ships and pretend to sail home to Greece.

Mother: So the Greeks got in their ships and pretended to sail away. When the Trojans saw that the Greeks were gone, they opened the gates and came outside.

Trojans: Hooray! The Greeks have gone home. And they left this wooden horse as a gift! Let's take it inside the gates.

Mother: That night, while the Trojans were sleeping, the Greek soldiers quietly climbed out of the wooden horse. Then they opened up the gates to the city of Troy. The Greek soldiers sent a signal to their ships, and all of the Greeks came back and entered the city.

Homer: The Trojans must have been very surprised!

Mother: Yes. By the time they woke up, it was already too late. The Greeks were inside the gates. They destroyed the city and took Helen home.

Narrator 1: The people of Troy learned a lesson from this.

Narrator 2: People today still remember the lesson they learned: Beware of Greeks bearing gifts!

Homer: But what about Odysseus? What happened to him?

Mother: That's another story. But it's time for you to go to bed.

Narrator 1: Homer went to bed, but he never forgot about the story. As he grew up, he told the story over and over to many people.

Narrator 2: He became so good at telling the story that people remembered the words he used, and wrote them down.

Narrator 1: People still read his words today, in a book called the *Iliad*. 📖

▼ The Greeks made a huge wooden horse as a gift to the Trojans.

Development of
GREEK CITY-STATES

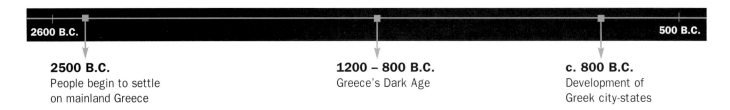

2600 B.C.			500 B.C.

2500 B.C.
People begin to settle
on mainland Greece

1200 – 800 B.C.
Greece's Dark Age

c. 800 B.C.
Development of
Greek city-states

City-states began to form in Greece when small villages formed alliances and banded together. Sometimes these villages came together for mutual protection. Other times they came together because they had similar religious beliefs. As trade increased between various villages, people began to organize themselves into units that were the foundation of the Greek city-state. The city-state or **"polis"** was one of the most important developments of ancient Greece.

Early History and Geography

One way to understand how different groups of people and their cultures have developed is to look at the physical area where people live. In what we now think of as ancient Greece, historians have discovered three groups of people that lived on the Greek mainland and the surrounding islands in the Aegean Sea.

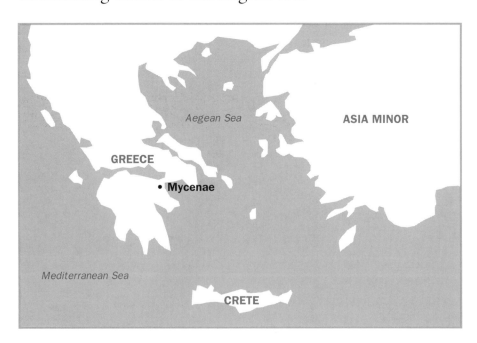

▶ In ancient Greece, three groups of people lived on the Greek mainland and the surrounding islands in the Aegean Sea.

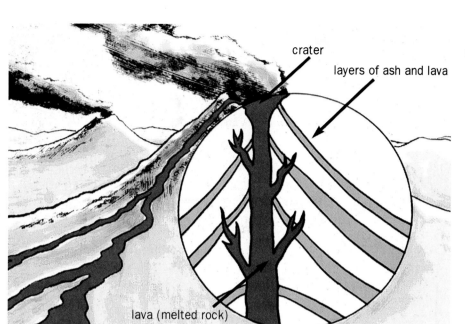

crater

layers of ash and lava

lava (melted rock)

◄ This diagram shows the major parts of a volcano.

Natural Disasters or War?

Starting about 2500 B.C., the first group of people spread over the **rugged** islands in the western part of the Aegean Sea. Eventually, this group of people faded away, and a second group appeared. The second group of people, the Minoans, lived on the island of Crete. About 1450 B.C., many cities on Crete were destroyed. Historians are not sure why this happened. Some believe **natural disasters** such as a volcanic eruption or earthquakes were the cause. However, the people who had been living on the mainland of Greece came to Crete and began to dominate the people living there.

The Mycenaeans

At this time, the people living in mainland Greece were centered around the city of Mycenae. The Mycenaeans were a warlike people whose civilization was found over all of the Greek islands, the Greek mainland, and on various parts of the coast of Asia Minor.

Although the Mycenaeans were powerful, they did not dominate the region for long. Around 1200 B.C., many Mycenaean cities were destroyed and their population was reduced by almost 90 percent. The cause of this destruction remains a **mystery**. Not only did the people abandon their forms of government, art, and cities, they also abandoned their writing. We have no written historical record of this time.

mystery: something that is unexplained, secret, or unknown

natural disaster: widespread destruction not caused by humans

polis: an independent, small city which ruled over the surrounding countryside

rugged: having a rough, irregular surface

The Greek Dark Age

The period of the next 400 years, from 1200 B.C. to about 800 B.C., is called the "Greek Dark Age." This time period gets its name because Greek civilization was in decline during these years. The information about this period is based on a few discoveries of ancient pottery and some evidence that the Greeks had changed from using bronze to iron. The most important documents from this time are two great epic poems, the *Iliad* and the *Odyssey*. You can read below a brief excerpt from the *Iliad*. In this excerpt, Andromache, wife of the Trojan hero Hector, is pleading with him not to fight the Greeks.

▲ This is a wood carving of Homer. Homer is considered by many to be the greatest writer of ancient Greece.

[She] stood close beside him, letting her tears fall, and clung to his hand and called him by name and spoke to him:
"Dearest, your own great strength will be your death, and you have no pity on your little son, nor on me, ... who soon must be your widow: for presently the [Greeks], gathering together, will set upon and kill you; and for me it would be far better to sink into the earth when I have lost you ... Please take pity upon me then, stay here ... that you may not leave your child an orphan, your wife a widow ...

Analyze the Source!

How did Andromache feel about the idea of her husband going to war? What concerns did she have? Do people today feel similar to or different from the way Andromache feels? Explain your answer.

Traditionally, both the *Iliad* and the *Odyssey* are thought to have been written by Homer. Today, however, most historians believe that these poems were the work of several men, all of whom contributed to the writing of these epics.

City-States Develop

Around 800 B.C., important changes started to take place in Greece. There was an increase in trade, agriculture, and art. This was also the time when the Greek city-states began to develop. Several areas in Greece showed a **rapid** growth in population.

No one knows exactly why the population increased, but the effects of the population growth were felt all over Greece. More people led to a larger number of towns and villages. This led to the expansion of trade. From the earliest records of Greek life, we know that the inhabitants of Crete, the Minoans, were very accomplished traders. Because of Crete's location between the Aegean and Mediterranean seas, the Minoans developed a very strong economy and traded with people from all over the area. One group from the mainland of Greece, the Mycenaeans, traded with the Minoans. As a result of this trading relationship, the Mycenaeans also began to adopt parts of the Minoan culture.

rapid: very fast

It's a FACT

The Minoans got their name from their famous king, Minos.

▲ The Minoans developed a very strong economy and traded with people from all over the Mediterranean area.

---

migration: the process of traveling to and settling in a new area

---

New Government

The growth in population also led to **migration** as people moved to new areas looking for better living conditions or more land to grow crops. The Greeks needed more agricultural land because mainland Greece was a hilly, rocky landscape with annual rainfall that was always uncertain. Most importantly, a larger population required a different kind of political system to govern the people.

Greek Culture and Civilization Spread

As the Greeks sailed around the Aegean Sea and the larger Mediterranean Sea, they traded goods with other groups. In the process, they spread Greek culture and ideas. People in other areas began to enjoy Greek goods and learn about Greek ideas, including ideas about the Greek polis. The spread of Greek ideas had an important influence on the development of Western civilization. 📖

What Do You Think?

1. What is the Greek word for city-state?

2. What happened in Greece around 800 B.C.?

3. Why do you think historians refer to a period of decline as a "dark age" and a period of growth and development as a "golden age"?

OLIGARCHY, TYRANNY, AND DEMOCRACY

At first, a king ruled each of the early Greek city-states. A government ruled by a king or a monarch is called a monarchy. By 800 B.C., however, the Greeks began to experiment with different forms of government.

Oligarchies and the Rise of Tyrants

One kind of government the Greeks tried was an oligarchy. In an oligarchy, only a few people, usually aristocrats, govern. Aristocrats were the nobles in Greek society. The English word *aristocrat* comes from the Greek word *aristoi*, which means "the best." Most Greek city-states were ruled by an oligarchy. At times, however, one of the men in an oligarchy would decide that he wanted to have more power. The population might support this person. In Greece, this person was known as a *tyrrano* or **tyrant**. Tyrants were mostly members of the aristocratic or noble class. Sometimes, tyrants came to power when a city-state was facing a crisis. For example, the city-state might be under attack by an enemy, and the people believed they needed a strong ruler to guide them. In early Greece, a tyrant who seized power often had the support of the people. Many tyrants tried to pass on their power to their sons or other family members. This attempt to create a hereditary rule caused many tyrants to lose power.

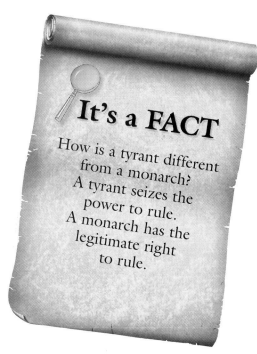

It's a FACT

How is a tyrant different from a monarch? A tyrant seizes the power to rule. A monarch has the legitimate right to rule.

tyrant: a ruler who governs without constitutional or other restrictions; the word *tyrant* has come to mean "a ruler who uses power in a harsh, cruel way"

HEREDITARY SUCCESSION

| Ruler | Ruler Dies | New Ruler |

▲ According to hereditary succession, the ruler's child or other relative becomes the next ruler.

What Do You Think?

1. What are the three forms of government discussed in this article?

2. Which form of government is most like our own American government?

3. How is the Greeks' idea of democracy different from the American idea? Give examples.

4. Is the idea of "equality before the law" applied equally today? Does it apply to citizens and non-citizens alike? Should it? Why or why not?

Democracy in Greek City-States

Another kind of government the Greeks experimented with was democracy. In a democracy, the people—or *demos* in Greek—govern. It is important to understand that democracy in ancient Greece was nothing like the democracy that we have in the U.S. today. Modern American democracy is a representative form of government—we elect men and women to represent us at the local, state, and national levels. In ancient Greece, a democracy meant that citizens assembled and voted directly on issues. Citizenship was limited to free-born men. Women, slaves, and foreigners were not allowed to participate. In ancient Greece, Athens was the first city to put into place a democracy.

Conflicts between Classes

Regardless of the form of government, conflicts arose between the different classes of people in every polis. And even though the Greeks were the first people to establish the idea of "equality before the law," it was not applied equally to all people, especially non-citizens. 📖

▼ Beginning in 487 B.C., Greek citizens could vote for the person they considered the most dangerous to their democracy. The person who "won" this vote was forced to leave the city for 10 years. This process is called ostracism.

DEMOCRACY
in Sparta

Sparta was one of the most powerful cities in ancient Greece. In Sparta, the central idea was to be a strong military state. Sparta might be described as having had democratic rule. However, Sparta had a very different idea of what a democracy meant.

Sparta—A Growing Power in Greece

The people of Sparta had been very successful in fighting wars. As a result, the Spartans controlled a large territory. They also controlled the people in these conquered territories. One reason Sparta fought wars was to gain land for agriculture. After the Spartans had gained new territory, they began to divide this land among some Spartan citizens. They forced the conquered people in these lands to work for them. These workers were called helots. The poet, Tyrtaeus (c. 650 B.C.), described the life of helots: "Like donkeys worn out with huge burdens … they bring to their masters a half of all the fruits of the earth." Not surprisingly, helots hated the Spartans and looked for any opportunity to revolt against them.

▲ Sparta was one of the most powerful of the Greek city-states.

Loyalty to the State

When the Spartans went to war to conquer additional territory and were almost defeated, they made each Spartan take a **pledge** of loyalty to Sparta. In return for their loyalty to the state, poorer citizens gained the right of equality before the law. They also gained a portion of the land.

pledge: a promise

Women, small farmers, most merchants, and helots did not have any political rights and could not be citizens. As a result, only about 10 percent of the people of Sparta were citizens. Spartan citizens were all equal by law, and all were citizen-soldiers. Sparta was ruled by five elected officials called ephors, two kings, a group of about 30 men, and an assembly of all of its citizens.

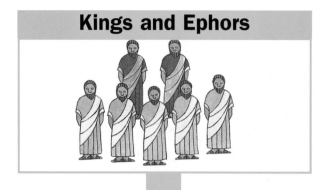

Kings and Ephors

Senate

Assembly

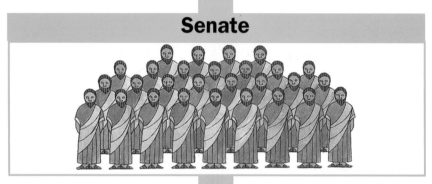

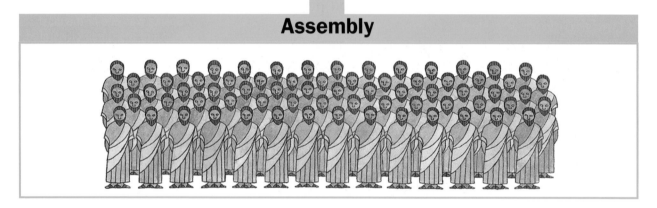

▲ Sparta was ruled by two kings, five officials called ephors, a senate, and an assembly.

Sparta—A Military City-State

In other Greek city-states, a citizen's occupation might be a landowner or artisan. However, this was not the case in Sparta. In Sparta, every male child, starting from the age of seven, was trained to become a soldier. For the next 13 years, every young boy went through strict military training. Spartans did not have any luxuries or enjoy what we would call leisure activities. Discipline and self-denial were the normal, accepted behaviors. Each individual lived and died for the state. This devotion to Sparta by its citizens helped make Sparta a **stable** society.

▲ From age seven, Spartan boys trained to be soldiers.

prestige: respect for a person or people resulting from past achievements and reputation

stable: not likely to fall apart or be thrown off balance

Spartan Women

Sparta's control over its citizens extended to Spartan women. In one way, Sparta granted women more freedom than did other Greek city-states of the time. Spartan women did not go through military training, but they were required to go through intense physical training. Part of the training included teaching women that their lives should be dedicated to the state. Spartan women were allowed much more freedom in the home than other Greek women because Spartan men did not live at home. They lived at a military camp from age seven to 50.

The Most Powerful City-State in Greece

Because of their "Spartan way of life" and their great success in war, other Greek communities admired and feared the Spartans. Sparta used its **prestige** to form alliances with other nearby groups on the Greek mainland. By about 490 B.C., Sparta was the most powerful city-state in Greece. At that time, it was much more powerful than its northern neighbor, Athens. 📖

What Do You Think?

1. How did Sparta gain new territory?

2. What happened to the people in the territories that Sparta conquered?

3. How would you describe democracy in Sparta?

4. How are the lives of ancient Spartan women like women today? How are they different?

DEMOCRACY
in Athens

700 B.C.   500 B.C.

640 – 559 B.C.
Solon

594 B.C.
Solon is elected as
an Athenian judge

At first, a king ruled over Athens. However, the king's power slowly faded and a council of nobles replaced him. Nine members of this council were elected to govern. Over time, Athens developed a form of democracy that had a **profound** effect on the world. Athenian ideas about democracy continue to influence our lives today.

▲ Solon is often considered as one of the seven wisest men in Greek history.

Athens in Crisis

For a period of time, Athens did not experience the same problems as other Greek city-states. The Athenians managed their population growth and enjoyed economic **prosperity**. Athens had much rich farmland and a port that allowed Athenians to trade with other groups around the Aegean Sea. However, as members of Athens' governing council became wealthier, they gained more and more political power. Over time, **middle-class** Athenians became unhappy with the way this system was working. Farmers found themselves in debt to wealthy landowners. In many cases, farmers had to sell their children into slavery to pay the money they owed to the wealthy landowners. As this situation worsened, Athens was on the verge of **revolution**.

The Reforms of Solon

As the situation in Athens reached a critical point, the citizens and the governing council decided to give control of the government to a single individual named Solon. Solon had three goals. First, he wanted to reform the government. Second, he wanted to help farmers get out of debt. And third, he wanted to make sure this situation did not happen again. He said, "I stood there holding my **sturdy** shield over both the parties; I would not let either side win a victory that was wrong."

Solon's Actions

Solon's first acts were to **cancel** all debts and to free as many Athenians as possible from slavery. Solon also divided the Athenians into four classes based on wealth. The two wealthiest groups were allowed to serve on the governing council. The third group made up an elected council of 400. The fourth group was allowed to participate in an assembly that voted on items brought to it by the council of 400.

Solon also believed that the laws should be written down. You can read below what a famous ancient Greek writer, Euripides, wrote about why this was important.

> When the laws are written down, weak and rich men get equal justice; the weaker, when abused, can respond to the prosperous in kind, and the small man with justice on his side defeats the strong.

Analyze the Source!
Read what Euripides said about written laws and tell in your own words what he meant. Do you agree or disagree with this viewpoint? Why?

The citizens of Athens thought of Solon as the great man of their state. They were proud of his reforms.

Pisistratus and Hippias

The government structure Solon put into place did not last very long. When Athens found itself in another crisis, a nobleman named Pisistratus came to power. Although this created a tyranny, he had the support of the people. While he was in power, Pisistratus encouraged annual literature festivals, built public works to beautify the city, and constructed a system to bring fresh water to Athens' marketplace. However, Pisistratus wanted to be a king. He also wanted to pass on his position to his son. When Pisistratus died, his son, Hippias, became ruler of Athens. At first, Hippias had the support of the people and the nobles. However, after his brother was killed, Hippias began to **exile** his **opponents**. Some of the people he exiled asked the Spartans for help in overthrowing Hippias. In 510 B.C., Hippias was overthrown and fled to Persia.

cancel: to erase, do away with, invalidate

exile: to force a person to leave his or her own country

middle-class: not poor, but not rich either

opponent: one who goes against another or others in a battle, contest, controversy, or debate

profound: very great; significant

prosperity: success; wealth

revolution: any complete change of a system of government or other method or condition

sturdy: strong

What Do You Think?

1. What word does the author use to describe the influence that the Athenian government had on the world? What does this word mean?

2. What advantages did Athens have that allowed the city-state to grow rich?

3. Why do you think that after 80 years of living under Solon's constitution, the citizens of Athens did not want to be ruled by a small group of people?

▲ After his brother was killed, Hippias began to force his opponents into exile.

The Beginning of Athenian Democracy

After Hippias was thrown out of power, many of the old Athenian nobles wanted to return to the kind of government they had before—an oligarchy. They wanted a government that kept power in the hands of just a few families. However, after 80 years of living under Solon's constitution, the citizens of Athens did not want to hand over their government to a small group of people. At this point, an Athenian came forward. He offered a series of reforms that became the foundation of democracy in Athens. His reforms gave all free men living in Athens and the surrounding area the right to vote. A council was formed that ran the government. An assembly was given the right to cancel any action taken by the council. Using this system of government, Athens dominated Greece for the next 100 years. ▢

THE PERSIAN EMPIRE

700 B.C.   450 B.C.

630 – 550 B.C.
Zoroaster

550 – 529 B.C.
Cyrus the Great rules
Persia

521 – 486 B.C.
Darius I rules
Persia

490 B.C.
Battle of Marathon

About 3,000 years ago, two groups of people, the Medes and the Persians, migrated to the large area in southwestern Asia that we now know as Iran. At first the Medes were the stronger group. Over time, however, the Persians created the largest and most powerful empire in the region.

Cyrus the Great

Around 550 B.C., a man named Cyrus led the Persians in a **revolt** against the Medes. He then became ruler of the Persian Empire. He became known as Cyrus the Great. He created a vast Persian Empire that stretched from the Mediterranean Sea to modern Afghanistan, south to the Arabian Sea and as far north as the Caspian Sea.

> **revolt:** rebellion; strong protest

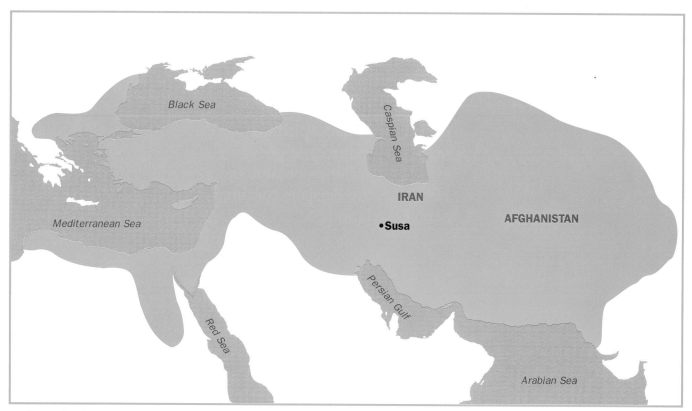

▲ Cyrus the Great created a vast Persian Empire.

inevitable: sure to happen; not able to be prevented

prophet: a person who is believed to speak for a god or who brings a god's message to people

standard: an agreed-upon measure of comparison

Governing the Empire

The Persians were very good at governing the land they conquered. Cyrus allowed his subjects to practice their own religion and to follow their own traditions and customs. Cyrus freed the Jews from their captivity by the Babylonians and allowed them to return to their homeland. His willingness to understand and tolerate the differences in people made him a unique ruler at that time.

The next great Persian king was Darius I. He expanded the Persian Empire even further. He also improved the methods for governing this vast territory. From his capital in Susa, Darius collected tribute from all the areas he controlled. He managed his government through officials called satraps. He gave satraps the authority over different parts of the empire. Darius made other improvements to the Persian Empire as well. He built a large network of roads and created a **standard** currency. These actions encouraged trade throughout the Persian Empire.

The Prophet Zoroaster

An important aspect of the Persian Empire was its religion. The Persians followed the teachings of a **prophet** named Zoroaster. According to Zoroaster, the world was in constant struggle between the forces of good and evil. Zoroaster taught that all good things come from the "Lord Wisdom," Ahura Mazda. The forces of evil were found in the dark spirit of the god, Ahriman. Zoroaster said that the forces of good would overcome the forces of evil. His teachings became the official religion of Persia. However, the Persians continued to be tolerant of other people's religions.

The Battle of Marathon

The Persians wanted to expand their empire. They began to look toward the Greek mainland as a place for expansion. The Greeks wanted their cites to remain free. A conflict between these two groups seemed **inevitable**.

Led by Darius, a Persian army landed at the city of Marathon in 490 B.C. An army of 10,000 Greeks, led by the Athenian general Miltiades, faced a much larger Persian army of 25,000 soldiers. Miltiades sent a man named Phidippides to call for more Greek soldiers.

Running to Sparta

Phidippides ran 240 miles, from Marathon to Sparta, to ask the Spartans to join the Athenians in battle against the Persians. However, the Spartans were celebrating a religious festival and said they would come later. When Phidippides returned with this news, Miltiades knew he could not wait. He came up with a daring plan to defeat the Persians.

The Battle Begins

The battle began and at first it looked like the Persians would win. However, Miltiades's plan worked, and after only a few hours, the battle of Marathon was won. The Greeks had lost less than 200 men. More than 6,000 Persians were dead. The remaining Persians returned to their ships. They intended to sail to Athens and attack the undefended city.

Nike!

According to the traditional story, Miltiades sent Phidippides to Athens to let them know that the Greeks had won the battle of Marathon. Phidippides, although exhausted, is said to have run about 26 miles from Marathon to Athens. When he finally arrived in Athens, Phidippides said only one word: *Nike.* Nike is the name of the Greek goddess of victory. For Athenians, this meant that the Greeks had won the battle of Marathon. Miltiades and his army were not far behind. They marched to Athens in less than eight hours and protected Athens from the Persian fleet. The victory at Marathon gave the Greeks the belief that their foot soldiers, called hoplites, were better fighters than the Persian soldiers.

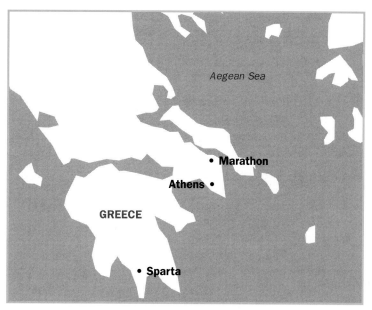

▲ Phidippides ran 240 miles, from Marathon to Sparta, to ask the Spartans for help in the battle against the Persians.

▼ Greek soldiers were called hoplites. Hoplites wore helmets and armor on their legs. Each hoplite overlapped his shield with the shield of the men standing on either side of him. As a result, hoplites went into battle well-protected.

▲ This drawing shows Miltiades leading the Greek army to victory against the Persians.

What Do You Think?

1. How are Zoroaster's ideas about religion similar to other religious ideas you know about? How are they different?

2. Why do you think the Persians' tolerance of other religions helped them govern their empire?

Fighting Continues

In 479 B.C., about 10 years after the battle of Marathon, the Persian army returned to Greece. This time the Persians made it all the way to Athens. The Athenians withdrew from their city to a nearby island. When the Persian fleet sailed into the water between the mainland and the island, the Greeks destroyed almost half of the Persian ships by ramming them with warships that had iron-tipped bows. Fighting between the Persians and Greeks continued for several more years. However, the Persians never again were a major threat to Greece. ▭

THE PERSIAN WARS

| 500 B.C. | | | | 450 B.C. |

499 – 479 B.C.
Persian Wars

490 B.C.
Battle of Marathon

480 B.C.
Battle of Salamis

Over time, Athens developed into a center for trade in the Mediterranean region. Sparta dominated the southern part of Greece and had a strong military. Over time, other cities developed around the coastal areas of the Aegean Sea. The people who lived in these cities shared many of the values of mainland Greeks. Between 550 B.C. and 500 B.C., Athens and Sparta established themselves as the two cities that would control and defend Greece.

The Persian Empire

To the east of Greece was the great empire of Persia. For a long time, the Persians had not been too concerned about the Greeks. After all, to the Persians, a few Greek city-states in **Anatolia** did not pose much of a threat. However, this changed as the Persians began to expand west. Several coastal cities that were once loyal to Athens came under Persian rule. The Athenians sent an armed fleet of ships to help the people rebel against the Persians. The king of Persia, Darius, stopped the revolt. Then he demanded that the Greeks pay **homage** to him. He sent officials to several Greek cities demanding that each city acknowledge his rule. Most Greek cities did as they were asked. The Athenians and Spartans responded by killing Darius's officials.

Anatolia: the area that generally comprises modern-day Turkey; Asia Minor

homage: special honor or respect shown publicly

The Battle of Marathon

At the battle of Marathon in 490 B.C., the Athenian army turned back the Persian army that had about 25,000 fighting men. The Athenian army was fighting to defend its homeland, which gave it an advantage. For the Greeks, the battle of Marathon was a great victory. Greek writers composed poems and plays portraying Greeks as heroes.

corpse: a dead body

glut: to flood or fill beyond capacity

league: individuals or groups working together in a common action

rivalry: a competition

strait: a narrow channel joining two larger bodies of water

The Empire Fights Back

For Persia, the defeat at Marathon was not very significant. However, the Persians never forgot the loss. Ten years later, a new Persian king, Xerxes, returned to Greece with a larger army. He was determined to punish Athens. The Athenians had been preparing for a battle with the Persians. They had been building a navy and boasted a fleet of approximately 200 ships. The Persians entered Greece by crossing a narrow **strait** of water that separates Greece from Asia Minor. The Persian leader, Xerxes, had an army of about 150,000 and almost 600 ships. When the right time came, the Greeks used their own warships, equipped with iron-tipped bows, to ram the Persian fleet. The Greeks destroyed almost half of the Persian navy.

The Battle of Salamis

In the battle of Salamis in 480 B.C., the Spartans and Athenians joined together to defeat the Persians. You can read below how the Greek writer Aeschylus described the battle.

> The Grecian warships, calculating dashed
> Round, and encircled us; ships showed their belly:
> No longer could we see the water, charged
> With ships' wrecks and men's blood.
> **Corpses glutted** beaches and the rocks. ...
> ... never in a single day
> So great a number died.

The Persians lost the battle. The two city-states, Sparta and Athens, had successfully defended Greece. Sparta had more soldiers than Athens. However, as a land-locked city, Sparta could offer no help defending many of the smaller, coastal city-states now seeking protection against the Persians should they return. Athens, with a powerful navy, was in position to help defend these smaller city-states. As a result, the city-states in the south came under the protection of Sparta; the city-states around Athens and those located on islands looked to Athens for leadership.

▲ In the battle of Salamis, the Spartans and Athenians joined together to defeat the Persians.

The Delian League

Leaders from Athens and Sparta met to form an alliance. They agreed to defend one another. This new alliance was called the Delian **League**, after the name of the island, Delos, where the league kept its money. Athens and Sparta had come together to fight their common enemy, the Persians. In the years that followed, however, the cities competed bitterly, and the **rivalry** between them resulted in war. 📖

What Do You Think?

1. Which two city-states were most important to Greece's defense?

2. What eastern empire was of greatest concern to the Greeks?

3. Why do you think the battle of Marathon was so important to the Greeks?

4. What lessons can you draw from the Persian Wars?

HERODOTUS
Father of History

| 500 B.C. | | 400 B.C. |

499 – 479 B.C. **c. 484 – 420 B.C.**
Persian Wars   Herodotus

Herodotus was a Greek storyteller. He was also the world's first historian. We don't know very much about his life. What we do know comes partly from his own writing, but mostly from the writings of others. We know that Herodotus was born about 484 B.C. in Halicarnassus, a Greek city in Asia Minor. At the time, the Persians ruled this part of the world.

▲ Herodotus was exiled from Halicarnassus for plotting against Persian rule.

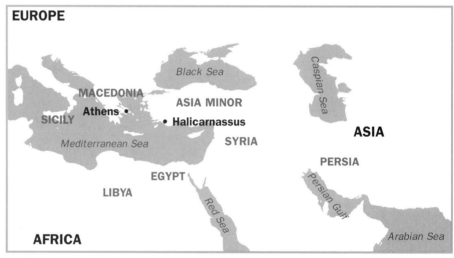

▲ Herodotus was born in Halicarnassus (present-day Bodrum, Turkey) around 484 B.C.

A Traveling Man

Herodotus traveled to many places during his lifetime. Through his travels, he gained valuable, **firsthand** knowledge of almost the entire ancient Middle East. He traveled through most of the Persian Empire, Libya, Syria, and Egypt. When he was in Egypt around 450 B.C., he observed how Egyptians made mummies. He wrote, "As much as the brain as possible is extracted through the nostrils with an iron hook." He went on to describe the entire process in great detail. Modern scientists say that his description was very accurate.

Writing History

Herodotus also traveled to Macedonia and north towards the Danube River. Since there wasn't any modern transportation, his travels would have taken many years. About 447 B.C., Herodotus went to Athens, the center of Greek culture. While he was there, Herodotus won the admiration of many important Athenians, including the great statesmen, Pericles. In 443 B.C., Herodotus went to live on the island known today as Sicily. He devoted the rest of his life to writing his great work, entitled *History*. The word *history* comes from a Greek word meaning, "I have seen."

The Beginning of Modern History

Herodotus's *History* tells about the wars between Persia and Greece (499–479 B.C.). This work is the first known attempt to write history. Many people have praised *History* because it is so easy to read. The writing is very clear, and Herodotus uses short stories to tell about the wars between Persia and Greece. The book is divided into nine parts. The first six parts talk about customs, legends, and traditions in the ancient world. The last three parts describe the actual fighting between Greece and Persia.

In *History*, Herodotus writes about the development of civilization and how the world was moving towards a **clash** between eastern (Persian) and western (Greek) cultures. Throughout his writing, Herodotus shows that he knows a great deal about Greek literature. He also reveals his belief that **fate** and chance rule the world. However, Herodotus says that moral choice is still important because the gods punish people who are very proud. His attempt to create moral lessons from the study of great events forms the basis of Greek and Roman historical traditions. Herodotus is thought of as the founder of these traditions.

The "Father of History"

We are not sure when Herodotus died. We believe his death occurred sometime between 430–420 B.C. Herodotus's work is valuable to us because it provides important details about the time in which he lived and the places he visited. Herodotus wrote the first historical account, which is why we think of him today as the "father of history." 📖

clash: a conflict with another person or group

fate: a supposed force or power that predetermines events

firsthand: obtained directly from the original source

 What Do You Think?

1. When and where do historians think Herodotus was born?

2. What did Herodotus observe when he was in Egypt?

3. Do you think Herodotus should be considered the "father of history"? Why or why not?

4. How does a person's idea about the size of the world influence his or her thinking?

THE PELOPONNESIAN WAR

500 B.C.   400 B.C.

460 – 429 B.C.
Pericles leads
Athens

431 – 404 B.C.
Peloponnesian War

After the end of the Persian Wars, Athens became the most important city in Greece. The wealth and power of Athens increased tremendously for two reasons. First, Athens controlled the trade routes. Second, other city-states who were members of the Delian League paid tribute to Athens. At the time, it seemed as if all the wealth and power in the world was centered in Athens. Over time, however, Athens did not use its power to defend the other cities, but to dominate them. When Athens began to form alliances with some of Sparta's enemies, the Spartans became concerned. The war between Athens and Sparta began in 431 B.C. and was fought off and on for almost 30 years. This war is called the Peloponnesian War.

▲ Pericles was one of the greatest statesmen of ancient Greece.

Pericles—An Athenian Leader

Just before the beginning of the Peloponnesian War, an Athenian named Pericles came to power. Under his leadership, Athens enjoyed a golden age. Historians refer to the "age of Pericles" as a time when most of the great accomplishments in ancient Greek drama, architecture, and philosophy took place. This also was the time when Athens came closest to our modern idea of democracy. Pericles **championed** important democratic government reforms. For centuries, historians have quoted his ideas about citizenship.

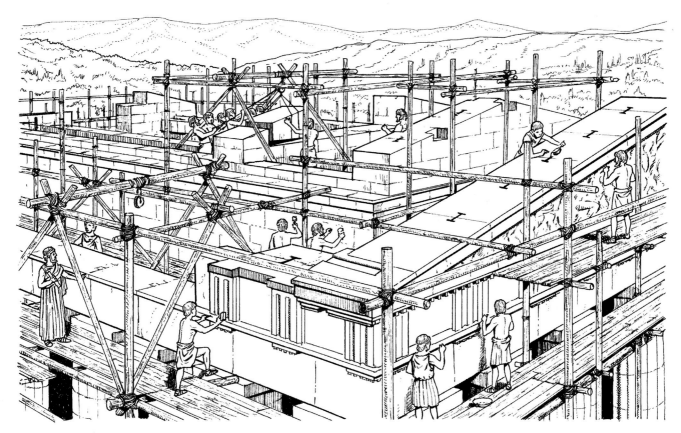

▲ Pericles started great building projects in Greece. The Parthenon was one of the buildings built during this time.

Pericles and the Funeral Oration

We do not have any records of Pericles's own writing. However, we do have a report about one of his most famous speeches—"**Funeral Oration.**" Pericles gave this speech in 431 B.C. In it, he praised the Athenians who had died during the first year of the Peloponnesian War. He honored the dead by celebrating the Athenian values for which they had given their lives. Pericles talked about the democratic system of Athens. He commented on how every citizen is equal before the law and said that Athens stands as an "education to Greece." You can read an excerpt from this speech on the next page.

champion: to defend or support a cause or another person

funeral: ceremonies held in connection with the burial or cremation of a dead person

oration: a formal speech, especially one given on a ceremonial occasion

Analyze the Source!

What does Pericles's speech tell us about this time in Athenian history?

[O]ur system of government does not copy the institutions of our neighbors. ... Our constitution is called a democracy because power is in the hands not of a minority but of the whole people. When it is a question of settling private **disputes**, everyone is equal before the law; when it is a question of putting one person before another in position of public responsibility, what counts is not membership of a particular class, but the actual ability which the man possesses. ...

Our city is open to the world ... This is because we rely, not on secret weapons, but on our own real courage and loyalty. There is a difference, too, in our educational systems. The Spartans, from their earliest boyhood, are submitted to the most laborious training in courage; we pass our lives without all these restrictions, yet are just as ready to face the same dangers as they are. ... Our love of what is beautiful does not lead to extravagance; our love of the things of the mind does not make us soft. ... Taking everything together then, I declare that our city is an education to Greece. ... This, then, is the kind of city for which these men, who could not bear the thought of losing her, nobly fought and died.

It's a FACT

Another name for the Peloponnesian Peninsula is the Peloponnesus. The Peloponnesus is about 8,400 miles in area.

Of course, it is important to remember that the Athenian democracy Pericles was talking about only applied to male Athenian citizens, who were only about half of the population. The other half—women, children, slaves, and foreigners—were not considered citizens. However, understood in its own time, Pericles's Athens was a remarkable and unique place.

A Disaster for Athens

Despite the fine words of Pericles, the Peloponnesian War was a disaster for Athens. At the end of the first phase of the war, neither Athens nor Sparta had the advantage. They signed a peace treaty that was supposed to last for 50 years. However, after only five years, the two city-states began the conflict again. Sparta gained unexpected help due to a plague that swept through Athens and killed as much as one-third of the population, including Pericles.

▲ Athens and Sparta fought against one another in the Peloponnesian War.

Starving Athenians

The new Athenian general, Alcibiades, then led a failed attack on the city of Syracuse, on the island of Sicily. When Alcibiades was ordered to return to Athens, he joined the enemy, Sparta, and tried to help them defeat the Athenians. When the Spartans destroyed the Athenian **fleet** of ships, the grain supply for Athens was cut off. Soon, Athenians were starving and could no longer defend themselves.

Athens Surrenders

In 404 B.C., Athens surrendered. The Spartans destroyed the walls of the city and forbade Athens from ever again having a **naval** fleet. Even worse for the Athenians, the Spartans set up their own government to rule Athens. The age of Pericles and the golden age of Athens had come to an end. 📖

What Do You Think?

1. Who was Pericles?

2. How long did the peace treaty last between Sparta and Athens before fighting began again?

3. What does it mean that neither Sparta nor Athens had the advantage?

THUCYDIDES
Greek Historian

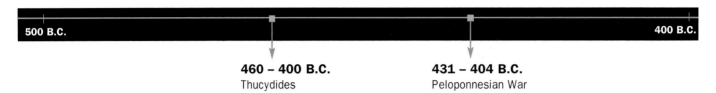

| 500 B.C. | | | 400 B.C. |

460 – 400 B.C.
Thucydides

431 – 404 B.C.
Peloponnesian War

O ne of the most important events in Greek history is the Peloponnesian War. Much of what we know about this war comes from the writings of a Greek historian, Thucydides. Thucydides was born near Athens about 460 B.C. His father was an aristocrat who owned gold mines and other property in Thrace, an area in northeastern Greece.

▶ Thucydides was born near Athens about 460 B.C.

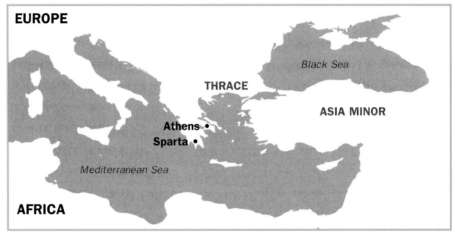

▲ This is a drawing of the Greek historian Thucydides.

Thucydides Goes to War

When the Peloponnesian War began in 431 B.C., Thucydides was in his late twenties. He recognized how important the war was going to be, and he knew he wanted to write about it. However, at about this same time, a plague began to spread throughout Greece. Many Athenians died in this plague. Thucydides became sick from the disease, but he survived.

Writing in Exile

In 424 B.C., Thucydides was given command of a group of Athenian ships. His job was to protect an important city from capture by the Spartans. However, the Spartans were too strong and Thucydides was unable to protect the city. As punishment, he was exiled from Athens. Thucydides went to Thrace and lived there for almost 20 years. It was during this period that he wrote a historical account of the Peloponnesian War.

History of the Peloponnesian War

During the period in which he was exiled from Athens, Thucydides traveled to many Greek **colonies**. As a result, Thucydides was able to gather information about the war from many different viewpoints. At the beginning of his history, he explained why he thought that this war was the most significant one in which the Greeks were ever involved. He also emphasized that he only included two kinds of information. One was information that came from his own firsthand knowledge. The other was information that came from sources he judged very **reliable**.

In his history, Thucydides **rejected** any ideas that some supernatural power was at work in how the events of the war turned out. Thucydides believed that human nature was the basic explanation for historical events. He believed that his *History of the Peloponnesian War* would be helpful to those people who wanted to understand the way things happen. And since he did not believe that human nature changed, he thought similar events would take place in the future.

Pericles and the Funeral Oration

In his account of the war, Thucydides included a famous speech given by Pericles, the general and leader of Athens. This speech, called the "Funeral Oration," honored Athenian citizens who had been killed in the war. Pericles's Funeral Oration includes almost all of the Athenian ideas about democracy and citizenship, and their belief in the greatness of Athens. 📖

---

colony: a territory or settlement controlled by another country

reject: to refuse to accept

reliable: trustworthy

What Do You Think?

1. What war did Thucydides think was the most significant one the Greeks had ever been involved in?

2. How did Thucydides spend his time in exile?

3. Why do you think Thucydides included the speech by Pericles, the Athenian leader, in his history of the Peloponnesian War?

4. What speeches are important in American history? Do they express the ideas that Americans have about important issues? Give examples.

Socrates, Plato, and Aristotle
GREEK PHILOSOPHERS

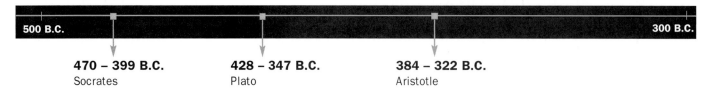

500 B.C.			300 B.C.

470 – 399 B.C.
Socrates

428 – 347 B.C.
Plato

384 – 322 B.C.
Aristotle

Perhaps the three most well-known Greeks in history are Socrates, Plato, and Aristotle. Together, their thinking and writing form much of the foundation of Western philosophy. The word *philosophy* means "love of wisdom" or "love of truth." To find truth or wisdom, each of these men sought the answer to the most basic questions such as: What is the purpose of human existence? What form of government is truly the best? What is the universe made of?

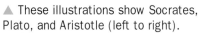 These illustrations show Socrates, Plato, and Aristotle (left to right).

unexamined: not looking at or analyzing; lacking self-reflection

Socrates

When historians write about ancient Greece, they focus mainly on Athens. Greece's greatest writers, sculptors, architects, and philosophers were all Athenians. The citizens of Athens were willing to question traditional values. They wanted to understand the world in which they lived and began to ask searching questions. What is the correct way to behave? How would correct behavior help improve society? One man who had many, many questions, but almost never gave any answers, was Socrates.

Socrates: "Know Thyself"

Socrates believed that people must examine their own lives. His message was, "know thyself." He believed that an **unexamined** life was not worth living. Though Socrates was a teacher, he would never accept any money for teaching. He would say he knew nothing and, therefore, should not accept any payment. Socrates's method of teaching was different than any other person of his time. He would casually approach groups of educated people and ask what seemed to be very simple questions. The questions were meant to make people think about and defend their beliefs. Socrates did not write down any of his ideas. As a result, we have to rely on what his opponents and his students said about him. Socrates spent his life searching for the truth. Ironically, his life ended when he was falsely accused of corrupting the youth of Athens and of believing in false gods. Rather than run away, Socrates drank poison hemlock and died.

▲ Socrates died by drinking poison hemlock. Hemlock is a type of plant.

Plato

Socrates's most famous student was Plato. It is from Plato's writings that we know about Socrates's trial and death. The death of Socrates shocked Plato. Plato had grown up during the Peloponnesian War and developed a distrust of Athenian democracy. He did not think ordinary people had the ability to make the best decisions for society.

Plato wrote many different works, but his most famous is the *Republic*. In this book, he argued that only philosopher-kings could tell the difference between what is real and what is not. At one point, Plato traveled to Sicily to observe different forms of government.

▲ This drawing shows Plato talking about his ideas with other Greeks.

What Do You Think?

1. Who are the three most famous philosophers of ancient Greece?

2. How do we know about Socrates's ideas? What are the sources?

3. Why is it difficult for people to think about and defend their beliefs?

4. Plato did not think ordinary people had the ability to make the best decisions for society. Do you agree or disagree with this idea? Why?

Plato's Academy

When he returned to Athens, he started a school called the Academy. Plato's school is the **forerunner** of the modern university. Its purpose was to teach the young men of Athens what Plato believed was right and good for society. Plato's view was that people could not gain true knowledge if they continued to focus on the ever-changing world of human experience. He believed people can only have true knowledge of those things that are eternal, perfect, and beyond the reach of their **five senses**. Plato said that when we think that we know somebody to be a "truly good person," what we really recognize is the **everlasting** idea of "goodness." And because we all have a memory of "goodness," we recognize it in others when we see it. Plato's ideas are very important in philosophy. However, his greatest student, Aristotle, had different ideas about knowledge and knowing.

Aristotle

Aristotle was born in the northern part of Greece. He was a student at Plato's Academy for about 20 years. However, Aristotle decided that the best approach to knowledge was very different than that of Socrates and Plato. Aristotle believed that knowledge came from observation—people gained knowledge by looking at as many examples as possible of all sorts of things. He collected shells, fish, and other kinds of sea animals. He also collected over 100 versions of the constitutions of Greek cities. After he had collected as many examples of an item as he could find, he would create a system to put them in order.

Aristotle's approach to understanding government was the same approach he used to understand fish or types of flowers. Aristotle did not care as much about the types of government. He was more concerned with whether the government took a balanced approach to its conduct. He believed that moderation in all things, both personal and public, was the key to a stable society. Aristotle said, "Study seems to be the only activity which is loved for its own sake." He believed that "a life guided by intelligence is the best and most pleasant …" By the time of his death, the system of the Greek polis was also dying. 📖

ALEXANDER THE GREAT

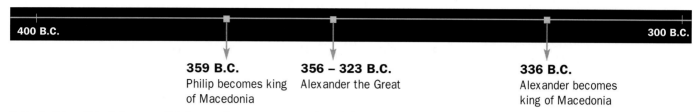

| 400 B.C. | | | 300 B.C. |

359 B.C.
Philip becomes king
of Macedonia

356 – 323 B.C.
Alexander the Great

336 B.C.
Alexander becomes
king of Macedonia

Philip II, king of Macedonia, watched his son Alexander tame a huge, fierce black horse. At that moment, Philip saw greatness in his 10-year-old son and gave him the following advice: "Find yourself a kingdom equal to and worthy of yourself for Macedonia is too little for you."

Philip—King of Macedonia

Philip was a good leader and a great warrior. Within a few years he had united all of Macedonia. Philip became king of Macedonia in 359 B.C. One reason for his success was that he developed a new type of army. The men in Philip's army served on a year-round basis. Before this time, soldiers had gone home after a battle or series of battles. Philip also developed the idea of bringing together in one army both foot soldiers and soldiers on horseback.

Philip's army relied on the Macedonian phalanx, which consisted of 256 men. A phalanx is a special arrangement of soldiers. Usually the phalanx was arranged in the shape of a square. However, a phalanx also could form the shape of a line or a wedge. The phalanx was trained to respond to signal flags or trumpet calls.

Macedonia Conquers Greece

In 338 B.C., less than 100 years after the end of the Peloponnesian War (431–404 B.C.), the Macedonians completed their conquest of Greece. The Greeks had mostly ignored the growing threat of Macedonia to their north. Philip took advantage of their disregard. Even the united Greek cities of Athens, Sparta, and Thebes could not hold off Philip's army. The Macedonian victory at the battle of Chaeronea in 338 B.C. meant the end of the influence of the Greek city-states. Greece remained a power for some time, however, its power came from its king—Alexander.

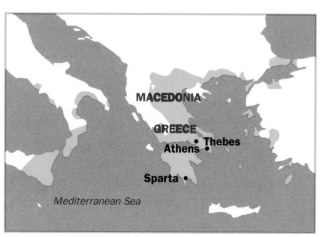

▲ This map shows the extent of the Macedonian kingdom in 338 B.C. under Philip's leadership.

▲ Alexander was just 20 years old when his father was killed.

Alexander Becomes King

Alexander was just 20 years old when his father was murdered in 336 B.C. Among other things, he inherited a powerful army. Alexander's first task was to restore order to Greece and Macedonia. People in both areas had begun to rebel against Macedonian rule. They knew a young boy was now king, and they thought he would be inexperienced.

Alexander marched to Thebes and demanded that the leaders of the rebellion be turned over to him. When the Thebans refused, he destroyed their city. Soon after, the citizens of Athens and Corinth named Alexander the person to lead them into battle against the Persians.

▶ Alexander was always in the front lines of battle, leading his army bravely.

Battling the Persians

In 334 B.C., Alexander's army crossed the **Hellespont**. The war against the Persians had begun. Over the next three years, Alexander's army fought a series of battles against the Persian army. In each battle his army faced a much larger Persian force. In each battle Alexander was victorious. Alexander's soldiers greatly admired him because of his personal courage.

At different times, the Persian king Darius had tried to **negotiate** a peace settlement. Each time, Alexander rejected his offer. After defeating a large part of the Persian army at the battle of Issus, Alexander moved his army along the coast of the Mediterranean toward Egypt. The Egyptians were not happy being ruled by the Persians. As a result, they welcomed Alexander's arrival. In Egypt, Alexander founded a city he called Alexandria. This city became one of the greatest cities of the ancient world.

Hellespont: the ancient name for the Dardanelles, a strait that is 37 miles long and four miles wide and that links the Sea of Marmara and the Aegean Sea

negotiate: to trade one thing for another

Conquering the Persians

When he left Egypt, Alexander marched his army toward a broad flat area of Mesopotamia. This is where Darius's army was camped. Darius believed that the Persian army had a much better chance of victory on this type of terrain. Again, Darius was wrong. Alexander won the battle. Darius fled east leaving everything behind.

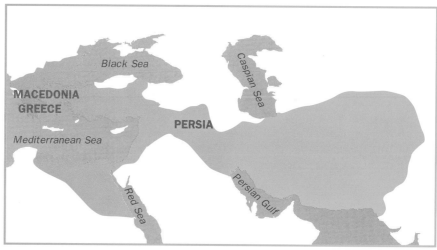

▲ This map shows the extent of the Macedonian kingdom under Alexander's leadership.

Within just three years, Alexander had conquered the entire Persian Empire. He had taken control of everything Darius had valued, including his land, his family, and his treasury. Shortly after Alexander took control of Persia, Darius was found murdered by his own men.

imitate: to copy; to try to be similar to

Alexander Marches East

By all accounts, Alexander was a great battlefield general. Over the next six years, Alexander and his army marched across present-day Iran, over the Khyber Pass, and as far east as the Indus Valley in India. He and his army had traveled more than 22,000 miles. They fought many battles along the way, never losing one fight.

On his return march from the east in 323 B.C., Alexander became ill and died in Babylon. He was only 32 years old. He had made no plans for anyone to take over his empire when he died. Instead, he believed that all that he had conquered should go to the strongest man. History books refer to him as Alexander the Great—the man who conquered Greece, the Persian Empire, and Egypt.

The Spread of Greek Culture

The Hellenistic period in Greek history begins in 336 B.C., the first year of Alexander's rule. The word *Hellenistic* comes from the Greek word *Hellas*, which means "Greece." Why does an entire period of Greek history begin with Alexander's reign? Why is Alexander considered important in the spread of Greek culture? Alexander developed a love for Greek culture from a very early age. The Greek philosopher Aristotle was young Alexander's personal teacher. Aristotle taught Alexander about Greek literature, philosophy, and science. As Alexander grew up, he learned about and came to appreciate Greek culture.

By the time he was in his early twenties, Alexander already was on his way toward building an empire. He brought his appreciation for Greek culture to the lands he conquered. Alexander built cities in the conquered areas that **imitated** Greek cities. For example, Alexander built the city of Alexandria in Egypt. During ancient times, Alexandria was the center of Greek culture. It was home to the greatest museum and library of the ancient world. Many of the great scientists, mathematicians, and philosophers of the time met in the Greek-influenced city of Alexandria.

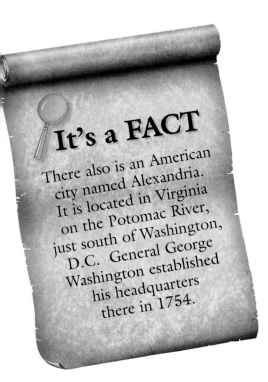

It's a FACT

There also is an American city named Alexandria. It is located in Virginia on the Potomac River, just south of Washington, D.C. General George Washington established his headquarters there in 1754.

▲ This drawing shows the waterfront city of ancient Alexandria, the center of Greek culture. The spread of Greek culture occurred mostly in the cities. In the rural areas, people continued as they always had.

Spreading Greek Influence

Alexander also appointed Greek officials to rule some of these conquered lands. As a result, people in these areas learned to speak Greek and appreciate Greek literature. Some even began to worship Greek gods. Alexander spread Greek culture throughout the Persian Empire and to places as far away as India and Ethiopia. Today, you can see the influence of Greece in buildings and statues in these places and throughout the world. 📖

What Do You Think?

1. What was one important reason for Philip's military success?

2. What is a phalanx?

3. Why do you think Alexander did not want to negotiate a peace settlement with Darius? If you had been Alexander, what would you have done?

4. The author says that Alexander's men admired him because of his personal courage and because he led them into battle. What qualities do you admire in leaders today?

What We Have Learned
FROM THE GREEKS

Why are the ancient Greeks important? Why should people today learn about the lives and ideas of the ancient Greeks? One reason is that reading about the ancient Greeks is a way to understand how people of an earlier time lived and what they thought was important. Another reason is that the ancient Greeks have greatly influenced Western civilization. As we learn about the Greeks, it is possible to see many traces of this ancient civilization in our lives today.

▲ This is how one artist portrayed Zeus.

The Influence of Greek Myths

A **myth** is a traditional story, retold over and over. Myths often are about gods and heroes who have supernatural powers. Throughout the world, people have used myths to explain and make sense of their ideas and beliefs about the world. In Greek myths, gods were immortal, which means they lived forever. Greek gods were not bound by the same physical limits as ordinary people. For example, Greek gods could travel great distances instantly. They also could disguise themselves in different shapes or forms. In Greek **mythology**, gods interacted with human beings. Often, Greek gods either punished or rewarded the people with whom they came into contact.

The influence of ancient Greek myths is all around us. For example, think about the names of **constellations** in our sky. Andromeda is a constellation in the Northern Hemisphere. This constellation is named after Andromeda, the daughter of a Greek king. Andromeda married Perseus, the son of Zeus. One of the most famous stories about Perseus tells how he saved the beautiful Andromeda from death. You can read a version of this story on the next page.

Perseus and Andromeda

Cassiopeia, Andromeda's mother, was very beautiful and she was not shy about letting people know what she thought of herself. She said she was more beautiful than the daughters of one of the sea gods. This angered Poseidon, the most powerful sea god. He flooded the land where she lived and sent a sea monster to terrorize the people living there.

Cepheus, Andromeda's father, was king of this land. He decided to ask for advice from an oracle, someone who could tell the future. What should he do? The oracle told him to chain his daughter to a rock and let the sea monster kill her. That would satisfy Poseidon.

According to the myth, Perseus saw Andromeda chained to the rock. It was love at first sight. He told Cepheus that he would kill the monster. But Perseus had one condition. If he killed the monster, he wanted to marry Andromeda. Cepheus agreed. Perseus put on a cap that allowed him to be invisible and sandals that allowed him to fly. He picked up his sword and killed the monster. Then he married Andromeda.

constellation: a group of stars

cower: to shrink away or hide because of fear

myth: a traditional, ancient story that deals with supernatural beings, ancestors, or heroes that serves as a way for people to explain the world

mythology: a collection of myths

Greek Influences on America

Ancient Greece has greatly influenced our democratic form of government, as well as the architecture of many of our public buildings. And, in modern times, every four years, athletes from around the world compete in the Olympic Games. These games began in ancient Greece about 776 B.C. and were first held in Zeus's sacred city of Olympia. The winners of the games were so important that poets wrote poems about their accomplishments. Winners were treated as honored guests wherever they went. Statues of them were created because they were heroic figures. On the other hand, losers faced disgrace. Here is what the poet Pindar (c. 522–440 B.C.) said about the young men who did not win.

> They, when they meet their mothers,
> Have no sweet laughter around them, moving delight.
> In back streets, out of their enemies' way,
> They **cower**; for disaster has bitten them.

▼ The Parthenon, a famous Greek temple, inspired the architecture of many modern buildings.

contemporary: current or modern

overstatement: an exaggeration

Greek Influences on Language

Americans use many words that originally referred to something in Greek life. For example, *Nike* is the name of the Greek goddess of victory. It is also the first word that was spoken by Phidippides, the Athenian soldier who ran from Marathon to Athens to let the Athenians know that their army had defeated the Persians. Phidippides's famous run inspired the name of the modern 26-mile race—the marathon.

Another example is the word *titan*. In Greek mythology, the titans were the first 12 gods—the children of Uranos and Gaia. Something of great size is said to be "titanic." The modern world has given this name to an ocean liner, as well as professional and amateur sports teams. The Greeks believed that the titans populated the world with lesser gods, one of whom was named Atlas. According to a Greek myth, Atlas and his brother went to war against Zeus and lost. As his punishment, Atlas was sent to forever hold up the western end of the sky—to keep heaven and earth separate. *Atlas* is also the word we use to refer to a group of maps.

Greek Influences on Literature and Popular Culture

The Greeks had an important influence on many **contemporary** works of literature and film. Traditionally, the Greek author, Homer, is credited with writing the two most important accounts of the ancient world, the *Iliad* and the *Odyssey*. These works of literature gave later authors the storylines and many of the characters for their modern works. For example, the 20th-century Irish novelist, James Joyce, wrote *Ulysses*, a book that has many similarities to the journey home faced by Odysseus in Homer's *Odyssey*. In addition, Homer's account of the Trojan War in the *Iliad* has been made into several plays and films.

It's a FACT

Ancient Greeks used the word *agonia* to describe playing sports. From this Greek word, we get the modern word *agony*, which means "to suffer greatly."

The Greeks Were First

It is not an **overstatement** to say that the ancient Greeks had a tremendous influence on the modern world. Government, literature, astronomy, and competitive sports have all developed in part from how the Greeks first thought about and did these things. They have taught us a great deal and shaped the way we think.

▲ Storytellers throughout the ages have wanted to tell the story of the war between Greece and Troy, and audiences throughout the ages have wanted to hear it.

What Do You Think?

1. What is a myth?

2. Why do people create myths?

3. What evidence does the author use to support the argument that the Greeks had an important influence on modern life? Which piece of evidence do you think is the strongest or most persuasive?

4. Of all the Greek influences on modern life today, which do you think is the most significant? Why?

SCIENTIFIC ADVANCES
in Hellenistic Greece

400 B.C.			0

336 – c. 27 B.C.
Hellenistic period

325 – 250 B.C.
Euclid

Greece enjoyed a golden age during which Greek thinkers made many scientific advances. Euclid was one of the most famous men of this age. He continues to be remembered for his work in astronomy and mathematics.

▲ This drawing shows Euclid, one of the most famous mathematicians of ancient Greece.

Alexandria during the Hellenistic Period

Alexandria, Egypt was an important Greek city-state during a part of Greek history known as the Hellenistic period. Traditionally, historians use the date of 336 B.C. as the beginning of the Hellenistic period. This was the year when Alexander the Great came to power. The Hellenistic period continued for about 300 years.

Alexander himself established the city of Alexandria. The city was once the world's largest **commercial** center. During the Hellenistic period, great advances were made in many areas of science such as astronomy and mathematics. For example, during this time it was discovered that the planets moved in regular patterns and that the earth **rotated** on its own **axis**.

▶ Alexandria was the largest commercial center of this period.

Euclid of Alexandria

In the field of mathematics, Euclid of Alexandria is credited with several important achievements. Most likely, Euclid received his education in Athens from Plato's Academy. Later he became a teacher in Alexandria at a school known as the Museum.

While in Alexandria, Euclid wrote his most important book, *The Elements*. In this 13-volume work, Euclid wrote down much of the mathematical knowledge known at this time. *The Elements* was the standard textbook for many centuries. Euclid's student, Apollonius, is also known as one of the great thinkers in the area of **geometry**. 📖

▲ Archimedes of Syracuse (287–211 B.C.) invented calculus and calculated the value of *pi*.

What Do You Think?

1. What period of time are historians referring to when they talk about the Hellenistic period?

2. Euclid wrote about a book that contained all the mathematical knowledge known at that time. Why do you think he did that? Why do people record knowledge in books?

3. What is the purpose of textbooks? Discuss the benefits and possible drawbacks.

HYPATIA

A.D. 300 — A.D. 500

c. A.D. 370 – 415
Hypatia

Alexandria was one of the most important intellectual and commercial centers of the Mediterranean world during ancient times. Alexandria was known for its great museum and library. It was also known as the home to many highly respected teachers. One of these teachers was a woman named Hypatia.

▲ Hypatia taught mathematics and astronomy in ancient Alexandria.

It's a FACT

Hypatia's father, Theon, was one of the most educated men in all of Alexandria. Theon believed that Hypatia should develop a strong and healthy body.

The Daughter of an Educated Man

Hypatia was the daughter of a well-known philosopher and mathematician. She received training in philosophy and **rhetoric**, as well as in science. Over time, she became recognized for her work in mathematics and astronomy. Many people came to Alexandria to learn from her.

A Non-Christian Philosopher in a Christian City

At the time Hypatia lived in Alexandria, Christianity was becoming increasingly popular in the Mediterranean world. In many cites, including Alexandria, philosophers were expected to have a public role in advising the city leaders as to the correct actions to take. In the Christian city of Alexandria, Hypatia was the most consulted and admired non-Christian philosopher.

A Crisis in the City

In A.D. 415, riots broke out in Alexandria when the Christian Archbishop Cyril tried to force the city's large Jewish population to leave Alexandria. A man named Orestes opposed the religious leader's actions. Orestes was the **civil** authority in the city. He also was a well-known supporter of Hypatia. When Orestes said the violence against the Jews should stop, Cyril's supporters tried, unsuccessfully, to kill Orestes.

Religious Intolerance

Shortly after this incident, it is believed that some of Cyril's supporters spread a rumor that Hypatia had used "**mystical**" powers to influence Orestes. They claimed she was responsible for keeping Cyril and Orestes from working out their disagreement.

Christians were the majority of the population in Alexandria. Sometimes they used violence as a way to solve problems. During the spring of A.D. 415, a Christian mob attacked and killed Hypatia for the role they believed she had played in the incident between Cyril and Orestes. Later scientists such as René Descartes and Isaac Newton used some of Hypatia's ideas as the basis of their own work. 📖

civil: having to do with the general public, not the military forces or an organized religion

mystical: having spiritual meaning or symbolism

rhetoric: the ability to speak and/or write well in order to persuade others

◀ Issac Newton used some of Hypatia's ideas in his own scientific work.

What Do You Think?

1. What was the city of Alexandria known for?

2. What religion was becoming popular in the Mediterranean world during Hypatia's lifetime?

3. Why do you think city leaders during this period looked to philosophers for help in understanding the correct actions to take?

4. Who do city leaders look to today for help in understanding the correct actions to take?

COMING TO AMERICA

The Beginnings of the Maya Civilization

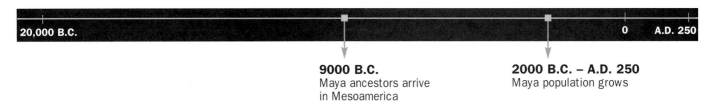

20,000 B.C. | 0 | A.D. 250

9000 B.C.
Maya ancestors arrive
in Mesoamerica

2000 B.C. – A.D. 250
Maya population grows

Not that long ago, a young boy was on a picnic outside **Guatemala City**. While exploring the area, he found a small black stone. It looked like something a hunter would put on the tip of a spear. Later, an archaeologist looked at the stone and knew it was made of obsidian. By studying the way the stone was chipped, the archaeologist concluded it had been made almost 9,000 years ago. This chipped stone is one of the earliest artifacts ever found in the area where the Maya civilization developed. How did it get there?

▲ Hunters tied chipped stones to the tips of spears.

Coming to the Americas

The earliest people in the Americas probably came from Asia across a land bridge. You can't see the land bridge today because it is under water. During the last Ice Age, however, a lot of sea water froze into ice. As the water level in oceans dropped, a land bridge between Asia and North America was exposed. Some experts think people may have started to walk across this land bridge 20,000 or even 40,000 years ago. We know for sure that people were crossing this bridge at 13,000 B.C. When the climate warmed up, the ice melted. By around 8000 to 6000 B.C., the land bridge was covered by water. People could no longer come to the Americas by this route. Experts do not agree about the exact dates when human beings began coming across the Bering land bridge. New information may change our understanding of this issue.

◀ Today, the land bridge is covered by water. The narrow waterway covering this land bridge is called the Bering Strait.

The Early People of Mesoamerica

Some of the people who crossed the land bridge moved eastward across North America. Others, including the ancestors of the Maya, went south. The Maya's ancestors arrived in **Mesoamerica** around 9000 B.C. These early people of Mesoamerica were hunters and gatherers. They lived in small family groups. They moved from place to place searching for food. The ancestors of the Maya shared many cultural traditions with other people in Mesoamerica. They had similar religious beliefs, building styles, and farming methods. They also ate similar foods. Some of these people—especially the Olmecs, one of the first American civilizations—had a strong influence on Mesoamerican culture.

Mesoamerica (shaded area) refers to both a geographical and cultural area. The area where the Maya civilization developed is part of Mesoamerica.

Growing Maize

Around 2600 B.C., **Mayan**-speaking people settled in the area that now covers Belize, Guatemala, and parts of El Salvador, Honduras, and Mexico. Like other groups in Mesoamerica, the Maya were mostly hunters and gatherers until around 2500 B.C. Then their way of life began to change. They still hunted and gathered food. Increasingly, however, they depended on farming. They grew **maize**, beans, **squash**, and **chile peppers**. Like other Mesoamerican farmers, they used a farming method called "slash and burn agriculture." They chose an area of land in the rain forest, cut down the trees and plants, and burned the cut trees and plants until there were only ashes. The ashes made the soil richer. By 2000 B.C., maize was the most important food in Mesoamerica.

chile pepper: the fruit of a plant used to flavor food

Guatemala City: the capital of Guatemala, a Central American country

maize: corn

Mayan: the language spoken by the Maya

Mesoamerica: the geographical area from present-day central Mexico to northern Costa Rica

squash: a fleshy vegetable with a hard skin

The Beginnings of the Maya Civilization

As the Maya focused more on agriculture, their food supply increased and became more dependable. They could stay in one place and build more permanent homes. From about 2000 B.C. to A.D. 250, the Maya population grew. Small villages developed. During this time period, most Maya men were farmers. Most Maya women looked after the children, prepared the family's food, and made clothes for the family.

Some Maya men and women also began to do more specialized work. Some people worked as artists, weavers, carvers, laborers, and basket and pottery-makers. Others became merchants and traders. Some Maya men were scribes, architects, and religious leaders. A few became political leaders. The Maya needed leaders to organize workers. Large groups of workers were needed to clear the land for planting, bring water to the fields, and build large buildings. □

What Do You Think?

1. Maya men and women did many different kinds of work in their society. Who do you think had the most important job? Why?

2. Why do you think experts believe the earliest people in the Americas came from Asia across a land bridge? What kind of information might help us understand some of the issues surrounding the Bering land bridge?

3. Why was it important to the Maya to have a dependable supply of food that could be stored? Is this important today? Why?

IN THE ZONE
The Geography of Maya Country

Maya country—the area where the Maya lived—covered three different **geographical zones**. Some Maya lived on the flat land along the Pacific coast in the south. This area is called the "Pacific coastal plain and **piedmont**." The Maya also lived in the highlands area above the Pacific coastal plain and piedmont. The highlands are **parallel** to the Pacific coastal plain. Other Maya lived in a third geographical zone—the lowlands. The lowlands stretch from the border of the highlands across the Yucatan Peninsula.

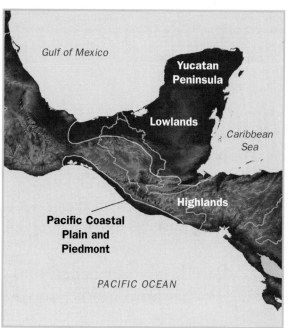

▲ This map shows the three major geographical zones in which the Maya lived. The Maya traded with one another for the different resources available.

Influencing Maya Way of Life

The different environments in these geographical zones influenced the Maya's way of life. Along the Pacific coast, the Maya enjoyed a rich source of food from the sea, including fish, shellfish, sea turtles, and sea birds. In the highlands, the Maya could get obsidian to make into cutting tools. They also had good rocks they could make into special stones used to grind maize. The lowlands were covered with rain forests. These rain forests were filled with plants used for food, flavorings, and medicine. These three geographical zones contained many different plants and animals. 📖

geographical zone: an area distinct from others because of its physical features, climate, vegetation, and animal life

parallel: located side by side; areas that do not cross

piedmont: the area at the bottom of a mountain or highlands

What Do You Think?

1. How does the environment in which you live affect your way of life?

2. If you were Maya, in what geographical zone would you want to live? Why?

DEEP IN THE FOREST

The Maya Kingdom of Palenque

A.D. 200   **A.D. 2000**

A.D. 250 – 900
Maya kingdoms
flourish

A.D. 1700 – 1800
Explorers discover
Palenque ruins

By 250 A.D., small Maya villages had developed into 50 or more large, independent kingdoms. Each independent Maya kingdom was ruled by an *ahau* (AH-haw) or "god-king." The kingdoms were never united under one ruler, but they were all part of the Maya civilization. The Maya shared a common language and culture. Their economy was based on agriculture. Maize was the most important crop. The Maya traded and fought with one another. They shared religious beliefs and followed the same calendar. Marriages were made between important people in different kingdoms.

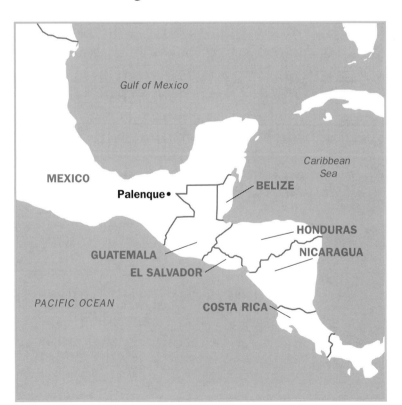

▶ Palenque is located in present-day Mexico.

The Kingdom of Palenque

Palenque (puh-LENG-kay) was one of these independent kingdoms. It was not the largest Maya kingdom, but it may have been the most beautiful. Palenque is located deep in the rain forests of the lowlands in Mexico. Palenque flourished along with other Maya kingdoms until A.D. 799. At that time, it was **abandoned** and slowly buried by jungle growth. Then, in the 1700s and 1800s, explorers accidentally rediscovered Palenque's magnificent buildings. These explorers were sure they had found the lost city of a highly advanced civilization.

▲ The ancient Maya were great architects and builders. They built stone structures like the one above throughout Mesoamerica—with no iron tools! This photograph shows a palace. Some experts believe the tower was used to observe the movement of the stars and planets.

A Political and Religious Center

Maya cities were important political and religious centers. Archaeologists believe the cities had control over people living in nearby villages. Most Maya cities were about 18-30 miles apart. The cities did not have streets, but various parts of the city were connected by **causeways**. Some of the bigger cities might have had populations of 50,000 or more. A smaller city such as Palenque probably had only 10,000 to 20,000 people.

A Spanish church leader wrote in the 1500s, "The Maya lived together in towns in a very civilized fashion … in the middle of the town were their temples with beautiful **plazas**, and all around the temples stood the houses of the lords and priests, and then the most important people." This may have been how ancient Maya cities were arranged. Most people lived outside the city. They only came to the city to visit the markets or for religious ceremonies. ▯

---

abandon: to leave

causeway: a raised path, usually over water or marshy land

plaza: a public square or open area

What Do You Think?

1. Why do you think explorers in the 1700s and 1800s thought Palenque was the lost city of a highly advanced civilization?

2. Imagine that you are a common person living in the kingdom of Palenque. What would it have been like to go into the city? Describe what you might see and how you might feel.

LADY KANAL-IKAL

First Woman to Rule Palenque

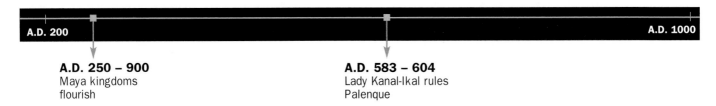

A.D. 200		A.D. 1000

A.D. 250 – 900
Maya kingdoms
flourish

A.D. 583 – 604
Lady Kanal-Ikal rules
Palenque

At first, ahaus were probably the best and strongest warriors in the group. Over time, rulers came from royal families. All of the Maya royal families believed they were close to the gods. They surrounded themselves with symbols of power.

▲ Lady Kanal-Ikal ruled the kingdom of Palenque from A.D. 583 to 604. Palenque was located in the far northwest region of Maya country. The shaded area shows where the Maya civilization developed.

An Exception to the Rule

The Maya believed in hereditary succession. This meant that when a Maya king died, his son was the next in line to become king. This method of succession is called *patrilineal* because the succession went through male family members. But what happened if the king did not have a son or brother or other male relative? That was the problem facing Lady Kanal-Ikal's father. He had a daughter, but no sons. His brother did not have any sons either. So, they made an **exception** and Lady Kanal-Ikal became the ruler of Palenque on December 23, 583.

Elite Woman—An Important Role

Elite women, like Lady Kanal-Ikal, played an important role in Maya society. Through marriages with other elite families, they helped create important political connections between families and kingdoms. They raised their children to assume adult roles in society. Elite women also were important figures in Maya rituals and ceremonies. They made offerings to their gods during religious rituals. They also organized and participated in public ceremonies such as when a husband took an important public role. But, elite women usually did not become rulers.

A Remarkable Maya Ruler

Very little is known about Lady Kanal-Ikal. We know that she became the first woman to rule Palenque. She lived in a palace in the heart of the city of Palenque. Like other elite women, she wore beautifully decorated clothes and sandals. We know she married a man who was not a member of the royal family, and she had at least one son. We also know that Lady Kanal-Ikal ruled for 20 years, until her death in A.D. 604. Lady Kanal-Ikal's son became king, which started another line of male descendants.

Most archaeologists and historians agree that Lady Kanal-Ikal must have been a **remarkable** and **charismatic** woman to come to the throne in Palenque. She is only one of two women we know for certain ruled in Palenque. But why is there so little known about her? Perhaps much of her history is still waiting to be uncovered in some part of Palenque that remains undiscovered. Perhaps we will find more inscriptions that tell about her life and her rule of Palenque. Until then, her past remains a mystery. 📖

charismatic: having the ability to get many people to follow

elite: member of the social group considered the best or most skilled

exception: a case that does not follow the general rule

remarkable: worthy of notice; amazing

What Do You Think?

1. Do you think being the first woman to rule Palenque was easy? What challenges do you think Lady Kanal-Ikal had to overcome?

2. Why do you think historians believe Lady Kanal-Ikal must have been a remarkable and charismatic person? Is their conclusion a fact, an opinion, or a reasoned judgment?

3. How are your ideas about beauty similar or different from the Maya?

▲ Lady Kanal-Ikal's great grandson had pictures of her carved on his tomb. Lady Kanal-Ikal reflects the Maya's idea of beauty.

MAYA SOCIAL CLASSES

Who's Who in Maya Country?

Everyone in Maya society had a particular status based on his or her social class. All the information we have suggests there were two major classes in Maya society. A few people were members of the elite class, but most people were commoners. Slaves were at the bottom of Maya society.

▲ Most Maya were commoners. They worked as artisans, weavers, carvers, pottery-makers, and farmers.

How Did Social Classes Form?

Historians think that in their early history some Maya became known for their skills as leaders or warriors. Over time, this distinction became hereditary. These elites married other elites. The elites also tried to gain more wealth to make them different from other people in the rest of society. "Being different" from other members of society was important. Their power and wealth increasingly set them apart from other people in Maya society—the commoners. Commoners were the artisans, weavers, carvers, pottery-makers, and farmers.

Slaves were another group of people in Maya society. Slaves were at the bottom of Maya society. People could be born slaves. They could become slaves as a punishment for stealing. Captured prisoners of war also could become slaves. Important prisoners of war and child slaves often were used as human sacrifices in Maya religious ceremonies. But, it also was possible for slaves to buy their freedom.

How Could You Tell Classes Apart?

Historians believe the nuclear family—a mother, father, and their children—was the basic social unit of Maya society. Most men had only one wife. However, elite men sometimes had several wives. Elite families had more and better food and resources than commoners. You could tell elites from commoners by their clothes as well as the location and size of their homes.

Where Did People Live?

During the height of the Maya civilization, Maya cities were important political and religious centers that had control over the people living in surrounding villages. From written accounts in the 1500s, we know that elites lived in the middle of the cities where there were beautiful temples and plazas. The most important elites lived in houses with roofs made of palm leaves or other plant material.

▲ Maya elite lived in the middle of cities such as Palenque, shown here. Commoners came into the city only on religious occasions.

Clothes Make a Man

All Maya men wore similar kinds of clothes. Elite men had clothing made from better material, and the cloth was more highly decorated. Maya men wore a piece of cotton cloth that wrapped around the waist and passed between the legs. This kind of clothing is called a loincloth. An elite Maya man's loincloth might have been decorated with beautiful embroidery and even feathers. Sometimes Maya men also wore a square piece of cotton cloth on their shoulders. This garment is called a *pati*. A commoner's pati would not be very fancy. Men also wore sandals. During ceremonies, they wore elaborate headdresses. 📖

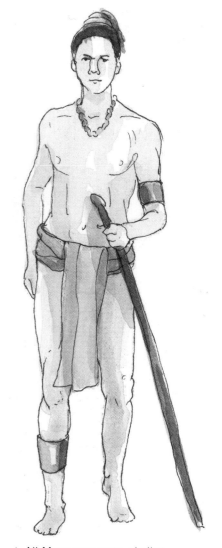

▲ All Maya men wore similar kinds of clothes.

LETTERS AND NUMBERS

The Maya Calendar and Writing System

| 0 | | | A.D. 1000 |

A.D. 199
Earliest example of
Maya writing

A.D. 250 – 900
Maya kingdoms
flourish

Not only did the ancient Maya have the most advanced writing system in the Americas, they developed a number system and studied astronomy to create calendars and track dates.

▲ Experts believe Maya scribes probably wrote thousands of books like the one pictured above. Only four Maya codices have survived. Some were destroyed by the weather. Others were destroyed by Spaniards who wanted the Maya to give up their culture and religious beliefs. Maya codices include brightly colored symbols or "glyphs." The plural of *codex* is *codices.*

An Advanced Writing System

The earliest example of Maya writing is on a stone monument archaeologists have dated to A.D. 199. Only Maya scribes knew how to read and write. They carved inscriptions on stone monuments. They also used brushes or feather pens dipped in black or red paint and wrote on long strips of paper. This paper was made from tree bark. They folded the paper into books. This kind of book is called a codex. Some codices were covered with **jaguar** skin. Maya scribes probably wrote thousands of books about Maya history, science, trade, religious beliefs, and family histories. However, only four Maya codices have survived. The other books were destroyed on purpose or by the weather.

Deciphering Maya Writing

For a long time, scholars were not sure what the Maya's writing meant. Over the past 30 years, however, almost all the Maya's writings have been **deciphered**. Scholars can now read and understand the four surviving Maya books. They also can read the inscriptions on Maya buildings and monuments. These inscriptions list the names of kings, the dates when people became ahaus, and when ahaus died. The inscriptions also tell about great battles, the marriages of important people, and stories about rulers and their families.

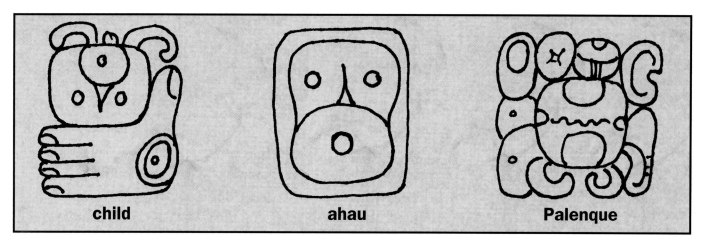

| child | ahau | Palenque |

Numbers, Dates, and Stars

The Maya number system is based on the number "20." This is different from our number system, which is based on the number "10." Numbers were important for Maya traders and merchants. However, they were most important to Maya priests. The priests kept track of the days. They wanted to learn which days were lucky or unlucky. They had different calendars to help them. They used a 260-day calendar to plan daily life. The priests studied this calendar and gave advice about how to influence the gods.

Another Maya calendar was 365-days long. This is the amount of time it takes for the earth to circle the sun. The Maya's skill in astronomy helped them accurately **calculate** this calendar. This Maya calendar had 18 months with 20 days each. The five "leftover" days at the end of the year were considered unlucky.

calculate: to figure out something, often by using numbers and mathematics

decipher: to interpret or make sense of something

jaguar: a large wild cat with black-spotted, golden fur

Maya Symbol	Arabic Numeral
⬭	0
•	1
—	5
• —	6
•••• — — —	19

▲ In the Maya number system, a flattened circle means "zero," a dot means "one," and a bar means "five." The chart above also shows how they made larger numbers.

fixed: staying in one place; not moving

The Long Count Date

The Maya developed another important way of using numbers to keep track of dates. They used a **fixed** point in the past to date events. Their system is called the "Long Count." The fixed point the Maya chose to begin the Long Count was their idea of the beginning of creation. According to their beliefs, the world was created about 5,000 years ago. Scholars have matched the Long Count dates to the system of dates we use today. This is how we know the date when Lady Kanal-Ikal became ahau of Palenque.

What Do You Think?

1. Why do you think people would want to destroy books on purpose?

2. What are the advantages of having a fixed point in the past to date events?

▲ Experts have matched the Maya Long Count dates to the calendar we use today. That is how we know that Lady Kanal-Ikal became ahau of Palenque on December 23, 583.

SPIRITS IN THE TREES

Maya Religious Beliefs

| 0 | | A.D. 1000 |

A.D. 250 – 900
Maya kingdoms
flourish

c. A.D. 642
Temple of the Sun in
Palenque is built

The Maya's writings tell about their religious beliefs. The Maya believed in hundreds of gods, but they thought one god was most powerful. Religious beliefs had an important effect on Maya society.

Important Religious Beliefs

The Maya thought all trees, rocks, water, stars, planets, and animals had spirits. They believed the most powerful god invented writing and supported learning and the sciences. They believed this most powerful god's wife was the goddess of weaving, medicine, and childbirth. The Maya believed the ahau was a living god. The ahau was the chief religious leader of a Maya kingdom.

◀ Experts believe the Maya began building the Temple of the Sun in Palenque (the building on the left) in A.D. 642. The temple was built to honor the Maya's gods.

▶ The Maya believed ahaus were living gods. The woman (right) in this picture is the wife of an ahau. As part of a religious ceremony, she is pulling a rope through her tongue. The Maya believed that blood would satisfy the gods and bring prosperity.

astronomy: the study of the universe, including the stars and planets

sacrifice: to kill or give up for a higher purpose

satisfy: to meet a need or expectation; to keep happy

What Do You Think?

1. How were science and religion connected in Maya society?

2. Are science and religion connected in American society today? Explain your answer.

Roles of the Priests

As Maya society grew larger, priests were needed to help **satisfy** the gods. The priests looked to the skies to guide them. They watched how stars and planets moved. They believed they were watching the gods at work. By observing the skies, they learned a great deal about **astronomy**. Priests kept track of the calendars and told about things in the future. They taught young priests about the gods. They also conducted religious rituals, which are ceremonies that take place the same way every time.

Satisfying the Gods

Blood was an important part of Maya religious rituals. The ahau and family members offered their own blood to the gods. Often, animals were **sacrificed** during the ceremonies. The Maya also sacrificed human beings— usually slaves or prisoners of war—to the gods. The Maya thought it was an honor to be sacrificed to the gods. The Maya believed the blood they offered would keep their society healthy and prosperous. 📖

TRADE AND WARFARE

Maya traders and merchants traveled all over the region trading goods such as gold and silver, **jade**, obsidian, jaguar fur, **cacao beans**, salt, honey, and brightly colored feathers. Traders carried these goods on their backs or loaded them into canoes. They traveled through jungles and swamps and along the region's many rivers. Having a common language helped trade flourish. Traders brought information and new ideas from place to place, which helped connect the various Maya kingdoms. These connections gave the people of the region a common identity as Maya people.

Maya Warfare

When other people threatened them, the Maya came together. However, the Maya also went to war against one another. When kingdoms fought, ahaus led the warriors in battle. Maya soldiers were armed with bows and arrows, spears, blow guns, and wooden swords. They did not have iron weapons. Warriors painted their faces. They went into battle shouting and **hissing**. They wanted to frighten their enemies. The goal of battle was to get prisoners. Prisoners were brought back to the winner's kingdom. Some prisoners were forced to play a ball game. We do not know how the game was scored, but we know prisoners always lost. Some prisoners were sacrificed as part of the Maya's religious rituals. Other prisoners became slaves. 📖

cacao bean: a bean used in making chocolate; also used as a form of money

hiss: sharp "s" sound made by blowing air across the tongue

jade: a green stone

What Do You Think?

1. Why might people fight among themselves, but then join together to fight against an outside enemy?

2. Having a common language helped trade flourish for the Maya. How does speaking the same language help people today?

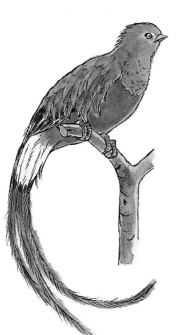

◀ The Maya especially liked feathers from quetzal (ket-SAHL) birds, a Central American bird with gold-green and red feathers. They used feathers to decorate headdresses, shields, and other objects. Quetzal feathers were highly prized trade items.

THE POPUL VUH

A Maya History of the Maya

The buildings and artifacts of the ancient Maya give us important clues to their lives. However, it is the written accounts of their way of life that help us understand what the Maya cared about and what they believed in. The *Popul Vuh*, which means "Council Book," gives us such a written account. Originally, the stories and songs that make up the *Popul Vuh* were part of the oral tradition of the Maya. The Quiche people, descendants of the ancient Maya in the Guatemalan highlands, wrote down these songs and stories 30 years after the Spanish arrived in the region. No one knows exactly who wrote the *Popul Vuh*. However, this 9,000-line poem is considered one of the finest examples of American Indian literature. The original was lost in the 1800s, but copies of it have survived. The *Popul Vuh* begins with the story of how the world began. You can read below a translation of the opening lines of this important source. 📖

From the *Popul Vuh*

Before the world was created, Calm and Silence were the great kings that ruled. Nothing existed, there was nothing. Things had not yet been drawn together, the face of the earth was unseen. There was only motionless sea, and a great emptiness of sky. There were no men anywhere, or animals, no birds or fish, no crabs. Trees, stones, caves, grass, forests, none of these existed yet. There was nothing that could roar or run, nothing that could tremble or cry in the air. Flatness and emptiness, only the sea, alone and breathless. It was night; silence stood in the dark. In this darkness the Creators waited ... They were there in this emptiness, hidden under green and blue feathers, alone and surrounded with light. They are the same as wisdom. They are the ones who can conceive and bring forth a child from nothingness. And the time had come. The Creators ... argued, worried, sighed over what was to be. They planned the growth of thickets, how things would crawl and jump, the birth of man. They planned the whole creation ... Then let the emptiness fill! They said.
Let the water weave its way downward so the earth can show its face! Let the light break on the ridges, let the sky fill up with the yellow light of dawn! Let our glory be a man walking on a path through the trees! 'Earth!' the Creators called.

Analyze the Source!
1. Read the excerpt and tell in your own words what it says.
2. What conclusions, if any, can you draw about the Maya's religious beliefs from this excerpt?
3. Based on this excerpt, do you agree that the *Popul Vuh* is fine literature? Why?

MAYA CIVILIZATION FADES

| 0 | | | A.D. 2000 |

A.D. 900
Southern Maya
abandon their cities

c. A.D. 1500
Spaniards arrive in
the Americas

The Maya civilization flourished from about A.D. 250 until around A.D. 900. During this time, the Maya produced remarkable architecture, advanced calendars and writing and number systems, and advanced ideas about astronomy. By the time the Spaniards arrived in the Americas in the early 1500s, the Maya civilization had faded.

What Happened to the Maya?

By A.D. 900, the Maya in the southern area had abandoned their cities. The Maya in the north began to blend with another Mesoamerican culture. No one is sure exactly what happened. Archaeologists have found walls built around Maya cities during this time and believe the Maya were trying to defend themselves from outside enemies. Some experts think the Maya population may have grown too large, and farmers could no longer grow enough food for everyone. Maybe there wasn't enough rainfall and the crops died. Other experts think it became too difficult for the common people to support the elite people.

The Spaniards Arrive

Whatever the reason, when the Spaniards arrived in the Americas in the early 1500s, the Maya civilization had faded. The descendants of the Maya went through a sad and cruel period under Spanish rule. One Maya account in the 1500s describes "mighty men" arriving from the east. The Spaniards had guns and iron swords. They also unknowingly brought diseases that were deadly for Mesoamerican people. The Spaniards wanted the Maya and other Mesoamerican people to give up their religious beliefs and culture. They burned the Maya's books and **belittled** their beliefs. They tried to make them forget their past. 📖

▲ Scholars are still trying to unfold the mysteries of the Maya. Scholars have deciphered the writing on this stela and know it was carved in A.D. 782. It stands in the main plaza of the ruins at Copán in modern-day Guatemala. The figure is of a woman wearing a jaguar skirt. Who is she? No one yet knows.

belittle: to cause to think something is not important or special

The Long History of
ANCIENT ROME

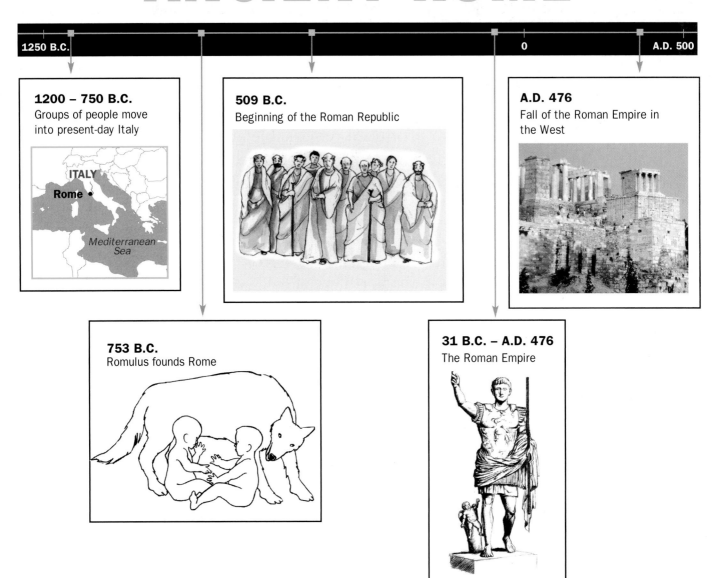

1250 B.C.   0   A.D. 500

1200 – 750 B.C.
Groups of people move into present-day Italy

ITALY
Rome •
Mediterranean Sea

509 B.C.
Beginning of the Roman Republic

A.D. 476
Fall of the Roman Empire in the West

753 B.C.
Romulus founds Rome

31 B.C. – A.D. 476
The Roman Empire

Have you heard the story about the two babies, Romulus and Remus, who were abandoned by their mother and raised by a wolf? Did you know that a woman named Lucretia is thought to have played a key role in the founding of the **Roman Republic**? Do you wonder who people like George Washington admired? One of his heroes was a man named Cincinnatus. Cincinnatus was a farmer who saved the Roman Republic. Have you seen pictures of the Roman Colosseum? This is the place where men fought other men and animals to entertain the public. Did you realize that over time emperors began to rule Rome? What important ideas and values do we get from the ancient Romans?

▲ This is what the Roman Colosseum looks like today.

History Tells Us Stories

The world we live in today was shaped by the people who lived before us—the kings and queens, writers, traders, slaves, scholars, farmers, and religious leaders. History tells us their stories. History reveals the challenges they faced, their victories and tragedies, and their ideas and beliefs.

Changes in Ideas and Life

As you study ancient Rome, remember that ancient Rome spanned almost 1,000 years. In contrast, the United States is less than 300 years old. Just as we have seen many changes in American history since its founding, many things changed over the period of Rome's 1,000-year history. As you read about the founding of Rome, the Roman Republic, and the **Roman Empire**, think about how Roman ideas and Roman life changed. Also think about how ancient Romans influence our ideas today. 📖

Roman Empire: the time in ancient Roman history after the Roman Republic when Roman emperors governed and controlled Rome and territory throughout the Mediterranean region (31 B.C.–A.D. 476)

Roman Republic: the time in ancient Roman history when people elected leaders to govern (509–31 B.C.)

ROMULUS AND REMUS
The Mythical Founding of Rome

1250 B.C.			700 B.C.

1200 – 750 B.C.
Groups of people move
into present-day Italy

753 B.C.
Romulus founds Rome

People have always wanted to know where they came from. Who were their ancestors? When did their civilization begin? Sometimes we have information to answer these questions, but oftentimes we do not. In many civilizations, people have myths and legends to explain their origins or other past events. Myths and legends are stories that have been told for generations and generations. They may contain facts, but they also include ideas from an author's imagination. Often people tell different versions of the same myth or legend. The central idea is always the same, but the details may change depending on who is telling the story. Throughout history, people have used myths and legends as a way to help them understand how the world or their civilization began. This mythical story is about two boys, Romulus and Remus.

It's a FACT
The earliest Romans were farmers. They respected people who were strong, serious, and disciplined. We get the word *gravitas* from the Latin word for "dignity" or "weightiness."

Who Will Be the Next King?

According to this myth, a very long time ago, a king died and left two sons. By tradition, the older son should have become the new king. That's the way things had always been done. But the younger son had a different idea. He wanted to become king. He pushed his older brother aside and made himself king. However, there was a problem. The older brother and his wife had given birth to **twin** sons. The new king became worried. What if the twin boys grew up and pushed him aside? The new king thought he had the solution—he would throw them into the Tiber River! Surely, the babies would drown and never bother him again.

Found by a Wolf

The twins' mother was very smart. To protect the boys, she put them in a basket that floated on the river. According to the myth, a female wolf heard the two babies crying. She felt sorry for them and began licking the mud off them and feeding them. Later, a shepherd found the two boys and named them Romulus and Remus. When the boys grew up, they learned about their father. They found out that he was supposed to have been king. They also heard about how their mother saved their lives.

▲ According to the myth, the twins' mother placed them in a basket on the Tiber River to save their lives.

Building a Town

The boys decided to build a town of their own. The problem was that they couldn't agree on where to build it. There were seven hills in the area. Romulus thought the town should be built on Palatine Hill. Remus wanted to build the town on Aventine Hill.

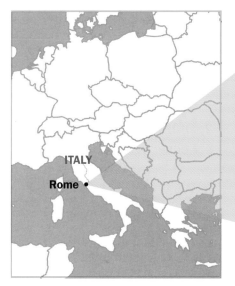

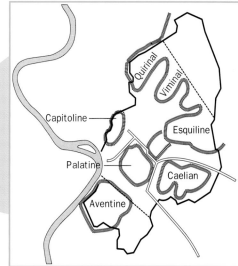

▲ Palatine Hill is one of the seven hills in Rome.

mock: to make fun of; ridicule; to treat with scorn

It's a **FACT**

Etruscan ideas probably influenced the legend of Romulus and Remus. The Etruscans strongly believed that boundaries such as walls were a way to keep out evil.

Town Walls

Many people decided to help Romulus build the town. They also decided that Romulus would be a good leader to rule over the town. Soon they began building the walls around the new town. Romulus said that everyone must respect the town walls. If they wanted to enter or leave the town, they had to use the gates.

Remus was not very happy about his brother's success and popularity. He was jealous of his brother. He decided to show Romulus what he thought of the new town walls. Remus did not use the gates. Instead, he jumped right over the wall and **mocked**, "You don't really think these walls are going to protect your town, do you?" He laughed and laughed.

Romulus's City—Rome

According to the story, Romulus became very angry with his brother. Town walls were serious business. Remus did not show them the respect they deserved. In fact, the myth says that Romulus was so angry that he killed Remus. Romulus is supposed to have said, "So will die whoever else shall leap over my walls." According to this myth, Romulus founded the town in 753 B.C. and named it after himself. This is the myth of the founding of Rome. 📖

 What Do You Think?

1. Which parts of this story might be true? Which parts might be someone's imagination?

2. Of the two brothers in this myth, which one seems more serious? Which one respects the law?

3. What does this myth tell you about what ancient Romans thought was important?

4. What do you think is the central idea of this story?

LUCRETIA
and the Founding of Rome

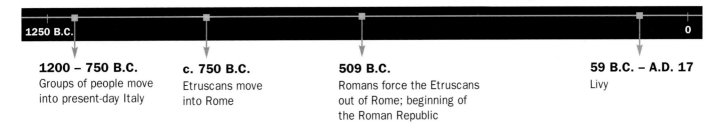

1250 B.C. **0**

1200 – 750 B.C.
Groups of people move
into present-day Italy

c. 750 B.C.
Etruscans move
into Rome

509 B.C.
Romans force the Etruscans
out of Rome; beginning of
the Roman Republic

59 B.C. – A.D. 17
Livy

This is the story of Lucretia, the wife of a Roman noble who lived at the time when Etruscans ruled Rome. According to Titus Livy, one of ancient Rome's most famous historians, Lucretia's death played a key role in the founding of the Roman Republic in 509 B.C. Lucretia's story also reveals what the Romans thought were important Roman values.

▲ The Etruscans moved from Etruria into Rome.

Who Has the Better Wife?

Between 1200 and 750 B.C., groups of people moved into what is present-day Italy. The Etruscans were one of these groups. Around 750 B.C., the Etruscans moved into the Roman settlement. Over time, Etruscan kings ruled all the people of Rome. The story of Lucretia begins during the rule of the Etruscan king Tarquin.

"By **Castor**, you're a good swordsman," the Etruscan shouted to his Roman friend. The two men were at a party, eating, drinking, and talking. After a while, the men began bragging about their wives. The Etruscan man was the king's son. His name was Sextus Tarquin. He boasted to his Roman friend, "I have the best, most faithful, and **virtuous** wife in the world." The Roman, a man named Collatinus, laughed and laughed. "You are fooling yourself. No one in all of Rome has a better or more virtuous wife than my lovely Lucretia."

Castor: according to Greek mythology, Castor and Pollux were the twins that Zeus changed into the constellation called Gemini

virtuous: having good moral character; being modest and pure

penalty: punishment for a crime

villa: a Roman country house, usually quite large

It's a FACT

Livy wrote stories about individual people to teach Romans lessons about how to have good Roman values.

A Surprise Visit

The two men were very competitive. They argued about who had the better wife. Finally, they agreed to settle the argument. They would pay a surprise visit to their wives. This would be the test to see which man had the better wife. Off they rode to Rome.

First they went to the Etruscan's **villa**. Sextus Tarquin found his wife eating and talking with her friends. She ignored her husband. She was too busy with her friends to pay him any attention. She greeted her husband's friend Collatinus briefly, but you certainly wouldn't say she was a very good hostess. Sextus Tarquin knew this wasn't a good sign. Maybe, he thought, Collatinus's wife would behave the same way—or worse!

Lucretia's Husband Wins the Bet

Off they rode to the Roman's villa. When they arrived, they found Collatinus's wife, Lucretia, busy spinning wool and watching her children write their letters. When she heard Collatinus enter the garden, she stopped her work immediately. "Collatinus, dear husband, we had not expected you so soon. How happy I am to see you." She moved gracefully to her husband and gently brushed his cheek with a kiss.

"Greetings to you, Sextus Tarquin. My husband's friends are always most welcome in our home. Please be seated." She motioned for him to sit on a comfortable bench near a small fig tree in the garden. "I will see to it that food and drink are brought to you immediately," she said. Then off she went to arrange for refreshments.

Collatinus smiled broadly at his Etruscan friend. Collatinus knew this was a good sign. He knew he had won the bet. Of course, Sextus Tarquin knew that, too, but he wasn't thinking about the bet anymore. He was thinking about what a beautiful, kind, and virtuous woman Lucretia was. Clearly, the Roman had the better wife!

An Unpleasant, Surprise Visit

Still, Sextus Tarquin was a very competitive man. He came up with a plan to make himself the winner and to show Collatinus that Lucretia wasn't a very good or virtuous wife. Several days later, Sextus Tarquin made a surprise visit to Lucretia. Lucretia welcomed Sextus Tarquin into her home. "Welcome to our home, Sextus Tarquin. My husband is not here, but let me offer you refreshments from your long journey." Lucretia did not suspect that Sextus Tarquin was up to no good. But he was. While he was a guest in her home, Sextus Tarquin forced Lucretia to take him to her bedroom. When she screamed, he said, "Silence, Lucretia. I am Sextus Tarquin. I have a sword in my hand. If you say a word, you will die." After he had forced himself on Lucretia, he said, "If you tell anyone about this, I will say that you were a willing participant. I will tell your husband that you desired me." And then he laughed. Lucretia was in tears. Sextus Tarquin was proud of himself. He had dishonored Lucretia, and Collatinus, too.

Death Before Dishonor

After Sextus Tarquin had left, Lucretia sent messages to her father and husband. She begged them to come home from their travels immediately. When they arrived at the villa, Lucretia's father and Collatinus saw that Lucretia was upset. "What is wrong, Lucretia? Are you ill?" She replied, "What can be well with a woman when her honor is lost?" She told them what happened. She made them promise to punish Sextus Tarquin for dishonoring her. Collatinus said, "It is not your fault for what that man did to you." Her father said, "Lucretia, you have no reason to feel guilty. I know you would never have agreed to this. All of Rome knows that."

However, when they looked away, Lucretia pulled a small knife out of the folds of her robe. Then she plunged the knife into her heart. The two men tried to stop her, but it was too late.

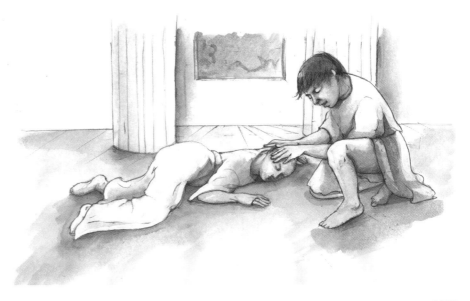

▼ As she lay dying, Lucretia said, "Although I know I am not guilty of the sin, I do not free myself from the **penalty**."

Forum: the main public square and marketplace in ancient Rome

The Roman Republic

Lucretia's family carried Lucretia's body to the Roman **Forum**. They told everyone they met about what had happened. The Romans were horrified. They would not stand for this dishonor. They decided they had to drive the Etruscans out of Rome and they did. According to Livy, in place of Etruscan kings, the Romans decided to establish a republic, the Roman Republic.

>
>
> ### What Do You Think?
>
> **1.** What are some examples of good (virtue) and evil (vice) in this story?
>
> **2.** Some people believe the moral or lesson of this story is "death before dishonor." Do you think this is a good moral for this story? Why or why not?
>
> **3.** The story of Lucretia occurred almost 500 years before Livy was born. What problems do people face when they write about events that happened long before they were born?

CINCINNATUS
A Roman (and American) Hero

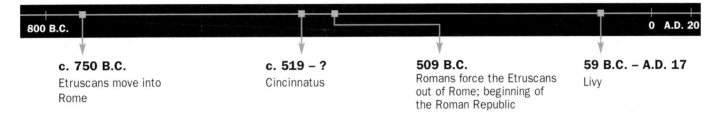

| 800 B.C. | | | | 0 A.D. 20 |

c. 750 B.C.
Etruscans move into Rome

c. 519 – ?
Cincinnatus

509 B.C.
Romans force the Etruscans out of Rome; beginning of the Roman Republic

59 B.C. – A.D. 17
Livy

This is the story of Lucius Quinctius Cincinnatus, a man who lived during the time of the Roman Republic. Thousands of years ago, the Roman historian, Livy, wrote about Cincinnatus. Throughout history, Romans have considered Cincinnatus a role model. America's founding fathers, including George Washington, also greatly admired him. Many Americans today still regard Cincinnatus as a hero and a model citizen. What is heroic about this man who lived 2,500 years ago?

A Citizen of the Roman Republic

Cincinnatus was born around 519 B.C., a time when Etruscan kings still ruled Rome. When he was 10 years old, in 509 B.C., the Romans forced the last Etruscan king to leave. They no longer wanted a king to rule them. They decided they wanted to choose their own leaders. This kind of government is called a republic. Cincinnatus lived most of his life during the time when Rome was a republic.

▲ This a statue of George Washington dressed as Cincinnatus. Similarities are often drawn between Cincinnatus and George Washington.

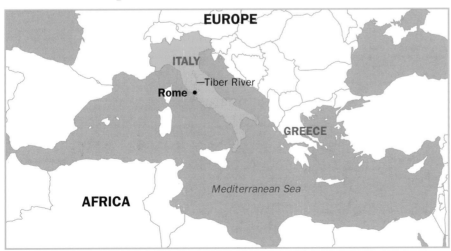

▲ Cincinnatus lived along the Tiber River in Rome.

A Roman Farmer

Cincinnatus came from a good Roman family who lived modestly in the Roman countryside. Cincinnatus loved the land and enjoyed the life of a farmer. After he married, he lived with his wife Racilia and their children on a small farm alongside the Tiber River. Cincinnatus was not rich, but his fellow Romans respected his strength, hard work, gravitas, and loyalty to the republic. Cincinnatus lived a happy life on his farm. However, his **contentment** was interrupted in 458 B.C.

▲ This is the Tiber River today.

A Crisis in Rome

There was a **crisis** in Rome. Enemies had surrounded a Roman army outside the city. If the enemies defeated the Roman army, the Roman Republic might be destroyed. Members of Rome's Senate quickly met to talk about what they should do.

They decided that Cincinnatus was the only person who could save the trapped Roman army. A group of **senators** rode to Cincinnatus's farm. According to Livy's account, the senators found Cincinnatus working in his fields. Livy says that Cincinnatus was surprised by their visit and that "... he cried, 'Is all well?' and bade his wife Racilia to hurry and fetch his toga from the cottage." After Cincinnatus wiped away the dust and sweat and put on his toga, the senators explained the terrible situation. They greeted Cincinnatus as **dictator** and told him he needed to leave for Rome immediately. As dictator, he would have complete power to lead Rome in this crisis.

It's a FACT

Livy wrote his history hundreds of years after Cincinnatus and other people of the Roman Republic lived.

The Ohio city of Cincinnati is named in honor of Cincinnatus.

▲ Roman men wore a long, flowing garment called a toga.

Rome's Military Commander

Livy reported that Cincinnatus did not hesitate to do what he saw as his duty. He dropped his plow and told his wife that he would be back as soon as he could. Within that moment, this Roman farmer had become Rome's military commander. He was now the person in charge of all of Rome's military forces.

A Roman Hero

Cincinnatus ordered all Romans who were old enough to fight to bring weapons and supplies to a meeting place. Then he marched this army of citizens throughout the night. By morning, Cincinnatus and his citizen army had arrived at the battleground ready to face the enemy. It was no longer one enemy army against one Roman army. Now there were *two* Roman armies and the enemy army was pinned between them. Livy wrote that within 16 days, the enemy army surrendered. Cincinnatus was a **victorious** general. People called him a great Roman hero. He could have remained as **consul** and become rich and powerful. But that's not what Cincinnatus did. Instead, he went back to his farm.

About 20 years later, in 439 B.C., Romans once again asked Cincinnatus to leave his farm to serve the Roman Republic. Once again, he did so willingly. When his duty was done, once again, he went back to his family farm. Cincinnatus believed it was the responsibility of all citizens to serve their country in time of need. He was not interested in wealth or power. When he completed his duty as a citizen, he willingly gave up his position of power and went back to his farm. 📖

consul: a general elected each year to lead the army and protect the city of Rome

contentment: a feeling of calm satisfaction

crisis: a critical time; an unstable condition

dictator: a ruler who has complete power in government; in ancient Rome, a dictator could be appointed for a short period of time to deal with a crisis

senator: a man who made laws and helped govern ancient Rome

victorious: winning

 What Do You Think?

1. Who is the hero of the story? What are the qualities of a Roman hero?

2. Livy wrote stories about the lives of various people. He wanted these stories to help Romans learn about good Roman values. What lesson do you think he was trying to teach through the story of Cincinnatus?

3. Why do you think people such as George Washington admired Cincinnatus? Why did America's founders think of Cincinnatus as an ideal or model citizen? What makes an ideal or model citizen?

WRITTEN LAWS
The Law of the Twelve Tables

520 B.C.   400 B.C.

509 – 31 B.C.
Roman Republic

494 B.C.
Roman Republic
gives plebeians the
right to elect tribunes

450 B.C.
Senate writes laws
on bronze tablets

In ancient Rome, patricians were rich landowners and army leaders. They came from old, wealthy Roman families. There were not very many of them. Patricians made up only about 10% of Rome's population, but they were the most powerful group. Patrician men elected consuls and senators to govern Rome. They served as leaders in the army.

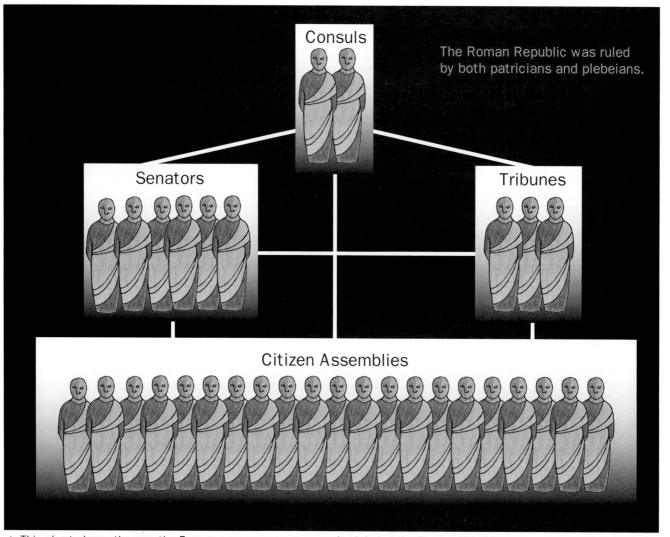

Consuls

The Roman Republic was ruled by both patricians and plebeians.

Senators

Tribunes

Citizen Assemblies

▲ This chart shows the way the Roman government was organized during the Roman Republic.

The Plebeians

Most Romans were artisans, small farmers, traders, and laborers. These people were called plebeians. Like the patricians, they were Roman citizens and paid taxes. Plebeian men served in the army. However, plebeians did not have many important rights. As some plebeians became richer and more powerful, they began to demand more rights. In 494 B.C., they gained the right to elect people to represent them and to protect their rights. These elected officials were called "tribunes."

Written Laws

During the early part of the Roman Republic, Roman laws were not written down. Only consuls and senators—the patricians—knew what the laws were. Plebeians did not think this was fair. They wanted the laws written down so everyone would know what they were. Around 450 B.C., they gained this right. The Senate wrote the laws on 12 bronze tablets. This was a great victory for the plebeians. These written laws are known as the Law of the Twelve Tables.

The Law of the Twelve Tables stated the basic rights of all free citizens. The laws covered **private,** criminal, religious, and **public** matters.

Why is the Law of the Twelve Tables important? First, it meant the laws were written down and available to everyone to read. Second, in theory, it established the principle of equality before the law. In other words, all citizens would be held to the same laws. You can read on the next page some of the laws that were included in the Law of the Twelve Tables. 📖

private: personal; not available for public use

public: for the use of everyone

It's a FACT

Tribunes had the power to stop discussions in the Senate about laws they didn't like. All they had to do was shout "Veto!" which means, "I forbid."

◀ According to one of the laws, this man has a legal right to remove his neighbor's tree.

bystander: a person who is present at an event, but not participating in it

slain: killed

summon: to send for

witness: a person who has seen or heard something

Analyze the Source!

Choose one of the laws above and tell in your own words what the law means. Then give reasons why you agree or disagree with the law. Compare this law with a law today.

Law of the Twelve Tables

Table I
• If anyone **summons** a man before the judge, he must go. If the man summoned does not go, let the one summoning him call the **bystanders** to witness and then take him by force.

Table II
• He whose **witness** has failed to appear may summon him by loud calls before his house every third day.

Table VII
• Let them keep the road in order. If they have not paved it, a man may drive his team where he likes.
• Should a tree on a neighbor's farm be bent crooked by the wind and lean over your farm, you may take legal action for removal of that tree.
• A man might gather up fruit that was falling down onto another man's farm.

Table VIII
• If one is guilty of insult, the penalty shall be twenty-five coins.
• If one is **slain** while committing theft by night, he is rightly slain.

What Do You Think?

1. Why did the plebeians want the laws written down?

2. What important right did the plebeians gain in 494 B.C.?

3. What does the author mean by the statement, "in theory, it established the principle of equality before the law"? What is the difference between theory and practice? Give an example of the principle of equality before the law.

WHAT A GOVERNMENT THOSE ROMANS HAVE

A Greek Historian Writes about Systems of Government

520 B.C.   100 B.C.

509 – 31 B.C.
Roman Republic

200 – 118 B.C.
Polybius

More than 2,000 years ago, the Greek historian Polybius asked, "Who is so thoughtless and lazy that he does not want to know in what way and with what kind of government the Romans in less than 53 years conquered nearly the entire inhabited world and brought it under their rule—an achievement previously unheard of?" Of course, the Romans had not conquered China or many other areas of the world, but they had conquered most of the Mediterranean region that Polybius was familiar with.

An Eyewitness to Roman History

Polybius saw that the Romans had developed an effective way to govern themselves. He was an eyewitness to Rome's rise to power. He traveled to Rome from his native Greece. Romans admired Greek ideas and culture. Many Romans wanted his friendship. Polybius went with one of Rome's greatest generals on military campaigns in Spain and North Africa.

A Mixed Government

Polybius described three kinds of governments: **monarchy**, **aristocracy**, and **democracy**. He believed each of these kinds of governments may start out all right, but over time each ends up badly. For example, he thought a monarchy eventually turns into a dictatorship. He thought an aristocracy becomes controlled by a few ruling families. He also thought a democracy declines into mob rule.

aristocracy: a ruling class or nobility

democracy: rule by the people

monarchy: rule by one person—a king, queen, or other monarch

Polybius believed that the Roman Republic avoided these problems by having a "mixed" government. Read below how he described the Roman government. ▭

Polybius said ...

All the aspects of the administration were, taken separately, so fairly and so suitably ordered ... that it was impossible even for the Romans themselves to declare with certainty whether the whole system was an aristocracy, a democracy, or a monarchy.

In other words ...

What did Polybius mean?

Polybius meant that Rome took parts of all three kinds of governments. The consuls (elected by the Senate) were a kind of monarchy. The Senate was drawn from the aristocracy. The assemblies allowed a voice for the people.

Polybius said ...

... When one part [of the government] having grown out of proportion to the others aims at **supremacy** and tends to become too predominant, it ... can be ... **thwarted** by the others. ...

In other words ...

What did Polybius mean?

Polybius believed these three parts of government provided a system of checks and balances. He thought that Rome's government avoided many of the mistakes other empires had made.

Analyze the Source!

1. What ideas about government do you think America's founders might have gotten from the Roman Republic?

2. Compare the parts of government in the Roman Republic with America's branches of government.

supremacy: having the greatest power

thwart: to prevent from taking place

THREE KINDS OF GOVERNMENT

MONARCHY	ARISTOCRACY	DEMOCRACY

Ruled by one person	Ruled by a few people	Ruled by many people

What Do You Think?

1. How did Polybius learn about the Roman government?

2. Explain how the Roman Republic took parts of all three kinds of governments—an aristocracy, a democracy, and a monarchy.

HANNIBAL
The Man Who Crossed the Alps with Elephants

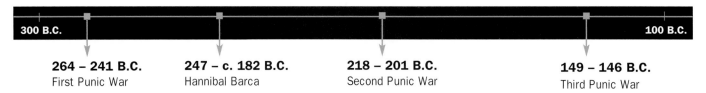

300 B.C.				100 B.C.
264 – 241 B.C. First Punic War	**247 – c. 182 B.C.** Hannibal Barca	**218 – 201 B.C.** Second Punic War	**149 – 146 B.C.** Third Punic War	

Carthage and Rome were two great superpowers of the ancient world. They fought over control of the trade routes and ports. They also fought to become the richest economic power in the Mediterranean world. Carthage and Rome clashed in a series of three wars called the **Punic** Wars. One of the heroes of the Punic Wars was a man named Hannibal. We remember him as the man who led an army across the Alps using elephants.

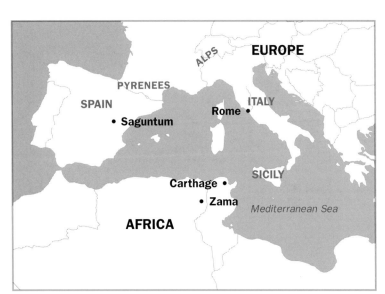

▲ The Phoenicians established trading centers around the Mediterranean Sea. Carthage began as one of these trading centers.

Ancient Rivals

The Phoenicians were a seafaring people who came from an area in the eastern Mediterranean. As they sailed around the Mediterranean Sea, they established trading centers, including one in Carthage. Carthage was located in northern Africa in what is known today as Tunisia. Over time, Carthage became a powerful city-state, more powerful than Rome at the time. Sometimes Rome and Carthage joined their forces against the Greek cities of Italy. Eventually, however, Rome and Carthage went to war against one another.

The Carthaginians and Romans fought each of three Punic Wars for a different reason. The First Punic War lasted from 264 to 241 B.C., when the Romans forced the Carthaginian general Hamilcar Barca to **surrender**. At that time, Rome and Carthage signed a treaty—an agreement that described the conditions for peace.

▲ The Alps are a range of mountains in Europe that stretch across Italy, France, Switzerland, Austria, and Germany.

Rome's Enemy Forever

According to a legend, Hamilcar Barca made his nine-year-old son Hannibal promise to be Rome's enemy forever. As he grew up, Hannibal's father taught him how to be a soldier. Hannibal dedicated his life to fighting against Rome. This was Hannibal's way to honor his father and also to do his duty as a citizen of Carthage. He believed that citizenship required him to defend Carthage's honor. He also thought it was his duty to fight against Carthage's enemies.

The Second Punic War

Around 221 B.C., when Hannibal was just 26 years old, he became leader of the Carthaginian army. His first goal was to conquer territory in Spain. He moved his troops into Saguntum, an independent city that had a treaty with Rome. After months of fighting, Saguntum finally surrendered to the Carthaginians. Rome **protested**. Roman leaders said that Carthage had **violated** the treaty that had ended the First Punic War. Rome demanded that Hannibal surrender. When he refused, the Second Punic War began. The year was 218 B.C.

protest: to complain or object

Punic: the Latin word for Phoenician; "Punic" refers to ancient Carthage and its people

surrender: to give up

violate: to fail to keep; to break (a law or regulation, for example)

It's a FACT

Hannibal's elephants were not much use in battle. They became frightened easily and ran in many directions, including back through Hannibal's soldiers!

Crossing the Alps on Elephants

Hannibal spent a winter getting ready to bring his army to Italy. He decided to attack from over land instead of by sea for two main reasons. First, he wanted the people who lived in the region to help him. Second, he thought an overland attack would surprise the Romans. To get to Italy he had to cross two mountain ranges—first the Pyrenees and then the Alps. Hannibal and approximately 35,000 soldiers crossed these mountain ranges with the help of horses and 37 elephants. After a long and difficult journey over the Alps, Hannibal's army arrived in northern Italy. The Carthaginians' first battles against Rome were successful. They conquered several Roman cities and could have marched on to Rome. However, Hannibal decided to let his soldiers rest. This gave Rome time to come up with a plan. The Roman armies decided not to fight in one great battle against Hannibal's army. Instead, they fought small battles against his soldiers on the edge of the territory he controlled.

▲ To get to Italy, Hannibal and his army had to cross two mountain ranges.

Defeat at the Battle of Zama

Hannibal was running out of food and other supplies for his soldiers. To make matters worse, the food, supplies, and new soldiers he had hoped to get from Carthage never arrived. This situation dragged on for several years. Meanwhile, Rome started an attack on the city of Carthage. Hannibal decided to leave Italy and return home to protect Carthage. He arrived in Carthage in time to fight a battle against the Romans. At the **decisive** battle of Zama, Hannibal lost 20,000 of his soldiers, but he escaped with his life.

A Carthaginian Hero

Rome and Carthage signed another treaty, but this was not the result Hannibal wanted. He had one last opportunity to fight against Rome. He led an army for the king of Syria. This time most of the fighting was at sea. The Romans defeated Hannibal and demanded his surrender. He could not escape and refused to give up. Instead, he poisoned himself. The year was probably 182 or 183 B.C.

Today, Hannibal is remembered as a brave general who led thousands of soldiers and a pack of elephants across the Alps. He fought against Rome to avenge his father's loss in the First Punic War, to uphold the honor of his country, and to protect Carthage's control of the trade routes, ports, and economy. 📖

decisive: having the power to settle a dispute or doubt; unmistakable

What Do You Think?

1. Hannibal is considered one of Carthage's most famous sons. Why do people remember him? What significant things did he do with his life?

2. What did Hannibal think that citizenship demanded? What do you think are the duties of a citizen today?

3. Hannibal was a strong leader. Are the qualities of a leader today different than the qualities of a leader from 1,000 or 2,000 years ago? Why or why not?

The Punic Wars	Dates	Reason for War
First Punic War	264–241 B.C.	Rome and Carthage fought over a town in Sicily.
Second Punic War	218–201 B.C.	Carthage captured Saguntum, a city in Spain that had a treaty with Rome. The terms of the treaty between Carthage and Rome were not followed.
Third Punic War	149–146 B.C.	Carthage attacked Rome again. Rome used this reason to destroy the city of Carthage.

CATO THE ELDER

A Self-made Man

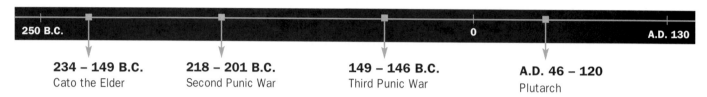

250 B.C.   0   A.D. 130

234 – 149 B.C.
Cato the Elder

218 – 201 B.C.
Second Punic War

149 – 146 B.C.
Third Punic War

A.D. 46 – 120
Plutarch

Marcus Cato, better known as Cato the Elder, was a wealthy Roman. He also was a strong supporter of traditional Roman values. He served in many different positions in the Roman government. He also was a successful military leader.

▲ Cato the Elder often said this about Roman men: "All other men rule their wives; we rule all other men, and our wives rule us."

▼ Rome greatly expanded its borders between 264 and 133 B.C., bringing great wealth to the Roman Republic. Cato was concerned that this wealth was corrupting the Romans.

A Self-made Man

Marcus Cato was born to a plebeian family in 234 B.C. We have learned much about Cato's life from Plutarch, a Greek historian, who lived in Rome and wrote biographies about people in Roman history. Plutarch described Cato as having a reddish-colored complexion and gray eyes. He praised Cato for making himself **"eminent** by his own **exertions."** In other words, Cato wasn't born into a family with high social rank and privilege. He was a self-made man. Cato was very intelligent and also a very hard worker.

Carthage Must Be Destroyed!

Beginning around 218 B.C., the famous Carthaginian general, Hannibal, invaded Italy. Cato was only a teenager at the time, but he fought with Roman forces against Hannibal's armies. Cato's experience fighting against the Carthaginians strongly affected him. Later when he became a Roman senator, Cato warned his fellow senators about the danger of the Carthaginians. He thought Carthage was the main **threat** against Rome. According to Plutarch, Cato ended each speech he gave with the same words: "Carthago delenda est!" This means, "Carthage must be destroyed!"

Traditional Values

Because of his leadership abilities, courage, and hard work, Cato became a leader in the military. He also held many important government positions. He believed in the traditional values of the early Roman Republic. He thought Romans should live on farms the way they did in earlier times. He thought life in the countryside was better than life in the city. Cato was worried about what he saw happening in Roman society during his lifetime. The Romans were busy conquering the entire Mediterranean region. This brought great wealth to Rome. Cato was afraid this new wealth was **corrupting** Romans. He thought they were becoming too interested in material goods and luxury. In describing Romans of his time, Cato said the Roman people were like sheep: "When single, [they] do not obey, but when altogether in a flock, they follow their leaders."

A Republic on Its Way to an Empire

Cato died in 149 B.C. Rome remained a republic for many decades, but the Romans already had begun conquering an empire. Eventually, Rome would move away from a republican form of government to one that was ruled by emperors. 📖

corrupt: to destroy or undermine honesty and integrity; to cause to become rotten or spoiled

eminent: outstanding

exertion: a strong effort

threat: something or someone thought to be a possible danger

What Do You Think?

1. Rome's conquests meant new wealth and power, but Cato thought that the conquests were having a negative effect, too. How did Cato see the conquests hurting Rome?

2. What do you think Cato thought of people such as Lucretia and Cincinnatus? Explain your answer.

3. What do you think Cato meant when he described the Roman people as sheep?

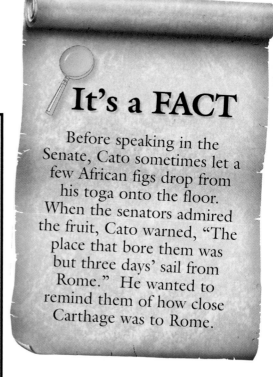

It's a FACT

Before speaking in the Senate, Cato sometimes let a few African figs drop from his toga onto the floor. When the senators admired the fruit, Cato warned, "The place that bore them was but three days' sail from Rome." He wanted to remind them of how close Carthage was to Rome.

JULIUS CAESAR
A Roman General and Statesman

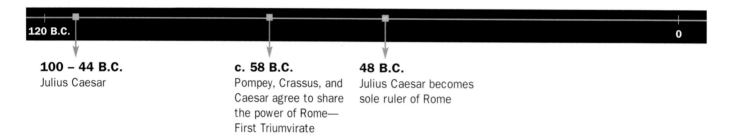

120 B.C.   0

100 – 44 B.C.
Julius Caesar

c. 58 B.C.
Pompey, Crassus, and
Caesar agree to share
the power of Rome—
First Triumvirate

48 B.C.
Julius Caesar becomes
sole ruler of Rome

More than 100 years before Julius Caesar was born, Romans were fighting and conquering lands throughout the Mediterranean region. When Julius Caesar was born in 100 B.C., however, Romans were spending much more time and energy fighting one another. Romans fought these civil wars to gain power in Rome. Julius Caesar grew up and lived during this troubled time. His family was not rich or important, but it was part of the patrician class. When Caesar was 15, his father died. Soon after that, Caesar married the daughter of an important Roman senator. Caesar's new father-in-law was not happy about the marriage. He wanted Caesar to end the marriage. Caesar refused. To avoid punishment, Caesar left Rome and became a soldier. When his father-in-law died in 78 B.C., Caesar returned to Rome.

▲ Caesar was born in the Roman month of Quintilis. This month was renamed "July" in his honor.

▲ Under Julius Caesar's leadership, Rome set up a permanent Roman base in what is now England.

A Proud and Determined Man

One story about Julius Caesar shows that he was a proud and **determined** man. While he was sailing to Greece in 75 B.C., **pirates** captured the ship on which he was sailing. The pirates agreed to trade Caesar for 20 pieces of gold. Caesar told them that he was worth at least 50! Throughout his capture, he was friendly with the pirates. However, he promised to track them down and kill them after the money was paid. And that's just what he did.

A Rising Leader

Beginning in 72 B.C., Caesar was elected to one important political office after another. He even served as a governor in what is now Spain. By about 58 B.C., Caesar had a group of very important political friends. One of the men was Pompey, a Roman general. Another was Crassus, a rich patrician. Together, Pompey, Crassus, and Caesar had the most power in Rome's government. Caesar continued to be an important military leader. He and his army conquered Gaul (present-day France). He also was the first Roman leader to cross the English Channel. He set up a permanent Roman base in what is now England.

Caesar and Cleopatra

Over time, Caesar, Pompey, and Crassus began to distrust one another. They were all very ambitious and willing to **betray** one another for personal gain. When Crassus was killed in a battle, the **tension** between Caesar and Pompey increased. Eventually, Caesar went to war against Pompey. Caesar crushed Pompey's army in 48 B.C., and Pompey fled to Egypt. Caesar followed him to Egypt. However, when he arrived, he found that Pompey was already dead. The young Egyptian king, Ptolemy XIII, had ordered him killed. While in Egypt, Caesar met and began a romantic relationship with the king's sister and co-ruler, Cleopatra. She soon was named queen of Egypt. Caesar and his army fought various groups of Egyptians who did not want Cleopatra to become queen of Egypt.

betray: to be disloyal; to give help to an enemy

determined: having a firm purpose

pirate: a person who steals at sea; a robber

tension: a strained (tense) or barely controlled dislike between people or groups

It's a FACT

When Julius Caesar defeated a group of people in Asia Minor, he said, "Veni, Vidi, Vici." This means, "I came, I saw, I conquered."

▶ Cleopatra charmed Julius Caesar into helping her gain control of Egypt. After six months of terrible warfare between Ptolemy's forces and Cleopatra's army, Ptolemy's army was defeated.

dictatorship: rule by one person (a dictator) who has complete power in government

exotic: from another place; unusual or unfamiliar

scandal: a situation that brings disgrace or is considered shameful by a community

suspicious: thinking that something is wrong, even though there is no proof

A Roman King?

When Caesar returned to Rome, Cleopatra followed him there with their son, Caesarean. Cleopatra's visit caused a **scandal** in Rome. Caesar was already married, and the Romans were **suspicious** of this **exotic** queen from the East. Would she encourage Caesar to declare himself "king" of Rome? Some Romans were very concerned about the power he already had. Rome had been a republic for many, many years. The citizens of the Roman Republic wanted nothing to do with kings.

Some Roman senators were afraid that Julius Caesar was going to do away with the Roman Republic. They thought he would try to make himself king of Rome. To save the Roman Republic from becoming a **dictatorship**, a group of senators stabbed him as he entered the Senate on March 15, 44 B.C.

The Greek historian Plutarch wrote about this event. He said the men who killed Caesar had agreed that "each of them should make a thrust at him." After he died, Caesar's will was read. In it, Caesar named his nephew Octavian as his heir. He also left large amounts of money to the city and to individuals. After his death, the people of Rome honored him. Some of his closest friends agreed to track down and punish the men who had killed Caesar. 📖

What Do You Think?

1. What is the difference between a war to conquer other lands and a civil war? How are they similar?

2. Who was Julius Caesar's heir?

3. How do you think Cleopatra's visit to Rome affected senators who were already worried that Julius Caesar wanted to make himself a king?

4. Why do you think average Romans honored Julius Caesar?

▲ According to one account, on the day Julius Caesar was killed, a fortune teller stopped him and said, "Beware the Ides of March." In the ancient Roman calendar, this was March 15, the day Caesar was killed.

CLEOPATRA
Queen of the Nile

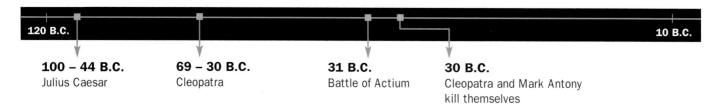

| 120 B.C. | | | | 10 B.C. |

100 – 44 B.C.
Julius Caesar

69 – 30 B.C.
Cleopatra

31 B.C.
Battle of Actium

30 B.C.
Cleopatra and Mark Antony
kill themselves

Cleopatra, the woman we call the "Queen of the Nile," was born in 69 B.C. in Alexandria, the capital city of Egypt. Cleopatra was not Egyptian. Her family was from Macedonia, an area in Greece. Her father was the ruler of Egypt, which was a wealthy, **independent** state in the Mediterranean world. It was one of the few areas that Rome had not yet conquered. Cleopatra grew up as a princess.

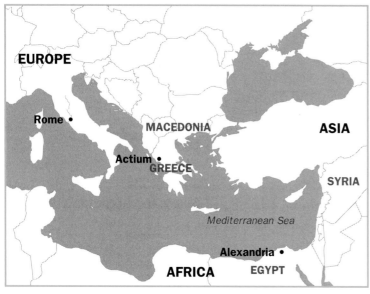

▲ Cleopatra's family was from Macedonia, an area in Greece.

Queen Cleopatra

After her father's death, the 18-year-old Cleopatra and her 10-year-old brother, Ptolemy XIII, became co-rulers of Egypt. However, since Cleopatra was a woman, her brother was the **primary** ruler of Egypt. Several of Ptolemy's advisors wanted to rule Egypt on the young king's **behalf**. Cleopatra had a different idea. She wanted to rule Egypt herself. She did not want Egypt to be one of many kingdoms that were part of the Roman Empire. She dreamed of returning Egypt to its previous position of power in the world.

Cleopatra and Caesar

Cleopatra and her brother's advisors disagreed about how Egypt should be ruled. Within two years, the advisors forced her to leave Egypt. She went to nearby Syria and convinced an army to help her gain control of Egypt. While she was in Syria, Julius Caesar, a great Roman general, arrived in Egypt.

Sole Ruler of Egypt

When Cleopatra returned to Egypt, Caesar tried to persuade Cleopatra and her brother to rule together peacefully. However, that seemed impossible. Cleopatra, now 20 years old, charmed the 52-year-old Julius Caesar. After six months of fighting, Cleopatra's army defeated Ptolemy's forces. Ptolemy died while fleeing Julius Caesar's army. Cleopatra then became queen and **sole** ruler of Egypt.

Cleopatra in Rome

Soon, Julius Caesar and Cleopatra began a love affair. When Caesar returned to Rome, Cleopatra followed him to Rome with their son, Caesarean. However, Romans did not welcome her to the city. Caesar was already married, and they did not approve of Cleopatra's relationship with him. Her customs and traditions were different from theirs. They were proud of the Roman Republic and were suspicious of this queen from the East. Some Romans thought Julius Caesar was going to make himself king of Rome. This fear was so great that several senators decided Caesar must die.

On March 15, 44 B.C., a group of senators stabbed Caesar to death as he entered the Senate. This left Cleopatra in a difficult position. What should she do? She had no friends in Rome and was afraid she would be killed, too. She quickly left Rome and returned to Egypt.

behalf: interest, benefit

independent: self-governing; not guided or controlled by another

primary: being first; basic or most important

sole: the only one

▲ This wall carving of Cleopatra and her son Caesarean can be seen on the outside of the Temple of Hathor in Egypt.

▲ This is a photograph of a modern-day actress playing Cleopatra in a movie. Of Cleopatra, the Greek historian Plutarch said, "Plato admits four sorts of flattery, but she had a thousand." In other words, most people had only a few ways to flatter people, but Cleopatra had 1,000 ways.

avenge: to take revenge; to get back at

maturity: fully grown (or mature); ripeness

What Do You Think?

1. Why did Cleopatra's visit to Rome create a scandal? Why do you think the Romans were suspicious of her?

2. What does the author mean by the statement, "She dreamed of returning Egypt to its previous position of power in the world"? When was Egypt a powerful empire?

3. Most of what we know about Cleopatra is from the Roman perspective. Most of what the Romans had to say about her was not very flattering. Why do you think their image of Cleopatra was negative?

▶ Cleopatra killed herself in 30 B.C. Some believe she ordered a servant to bring her a poisonous snake hidden in a basket of figs.

Cleopatra and Mark Antony

After Caesar's death, three of his closest friends—Octavian, Mark Antony, and Lepidus—decided to **avenge** his murder. While he was fighting in the eastern part of the Roman Empire, Antony met Cleopatra. She still wanted Egypt to become a world power and she thought Antony could help her. Antony wanted to become the most powerful man in the Roman Empire. He thought Cleopatra and her Egyptian armies could help him. The Greek historian Plutarch says that when Antony and Cleopatra met she was "in the time of life when women's beauty is most splendid and their intellects are in full **maturity**." They joined political and military forces. Soon, they also began a romantic relationship. Plutarch said that Antony was "captivated by her."

Eventually, Cleopatra and Antony fought Octavian to decide who would rule Rome and Egypt. In the decisive battle of Actium, Octavian's military defeated Cleopatra and Antony's forces. They fled to Egypt. Within a year, they killed themselves. Soon after, Octavian became Augustus, the first emperor of the Roman Empire.

Cleopatra was an intelligent and powerful woman. She did not achieve her dream of returning Egypt to its previous position as a world power in the world, but she came very close. 📖

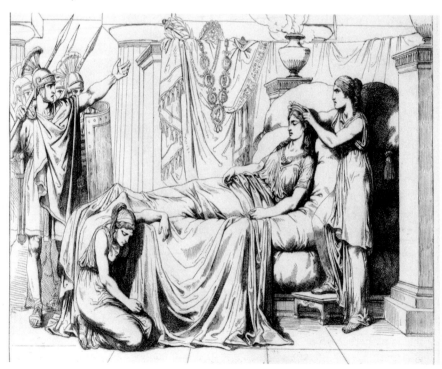

MARK ANTONY
A Fight for Power

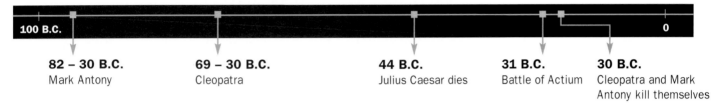

100 B.C. 0

82 – 30 B.C.
Mark Antony

69 – 30 B.C.
Cleopatra

44 B.C.
Julius Caesar dies

31 B.C.
Battle of Actium

30 B.C.
Cleopatra and Mark
Antony kill themselves

The year was 44 B.C. Julius Caesar was dead. Who would lead Rome? Who should lead Rome? Mark Antony thought he had the answers to these questions.

Mark Antony's Claim to Leadership

Mark Antony, the son and grandson of military leaders, thought he should be Rome's new leader. The Greek historian Plutarch said Antony had "a very good and noble appearance ... a bold, masculine look that reminded people of the faces of **Hercules** in paintings and sculptures." Antony had served with Caesar when he conquered Gaul. While Caesar had to be away from Rome, he left Antony in charge. After Caesar's death, Antony persuaded ordinary Romans to take out their anger on the men who had killed Caesar. He wanted people to see him as Caesar's successor. After all, Antony had fought many battles at Caesar's side.

However, in his will, Caesar named his nephew Octavian as his heir. Antony did not want to recognize Octavian as Caesar's successor. He thought Octavian was just a young man who happened to be related to Caesar. At first, most people did not think that 18-year-old Octavian was a match for a man such as Antony. They were wrong.

Hercules: a Roman mythological hero; the son of Jupiter and a mortal woman, Alcmene; known for his courage and great strength

▼ Mark Antony, Cleopatra, and their forces fought Octavian at the decisive battle of Actium.

Antony and Octavian

During the fall of 43 B.C., Octavian asked the men who had served in his uncle's army to help him. Because of their loyalty to the name of Caesar, the soldiers agreed. This gave Octavian an army. After a short time, Octavian and Antony agreed to join forces to avenge Julius Caesar's death. Octavian, Antony, and Lepidus, another Roman general, decided to go after the men who had killed Caesar.

Then the three men agreed to rule Rome together. They divided the Roman Empire into three areas. Octavian would rule the western provinces, Lepidus the provinces in Africa, and Antony the eastern provinces. This sharing of power didn't last long, and Lepidus was soon forced out. This left only Octavian and Antony in positions of power. A showdown between the two men seemed bound to happen. Octavian had gained a great deal of power and had a large army. Still, Antony wasn't worried. He had a strong ally in Egypt.

▼ Plutarch said that with Cleopatra, Antony was "like a boy ... fooling away ... that most costly of all valuables, time."

Antony and Cleopatra

As Roman ruler of the eastern part of the Roman Empire, which included Egypt, Antony had gotten to know Queen Cleopatra of Egypt. In fact, they had formed an alliance based on love and politics. Plutarch writes that Antony was "captivated by her."

However, Antony and Cleopatra were not just a couple in love. They shared the goal of conquering Rome and creating an empire that would rule the Western and Eastern worlds. This was not going to be easy.

Of course, Octavian was doing everything he could to stop them. Octavian persuaded Romans to have a bad opinion of Antony. Antony's relationship with Cleopatra was scandalous. He was already married and Fulvia, his Roman wife, was Octavian's sister. Rumors also spread throughout Rome that Antony was helping Egypt to conquer Rome. The idea of an Egyptian queen ruling Rome was unthinkable to Romans.

The Battle of Actium

Octavian was very clever. He knew that Romans did not want any more civil wars. So, rather than declaring war on Antony, he declared war on Egypt. The final battle for control of the Roman Empire took place in Actium (in present-day Greece) in 31 B.C. Octavian had more soldiers and a better-trained army. However, Cleopatra believed that Egypt's navy could win the battle for Antony. Events turned out very differently. Antony and Cleopatra's forces were crushed.

Antony and Cleopatra fled to Egypt, and Octavian chased after them. When it was clear that they would be caught, Antony and Cleopatra killed themselves. This left Octavian as the ruler of Egypt and all the Roman Empire. The wealth of Egypt belonged to Octavian, who would soon be renamed Augustus. Antony had fought hard, but he lost the battle to the most powerful man in Rome.

What Do You Think?

1. How did Octavian hurt Mark Antony's reputation with the Roman people? Do leaders today try to influence people's opinions of other leaders? Explain your answer.

2. Why do you think Octavian declared war on Egypt? How did this action make Romans think this was Rome's war against Egypt and not a civil war between two Romans who wanted power?

▼ The battle of Actium was a decisive battle for Antony and Cleopatra.

CICERO
Rome's Greatest Orator

| 110 B.C. | | | | 0 |

106 – 43 B.C.
Cicero

100 – 44 B.C.
Julius Caesar

82 – 30 B.C.
Mark Antony

Before 50 B.C., Romans could gain fame and power in two ways. One way was to be born to a well-known and important family. Another way was to become a military hero. Cicero found a third way to gain fame and power. He was the first man to gain the most powerful positions in Rome based upon his ability to speak well in public. He is sometimes called Rome's greatest orator.

oratory: public speaking; from the Latin word *orare*, which means "to speak"

An Excellent Education

Cicero was born in 106 B.C. His family was not wealthy, but they were not poor either. As a young boy, Cicero and his brother were given a good education. Cicero's father insisted that he study with excellent teachers. His father understood that having a good education would allow Cicero to work in Rome's government. Cicero studied poetry, law, philosophy, and most importantly, **oratory**. Cicero thought education was very important. Later in his life, Cicero said, "What greater and better gift can we offer the Republic than to teach and to instruct our young?"

▶ Cicero was born in Italy about 60 miles southeast of Rome. He lived in Rome, but traveled to Greece and Sicily.

The Cost of Success

Because of his skill in public speaking, Cicero was asked to defend many people who were charged with crimes. When he successfully defended a man who was accused of murdering a person from an important Roman family, the family became very angry with Cicero. As a result, Cicero left Rome for about two years.

During this time, Cicero traveled to Greece and other eastern provinces controlled by Rome. He became very impressed with Greek philosophy. Cicero returned to Rome when he was about 30 years old. By this time, his public speaking ability was far greater than anyone else's in all of Rome. He decided to begin a political career. Over the next 20 years, Cicero argued many important law cases. He also wrote several essays on philosophy and public speaking. In addition, he served as a Roman senator and as a leader in one of Rome's provinces. He was even elected as a consul.

Roman Politics

During this time, Romans were fighting among themselves for control of Rome and all its territory. In these conflicts, Cicero sided with Pompey, one of Rome's great generals, and against Julius Caesar. Eventually, however, Julius Caesar defeated Pompey. Cicero was on the wrong side of this fight! As a result, he had to leave Rome again. Later, he returned when Caesar offered his friendship. For the next few years, Cicero lived as a private citizen.

After Julius Caesar was killed in 44 B.C., Cicero decided to return to political life. He spoke harshly about Mark Antony, one of Rome's new leaders. This decision cost Cicero his life. He was captured and killed by Antony's soldiers in 43 B.C.

▲ This is an artist's idea of what Cicero might have looked like. Nearly all of Cicero's ideas about philosophy are borrowed from the Greeks.

bud: an undeveloped person or thing

Words to Protect the Republic

Cicero is credited with preserving much of the original Greek philosophy that might otherwise have been lost to us. However, he is best remembered for his writing and speaking skills. Today, when people hear the name Cicero, they think of Rome's greatest orator. Before his death, Cicero wrote essays and hundreds of letters to his friends about events in Rome and about his thoughts and ideas. You can read some quotations from Cicero's writings below. □

Analyze the Source!

Select one of Cicero's quotations and tell in your own words what it means. Give reasons why you agree or disagree with the quotation.

- There is no place more delightful than home.
- Every evil in the **bud** is easily crushed; as it grows older, it becomes stronger.
- The more laws, the less justice.
- The mind of each man is the man himself.
- Philosophy, rightly defined, is simply the love of wisdom.

What Do You Think?

1. Why is Cicero still remembered today?

2. How did Cicero's travels to Greece affect him?

3. Cicero was one of ancient Rome's greatest orators. Who is one of the greatest orators today? Explain why.

SIX GREATEST MISTAKES

Cicero recorded what he considered to be the six greatest mistakes human beings make:

1. The idea that a person advances by crushing others.
2. The tendency to worry about things that cannot be changed.
3. Insisting that something is impossible because we cannot do it ourselves.
4. Refusing to set aside unimportant preferences.
5. Neglecting learning and neglecting to develop the habit of reading and study.
6. Attempting to make others believe and live as we do.

AUGUSTUS
First Emperor of Rome

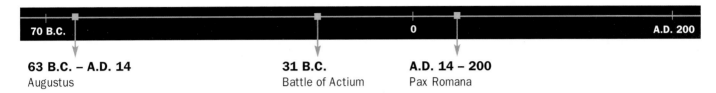

70 B.C.		0		A.D. 200

63 B.C. – A.D. 14
Augustus

31 B.C.
Battle of Actium

A.D. 14 – 200
Pax Romana

As a young boy, Octavian had no idea that his life would be very different than that of other boys around him. But Octavian's great uncle, Julius Caesar, took a liking to him. As a result, his life and the story of ancient Rome were changed forever.

Heir to Power

Octavian was born on September 23, 63 B.C. At birth he was given the name Gaius Octavius. As a young boy, he was taught basic military skills as well as how to think and debate. While Octavian was at school away from Rome, Julius Caesar was murdered by some Roman leaders who thought he was going to make himself king of Rome. When Octavian returned to Rome, he discovered that Caesar had named him as heir. Octavian then took the name Gaius Julius Caesar Octavius. In English, his name is shortened to Octavian.

▲ Augustus was born near Rome. He traveled throughout the Roman Empire (shaded area).

Avenging Julius Caesar's Murder

Octavian was very angry and upset about his uncle's murder. He persuaded the army to help him avenge Julius Caesar's death. He joined forces with Mark Antony, a popular and respected Roman military leader, and Lepidus, another Roman general. The three leaders made sure that Caesar's murderers were killed.

▲ Augustus brought peace to the Roman Empire.

aqueduct: a structure that helps move water in a certain direction

boast: something bragged about or said with pride

golden age: a period of time when something reaches its height of excellence

harken: to listen carefully

revered: very highly thought of

Control of Rome's Territories

The three men divided the Roman Empire into thirds. According to this plan, Octavian would rule the western provinces, Antony would rule the eastern provinces, and Lepidus would rule the provinces in Africa. The Greek historian Plutarch wrote, "And an agreement was made that everyone in their turn, as they thought fit, should make their friends consuls, when they did not choose to take the offices themselves." However, this arrangement did not satisfy either Octavian or Mark Antony for long. Both men wanted to control all of Rome's territories. Lepidus was soon forced out. Eventually, Octavian's forces defeated Antony and Cleopatra's forces at the battle of Actium (in present-day Greece) in 31 B.C.

From Octavian to "Augustus"

After the battle of Actium, Octavian returned to Rome at the age of 34. The Roman Senate gave him many titles and honors. One of the titles was "Augustus," which means "**revered** one." He is most often referred to as Augustus.

Augustus ruled the Roman Empire for about 40 years. During his reign, he expanded the Roman Empire to include Spain, Gaul (present-day France), and Egypt. Augustus provided many services for the people of Rome. He wanted to improve the life of average Romans. He ordered the building of many bridges, **aqueducts**, and libraries. He tried to strengthen the Roman family. He passed laws that emphasized traditional Roman values such as marriage and loyalty between husbands and wives. He developed a civil service—an organization of government workers—to help with the work of governing the Roman Empire.

A Golden Age of Latin Literature

Augustus also encouraged artists and writers. His reign is sometimes referred to as a **golden age** of Latin literature because he was a friend to poets and historians. Augustus supported the work of Virgil who wrote *The Aeneid* during this period. The Roman poet Horace wrote, "With Caesar [Augustus] the guardian of the state, not civil rage nor violence shall drive out peace …" In other words, after a long period of war and fighting, Augustus had brought peace to the empire.

▲ This is a photograph of Augustus's mausoleum.

The Pax Romana

During the rule of Augustus, the Roman Empire became more united. It also enjoyed a period of peace. The Roman people considered him a fair and wise ruler. Augustus said in a famous **boast**, "I found Rome a city of bricks and left it a city of marble."

When he died in A.D. 14, Romans worshiped him as a god. Augustus had brought peace, prosperity, and order to the empire. The peace, prosperity, and order continued for almost 200 years. This period of time is called the Pax Romana, which means "Roman peace." 📖

▲ Augustus built aqueducts to provide fresh water for the people of Rome.

What Do You Think?

1. What actions did Augustus take to improve the lives of Romans?

2. Toward the end of his life, Augustus said, "Young men, hear an old man to whom old men **harkened** when he was young." What do you think he meant?

3. How might peace and prosperity contribute to a golden age of literature?

AENEAS
A Mythical Founder of Rome

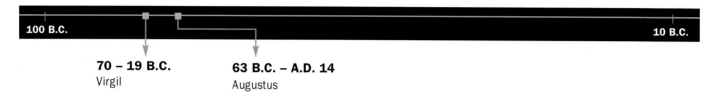

100 B.C.   10 B.C.

70 – 19 B.C.
Virgil

63 B.C. – A.D. 14
Augustus

Aeneas was one of many characters in Homer's *Iliad* and *Odyssey*. However, Aeneas became a mythical Roman hero when the Roman poet Virgil wrote about him in a famous poem called *The Aeneid*. According to the myth, Aeneas was the son of a Trojan prince, Anchises, and the goddess Venus. In *The Aeneid*, Venus and other gods became involved in events throughout Aeneas's life.

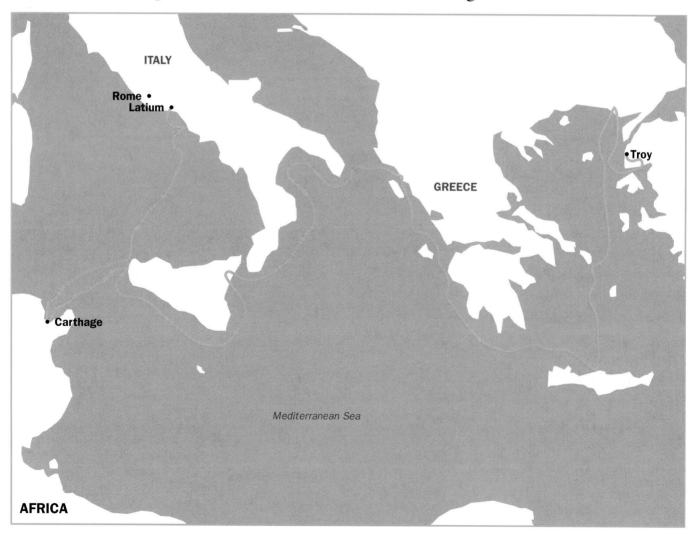

▲ The map shows the route taken by Aeneas as he fled Troy and started his travels across the Mediterranean.

Aeneas's Family Tree

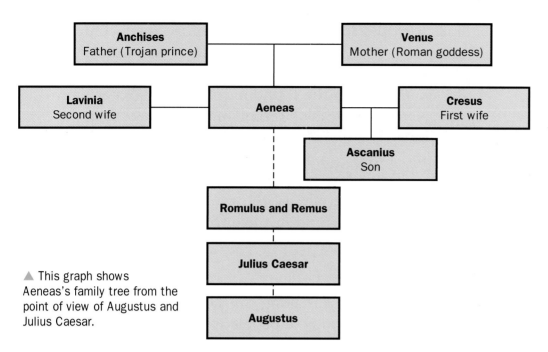

Anchises
Father (Trojan prince)

Venus
Mother (Roman goddess)

Lavinia
Second wife

Aeneas

Cresus
First wife

Ascanius
Son

Romulus and Remus

Julius Caesar

Augustus

▲ This graph shows Aeneas's family tree from the point of view of Augustus and Julius Caesar.

Escape from Troy

Aeneas was a great Trojan warrior and hero. Virgil's story of Aeneas begins just after the Greeks fought and destroyed the city of Troy. The gods had saved Aeneas from death twice during the war. They believed he had a mission in life and couldn't die in the battle for Troy. He escaped from the ruined city along with a small group of other Trojans. Aeneas carried his elderly father on his back and led his small son by the hand. As they were fleeing Troy, in the confusion of the battle, Aeneas's wife was lost. Where would Aeneas and the other escaping Trojans go? What was ahead for them?

A Journey, An Adventure

Aeneas and his group began a long journey. They traveled from island to island across the Mediterranean Sea. At each island, they experienced some adventure. Eventually, after surviving a storm, the group washed up on the coast of North Africa, near the city of Carthage. There, Aeneas met Queen Dido of Carthage. Dido fell in love with Aeneas almost immediately.

It would have been easy for Aeneas to stay with the queen of Carthage. However, Aeneas did not remain in Carthage. He continued his journey because he believed it was his duty to his people and his gods.

▲ Aeneas, his father, and his son fled Troy after the war.

descendant: offspring; child, grandchild, and so forth

prophecy: a prediction of something that will happen in the future

rival: a person who tries to equal or pass another person

underworld: according to Greek and Roman mythology, the world of the dead

What Do You Think?

1. Romans thought of Aeneas as an important symbol of Roman values. What are some of Aeneas's heroic qualities?

2. Why do you think the Romans wanted to make a connection between their own history and the heroic Greek past?

3. Compare Aeneas with Romulus or Lucretia. What qualities do they have in common? How are they different?

The Founding of Rome

In *The Aeneid*, Aeneas visited the **underworld** where he met with the spirits of people who had died. One of the people he met was his beloved father, Anchises. During this meeting, Aeneas heard the **prophecy** about the role he would play in the founding of Rome. According to *The Aeneid*, Aeneas's descendants would include Romulus, the mythical founder of the city of Rome. In the underworld, Aeneas learned about the future of Rome: "Your task, Roman, and do not forget it, will be to govern the peoples of the world in your empire." Of course, Aeneas would not live to see this future.

Landing in Latium

After years of wandering, Aeneas sailed to an area called Latium. This area is along the Tiber River in present-day Italy. Several groups of people were living in the region, including a group called the Latins. King Latinus was the leader of the Latins. Aeneas became friends with King Latinus and later married the king's daughter, Lavinia. But all did not go smoothly. Another man had wanted to marry Lavinia. When he heard that Lavinia married Aeneas instead, he began a war with Aeneas. The war ended when Aeneas defeated his **rival**.

A Timeless Story

The Aeneid is modeled after Homer's *Iliad* and *Odyssey*. Virgil thought *The Aeneid* would be to the Romans what Homer's *Iliad* and *Odyssey* were to the Greeks. He wrote *The Aeneid* while Augustus was emperor of the Roman Empire. Virgil's work praised Augustus. *The Aeneid* tells that Augustus was one of Aeneas's **descendants** and suggests that Augustus had many of Aeneas's heroic qualities. Aeneas was famous for his sense of duty and devotion to his country. His other important qualities included honor, sacrifice, and dedication.

The Aeneid is still read today, 2,000 years after it was written, because it is a beautiful poem. It also is read because it tells a timeless story about a human being who knew love, honor, defeat, disappointment, and duty. This story continues to touch the lives of people today. 📖

Reader's Theater
Presents

THE FALL OF THE REPUBLIC

Practice reading the script. When the script says, "PEOPLE OF ROME," everyone in the class joins in the reading. Read with expression! ➡️

ROLES

★ **NARRATOR 1**
★ **NARRATOR 2**
★ **DRUSUS**
★ **JULIA**
★ **CICERO**
★ **PEOPLE OF ROME (ALL)**

Narrator 1: Long ago, in 44 B.C., a young boy named Drusus and his sister Julia were walking through the ancient city of Rome.

Narrator 2: But Rome was a very large city and soon Drusus and Julia realized they were lost.

Drusus: Excuse me, but can anyone tell us where the Forum is?

Narrator 1: Everyone around them was in such a hurry that they wouldn't stop to answer his question. Drusus and Julia were getting worried.

Narrator 2: Then they saw an old man sitting on the side of the road.

Julia: I'm sorry sir, but we can't find our way to the Forum. Can you help us?

Narrator 1: Julia and Drusus didn't know it, but the old man's name was Cicero.

Narrator 2: Cicero was one of the greatest orators of all time.

Julia: Excuse me, sir, but can you help us?

▼ This is the Roman Forum today.

Cicero: Of course I can. But you're going in the wrong direction! The Forum is back the way you came, at the end of the road. Just go that way, and you'll find it soon enough.

Narrator 1: Julia and Drusus thanked him. They were about to walk away.

Narrator 2: But then they saw Cicero writing on a piece of parchment.

Drusus: Excuse me, but what's that you're writing?

Cicero: A speech. I'm going to talk to the Senate today.

Julia: The Senate! How exciting!

Cicero: Actually, it's a little scary.

Drusus: Why?

Cicero: Because they might not like what I have to say. You see, I have to warn them about Mark Antony.

Julia: Mark Antony? But my father says he's a hero! He got revenge against the people who killed Julius Caesar.

Cicero: Well, do you know why Caesar was killed?

Drusus: I suppose he must have had a lot of enemies.

Cicero: You're right. But he also had a lot of friends. In fact, the people of Rome loved him.

People of Rome: Hail Caesar! You have conquered many lands for Rome!

Cicero: They knew Caesar could protect them, so they gave him a lot of power.

People of Rome: We will make you our dictator! Then we'll always be safe.

▲ Julius Caesar was murdered because some Roman senators were afraid that he would make himself king of Rome.

Julia: Well, that makes sense. Why would anyone want to kill him?

Cicero: Because someone who has that much power is like a king.

Drusus: There aren't any kings in Rome! My mother says we're a republic.

Cicero: Do you know what a republic is?

Drusus: Not really.

Cicero: In a republic, what the people want is important. Even the Senate has to listen to what the people say.

Julia: What if they don't?

Cicero: Then we can veto their orders.

Julia: What's a veto?

Cicero: That's when the people stop the Senate from doing things they think are bad.

Drusus: That's a good way of doing things.

Cicero: I think so, too. But when Caesar became a dictator, the people couldn't veto him any more. He had too much power.

Drusus: I see! So that's why those people killed him.

Cicero: Yes.

Drusus: I still don't understand what this has to do with Mark Antony.

Cicero: Mark Antony is a lot like Caesar. He wants to be like a king, too. That's what I'm going to tell the Senate.

Julia: I'm on your side. We don't need any kings in Rome.

Cicero: I hope the Senate thinks so, too.

▲ Cicero was one of Rome's greatest orators.

Drusus: Well, we have to get to the Forum. Good luck!

Narrator 1: Drusus and Julia went on their way, and Cicero gave his speech to the Senate. Many people liked what Cicero said.

Narrator 2: It's true that Mark Antony never got the power he wanted, but pretty soon his friend Octavian did. Octavian became the first Roman emperor—which is a lot like being a king! 📖

ROMAN POETS

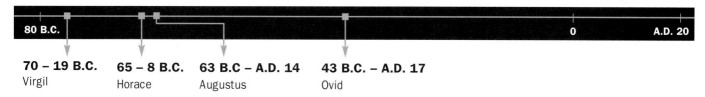

| 80 B.C. | | | | 0 | A.D. 20 |

70 – 19 B.C.
Virgil

65 – 8 B.C.
Horace

63 B.C – A.D. 14
Augustus

43 B.C. – A.D. 17
Ovid

Romans honored and admired men who wrote beautiful poems. Wealthy Roman leaders such as Augustus encouraged and supported writers. Roman poets wrote about many different topics. They praised the dignity of human beings and celebrated the pleasures of a peaceful and happy life. Roman poets also wrote about Roman gods and goddesses, but their central idea always had to do with human beings. Three of Rome's greatest poets, Horace, Virgil, and Ovid, lived during the golden age of Latin literature. During this period, Augustus was ruler of Rome.

Horace

Horace's family lived in the provinces outside the city of Rome. His family was not rich, but his parents had enough money to make sure that Horace had an excellent education. Augustus greatly admired Horace's poetry. One reason might be that Augustus was the hero in many of the poems. Horace's poems are filled with praise for Augustus and the period of peace that Augustus brought to Rome. Horace wrote the following lines about this idea:

HORACE
THE COMPLETE ODES
AND EPODES

> With Caesar [Augustus]
> the guardian of the state
> Not civil **rage** nor violence
> shall drive out peace,
> Nor **wrath** which **forges** swords
> And turns unhappy cities
> against each other.

forge: to give form or shape to; to create

rage: intense anger

wrath: intense anger

Virgil

Like Horace, Virgil came from a family of modest means. Virgil also had an excellent education. Virgil's early poems were about life in the countryside. Later, he began to write poems in praise of Augustus and the Augustan age.

The Aeneid

Virgil's most famous poem is *The Aeneid*. Virgil's poem tells the story of a Trojan hero, Aeneas, who travels throughout the Mediterranean. During his travels, Aeneas hears a prophecy about the future role of Romans in the world:

> Others will hammer out bronzes so gracefully that you would think that their statues breathed, and bring out the living features of a face from stone. They will plead cases better, better trace out the wanderings of the heavens with a compass, and name the rising stars. But you, Roman, remember these are your skills: to govern the peoples with power and to establish the habit of peace …

Ovid

Ovid's most famous work is *Metamorphoses*, a word that means "changes." In *Metamorphoses*, Ovid wrote:

> Wherever Rome's influence extends, over the lands it has civilized, I will be spoken, on people's lips: and, famous through all the ages, if there is truth in poet's prophecies,—vivam— I shall live.

At first, Ovid was popular with Augustus. However, his work made fun of Roman marriage, Roman warfare, and Roman life. Augustus did not think this was very funny. He sent Ovid away from Rome. Ovid spent his last years living in a Roman province far away from the city he loved. □

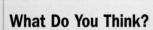

What Do You Think?

1. According to Virgil, what task did Romans have to accomplish?

2. What does the phrase "nor wrath which forges swords" mean?

3. Choose a phrase from Horace, Virgil, or Ovid's writing and explain what it means in your own words.

IT'S THE ECONOMY

As they gained new territories, ancient Romans enjoyed great wealth and new riches. They also had a huge influence on people throughout the Roman Empire. Romans gained this **economic prosperity** and exerted this influence for many reasons. Two key factors were the trade routes and the use of money.

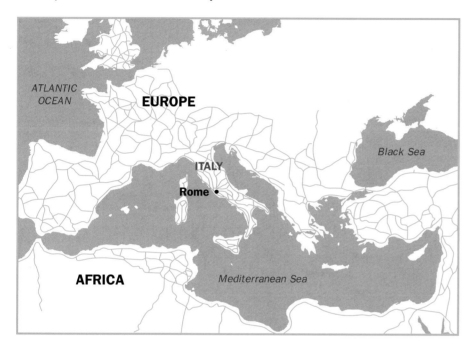

◀ At the height of the Roman Empire, around A.D. 200, a network of about 50,000 miles of roads spanned the Roman Empire. Towns often developed in the places where two roads came together.

Great Builders

Romans were great organizers and builders. Wherever they went, they built temples, aqueducts, baths, and public buildings. And, of course, the Romans also built roads. To build all these structures, many workers and lots of building materials were needed.

Trade Routes

The roads the Romans built connected all parts of the Roman Empire. These roads allowed people to trade goods from every corner of the empire. The trade brought people with different goods and different ideas into contact with one another. In this way, people exchanged both goods and ideas. This trade had a positive effect on the economy of the Roman Empire.

economic prosperity: growth and expansion of a country's ability to produce, develop, and manage wealth

circulate: to move around, as from person to person or place to place

coinage: a system of metal currency (money)

What Do You Think?

1. What two factors were important in Rome's economic growth?

2. What was placed on Roman coins?

3. How are ancient Roman coins like coins we use today? How are they different?

4. Is there a world coinage today? Explain your answer.

Roman Coins

Romans began making coins as early as 280 B.C. They got many of their ideas about coins from the ancient Greeks. Like the ancient Greeks, the Romans carefully planned and designed their coins. They knew that people all over the Mediterranean world would see the coins as something of value, but also something that showed the power and ideas of Rome itself. For this reason, Roman coins showed images of Roman leaders. Some women were portrayed on coins, but most showed images of men.

A World Coinage

Roman emperors wanted to have pictures of themselves circulating throughout the Roman Empire. It was certainly easier to transport coins around the empire rather than statues! One historian called Rome's currency "a world **coinage**" and said, "Perhaps no coins **circulated** so widely and in such large quantities as the gold and silver of Augustus bearing the figures of his grandsons. ..." Roman leaders used the back of the coins to place news about what was going on in the empire or moral principles. For example, a coin might show a province that was conquered or have a god or a symbol of a Roman value or tradition. 📖

▲ Ancient Romans placed official announcements and government information on coins. This way, people throughout the Roman Empire could keep up with the latest news. More importantly, the Roman government could present people with the information it wanted them to know about. Thousands or even hundreds of thousands of people might see a Roman coin as it circulated throughout the Roman Empire.

ROME EXPANDS

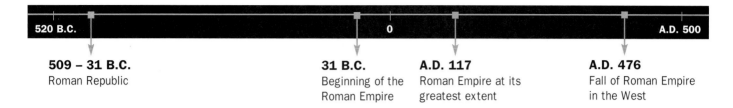

520 B.C.		0		A.D. 500

509 – 31 B.C.
Roman Republic

31 B.C.
Beginning of the
Roman Empire

A.D. 117
Roman Empire at its
greatest extent

A.D. 476
Fall of Roman Empire
in the West

According to an old proverb, "Rome wasn't built in a day." Over a long period of time, the Romans built impressive buildings, aqueducts, roads, and bridges. At first, however, there were no huge forums or paved roads. In fact, Rome probably looked a lot like many other small settlements along the Tiber River. However, by A.D. 117, the Romans had built an extraordinary city and ruled a vast empire. Why was Rome so successful in conquering other lands? Who did the Romans conquer?

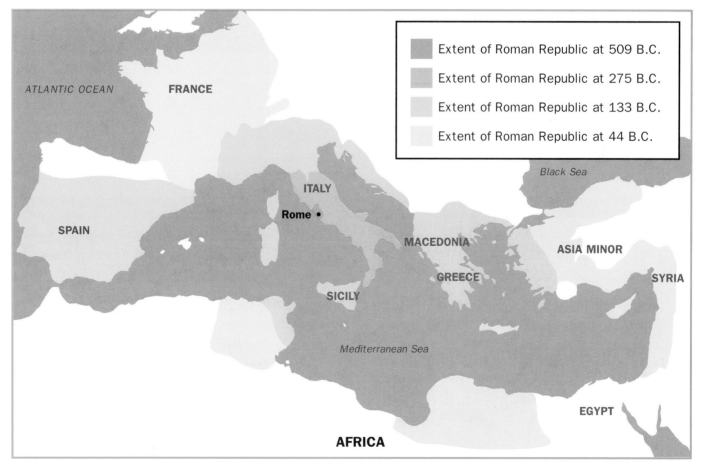

Extent of Roman Republic at 509 B.C.

Extent of Roman Republic at 275 B.C.

Extent of Roman Republic at 133 B.C.

Extent of Roman Republic at 44 B.C.

▲ Rome conquered vast territories during the time it was a republic.

Conquering the Mediterranean World

By 275 B.C., the Romans had conquered Etruria, a region in Italy where the Etruscans lived. Then the Romans turned their attention to the territories surrounding the Mediterranean Sea. This region is sometimes called the "Mediterranean world." During the three Punic Wars, between 264 B.C. and 146 B.C., Rome invaded Sicily, Sardinia, Corsica, Spain, and Carthage (in northern Africa). This gave the Romans control of much of the western Mediterranean.

With armies of well-trained soldiers, Rome went on to conquer other territories in the eastern Mediterranean region. By 133 B.C., Rome had conquered Macedonia, Greece, and part of Asia Minor. The Romans did not stop there. During the period of the Roman Republic, Rome continued to expand control over parts of northern Africa and southern France or Gaul, as it was known in those days. The Romans also expanded further east and conquered Syria and Jerusalem. By 44 B.C., the Romans controlled a large part of the Mediterranean world.

▲ Rome was successful conquering many territories because it had an army of well-trained soldiers.

Expansion During the Roman Empire

During the reign of Augustus (27 B.C.–A.D. 14), Rome expanded its empire even further. The Romans conquered all of North Africa and territories as far away as the Red Sea and Black Sea. After Augustus's death, the Romans conquered Britain in A.D. 43. The Roman Empire reached its greatest size under the Roman Emperor Trajan in A.D. 117. During his reign, Rome's territories extended further east to include both Armenia and Mesopotamia.

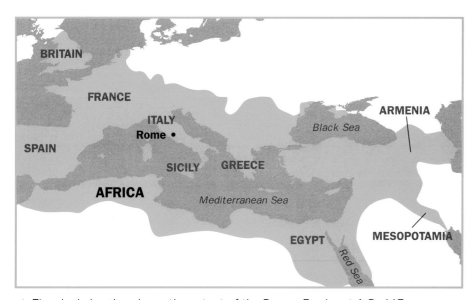

▲ The shaded region shows the extent of the Roman Empire at A.D. 117.

Successful Conquerors and Rulers

The Romans were able to conquer so many territories because they had a strong and well-trained military. And, after they conquered new territories, the Romans treated the people they conquered in ways that were very different from earlier conquerors. Instead of punishing them or making them slaves, the Romans allowed some of the leaders of the conquered groups to become Roman citizens. The Romans allowed the leaders and people who lived in these conquered territories to continue with their own traditions and laws. The Romans even encouraged the conquered people to be a part of Rome's success. All of the people in the territories Rome conquered had to pay taxes. The men were expected to serve in the military during times of war. In return, Rome offered the conquered people their protection. Sometimes, the Romans shared some of the riches they gained from wars with the people they had conquered.

border: the edge of an area that separates one region from another

flourish: to grow well; to thrive or do well

Germanic people: people from the northern part of Europe who have a common language and cultural traditions

What Do You Think?

1. What is the "Mediterranean world"?

2. What did the Romans do that was different from earlier conquerors?

3. Do you think wars were a good or bad thing for Rome? Why?

4. In your own words, tell what the old saying, "Rome wasn't built in a day" means.

An End to Expansion

As the eastern half of the empire was **flourishing**, the western half faced many problems. One of the greatest problems was that groups of **Germanic people** from the north and east began pouring into the empire. The Romans called these people "barbarians" because they did not speak Latin or have the same culture and traditions as the Romans. Some of these groups simply wanted to find a place to live. Others invaded because they wanted to create their own empires. The Roman Empire had become so large that it was hard to defend itself against these groups. Instead of conquering new lands, the Roman army now focused mainly on defending its **borders**. 📖

▲ "Barbarians" entering the Roman Empire caused problems for the Roman government. The Roman army fought these groups to defend the borders of the Roman Empire.

OUR LATIN ROOTS

Latium is an area in Italy that is south of Rome. When groups of people began to move into present-day Italy, some settled in this area. The word *Latin* refers to Latium and its people and culture. It also refers to their language. The Romans who established the city of Rome spoke Latin. Lucretia and Cincinnatus spoke Latin, and so did Cato the Elder, Cicero, Julius Caesar, and Marcus Aurelius. Latin was the language of ancient Rome.

Today, Latin is called a dead language because no one speaks it. However, many modern languages, including Italian, Spanish, French, and Portuguese, are all closely related to Latin. For example, *aqua* is the Latin word for "water." Speakers of Italian, Spanish, French, and Portuguese probably know that.

▲ Today, Lazio is the name used for the region in Italy that previously was known as Latium.

English Language, Latin Roots

Many English words also have Latin roots. In fact, more than half the words in the English language have Latin roots. *Familia* is the Latin word for "family." Was that too easy? What do you think the Latin word *libris* means? Did you guess "library"? If so, you're right! Knowing Latin words can help you figure out the meaning of many English words. You can find a short Latin-English glossary on the next page. Count how many Latin words you recognize. 📖

Latin Phrases/Latin Wisdom

Latin	English
Non multa sed multum.	Quality, not quantity.
Scientia est potestas.	Knowledge is power.
Spectemur agendo.	Let us be judged by how we act.
Verbum sat sapienti.	A word to the wise.
Veritas vos liberabit.	The truth shall set you free.
Carpe diem.	Seize the day.

What Do You Think?

1. Where does the word *Latin* come from?

2. Why is Latin called a dead language today?

3. How can knowing Latin help you understand English?

4. Choose one of the Latin phrases listed on the left and tell what it means in your own words. Give an example of the meaning of the phrase you chose.

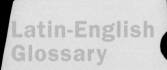

Latin-English Glossary

advocate: skilled speaker

amphitheater: arena

anno: year

aqua: water

atrium: a main reception area

bene: good

caldarium: "hot room" in the baths

canis: dog

caput: head

cena: dinner

circus: circle

codex: book

cognito: I think

de facto: in fact

deus: god

corpus: body

cremation: burning of a body

cubiculum: bedroom

ego: I

equus: horse

ergo: therefore

est: is

exempli gratia (e.g.): for example

frigidarium: "cold room" in the baths

habitat: the place where a plant or animal lives

hortus: garden

index: sign or indicator

iridis: rainbow

legere: to read

libris: library

litterator: elementary school teacher

locus: place

magnus: great; very good

mare: sea

memento: something that causes one to remember

mens: mind

murus: wall

musica: music

non: not

nota: note; remember

opus: work

orbus: world

per capita: by or for each unit of the population

per diem: a daily allowance

post mortem: after death

potestas: power

prima: first

sanus: healthy

servi: slaves

SPQR (Senatus Populusque Romanus): the Senate and people of Rome

status quo: the current state of being; unchanged

stilus: pen

sub poena: under penalty of law

tempus: time

urbis: city

vice versa: in reverse order

MARBLE AND CEMENT, ARCHES AND DOMES

Ancient Romans borrowed many ideas about architecture from the ancient Greeks. Romans thought the Greek architectural style showed harmony, order, balance, simplicity, and beauty. Romans also added their own ideas. They introduced the "arch" and the "dome." Romans used traditional building materials such as marble, but they also used new materials such as cement.

Classical Style

Today, we generally refer to the style of ancient Roman and Greek architecture as "classical" architecture. Some very distinctive features tell you a building is built in the "classical" style. For one thing, classical buildings are usually very big. Classical buildings also often have columns and arches. People often describe classical buildings with words such as balanced, ordered, in harmony, and simple yet beautiful.

Neoclassical Style

America's founders were very impressed with the political ideas of the Roman Republic. They agreed with the idea that people should elect their own leaders. They also liked the Romans' ideas about architecture. They were attracted to the harmony, order, balance, simplicity, and beauty of classical architecture. Many of the most important buildings in the United States today were influenced by the classical style. These buildings are called "neoclassical," which means "new classical."

Columns

The Greeks and Romans used columns in their architecture. A column is an upright post or pillar. Some columns in classical buildings help support the weight of the building. Others are simply there to make the building more beautiful. Columns can be smooth or they can have flutes, which are long parallel grooves. Some columns are set on bases.

▲ The United States Capitol building in Washington, D.C. is an example of neoclassical style.

Capitals

The top part of a column is called the capital. Capitals can be very simple or very elaborate. The chart below shows the three major types of columns that originated in ancient Greece. Ancient Romans used these Greek styles and also created new ones. The easiest way to tell the types of columns apart is to look at the capitals.

COLUMNS AND CAPITALS

One way to remember the order of columns (Doric, Ionic, and Corinthian) is to put them in order according to the number of syllables in their titles.

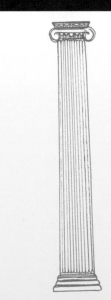

Doric has just two syllables. Doric is the plainest style. The Doric column has a very plain capital and no base.	Ionic has three syllables. The Ionic style is more elaborate. The Ionic column has a fancier capital. The twirls on it are called "volutes." The Ionic column is set on a base. This illustration shows a fluted column.	Finally, the Corinthian style is the most elaborate. And, of course, it also has the most syllables—four! The Corinthian column has a very elaborate capital. Instead of volutes (the twirls), it often has a flower pattern. This type of column is set on a base. This illustration shows a fluted column.
DORIC	**IONIC**	**CORINTHIAN**

Arches and Vaults

Ancient Romans used arches in their buildings. An arch is a curved structure at the top of an opening or a support. The Romans got their idea for the arch from the Etruscans. However, they created new ways to use it. They also developed a new kind of arch, a covered arch structure called a vault.

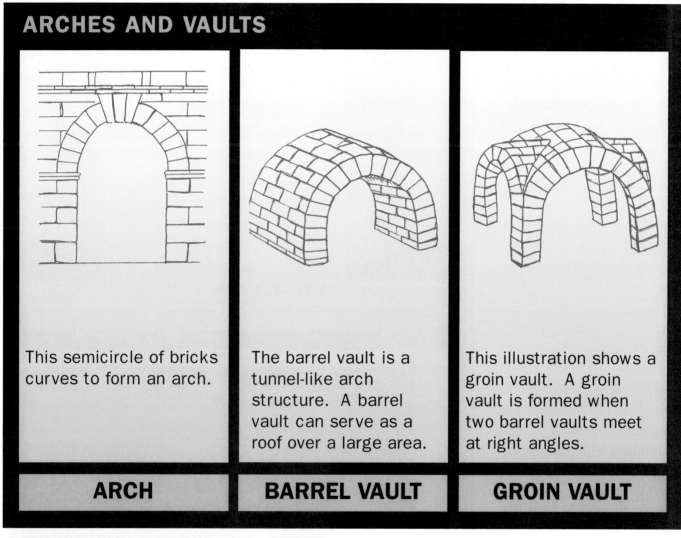

ARCHES AND VAULTS

This semicircle of bricks curves to form an arch.

ARCH

The barrel vault is a tunnel-like arch structure. A barrel vault can serve as a roof over a large area.

BARREL VAULT

This illustration shows a groin vault. A groin vault is formed when two barrel vaults meet at right angles.

GROIN VAULT

◀ The Arch of Constantine was built in A.D. 315 in honor of Emperor Constantine's victory in battle.

What Do You Think?

1. What kinds of building materials did ancient Romans use?

2. Where did ancient Romans get most of their ideas about architecture?

3. Choose an American building in the neoclassical style. Discuss how this building was influenced by Roman ideas about architecture. What elements make it "neoclassical"?

4. Choose a building in your community (e.g., your school, a nearby store, or local library) that is built in a different architectural style. What words would you use to describe this building? How is it different from the neoclassical building? Which building style do you prefer? Explain your answer.

Domes

The dome is a variation of the arch. The Romans are legendary for their engineering skill in creating monumental domes for buildings. 📖

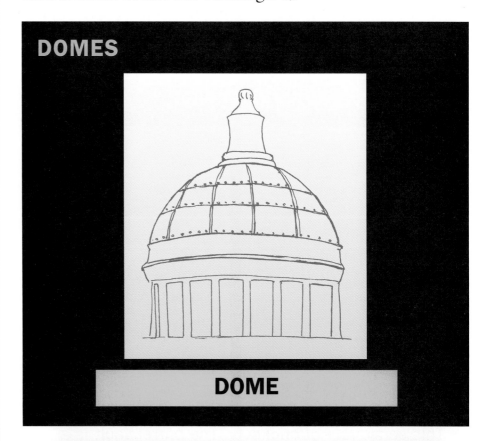

DOMES

DOME

▲ The Pantheon in Italy is one of the most beautiful buildings in the world. This photograph shows the interior of the dome.

MOSAICS
Beautiful and Practical Roman Art

Art was important in ancient Rome. One of the most beautiful forms of art created in ancient Rome was the mosaic—a picture made of small pieces of colored stone such as marble. Roman artists also used small pieces of glass, broken pieces of pottery, and other materials to create mosaics.

▲ This drawing shows a Roman man making a mosaic.

Skilled Artisans

The people who created these mosaics were skilled artisans. They had different ways to create mosaics. One method was to set tiny stones in wet cement. This required them to work fast and to know what they were doing!

Why Mosaics?

Ancient Romans hired artisans to create beautiful mosaics in their homes. They did this because they thought mosaics made their homes more beautiful. Romans admired beauty and having a beautiful home was important to them.

What Do You Think?

1. What is a mosaic?

2. Why do you think archaeologists and other experts are interested in mosaics?

3. What clues can mosaics reveal about the lives of ancient Romans?

Showing Roman Life

Archaeologists and other experts have found many ancient Roman mosaics. Some of these mosaics show scenes from Greek or Roman myths. For example, a mosaic in Rome shows a goddess riding a leopard. Other mosaics show Roman life. A mosaic in Pompeii, for example, shows a barking dog and the Latin phrase, *cave canem*. This phrase means "beware of dog."

From Floors to Walls and Ceilings

During early ancient Roman times, middle-class and wealthy Romans decorated the floors in their homes with mosaics. Mosaics made their homes more beautiful. They offered another advantage as well. Mosaic floors were easier to clean than dirt floors or rugs! Later Romans also placed mosaics on walls and ceilings.

Public Art

Mosaics were not only important in private homes. Mosaics were used in public buildings and churches. Some of the most beautiful mosaics were created in the Eastern Roman Empire—the Byzantine Empire—when Justinian was emperor. He and his wife Theodora were strong Christians. They hired artisans to create beautiful mosaics showing religious themes.

Today, you can see many mosaics created during ancient times in cities throughout the Mediterranean region. 📖

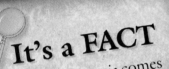

It's a FACT

The word *mosaic* comes from a Greek word *mouseious*, which means "belonging to the Muses." The Muses were the nine daughters of the Greek god Zeus. Each of the Muses was thought to inspire a different art or science.

▲ Erato is the Muse of love poetry.

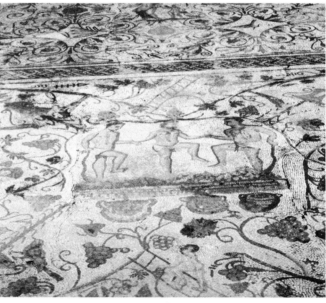

▲ This is a Roman mosaic. Romans got many of their ideas about mosaics from the ancient Greeks.

(A ROMAN) FATHER
Knows Best!

What makes a family? Today, we might say a family is a group of people who love one another. American families come in all shapes and sizes. You could say the same thing about Roman families in ancient times.

Family = People in the Household

Romans had definite ideas about what made a family. It included everyone who lived in a Roman household. The father was the head of the Roman family, which included his wife and their unmarried children. The Roman family also included any freed persons, slaves, and adopted children who lived in the household. Sometimes, relatives of the husband and wife lived in the household, but that was uncommon.

In general, Roman families were small. Usually, only two or three children survived beyond childhood. Parents seemed happy to have both sons and daughters. Parents arranged marriages for children when they were young. In general, girls married when they were 12-18 years old and boys married when they were 19-21 years old. But there were many exceptions!

▲ Roman girls usually married when they were very young. By law, however, they had to be at least 12 years old.

The Paterfamilias

The father in a Roman family was called the paterfamilias. He had almost complete authority over everyone in the household. The father could decide how the children would be educated and who they would marry. He could decide how they should be punished. Even adult sons with children of their own still had no independent legal status or property rights until after the death of the paterfamilias.

The paterfamilias could buy and sell the slaves. As the head of the family, he performed ceremonies in the family home to honor Roman gods. He could make all the decisions about the family's property and business. By tradition, he was expected to consult with older relatives on important matters, but he did not have to follow their advice.

▲ The Roman father had authority over everyone in the household.

Roman Mothers and Children

We do not know much about the lives of Roman women and children from their own writings. Historians have studied the messages Roman women placed on the **gravestones** of their husbands who died. One of these messages said, "To my sweet, well-deserving husband." Another said, "To my well-deserving husband with whom I lived without a **quarrel**."

Legally, Roman women and children had an **inferior status** to the paterfamilias. However, in practice, women seemed to have a lot of independence. A woman was still a member of her father's family. This meant she did not depend completely on her husband for financial support. Some Roman women were very wealthy. Both men and women could decide to divorce. 📖

gravestone: a stone marker that is set on or near the place where a person is buried; a tombstone

inferior status: lower in rank; less important

quarrel: argument

What Do You Think?

1. How much authority did the paterfamilias have in ancient Rome?

2. In ancient Rome, who usually married earlier, girls or boys?

3. How are ancient Roman families like families in the United States today?

4. How can reading messages on gravestones tell about life in ancient Rome? What do the messages in this story tell us about family life in ancient Rome?

▲ Women in ancient Rome seemed to have a lot of independence.

The Lives of
ROMAN WOMEN

How do we know about women's lives in ancient Rome? Archaeologists have found artifacts that give us some clues. We also have writings that tell about the women of ancient Rome.

Artifacts

Some artifacts tell us about the lives of wealthy Roman women. We know they bathed often either at home or in the public baths. They used mirrors, beauty creams, combs, tweezers, hairpins, hair coloring, and make-up. The Roman poet Ovid wrote a poem called "On Making Up a Woman's Face." It tells us about Roman women's concern about their appearance. Rich Roman women could afford expensive clothes, gold, and jewels such as opals, pearls, and emeralds. They wore earrings, necklaces, bracelets, and rings.

A Roman Woman's Love for Jewelry

Petronius, a Roman writer, made fun of a Roman woman's love for jewelry in a story he wrote: "The next thing I knew, Fortunata was undoing the bracelets … Then she undid her anklets, and finally her hair net … Trimalchio, who was observing this by-play with interest, ordered all her jewelry to be brought to him. 'Gentlemen,' he said, 'I want you to see the chains and fetters our women load themselves with … she must be wearing six and a half pounds of solid gold.'"

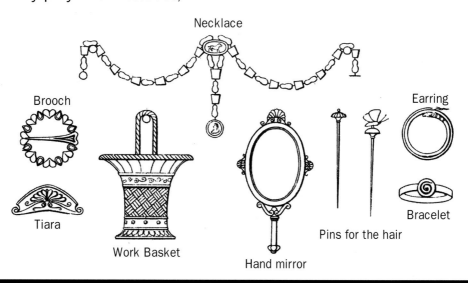

Necklace

Brooch

Earring

Tiara

Work Basket

Hand mirror

Pins for the hair

Bracelet

▲ Roman women did not leave many writings that tell about their lives.

Writings

Roman women did not leave many writings that tell about their lives. Archaeologists have found short messages Roman women wrote for their husbands' gravestones. These messages said things such as, "To my dear husband." One message said, "To my well-deserving husband with whom I lived without a quarrel."

Most of the written information we have about the lives of ancient Roman women comes from men. In A.D. 21, the Roman Senate discussed whether wives should go with their husbands when they went to govern the provinces. One senator said, "It is a good thing, a cause for rejoicing that much of the ancient harshness [toward women] has changed. … when [the Roman officials] come home after their efforts, what more honorable comforts can they enjoy than those provided by a wife?"

Family and Education

Most Roman women were married. Married women were responsible for raising their children and supervising the family's meals. They also performed some religious ceremonies. In wealthy families, Roman mothers helped make decisions about their children's education.

Many upper-class women were well educated. Like upper-class men, they went to school or were tutored at home at least for a few years. They learned reading, writing, and arithmetic, as well as spinning and weaving. Some women also studied history, geography, and science. Poor Roman women and slaves did not go to school. Children were not required to go to school. School was not free.

Independence

Some Roman women, especially women from wealthy families, had a great deal of independence. For example, after her husband's death in 154 B.C., Cornelia, daughter of the great Roman general Scipio Africanus, decided not to remarry. Instead, she managed her family's finances and helped guide her children's political careers.

A few women, called the Vestal Virgins, played an important role in Roman religious ceremonies. They served the goddess Vesta for 30 years, from the time they were seven or eight years old. After their service they could marry, but few did.

Public Life

Patrician and plebeian women were Roman citizens, but they did not have the right to vote or have a public career in government. Still, many Roman women had an important influence on Roman politics, law, and culture.

Julia Domna, for example, married the Roman Emperor Septimius Severus in A.D. 185. She brought artists and scholars to the royal court. Her interest in knowledge and her ability to reason earned her the nickname, "Julia the Philosopher." When her son, Caracalla, became emperor in A.D. 211, she played a larger role in governing the Roman Empire.

Empress Theodora

Empress Theodora played an important role helping her husband Justinian rule the Eastern Roman Empire. Theodora was an actress from a poor, circus family. During this time, people looked down on actresses. Justinian fell in love with her and had the laws changed so they could marry. Theodora was intelligent and had great courage. When a group of people began a riot in Constantinople in A.D. 532, Justinian's advisors told him to quickly leave the city. Theodora disagreed. She said, "If you wish to flee, well and good. You have the money. The ships are ready. The sea is clear. But I shall stay." Justinian decided to stay, the riots ended, and he continued to rule the Byzantine Empire. 📖

What Do You Think?

1. How were the lives of wealthy Roman women different from poor women or slaves?

2. Why do we know more about the lives of wealthy Roman women?

3. How do the lives of ancient Roman women compare with the lives of women today?

▲ The Empress Theodora played an important part in helping her husband rule the Eastern Roman Empire.

RELIGION IN THE ROMAN EMPIRE

A.D. 60

A.D. 150

A.D. 70
Romans destroy the Jewish
temple in Jerusalem

A.D. 135
Romans no longer allow
Jews to live in Jerusalem

Ancient Romans worshiped many different gods. They got many of their ideas about gods and religion from the ancient Greeks. Like the Greeks, ancient Romans believed their gods kept order in the world.

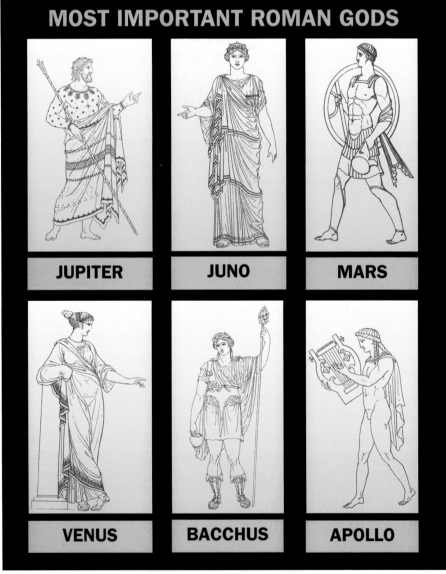

MOST IMPORTANT ROMAN GODS

| JUPITER | JUNO | MARS |

| VENUS | BACCHUS | APOLLO |

▲ This chart shows some of the important Roman gods.

Super Human Beings?

Ancient Romans thought their gods had much greater power than human beings. However, they also thought their gods were like human beings in some ways. For example, they believed their gods argued with one another, got married, had children, laughed, and played tricks. The most important Roman gods were Jupiter, his wife Juno, Mars (the god of war), Venus (the goddess of love), Bacchus (the god of wine), and Apollo (the god of light, music, and poetry).

Household Gods

Each family also had its own household gods. Ancient Rome did not have a separate group of priests. The father in each family—the paterfamilias—performed rituals to honor the family's ancestors and household gods. The wife also performed ceremonies to honor the household gods.

▼ The Roman government built many temples to the gods. The Temple of Venus, built in A.D. 123, was designed by Emperor Hadrian.

festival: celebration, event, fair

forged: faked; counterfeit

State-Supported Religion

Religion for ancient Romans was not so much about having a personal relationship with the gods. Ancient Romans thought of religion more as a public activity that brought the citizens together. That is why it was common for the Roman government to build temples to the gods and to support religious ceremonies and **festivals**. Important Roman officials were responsible for performing religious rituals for the entire state. These Romans were elected to religious offices.

Cults

Some Romans worshiped specific gods. They came together in a group to honor a particular god such as Apollo or Bacchus. We sometimes use the word *cult* to describe these religious groups. The Roman historian Livy (59 B.C.–A.D. 17) did not approve of the cult of Bacchus. He said:

Analyze the Source!

What did Livy mean? On what basis was he criticizing this cult? What does this tell us about the importance of authority and order in Roman life?

"The cult was also a source of false witnesses, **forged** documents and wills, ... dealing also in poisons and in wholesale murders."

The Roman Senate tried to stop this cult. It ordered the destruction of all shrines to Bacchus. Later, as the Roman Empire expanded, other cults developed. The cult of the Egyptian goddess Isis and the cult of Mithras, the Persian god of light and truth, became popular.

Judaism

Jews lived in areas throughout the Roman Empire. They had many settlements in the eastern territories that had been established in Greek times. Pompey, a powerful Roman general, allowed Jews to come to Rome from the eastern provinces. Julius Caesar allowed Jews to worship freely. Augustus also respected Jewish holy days and places of worship.

Problems between Jews and Romans

Later, however, problems arose between Jews and Romans. Some later Roman emperors tried to make Jews worship Roman gods. Some rulers allowed Jewish places of worship to be destroyed. When Jews in Jerusalem rebelled in A.D. 70, the Romans conquered the city. They destroyed the temple there and forced most Jews to leave the area. By A.D. 135, the Roman government said no Jews could live in Jerusalem or Judea. This forced exile is called the Diaspora, which comes from a Greek word that means "to scatter" or "to disperse."

Over time, Jews spread to all parts of the Mediterranean world, including Europe, North Africa, and beyond. Many went to Spain. A large number settled in Germany. Wherever they went, they usually organized themselves in small communities within larger cities. Jews continued to follow their own religious traditions.

Christianity—Belief in One God

Christians, like Jews, strongly believed that there was only one God. Generally, the Roman government tolerated different religious beliefs. However, Romans did not tolerate religious ideas that threatened Roman authority and order. Many Romans began to see Jesus and his followers as troublemakers. They thought Christians did not respect the Roman gods. This was a very serious issue for the Romans because they believed that as long as their gods were worshiped properly, Rome would be protected.

Like Jews, Christians believed in only one God and refused to worship the Roman gods. Romans believed that this threatened the welfare of Rome. As a result, Jesus and many of his followers were persecuted and killed. However, as Christians traveled throughout the Roman Empire, they shared their religious ideas with all the people they visited. Christianity appealed to many people—men and women, rich and poor, free persons and slaves, and Romans and Jews. It offered people forgiveness for their sins and a life in heaven after death. Soon, Christianity spread to Europe and other Roman territories, especially in the eastern parts of the empire. By the early 300s, more and more people in the Roman Empire became Christians, including Roman emperors in both the western and eastern parts of the empire.

What Do You Think?

1. Where did ancient Romans get many of their ideas about religion?

2. In ancient Rome, how were religious leaders chosen?

3. Why did the Roman government support religious activities? Do governments today support religious activities? Why or why not?

▲ Romans sometimes put condemned Christians into arenas to fight lions.

JESUS OF NAZARETH

| 100 B.C. | | 0 | | A.D. 40 |

63 B.C. – A.D. 14
Augustus

c. A.D. 4
Jesus is born

c. A.D. 37
Jesus is killed

Jesus is a **complex** historical and religious figure. For Christians who believe that the Bible is the word of God, the life of Jesus is very clear and easy to understand. For those who do not see this source as completely factual, the life of Jesus is more complicated.

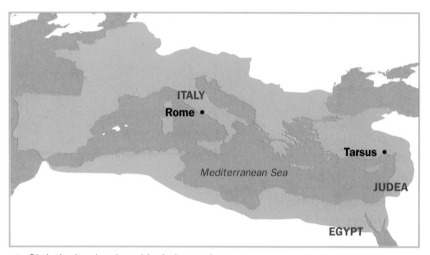

▲ Christianity developed in Judea and soon spread to other parts of the Roman Empire (shaded area).

It's a FACT
Augustus was the emperor of Rome when Jesus was born. Tiberius was emperor when Jesus was killed.

Written Accounts of Jesus

Most of what we know about Jesus comes from what others wrote about him. One way to understand his life is to look at the writings of these people. Some of the people who wrote about Jesus held traditional Roman beliefs in many gods. Some of the people who wrote about him were Jews. They believed in one God, but they didn't believe that Jesus was his son. Others who wrote about Jesus were Christians who believed Jesus was the son of God. Examining the writings of these different groups provides information about the life of Jesus.

What Romans Said about Jesus

When Christianity began, Romans controlled most of the Mediterranean world. To most Romans, however, Christianity was a just a small Jewish sect. Romans saw Christians as troublemakers. They thought Christians did not respect Roman gods. Several Romans shared this view in their writings. For example, the Roman historian Tacitus (A.D. 56–120) wrote about the death of Jesus by order of the Roman official Pontius Pilate. Tacitus described how Christianity developed in Judea and how it later became popular both in Judea and in Rome.

Early Christian Beliefs

Other Roman writers such as Suetonius and Pliny the Younger also wrote about Jesus and the early Christians. From their perspective, Romans should have gotten rid of Christianity at the very beginning.

However, Pliny commented on how Christians were strong in their beliefs. These sources provide evidence about early Christians and their beliefs. We can conclude from this evidence that Jesus lived. We also can conclude that many people worshiped Jesus as the Jewish Messiah (or "savior") described in the Bible.

What Jews Said about Jesus

Flavius Josephus, a Jewish historian, wrote about the life of Jesus. Josephus lived during the time that Jesus was alive, but he did not leave an eyewitness account of Jesus. His writings include information about John the Baptist, a follower of Jesus. Josephus also wrote briefly about the religious teachings of Jesus based on information from Jesus's life. Josephus did not become a Christian himself. Historians disagree whether the accounts of Josephus are true. His writings about Jesus's life are still the subject of argument.

What Christians Said about Jesus

Paul of Tarsus (also called St. Paul) wrote four letters that contain information about the life of Jesus. According to Paul's writings, Jesus was born to a poor family during the reign of the Roman emperor Augustus. At the time of his birth, his parents, Mary and Joseph, were traveling to Bethlehem to be counted in the **census**.

The Christian Bible tells many stories about the life of Jesus. Some stories tell about Jesus as a young man. They tell how Jesus used stories to teach people what he believed was important. One story was about "the golden rule," treating others as you would have them treat you. Another story was about the importance of loving others as you love yourself.

census: an official count of a population

complex: not easy; complicated

▼ Christians celebrate the birth of Jesus on December 25, but no one knows the exact date on which he was born.

▲ The Romans sentenced Jesus to death.

A Message

According to Christians, as more people came to listen to him, Jesus asked several men to help spread his message. These men were his disciples or followers. As the message of Jesus became more popular, Romans became concerned that the people of the Roman Empire would not worship Roman gods. Romans believed that worshiping their gods kept Rome safe and strong.

Jesus's Death and His Legacy

When Jesus was about 33 years old, he led a group of his followers into Jerusalem. They were going to celebrate the Jewish festival of Passover. Shortly after he arrived in Jerusalem, the Romans arrested him and sentenced him to death. He was nailed to a cross where he died. According to the New Testament in the Christian Bible, Jesus rose from the dead. Christians celebrate this event as Easter.

Christian Beliefs

People who follow Jesus's teachings—Christians—believe that Jesus is the son of God. They believe in salvation. This is the idea that all people can be forgiven for their sins. Christians believe in the Trinity. This is the idea that God, Jesus, and the Holy Spirit are unified into one divine God. Christians believe that three days after Jesus was killed, he was resurrected. In other words, he was raised from the dead and returned to life. Christians believe that all the dead will rise again and that there is life in heaven after death.

The ideas Jesus taught have had an important influence on people throughout the world. Today, Christianity is one of the world's largest and most influential religions. 📖

What Do You Think?

1. What sources provide information about Jesus?

2. In what part of the world did Jesus live? Who governed this area?

3. Why do you think historians would want to know what different groups of people said about Jesus?

4. Other figures in history, such as Confucius, believed in the "golden rule." Why do you think people in different parts of the world share some common beliefs?

THE TEACHINGS OF JESUS

0	A.D. 70

c. A.D. 4 – 37
Jesus

c. A.D. 67
Peter is killed

Jesus preached a message of peace and love of God in the Roman province of Judea. He taught that people should treat one another as they wished to be treated. He also taught that there was only one God and that it was important to love God and your neighbor. Many people became interested in and excited about his ideas. Over time, his teachings began to spread throughout the Roman Empire.

Was Jesus the Messiah?

In the Jewish religion, some people were thought to be interpreters of messages from God. Such people are called prophets. The Jewish prophets, including Abraham and Moses, said that God would send a Messiah to save them. The word *messiah* means "savior." Some Jews believed that Jesus was the Messiah that had been promised to them.

However, not all Jews thought Jesus was the true Messiah. Some thought his teachings were in conflict with their Jewish beliefs. Other people thought his ideas threatened the authority of the Roman Empire. Pontius Pilate, the Roman governor of the province, put Jesus on trial and sentenced him to death. The Romans thought this action would be the end of his teachings.

▲ Many people in the Roman Empire were interested in Jesus's ideas.

basilica: a church that has two rows of columns dividing the interior space; from the Greek word *basilike*, which means "royal court" or "royal portico"

blot: to wipe away

ignorance: a lack of knowledge

repent: to feel regret for past actions or wrongdoing

▲ Jesus had 12 disciples—Peter (or Simon), Andrew, James, John, Philip, Bartholomew, Thomas, Matthew, James (the younger), Thaddeus, Simon, and Judas.

What Do You Think?

1. What did the Romans expect would happen when they sentenced Jesus to die?

2. What do we call people who follow the teachings of Jesus?

3. Why do people want to share their religious ideas with others?

Jesus's Ideas Spread

Many people continued to believe Jesus was the Messiah the prophets said would come. They believed there was a kingdom in heaven for people who believed in him. Peter, one of Jesus's followers, began to lead these people. They became known as Christians.

Peter and others, especially Paul of Tarsus, traveled all over the Roman Empire telling people about Jesus and his teachings. Christians were eager to share their beliefs with others.

You can read on the next page an excerpt from the Christian Bible. Historians believe this represents Peter's teaching about Jesus. In this passage, Peter is saying that the people who put Jesus to death did not know any better. 📖

... I know that you [Pontius Pilate] acted in **ignorance**, as did also your rulers.

But what God foretold by the mouth of all the prophets, and that his Christ should suffer, he thus fulfilled.

Repent therefore, and turn again, that your sins may be **blotted** out, that times of refreshing may come from the presence of the Lord, and that he may send the Christ appointed for you, Jesus, whom heaven must receive until the time for establishing all that God spoke by the mouth of his holy prophets from of old.

Analyze the Source!

Read the passage and tell in your own words what Peter was saying. From this passage, how would you describe Peter's attitude toward Pontius Pilate and the Romans?

▲ This is a photograph of St. Peter's Basilica in Rome.

SIMON PETER—DISCIPLE

Peter was one of Jesus's 12 disciples. Peter's name was originally Simon. He was called Simon Peter. Sharing his beliefs cost Peter his life. Christians believe the Romans put him to death. They believe that St. Peter's **Basilica** in Rome was built on the exact spot where he died.

SAINTS

Early Christians believed Jesus gave Peter the power to govern the Christian Church. The Christian Church recognizes some people as having lived very holy lives, and after their deaths officially identifies these people as saints. Jesus's 12 disciples are considered saints. "St." is the abbreviation for the word *saint*.

PAUL OF TARSUS

On the Road to Damascus

| 0 | | A.D. 70 |

c. A.D. 4 – 37
Jesus

c. A.D. 5 – 67
Paul

Most of what we know about Paul of Tarsus comes from letters he wrote. His letters reveal the story of his life and how he decided to become a Christian.

▲ Paul was born in Tarsus.

▲ This is one artist's idea of what Paul looked like.

A Threat to Jewish Beliefs?

Paul was born a Roman citizen in the seaport city of Tarsus (in present-day Turkey) around A.D. 5. Tarsus was on the main East-West trade route. In his early life, Paul became a member of a Jewish group or sect called the Pharisees. The Pharisees thought it was important to follow carefully the laws that Moses had delivered to the Jews. Paul became a rabbi or teacher in this sect. He earned his living as a tent maker. Paul became aware of Christianity when people were just beginning to learn about it. At first, he thought Christianity was a threat to his strongly held religious beliefs.

On the Road to Damascus

In one of his letters, Paul writes about the events that made him decide to become a Christian. While he was traveling on the road to Damascus, he saw a vision of Jesus and temporarily lost his sight. This experience made him believe that Jesus was the son of God. It was the most important moment in his life.

After this event, Paul spent time alone in the desert to think. Then he began traveling throughout the Roman world telling people about Christianity. He started Christian communities everywhere he went. He went on three journeys around the Aegean coast and to Cyprus. He wanted to bring the ideas of Christianity to the places he visited.

Paul's Journeys

First, he went to the area that is now southeastern Turkey. Eventually, hundreds of Christian churches were built in this area. His second and third journeys were longer. During these journeys, he is thought to have written his famous letters to the Romans and Corinthians.

Arrested in Jerusalem

Paul wanted to make a fourth journey, this time to Spain. In his letter to the Romans he wrote, "But now that there is no more place for me to work in these regions, and since I have been longing for many years to see you, I plan to do so when I go to Spain. I hope to visit you while passing through and to have you assist me on my journey there, after I have enjoyed your company for a while. Now, however, I am on my way to Jerusalem. …"

However, in A.D. 56, he was arrested in Jerusalem. Many Christians were being **persecuted** at that time. The Romans thought the followers of Christian ideas were creating trouble for the Roman Empire. Eventually, Paul was taken to Rome for trial. It is not clear whether Paul was found innocent and released by the Romans. He may have been released, traveled again to the east, and arrested again. Whatever is the case, he was killed in Rome around A.D. 67.

Sharing of Christian Ideas

As Paul and other Christians traveled throughout the Roman Empire, they shared Christian ideas with all the people they visited. They wanted everyone—not just Jews—to know that they could become Christians.

persecute: to treat badly and unfairly

It's a FACT

Paul of Tarsus is also known as St. Paul.

Roman Catholics celebrate the feast day of St. Paul on June 29th.

◀ Most of what we know about Paul of Tarsus comes from the letters he wrote.

associate: to be involved with; to socialize

cling: to hold onto tightly

mourn: to feel sadness

rejoice: to feel happiness

What Do You Think?

1. What was Paul's relationship to the Roman Empire?

2. How did Paul spread the ideas of Christianity throughout the Roman Empire?

3. After Paul decided to become a Christian on the road to Damascus, he had a hard time persuading others that he really had changed his ideas. Have you ever changed your mind about something important and had a hard time getting other people to believe you? Why is it so difficult for others to believe that people can change?

The Spread of Christianity

Christianity appealed to many people—men and women, rich and poor, free persons and slaves, and Romans and Jews. It offered them forgiveness for their sins and a life in heaven after death. Soon, Christianity spread to Europe and other Roman territories, especially in the eastern parts of the empire. By the early 300s, more and more people in the Roman Empire became Christians, including Roman emperors in both the western and eastern parts of the empire.

A Christian Hero

Paul left a lasting mark on history. More than any other early Christian, he spread the news of Christianity across the Roman world through his travels and his letters. He believed it was his duty to tell all people, not just Jews, about the ideas of Christianity.

Some people believe Paul deserves credit for turning a small Jewish sect into a worldwide religion—Christianity. Today, he is called Paul of Tarsus or St. Paul. The letters he wrote are included in the Christian Bible. 📖

Paul's Letter to the Romans:

Love must be sincere. Hate what is evil; **cling** to what is good. Be devoted to one another in brotherly love. Honor one another above yourselves ... Bless those who persecute you; bless and do not curse. **Rejoice** with those who rejoice; **mourn** with those who mourn. Live in harmony with one another. Do not be proud, but be willing to **associate** with people of low position. Do not be conceited. Do not repay anyone evil for evil. Be careful to do what is right in the eyes of everybody. If it is possible, as far as it depends on you, live at peace with everyone.

Analyze the Source!

Read the passage and tell in your own words what Paul was saying. From this passage, how would you describe Paul's advice to people?

THE CITIZENS (AND OTHERS) OF ROME

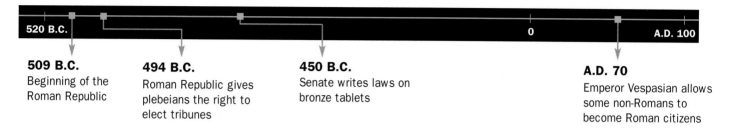

| 520 B.C. | | | | 0 | A.D. 100 |

509 B.C.
Beginning of the Roman Republic

494 B.C.
Roman Republic gives plebeians the right to elect tribunes

450 B.C.
Senate writes laws on bronze tablets

A.D. 70
Emperor Vespasian allows some non-Romans to become Roman citizens

According to one story about the history of Rome, Romulus chose 100 men to advise him. These 100 men were leaders of Roman families. Over time, their children and their children's children became known as patricians. Patricians were usually from older, richer families. Patrician men were leaders in the army and in the government. Other people living in Rome became known as plebeians. They were ordinary people—small farmers, artisans, merchants, and traders. Plebeian men served as soldiers in the army. Both patricians and plebeians were citizens, but patricians had more power in governing Rome. Patricians and plebeians over the age of 16 were Roman citizens. Citizens paid taxes. Male citizens served in the Roman army and could vote. In theory, all citizens—patricians and plebeians— were equal before the law.

Writing Down Laws

During the Roman Republic, there were many conflicts between patricians and plebeians over rights and privileges. At first, the patricians did not want any of the laws they passed to be written down. However, in 450 B.C., the plebeians forced the patricians in the Senate to write down the laws. These laws were written on 12 bronze tablets. They became known as the Law of the Twelve Tables.

▲ Plebeian men served in the army.

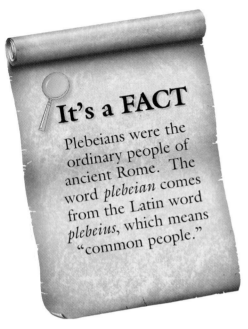

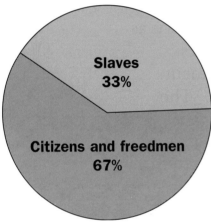

Slaves
33%

Citizens and freedmen
67%

▲ Some historians estimate that one-third to one-half of the people of the Roman Empire were slaves.

Changing Laws

For a long time, plebeians couldn't marry patricians. And, at first, plebeians could not hold any important offices. Over time, these laws were changed.

Over time, Romans also extended Roman citizenship to important people in the provinces they conquered. Around A.D. 70, Emperor Vespasian even let non-Romans who served in the army become Roman citizens.

Freedmen and Slaves

Roman society included more than just patricians and plebeians. There were also slaves and freedmen. Some historians estimate that one-third to one-half of the people of the Roman Empire were slaves. Most Roman slaves were people who had been captured during a war. Slaves were considered property, but they could marry other slaves. A slave owner could give slaves their freedom. Slaves also could buy themselves out of slavery. In this way, they would become freedmen. However, this did not make them Roman citizens. Generally, in order to be a citizen, a person had to be the child of a freedman. ▢

What Do You Think?

1. In ancient Rome, who could be a citizen? Did men and women citizens have the same rights and responsibilities? Give examples to support your answer.

2. What other groups of people lived in ancient Rome besides Roman citizens?

3. What were the advantages of Roman citizenship?

4. How does Roman citizenship compare with American citizenship?

CLAUDIUS EXTENDS ROMAN CITIZENSHIP

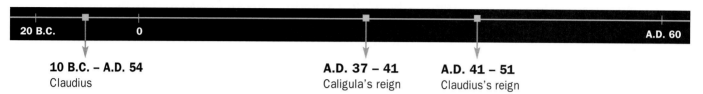

20 B.C.	0		A.D. 60

10 B.C. – A.D. 54
Claudius

A.D. 37 – 41
Caligula's reign

A.D. 41 – 51
Claudius's reign

Claudius, whose full name was Tiberius Claudius Caesar Augustus Germanicus, was born in 10 B.C. His family didn't think very much of young Claudius. They didn't pay very much attention to him either. Claudius had several physical disabilities—he was partially **paralyzed**, **stammered** when he spoke, and walked with a limp.

An Unexpected Emperor

Claudius spent most of his early life studying, reading, and writing. No one, including Claudius, ever thought he would become emperor of the Roman Empire. But he did become emperor. On January 1, A.D. 41, his nephew, the Roman emperor Caligula, was murdered. Roman soldiers found Claudius hiding behind a curtain. Claudius was sure he would be killed, too. Instead, he was named Roman emperor.

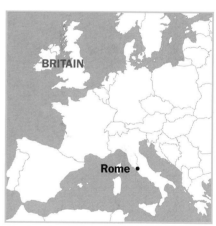

▲ Rome conquered Britain while Claudius was emperor.

A Good Ruler

Claudius surprised people. He showed that he was able to rule effectively. In A.D. 43, while he was emperor, Rome conquered Britain. Claudius even went to Britain to lead the Roman army. This action made him more popular with Romans. Claudius also established new provinces in North Africa and other areas in the Mediterranean region. He died in A.D. 54. Historians believe his wife poisoned him.

◄ This is a drawing of Claudius.

paralyzed: unable to move

stammer: to speak with pauses and repetitions

distinction: a difference; excellence

exclude: to prevent or keep from entering a group or place; from the Latin word *excludere*, which means "to shut out"

provincial: someone who lives in the provinces, which are areas outside the main city

Roman Citizenship

One of Rome's most important achievements was to give some of the people it conquered the chance to become Roman citizens. Claudius went even further. He allowed citizens from the provinces to become members of the Roman Senate. Many Romans disagreed with this decision, but Claudius defended his actions. You can read below how he explained his decision to allow non-Romans to become Roman senators. 📖

Surely both my great-uncle ... Augustus, and my uncle Tiberius Caesar, were following a new practice when they desired that all the flower of the colonies ... that is, the better class and the wealthy men—should sit in this senate house.

You ask me: Is not an Italian senator preferable to a **provincial**? ...

I think not even provincials ought to be **excluded**, provided that they can add **distinction** to this senate house.

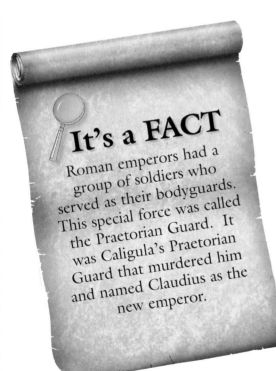

It's a FACT

Roman emperors had a group of soldiers who served as their bodyguards. This special force was called the Praetorian Guard. It was Caligula's Praetorian Guard that murdered him and named Claudius as the new emperor.

Analyze the Source!

Who was Claudius referring to in the phrase, "flower of the colonies"?

Why do you think some Romans were opposed to the idea of non-Romans in the Senate? Why do you think Claudius mentions Augustus in this passage?

What Do You Think?

1. How did Claudius become emperor?

2. What did Claudius do that went further than any earlier Roman emperor?

NERO
Fiddling While Rome Burns

A.D. 54
Nero becomes
emperor

A.D. 64
A huge fire
sweeps Rome

A.D. 68
Nero is killed

A.D. 476
Fall of Roman Empire
in the West

In 27 B.C., Augustus became the first emperor of Rome. In A.D. 476, the last Roman emperor, Romulus Augustulus, was forced out. There were many emperors in between. Some of them were good emperors, but others were terrible leaders. This is the story of Nero, the **notorious** Roman emperor who ruled Rome from A.D. 54 to 68.

A Weak, Self-Centered, Cruel Man

After Augustus died, there was peace in the Roman Empire. Some of the emperors who followed Augustus were good leaders, but not all of them. Rome was no longer a republic where people elected their leaders. Some of the leaders, including Nero, who came after Augustus were weak, self-centered, and cruel men. Nero became emperor in A.D. 54 when his adopted father, Emperor Claudius, died. Nero was just a boy at the time.

At first, Nero had good men to guide him. Over time, however, Nero became more interested in a life of pleasure than in good government. He ate fine food and drank the best wine. His clothes were made of the best material. His wife bathed in milk and wore gold and jewels. She spent her days gossiping with her friends, meeting secretly with other men, and going to parties. Nero and his wife had servants to do everything for them. They lived in the greatest comfort and luxury.

notorious: dishonorable; well known, but for evil rather than good

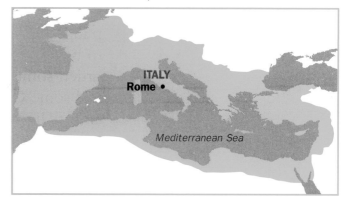
▼ Nero was the emperor of the Roman Empire from A.D. 54 to 68.

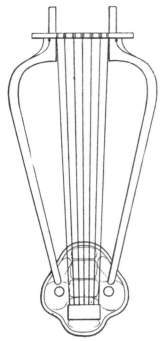

▲ Nero is often called the emperor who fiddled while Rome burned. In fact, fiddles had not yet been invented, so if Nero had been playing a musical instrument, it was most likely a lyre as shown above.

A Talented Musician?

Nero spent his days playing music and writing poetry. He thought he was very talented and was quite proud of himself. He punished anyone who yawned or who didn't applaud his songs or poetry. Nero also spent a great deal of his time planning "games" for the city's amusement. The games he planned were **spectacular** events where **gladiators** would fight other gladiators or wild animals to the death.

When people got in his way, Nero got rid of them. When his mother and wife became problems for him, he had them killed. He also was responsible for the horrible deaths of many Christians living in Rome while he was emperor. People today remember Nero as the Roman emperor who played music while Rome burned. Have you ever heard of the saying, "fiddling while Rome burns?" That saying refers to a great fire in Rome during Nero's rule.

A Fire in Rome

Throughout Rome's history, there were lots of fires in the city. However, in A.D. 64, a huge fire swept across Rome and destroyed many parts of the city. Somehow a **rumor** got started that Nero had set the fire himself so that he could rebuild the city according to his own plan. Some people today believe Nero really did set the fire, but we don't know for certain. What we do know is that Nero blamed the Christians for the fire.

Persecuting Christians

Many Romans were suspicious of Christians. They thought Christian beliefs were too different from the traditional religious beliefs. That made it easier for Nero to begin a **policy** of persecuting Christians. At Nero's order, some Christians were nailed to crosses. Nero also had some Christians covered with tar and then burned alive as human **torches**. Nero sent other Christians to the arena to be part of his "games." Lions and other wild animals killed these Christians while the crowds in the Colosseum shouted and cheered.

▲ Nero had Christians killed by lions.

An Enemy of Rome

Eventually, several Roman generals rebelled against Nero. The Senate called him an enemy of Rome. Rather than being captured and killed, Nero took his own life. It is reported that as he was dying, he said: "What an artist the world is losing in me!" 📖

gladiator: a person who fights another person or an animal as public entertainment

policy: course of action

rumor: a story or piece of gossip that may or may not be true

spectacular: amazing, fantastic, dramatic

torch: a light that is produced by a burning flame

 What Do You Think?

1. Based on this story, how do you think power and wealth had affected Rome?

2. What are Nero's qualities? Is he a hero? Compare what Lucretia said when she lay dying with Nero's words.

3. What do you think is the moral of this story?

TACITUS
and the Lessons of History

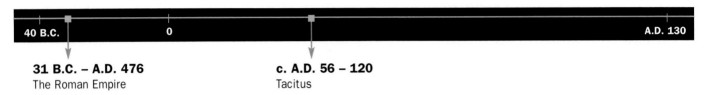

40 B.C.	0		A.D. 130

31 B.C. – A.D. 476
The Roman Empire

c. A.D. 56 – 120
Tacitus

Much of what we know about life in the Roman Empire and the emperors who ruled it comes from the work of the historian Tacitus. Tacitus was born to a wealthy family in northern Italy or Gaul (present-day France). He was well educated in public speaking and debate. He became a Roman senator and then a consul. Later he became the governor of a large Roman province in Anatolia (much of present-day Turkey). However, Tacitus is best known today as one of Rome's most brilliant historians.

▲ Tacitus wrote about Roman history.

A Brilliant Historian

Tacitus's two most famous works are *Histories* and *The Annals of Imperial Rome*. In his work, Tacitus wrote about government corruption and scandal. He wrote about how innocent people were ruined because of the emperor's power. Tacitus believed that too much power in the hands of one man resulted in corruption.

History Lessons

Tacitus thought history could guide people in making good decisions. He thought the past was filled with examples of good and bad decisions. By paying attention to those examples, he believed people could avoid mistakes and have a model for good behavior. You can read on the next page Tacitus's description of how Germanic peoples looked, how they selected their leaders, and where they lived. Many different groups of Germanic peoples lived beyond the **frontiers** of the Roman Empire. Romans did not consider them as equals in terms of culture, education, or government. Consider what lessons Tacitus may be giving Romans in this passage. 📖

They all have blue eyes, reddish hair, and large bodies; they do not submit patiently to work and effort and cannot endure thirst and heat at all, though cold and hunger they are accustomed to because of their climate. ...

They pick their kings on the basis of noble birth, their general on the basis of bravery.

It is well known that none of the German tribes live in cities. They live separated and in various places, as a spring or a meadow or a grove strikes their fancy. ...

Analyze the Source!

Read the passage and tell in your own words what lesson you think Tacitus was giving to Romans. Explain your answer.

frontier: border; boundary; edge

What Do You Think?

1. What positions did Tacitus have in the Roman Empire?

2. Why is Tacitus remembered?

3. Do you agree with Tacitus that history gives people both good and bad examples that they can use to guide their lives? Explain your answer.

MARCUS AURELIUS
The Stoic Emperor

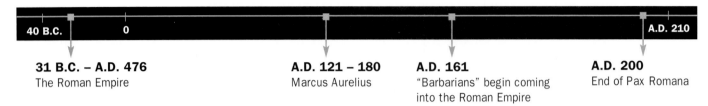

40 B.C.	0			A.D. 210

31 B.C. – A.D. 476
The Roman Empire

A.D. 121 – 180
Marcus Aurelius

A.D. 161
"Barbarians" begin coming into the Roman Empire

A.D. 200
End of Pax Romana

Of all the Roman emperors, only a few stand out from all the rest. We remember some for the good they did and some for the harm they caused. Marcus Aurelius stands out for the good he did. What made him different from so many other Roman emperors? Why is Marcus Aurelius admired as a heroic figure in Roman history? Many would say it is because he carried out his duties with courage and **integrity**.

▲ Marcus Aurelius was born in Rome, but he spent most of his life away from Rome on government business.

Early Life and Education

Marcus Aurelius was born in Rome on April 26, A.D. 121. His family was wealthy and politically important. His parents died when he was young, and the Emperor Hadrian became interested in his **welfare**. The emperor made sure Marcus received an excellent education and had teachers who were some of the greatest thinkers of the time.

Throughout his life, Marcus Aurelius loved learning, especially philosophy. Philosophy is concerned with questions about the world in which we live. How did the world begin? What is the purpose of life? Do human beings have free will or are their actions decided by fate or gods? What is right and wrong? How should people live their lives? Philosophers think about and discuss such questions. Different groups or "schools" of philosophy had different answers to these questions.

Emperor of Rome

Marcus Aurelius became emperor of Rome in A.D. 161 after serving in various government positions for about 20 years. During the time he was emperor, the Roman Empire faced several major problems. First, Rome was at war with the Parthians, a Roman enemy in the East. Marcus Aurelius and his army were victorious in battle against the Parthians.

Another problem was that the Roman soldiers returned from battle with a plague that spread throughout the empire. Many people became sick and died.

Tribes of Germanic peoples—people the Romans called "barbarians"—attacking the northern border of the empire were a third problem. Eventually, Marcus Aurelius was successful against these attacks. Later emperors would not be so successful.

Meditations

Marcus Aurelius wrote a book that today we call *Meditations*. The title Marcus Aurelius gave to this was a Greek phrase meaning, "to himself." This book tells us about Marcus Aurelius's views on the Roman Empire. It also gives us an idea of his values and beliefs.

Meditations is a kind of journal in which he wrote down his thoughts about events that happened, things he had read, and ideas that occurred to him. For example, he wrote that he should be careful of the frequent use of the words "I am too busy" in speech or correspondence, except in cases of real necessity. He said no one should **shirk** their obligations to society because they are busy.

Stoicism

In *Meditations*, Marcus Aurelius also reveals his belief in the Stoic philosophy. The Stoic philosophy or "Stoicism" is a system of moral principles that originated in Greece. It is a way of thinking about how human beings should behave and how they should live their lives. Some people call it a moral code.

Stoics believed that life should be lived in accordance with nature, and that people should be fair, self-disciplined, and courageous. Stoics were not interested in material things. Marcus Aurelius tried to live his life according to the principles of Stoicism. He avoided personal **luxuries**.

integrity: honor; honesty

luxury: something extra that is not needed, but makes life more comfortable or pleasant

shirk: to avoid or stay away from

welfare: benefit; happiness; well-being

▲ Marcus Aurelius was a peaceful man, but his rule of the Roman Empire was marked by constant war.

Moral Principles

Marcus Aurelius put the needs of the Roman Empire above his own needs. For example, he wrote, "avoid all actions that are haphazard or purposeless; and secondly let every action aim solely at the common good."

His beliefs in Stoicism helped him deal with the many problems he faced. These Stoic beliefs gave him moral principles upon which to make decisions and take actions.

The End of the Pax Romana

Late in his reign, Marcus Aurelius went to the eastern part of the Roman Empire. During this trip, his wife died. Marcus Aurelius wrote with great love and admiration about her in *Meditations*. In A.D. 177, Marcus Aurelius announced that his son, Commodus, would help him rule as emperor and become sole emperor when he died. Together, they returned to the northern borders of the empire. They planned to continue the expansion of the Roman Empire. However, Marcus Aurelius died in A.D. 180, far from Rome. With his death the period known as the Pax Romana came to an end. 📖

---

unembittered: not bitter or angry; accepting

 What Do You Think?

1. What advantages did Marcus Aurelius have as a young child?

2. What obstacles did he have to overcome?

3. How does having a moral code help a person deal with problems? Do you think it is important for leaders to have a moral code?

An Excerpt from *Meditations*:

Be like the headland against which the waves break and break: it stands firm, until presently the watery tumult around it subsides once more to rest. 'How unlucky I am, that this should have happened to me!' By no means; say rather, 'How lucky I am, that it has left me with no bitterness; unshaken by the present, and undismayed by the future.' The thing could have happened to anyone, but not everyone would have emerged **unembittered** ... So here is a rule to remember in future, when anything tempts you to feel bitter: not, 'This is a misfortune,' but 'To bear this worthily is a good fortune.'

Analyze the Source!

Read the excerpt from *Meditations* and tell what it means in your own words. Do you agree or disagree with the idea Marcus Aurelius expressed? Why?

"BARBARIANS" AT THE GATES!

A.D. 150   **A.D. 480**

A.D. 161
"Barbarians" begin coming
into the Roman Empire

A.D. 300
Waves of "barbarians"
create serious problems for
the Roman government

A.D. 476
Fall of Roman Empire
in the West

Beginning in A.D. 161, groups of people the Romans called "barbarians" began to come into the Roman Empire. The Romans did not think these groups of people had an advanced culture. The Romans thought they were uncivilized compared to the Roman culture. Some of these groups lived peacefully side by side with the Romans. Many joined the Roman army and helped to defend the borders of the Roman Empire. By the late 300s, however, the large number of "barbarians" wanting to come into the Roman Empire had become a serious problem for the Roman government.

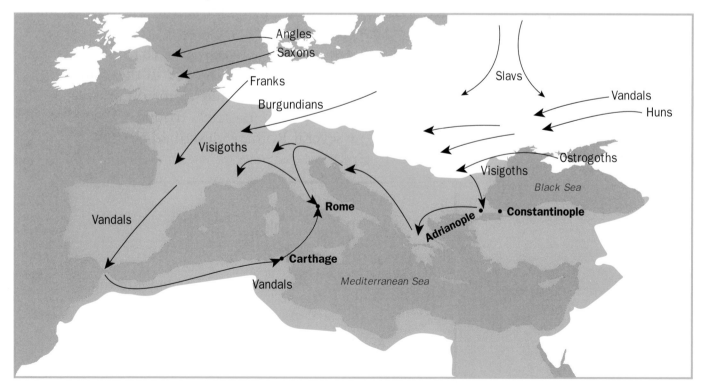

▲ This map shows some of the groups of "barbarians" that invaded the Roman Empire. The Visigoths, a Germanic people, attacked the city of Rome in A.D. 410. Then another Germanic group, the Vandals, attacked the city, destroying much of its art and beauty. The word we use to describe people who destroy property—vandals—comes from this group of people.

chaos: extreme confusion and disorder

competence: having ability or skill

dwell: to live

indomitable: not able to be defeated; from the Latin word *in*, which means "not" and *domitare*, which means "to tame"

invasion: the act of entering by force

race: a group of people classified together because they have similar history, nationality, and/or physical characteristics

retain: to keep

vigor: energy, power, strength; from the Latin word *vigere*, which means "to be lively"

▲ The Romans fought with many groups of "barbarians."

Settlers or Invaders?

Some of these groups wanted to settle down and begin new lives. Others, such as the Huns, Vandals, and Visigoths, wanted to conquer Roman territories for themselves. Some historians refer to the waves of people who entered the Roman Empire as the "barbarian **invasions**." Almost all historians agree that this situation created **chaos** for the people who lived in the Roman Empire. Romans no longer could count on the Roman government to keep law and order. You can read on the next page how several Romans described the "barbarian invasions." 📖

What Do You Think?

1. Why did groups of people begin coming into the Roman Empire?

2. What problems did the "barbarian invasions" create for Romans? How do you think the "barbarian invasions" affected the way people of the Roman Empire thought about Roman government?

Letter from the Leader of the Christian Community of Carthage

The leader of the Christian community in Carthage wrote a letter telling about his ideas around A.D. 250. You can read below an excerpt from his letter:

The world has grown old and lost its former **vigor**. ... Winter no longer gives rain enough to swell the sea, nor summer enough to toast the harvest ... the mountains are gutted and give less marble, the mines are exhausted and give less silver and gold ... the fields lack farmers, the seas sailors, the encampments soldiers ... there is no justice in judgments, **competence** in trades, discipline in daily life.

Ammianus Marcellinus on the Huns

In the late 300s, Ammianus Marcellinus, a retired Roman soldier, described the invasion of the feared Huns. This is an excerpt from his account:

The people called Huns ... are a **race** savage beyond all parallel. At the very moment of birth the cheeks of their infant children are deeply marked by an iron, in order that the hair, instead of growing at the proper season on their faces, may be hindered by the scars. ... The Huns grow up without beards, and without any beauty.

... They never shelter themselves under roofed houses ... they wander about, roaming over the mountains and the woods. ... There is not a person in the whole nation who cannot remain on his horse day and night. On horseback they buy and sell, they take their meat and drink, and there they recline. ...

None of them plow, or even touch a plow handle, ... but are homeless and lawless, perpetually wandering with their wagons, which they make their homes. ... This active and **indomitable** race, ... had suddenly descended ... and were ravaging and destroying everything which came in their way.

Procopius on the Vandals

Procopius, a Roman historian, wrote in the early 400s. This excerpt from his account describes the Vandal invasions in North Africa:

[The king of the Vandals] robbed [the Romans] of their estates, which were both very numerous and excellent, and distributed them among the nation of the Vandals ...

And it fell to the lot of those who had formerly possessed these lands to **dwell** in extreme poverty. ...

[T]he land that he did not deem worthy he allowed to remain in the hands of former owners, but assessed so large a sum to be paid in government taxes that nothing whatsoever remained to those who were able to **retain** their farms.

Analyze the Source!

Read the three excerpts. Choose one and tell in your own words what the person was saying.

THE BYZANTINE EMPIRE
The New Rome

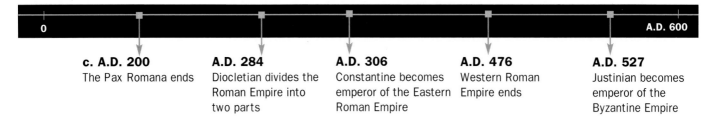

c. A.D. 200
The Pax Romana ends

A.D. 284
Diocletian divides the Roman Empire into two parts

A.D. 306
Constantine becomes emperor of the Eastern Roman Empire

A.D. 476
Western Roman Empire ends

A.D. 527
Justinian becomes emperor of the Byzantine Empire

By the late 200s, problems in the Roman Empire had become too great for one man to handle. In 284, Emperor Diocletian divided the Roman Empire in half, making himself ruler of the eastern half and another man ruler of the western part. The two halves were supposed to be equal, but the power had shifted to the east.

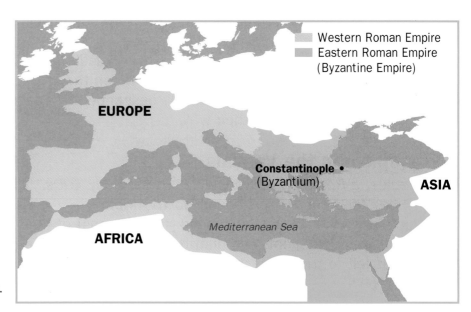

▶ Constantine made Constantinople the new capital of the Eastern Roman Empire. He called it the "new Rome."

Emperor Constantine

After Diocletian, Constantine became emperor of the Eastern Roman Empire in 306. Constantine built a new capital city—Constantinople—on the site of the old Greek city Byzantium. He called Constantinople the "new Rome." He reunited the eastern and western parts of the Roman Empire and decided to stay in the eastern half. Emperors after Constantine tried to keep the Roman Empire united. However, it slowly began to separate.

Fall of the Western Roman Empire

As the Eastern Roman Empire flourished, Rome and the Western Roman Empire faced problems. There wasn't enough money to pay for the army and government services. People were forced to pay high taxes. The government could not solve the problems people were facing. To make matters worse, Germanic groups from the north and east began invading.

Some of the Germanic groups wanted to find a place to live. Others, such as the Huns, came to conquer an empire. Historians generally agree that the Western Roman Empire officially ended in 476. In that year, Odoacer, a leader of a Germanic group, took control of Rome and forced out the last Roman emperor, Romulus Augustulus. By 500, Rome was in ruins and the Western Roman Empire was in chaos.

Constantine and the Byzantine Empire

The Eastern Roman Empire escaped many of the problems that confronted Rome. They defended themselves from invaders. The Eastern Roman Empire became known as the Byzantine Empire. It lasted for another 1,000 years after the Western Roman Empire lost power.

Constantine and the early rulers of the Byzantine Empire were Romans. Their Roman ideas and culture greatly influenced them as they ruled. They had a Senate in their government and organized their armies the way Romans did. They built arenas similar to the Colosseum, a stadium like the Circus Maximus, and buildings that were exactly like buildings in Rome. They even spoke Latin.

Over time, however, Rome's influence was not as great. Perhaps the most significant reason for this is that Constantinople was located on an important trade route between Europe and Asia. Most people there were not Roman; they were Greek or from other areas. The city was a crossroad for people from the East and the West.

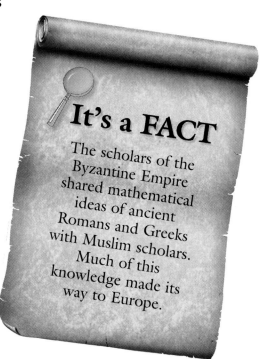

It's a FACT

The scholars of the Byzantine Empire shared mathematical ideas of ancient Romans and Greeks with Muslim scholars. Much of this knowledge made its way to Europe.

Religion and Government

One area of disagreement between Rome and the Byzantine Empire had to do with religion and government. The Byzantine Empire was a Christian empire. Constantine was a Christian, and Constantinople was filled with Christian churches. Christians in the Byzantine Empire did not all agree on the same teachings. However, they did agree the emperor should have power over the church. Religion was almost a branch of the government. Over time, Christians in the Byzantine Empire disagreed strongly with Christians of the old Western Roman Empire. One of the most important disagreements was about whose power was greater—the state or the church.

▶ Constantinople (present-day Istanbul) developed on two continents—Asia and Europe. A narrow passage of water called the Bosporus separates the Asian and European sides of the city.

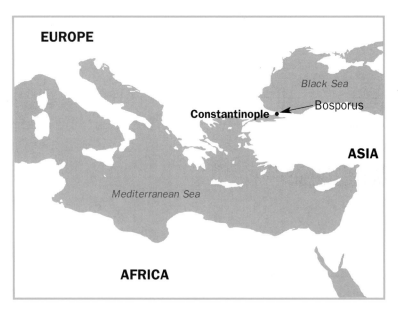

Justinian and the Byzantine Empire

Justinian became emperor in A.D. 527 and ruled the Byzantine Empire for almost 40 years. He was known as "the emperor who never slept" because he was ambitious and worked hard to restore the power and glory of the Roman Empire. His wife, Theodora, and generals, scholars, and administrators helped him to do this. Justinian's armies won back much of the Roman territory lost in the west—including land in Italy and North Africa. He also forced the Germanic groups out of Rome, but the city was left in ruins.

One of Justinian's most important accomplishments was the Justinian Code. He asked a group of scholars to organize all the Roman laws into one law code.

▲ Justinian is remembered as the greatest emperor of the Byzantine Empire. He is shown here with his wife, Empress Theodora.

THE JUSTINIAN CODE

Justinian knew to have good government, you needed to have good laws. He was responsible for making sure that the people followed the law. But what were the laws? The Byzantines had lots of good Roman laws—too many. Some were not useful, others confusing.

Justinian had an idea! He organized a group of people to look at the laws. The group included Latin and Greek scholars. They made sure the laws were clear. After all, people need to understand the laws if they are going to follow them. He asked the scholars to organize all the Roman laws into one law code. It was a lot of work, but they finished in 533. This law code is called the Law Code of Justinian or the Justinian Code. It stated people's rights and described Roman legal customs.

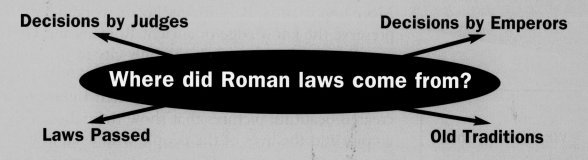

Decisions by Judges

Decisions by Emperors

Where did Roman laws come from?

Laws Passed

Old Traditions

▲ During Justinian's rule, the Hagia Sophia was a Christian church. However, when the Turks captured Constantinople in 1453, they converted it into a mosque. Today, people from all over the world visit the Hagia Sophia to admire its beauty.

Preserving Learning for the Western World

Education was important in the Byzantine Empire. Scholars thought the writings of people who lived before them—the ancient Greeks and Romans—should be kept safe. This was not important to the Germanic peoples who took power in the Western Roman Empire. Many of the writings in that part of the empire were destroyed. Some of the ideas and knowledge of the ancient Greeks and Romans would have been lost forever if not for the scholars of the Byzantine Empire.

It's a FACT

The Justinian Code is the foundation of most European legal systems.

During a riot in Constantinople in A.D. 532, Justinian's wife Theodora organized an army of 35,000 in just one day!

What Do You Think?

1. What were the similarities and differences between the Byzantine Empire and the Western Roman Empire?

2. Why is Justinian called the Byzantine Empire's greatest emperor?

3. What "gifts" did the Byzantine Empire give to the Western world? Which is most important? Why?

Constantinople

Constantinople was the capital of the Byzantine Empire. The city developed on both sides of a narrow waterway called the Bosporus. One part of the city was on the continent of Asia and the other was on the European continent. During Justinian's rule, Constantinople was a bustling city of as many as 350,000 people.

Scholars in the Byzantine Empire used their knowledge of mathematics, geometry, and physics to build wonderful buildings and roads. Constantinople was filled with markets, theaters, palaces, government buildings, an arena, baths, warehouses, bakeries, and inns. There were also many churches, including the Hagia Sophia, a stunningly beautiful Christian church built during Justinian's rule. More importantly, Byzantine scholars worked hard to preserve the knowledge of ancient Romans and Greeks.

Constantinople wasn't the only city in the empire. Many other cities—perhaps as many as 1,500—also were part of the Byzantine Empire. Talented Byzantine artists created beautiful pictures that show the riches of the empire and the lives of the people who lived in it.

The End of the Byzantine Empire

Emperor Justinian's accomplishments were great but very costly. When he died in 565, his successors did not have many resources left to rule the empire. However, the Byzantine Empire continued long after Justinian died. It didn't end until the year 1453, when the Turks captured the capital city of Constantinople. They renamed Justinian's magnificent city "Istanbul" and made it the capital of their Ottoman Empire.

Gifts to the Western World

The Western world owes a great debt of gratitude to the Byzantine Empire. When most of present-day Europe was in chaos (from the 500s through the 900s), the Byzantine Empire had an orderly government, central rule, and effective laws.

When some Europeans in the 1300s wanted to learn more about ancient Greek and Roman ideas, they looked to Constantinople for some of the works of Greek writers such as Plato and Homer. The Byzantine Empire preserved the Roman way of life and much Greek and Roman knowledge for the world. ▢

DR. MARTIN LUTHER KING, JR.
Changing America

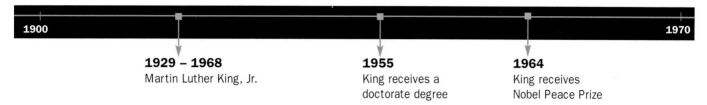

| 1900 | | | 1970 |

1929 – 1968
Martin Luther King, Jr.

1955
King receives a
doctorate degree

1964
King receives
Nobel Peace Prize

The life of Dr. Martin Luther King, Jr. illustrates how one man's dream can change a nation.

> *"... I have a dream that one day this nation will rise up and live out the true meaning of its **creed**: 'We hold these truths to be self-evident: that all men are created equal.'"*

These words rang loud and clear on August 28, 1963, when King delivered what is perhaps the most famous speech in American history. King's journey to become the greatest American civil rights leader was not an easy one.

The Influence of Religion

Martin Luther King, Jr. was born January 15, 1929, in Atlanta, Georgia. Martin's father was a Baptist preacher and the church was a major part of the King family's life. Throughout his childhood, Martin faced **racism** against black Americans. He learned early on that black Americans did not have the same rights as white Americans. This made young Martin angry. However, his parents always reminded him that "it was my duty as a Christian to love ...," even to love people who did not love him simply because of the color of his skin.

◀ This is a photograph of Dr. Martin Luther King, Jr. In 1983, Dr. King's birthday was made a national holiday.

creed: a statement of belief

racism: feelings or actions of hatred toward a person or persons because of their race

abuse: mistreatment; injury

boycott: a refusal to buy, use, or sell something

demonstration: a public show of opinion

discriminate: to treat differently

integrated: free and equal association; not segregated or separate

segregation: being set apart form the main group

theology: the study of religion

The Influence of Education

Before he could even read, young Martin surrounded himself with books. He also was fascinated by language and sounds and the way they could be used to inspire people. Martin skipped two grades and entered Morehouse College when he was 15 years old. He graduated college in 1948 and then studied **theology** at Crozer Theological Seminary. He attended graduate school at Boston University and received a doctorate in theology in 1955. While in Boston, he married Corretta Scott.

King became the pastor of Dexter Avenue Baptist Church in Montgomery, Alabama. King's religious beliefs and education convinced him that change was possible, and he began his journey to end racism and fight for equal rights for all Americans. Most importantly, King believed that these goals could be achieved through nonviolent actions.

Segregation

King believed that **segregation** was a major problem in society. He said, "Men often hate each other because they fear each other; they fear each other because they do not know each other; they do not know each other because they cannot communicate; they cannot communicate because they are separated." On December 1, 1955, a woman named Rosa Parks was arrested because she refused to give up her seat to a white person on a Montgomery city bus. Black civil rights leaders, led by Dr. King, decided to organize a **boycott** of the buses. The boycott lasted for more than a year, and finally ended when the United States Supreme Court ordered the city of Montgomery to provide **integrated** seating on public buses. This was a major step in the fight to end segregation, but it came with a price. During the boycott, Dr. King's home was bombed, he was arrested, and he received much personal **abuse**.

▲ Dr. King inspired many people to use nonviolent actions, such as marches, to bring about change.

A Civil Rights Leader

Dr. King was a powerful and inspirational public speaker. Both blacks and whites who believed in his cause joined the civil rights movement. He was elected president of the Southern Christian Leadership Conference, an organization formed to support the civil rights movement. As a civil rights leader, he organized many nonviolent **demonstrations** in the southern United States. People saw pictures of and read about Dr. King's demonstrations, and more and more people began to support his work.

"I Have a Dream"

In August 1963, Dr. King led a march of more than 200,000 people in Washington, D.C. He delivered his speech at the Lincoln Memorial, saying, "I have a dream that my four little children will one day live in a nation where they will not be judged by the color of their skin but by the content of their character." Dr. King's efforts helped convince Congress to pass the Civil Rights Act of 1964. This law made it illegal for businesses to **discriminate** against people because of race, color, religion, or national origin. This law also gave the attorney general the power to end segregation in schools. Dr. King's dream was beginning to come true.

The Work Continues

Dr. King's life was cut short on April 4, 1968, when he was shot and killed in Memphis, Tennessee. While Dr. King's life has ended, his dream lives on. Dr. Martin Luther King, Jr. continues to be an inspiration to all those who believe that change is necessary, and possible. In 1983, Dr. King's birthday was made a national holiday. 📖

▲ In January 1964, *Time* magazine chose Dr. Martin Luther King, Jr. as "Man of the Year." He was the first black American to receive this honor.

What Do You Think?

1. In what ways is Dr. Martin Luther King, Jr. similar to ancient world leaders you learned about this year? In what ways is he different?

2. What are your dreams? How can you make your dreams come true?

3. In what ways did Dr. Martin Luther King, Jr. change the world?

CESAR CHAVEZ

Changing the Lives of Migrant Workers

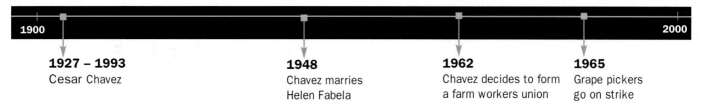

1900				2000

1927 – 1993
Cesar Chavez

1948
Chavez marries
Helen Fabela

1962
Chavez decides to form
a farm workers union

1965
Grape pickers
go on strike

Juana Chavez taught her children to help those less fortunate and never use violence against others. These are lessons that Cesar Chavez applied throughout his lifetime. Cesar Chavez was born March 31, 1927 near Yuma, Arizona. He was born in an apartment under the grocery store that his parents owned. When Cesar was 10 years old, the country was going through an economic decline known as the **Great Depression**. Many people lost their jobs and had little money. In 1939, Cesar's family had to sell their farm in order to pay the taxes they owed the government. Shortly after this happened, the Chavez family moved to California.

▲ Chavez helped migrant workers become citizens and register to vote.

Working in the Fields

In California, the Chavez family went to work. They became **migrant** workers, planting and picking crops in the fields. The men who grew the crops did not want to pay the workers very much money. Many workers needed jobs, so the growers were able to find people who would work for very little money. Every day the Chavez family picked crops such as grapes, cucumbers, and peaches under the hot California sun. They received only a small amount of money each week.

Facing Prejudice

The Chavez family didn't have a permanent home in California. Sometimes they slept in their car. Cesar moved around so much that he was always changing schools. He had gone to 37 different schools by the time he was in eighth grade. Many teachers and students were **prejudiced** against Mexican-American people and did not treat Cesar well. Cesar left school after eighth grade. He joined the Navy when he was 17 years old. He saw racism everywhere—at school, in the Navy, in movie theaters, and in restaurants. He saw signs that said, "No dogs or Mexicans allowed."

Empowering Migrant Workers

Chavez married a woman named Helen Fabela in 1948. The two of them moved around California looking for jobs. Around this time, Chavez's life began to change. He realized that he held the power to change not only his life, but the lives of all migrant workers. First, Chavez began to help migrant workers become citizens and register to vote. He knew this would **empower** them. They could help elect people who cared about their problems and would work to fix them.

Forming a Farm Workers Union

In 1962, Chavez decided to dedicate himself to forming a **union** for migrant workers. He thought an organized group could improve working conditions for migrant workers. Chavez's plans were not easy on his family. Helen had to work in the fields to make money for the family.

First Chavez met with individual workers and told them of his plan. Then he met with small groups, and eventually held large meetings. Chavez named his union the National Farm Workers Association (NFWA). By 1965, 1,200 migrant families were part of the union.

The Grape Strike

The union held a big meeting and the grape pickers decided to go on **strike**. Chavez sent workers all over the country to tell people to boycott grapes. Workers also held a 300-mile march to the California state capital to bring attention to their cause. Chavez always stayed true to his belief that change can come through nonviolent actions.

The grape strike lasted for five years. Finally, some growers agreed to pay the farm workers more money and improve their working conditions. Soon other workers joined forces and established the United Farm Workers (UFW). More growers gave in and agreed to meet the union's demands. When the strike was over, union workers were picking 85% of California grapes.

empower: to give power or authority to

Great Depression: a worldwide business decline that began in October 1929

migrant: a farm worker who moves from place to place to pick crops

prejudice: an opinion, usually unfavorable, formed before the facts are known

strike: to stop working as a group to get better pay and working conditions

union: an organization of workers

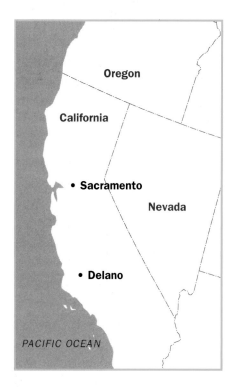

▶ A 300-mile march from Delano to Sacramento proved Cesar Chavez's belief that nonviolent actions can bring about a change.

fast: to stop eating for a period of time

A Life Dedicated to Change

Chavez spent the rest of his life using nonviolent methods to improve the lives of farm workers. He even **fasted** for 36 days to show his support for the workers. Throughout his life, Chavez carried with him the two very important lessons that his mother taught him. He dedicated his life to helping others, and he created change through nonviolent actions. He is an inspiration to many other people who want to change the world around them. Cesar Chavez died on April 23, 1993. ▯

What Do You Think?

1. In what ways is Cesar Chavez similar to ancient world leaders you learned about this year? In what ways is he different?

2. In what ways did Cesar Chavez change the world around him?

3. What are the most important lessons you have learned from your family?

4. Think of problems in your community. What could you do to help fix the problems?

▲ Cesar Chavez dedicated his life to helping others. He continues to be an inspiration to people who want to change the world around them.

GLOSSARY

A

abandon: (uh-BAN-dun) *v.* To leave.

absolute: (AB-suh-loot) *adj.* Not limited or restricted; total.

absolute date: (AB-suh-loot dayt) *n.* Exact or precise date based on a common measurement scale (such as a year).

abuse: (uh-BYOOS) *n.* Mistreatment; injury.

academic: (ak-uh-DEM-ik) *adj.* Having to do with school subjects such as history, literature, geography, and so forth.

accumulate: (uh-KYOOM-yuh-layt) *v.* To collect; to pile up or gather.

adversity: (ad-VUR-suh-tee) *n.* Hardship; troublesome time.

allegiance: (uh-LEE-jens) *n.* Loyalty.

alliance: (uh-LIY-uns) *n.* A formal agreement, partnership, or connection between people or groups.

alter: (AWL-tur) *v.* To change.

Anatolia: (an-uh-TOH-lee-uh) *n.* The area that generally comprises modern-day Turkey; Asia Minor.

aqueduct: (AK-we-dukt) *n.* A structure that helps move water in a certain direction.

aristocracy: (ayr-is-TOK-ruh-see) *n.* A ruling class or nobility.

artifact: (AHR-tuh-fakt) *n.* An object made and used by humans or early humanlike creatures.

assent: (uh-SENT) *v.* To agree.

assertion: (uh-SUR-shun) *n.* Claim; statement.

associate: (uh-SOH-see-ayt) *v.* To be involved with; to socialize.

astrological: (as-troh-LAWG-uh-kul) *adj.* Having to do with the position of the stars and planets in the sky.

astronomy: (uh-STRAHN-uh-mee) *n.* The study of the universe, including the stars and planets.

authority: (uh-THOHR-uh-tee) *n.* The rules giving one power.

avenge: (uh-VENJ) *v.* To take revenge; to get back at.

axis: (AK-sis) *n.* A straight line around which a body or geometric shape rotates.

axle: (AK-sul) *n.* The bar or rod on which a wheel turns.

B

basilica: (buh-SIL-i-kuh) *n.* A church that has two rows of columns dividing the interior space; from the Greek word *basilike*, which means "royal court" or "royal portico."

Bedouin: (BED-oo-in) *n.* A member of a group of nomadic peoples who traveled through and settled in the deserts of southwestern Asia.

behalf: (bi-HAF) *n.* Interest, benefit.

belittle: (bi-LIT-ul) *v.* To cause to think something is not important or special.

besieged: (bi-SEEJD) *n.* People who are under attack.

betray: (bee-TRAY) *v.* To be disloyal; to give help to an enemy.

biased: (BIY-ust) *adj.* Favoring one side; prejudiced.

biography: (biy-AHG-ra-fee) *n.* A written account of a person's life.

blot: (blot) *v.* To wipe away.

boast: (bohst) *n.* Something bragged about or said with pride.

border: (BOHR-dur) *n.* The edge of an area that separates one region from another.

boycott: (BOI-kot) *n.* A refusal to buy, use, or sell something.

bud: (bud) *n.* An undeveloped person or thing.

burst of creativity: (burst uv kree-ay-TIV-uh-tee) *n.* A sudden occurrence of imagination, originality, or expressiveness.

bystander: (BIY-stan-dur) *n.* A person who is present at an event, but not participating in it.

C

cacao bean: (kuh-KAH-oh been) *n.* A bean used in making chocolate; also used as a form of money.

calculate: (KAL-kyoo-layt) *v.* To figure out something, often by using numbers and mathematics.

cancel: (KAN-sul) *v.* To erase, do away with, invalidate.

captivity: (kap-TIV-uh-tee) *n.* The period in which someone or something is held as a prisoner.

caravan: (KAYR-uh-van) *n.* A group of people traveling together.

Castor: (KAS-tur) *n.* According to Greek mythology, Castor and Pollux were the twins that Zeus changed into the constellation called Gemini.

causeway: (KAWZ-way) *n.* A raised path, usually over water or marshy land.

cavalry: (KAV-ul-ree) *n.* Soldiers trained to fight while riding horses.

census: (SEN-sus) *n.* An official count of a population.

century: (SEN-chuh-ree) *n.* A period of 100 years.

champion: (CHAM-pee-un) *v.* To defend or support a cause or another person.

chaos: (KAY-ahs) *n.* Extreme confusion and disorder.

characteristic: (kayr-ik-tuh-RIS-tik) *n.* Feature; attribute; quality.

charismatic: (kayr-iz-MAT-ik) *adj.* Having the ability to get many people to follow.

chile pepper: (CHIL-ee PEP-ur) *n.* The fruit of a plant used to flavor food.

Christianity: (kris-tee-AN-uh-tee) *n.* The religion of Christians.

chronology: (kruh-NAHL-uh-jee) *n.* The order in which things occur.

circulate: (SUR-kyuh-layt) *v.* To move around, as from person to person or place to place.

civil: (SIV-ul) *adj.* Having to do with the general public, not the military forces or an organized religion.

civil service: (SIV-ul SUR-vus) *n.* All of the people who work for the government (except people in the military, the people who make laws, and the judges).

civil war: (SIV-ul wohr) *n.* Fighting between different groups in a country.

clash: (klash) *n.* A conflict with another person or group.

cling: (kling) *v.* To hold onto tightly.

coffin: (KOF-un) *n.* A box in which a dead body is placed before it is buried.

coinage: (KOI-nij) *n.* A system of metal currency (money).

colony: (KAHL-uh-nee) *n.* A territory or settlement controlled by another country.

commerce: (KAHM-urs) *n.* Business.

commercial: (kuh-MUR-shul) *adj.* Relating to the buying and selling of goods.

competence: (KAHM-puh-tuns) *n.* Having ability or skill.

complex: (kahm-PLEKS) *adj.* Not easy; complicated.

compromise: (KAHM-pruh-miyz) *n.* A settlement in which both sides give up some of the things they want.

constellation: (kahn-stuh-LAY-shun) *n.* A group of stars.

consul: (KAHN-sul) *n.* A general elected each year to lead the army and protect the city of Rome.

contemporary: (kun-TEM-puh-rer-ee) *adj.* Current or modern.

contentment: (kun-TENT-munt) *n.* a feeling of calm satisfaction.

corpse: (kohrps) *n.* A dead body.

corrupt: (kuh-RUPT) 1. *adj.* Dishonest; unfair. 2. *v.* To destroy or undermine honesty and integrity; to cause to become rotten or spoiled.

corruption: (kuh-RUP-shun) *n.* Dishonesty.

cower: (KOW-ur) *v.* To shrink away or hide because of fear.

creed: (kreed) *n.* A statement of belief.

crisis: (KRIY-sus) *n.* A critical time; an unstable condition.

crisis of conscience: (KRIY-sus uv KAHN-shuns) *n.* A time of extreme personal reflection in which a person thinks about and questions his/her beliefs, ideas, and/or actions.

cuneiform: (KYOO-nee-uh-fohrm) *n.* A series of wedge-shaped symbols used in the first forms of writing; these symbols were etched into clay tablets.

currency: (KUR-uhn-see) *n.* Money.

D

decipher: (di-SIY-fur) *v.* To interpret or make sense of something.

decisive: (di-SIY-siv) *adj.* Having the power to settle a dispute or doubt; unmistakable.

delta: (DEL-tuh) *n.* A deposit of sand and soil at the mouth of a river; usually shaped like a triangle.

democracy: (duh-MAHK-ruh-see) *n.* Rule by the people.

demonstration: (dem-un-STRAY-shun) *n.* A public show of opinion.

descendant: (di-SEN-dunt) *n.* Offspring; child, grandchild, and so forth.

determined: (di-TUR-mind) *adj.* Having a firm purpose.

devour: (di-VOWR) *v.* To eat up greedily; to destroy, consume, or swallow up.

devout: (di-VOWT) *adj.* Faithful; devoted.

dictator: (DIK-tay-tur) *n.* A ruler who has complete power in government; in ancient Rome, a dictator could be appointed for a short period of time to deal with a crisis.

dictatorship: (dik-TAY-tur-ship) *n.* Rule by one person (a dictator) who has complete power in government.

dike: (diyk) *n.* A raised portion of land used to stop or control the flow of water; commonly used in irrigation systems.

discard: (dis-KARD) *v.* To throw away.

discriminate: (dis-KRIM-uh-nayt) *v.* To treat differently.

dispute: (dis-PYOOT) *n.* A disagreement.

distinction: (dis-TINGK-shun) *n.* A difference; excellence.

domesticate: (di-MES-ti-kayt) *v.* To train to live with and be of best use to humans.

dwell: (dwel) *v.* To live.

dynasty: (DIY-nuh-stee) *n.* A series of rulers linked by a family relationship or by geographic location.

E

economic prosperity: (ek-uh-NAHM-ik prah-SPER-it-ee) *n.* Growth and expansion of a country's ability to produce, develop, and manage wealth.

economy: (i-KAHN-uh-mee) *n.* The production, development, and management of materials and goods.

elite: (i-LEET) *n.* Member of the social group considered the best or most skilled.

eminent: (EM-uh-nunt) *adj.* Outstanding.

empower: (em-POW-ur) *v.* To give power or authority to.

endless: (END-lis) *adj.* Being or seeming to be without an end; continuous.

epic: (EP-ik) *n.* A long story or poem of particular importance to a specific culture or people.

erupt: (i-RUHPT) *v.* To explode or blow up.

Eurasia: (yoo-RAY-zhuh) *n.* The continents of Europe and Asia.

everlasting: (ev-ur-LAS-ting) *adj.* Eternal; continuing indefinitely.

evidence: (EV-i-duns) *n.* Information that supports a judgment or decision.

exaggerated: (eg-ZAJ-uh-ray-tid) *adj.* Physically enlarged; emphasized; abnormally developed.

excavation: (ek-skuh-VAY-shun) *n.* A hole made by digging.

exception: (ek-SEP-shun) *n.* A case that does not follow the general rule.

exclude: (eks-KLOOD) *v.* To prevent or keep from entering a group or place; from the Latin word *excludere*, which means "to shut out."

exert: (eg-ZURT) *v.* To put forth; to bring; to bear.

exertion: (eg-ZUR-shun) *n.* A strong effort.

exile: (EG-ziyl) *v.* To force a person to leave his or her own country.

Exodus: (EK-suh-dus) *n.* The name of the second book of the Bible; the word *exodus* means "a departure from a place that involves large numbers of people."

exotic: (eg-ZAHT-ik) *adj.* From another place; unusual or unfamiliar.

F

fact: (fakt) *n.* Something known with certainty; something shown to be true.

famine: (FAM-in) *n.* A time when food is very scarce and people do not have enough to eat.

fast: (fast) *v.* To stop eating for a period of time.

fate: (fayt) *n.* A supposed force or power that predetermines events.

fatigue: (fuh-TEEG) *n.* Tiredness; exhaustion.

fertility: (fur-TIL-uh-tee) *n.* The ability to grow and develop; highly productive.

festival: (FES-tuh-vul) *n.* Celebration, event, fair.

fine: (fiyn) *adj.* Thin; slender.

firsthand: (FURST-hand) *adj.* Obtained directly from the original source.

five senses: (fiyv SEN-sus) *n.* Seeing, hearing, feeling, smelling, tasting.

fixed: (fixt) *adj.* Staying in one place; not moving.

flake: (flayk) *n.* A small, flat piece or layer that is broken off from a larger object.

fleet: (fleet) *n.* A number of warships operating together under one command.

flourish: (FLUR-ish) *v.* To grow well; to thrive or do well.

forebear: (FOHR-bayr) *n.* Ancestor; family member who lived in earlier times.

forerunner: (FOHR-run-ur) *n.* One that comes before.

forge: (forj) *v.* To give form or shape to; to create.

forged: (forjd) *adj.* Faked; counterfeit.

Forum: (FOHR-um) *n.* The main public square and marketplace in ancient Rome.

fossil: (FAHS-ul) *n.* Hardened remains of a plant or animal.

frenzy: (FREN-zee) *n.* Violent excitement; agitation.

frontier: (FRUN-teer) *n.* Border; boundary; edge.

funeral: (FYOO-nur-ul) *n.* Ceremonies held in connection with the burial or cremation of a dead person.

G

generation: (jen-uh-RAY-shun) *n.* All of the people who are born at approximately the same time.

geographical zone: (jee-uh-GRAF-i-kul zohn) *n.* An area distinct from others because of its physical features, climate, vegetation, and animal life.

geometry: (jee-AHM-uh-tree) *n.* The measurement or relationship between points, lines, angles, and surfaces.

Germanic people: (jur-MAN-ik PEE-pul) *n.* People from the northern part of Europe who have a common language and cultural traditions.

gladiator: (GLAD-ee-ay-tur) *n.* A person who fights another person or an animal as public entertainment.

glut: (glut) *v.* To flood or fill beyond capacity.

golden age: (GOHLD-un ayj) *n.* A period of time when something reaches its height of excellence.

gravestone: (GRAYV-stohn) *n.* A stone marker that is set on or near the place where a person is buried; a tombstone.

Great Depression: (grayt di-PRESH-un) *n.* A worldwide business decline that began in October 1929.

Guatemala City: (gwah-tuh-MAH-luh SIT-ee) *n.* The capital of Guatemala, a Central American country.

H

harken: (HARK-un) *v.* To listen carefully.

harvest: (HAR-vist) *v.* To gather a crop from the field where it is grown.

hearth: (harth) *n.* Fireplace.

heir: (ayr) *n.* A person who is next in line to assume a title or office.

Hellespont: (HEL-lus-pawnt) *n.* The ancient name for the Dardanelles, a strait that is 37 miles long and four miles wide and that links the Sea of Marmara and the Aegean Sea.

Hercules: (HUR-kyuh-leez) *n.* A Roman mythological hero; the son of Jupiter and a mortal woman, Alcmene; known for his courage and great strength.

hieroglyphics: (hiy-roh-GLIF-iks) *n.* A form of writing in which pictures are used to represent meaning and sound.

hiss: (his) *n.* Sharp "s" sound made by blowing air across the tongue.

homage: (HAHM-ij) *n.* Special honor or respect shown publicly.

hominid family: (HAHM-uh-nid FAM-lee) *n.* Includes mammals that walk upright and have comparatively large brains.

I

ignorance: (IG-nur-uns) *n.* A lack of knowledge.

imitate: (IM-uh-tayt) *v.* To copy; to try to be similar to.

imperial: (im-PIR-ee-ul) *adj.* Belonging to an empire or emperor.

implication: (im-pli-KAY-shun) *n.* An indirect indication; suggestion; inference.

independent: (in-di-PEN-dunt) *adj.* Self-governing; not guided or controlled by another.

indomitable: (in-DAHM-uh-tuh-bul) *adj.* Not able to be defeated; from the Latin word *in*, which means "not" and *domitare*, which means "to tame."

inevitable: (in-EV-uh-tuh-bul) *adj.* Sure to happen; not able to be prevented.

infamous: (IN-fuh-mus) *adj.* Well known in a negative way; notorious.

inferior status: (in-FEER-ee-ur STAT-us) *n.* Lower in rank; less important.

innovation: (in-uh-VAY-shun) *n.* A new way of doing things; a new process.

instability: (in-stuh-BIL-uh-tee) *n.* Not steady; lacking permanence; likely to change.

integrated: (IN-ti-grayt-id) *adj.* Free and equal association; not segregated or separate.

integrity: (in-TEG-ruh-tee) *n.* Honor; honesty.

intensive agriculture: (in-TEN-siv AG-ri-kul-chur) *n.* A kind of farming that is very concentrated in an area.

intermediate: (in-tur-MEE-dee-it) *adj.* In the middle; in between.

invasion: (in-VAY-shun) *n.* The act of entering by force.

irreversible: (ir-i-VUR-suh-bul) *adj.* Permanent; unable to be changed.

Islam: (IS-lum) *n.* The religion of Muslims.

isolation: (iy-suh-LAY-shun) *n.* A condition of being set apart from others; not to have any outside influences or contact.

Israelite: (IZ-ree-uh-liyt) *n.* A Hebrew; a member of any of the various groups who descended from Jacob, one of the Hebrew patriarchs.

J

jade: (jayd) *n.* A green stone.

jaguar: (JAG-wohr) *n.* A large wild cat with black-spotted, golden fur.

Jainism: (JIY-niz-um) *n.* A religion of India that teaches that the soul never dies and that there is no perfect or supreme god.

javelin: (JAV-lun) *n.* A light spear that is used as a weapon.

Jewish: (JOO-ish) *adj.* Relating to people of the Jewish religion; the ancient Hebrews were the ancestors of the Jews.

Judaism: (JOO-dee-iz-um) *n.* The religion of Jews.

judgment: (JUJ-munt) *n.* A reasonable decision based on facts and knowledge.

K

Kadesh: (KUH-desh) *n.* The fortress-like, walled Egyptian city where a great battle was fought between Ramses the Great's army and the Hittites.

L

launch: (lawnch) *v.* To begin; to start.

league: (leeg) *n.* Individuals or groups working together in a common action.

legacy: (LEG-uh-see) *n.* Something handed down or left behind after a person dies.

literally: (LIT-ur-uh-lee) *adv.* Really; actually.

luxury: (LUG-zhuh-ree) *n.* Something extra that is not needed, but makes life more comfortable or pleasant.

M

maize: (mayz) *n.* Corn.

material goods: (muh-TEER-ee-ul goods) *n.* Physical things such as clothing, supplies, dishes, cookware, tools, furniture, and so forth.

maturity: (muh-TYOOR-uh-tee) *n.* Fully grown (or mature); ripeness.

Mayan: (MAH-yun) *n.* The language spoken by the Maya.

merit: (MER-it) *n.* Ability; deserving of reward or praise.

Meroitic: (mer-oh-IT-ik) *n.* The language of the people of Kush.

Mesoamerica: (mez-oh-uh-MER-i-kuh) *n.* The geographical area from present-day central Mexico to northern Costa Rica.

middle-class: (MID-ul klas) *adj.* Not poor, but not rich either.

migrant: (MIY-grunt) *n.* A farm worker who moves from place to place to pick crops.

migrate: (MIY-grayt) *v.* To move from one place or region to another.

migration: (miy-GRAY-shun) *n.* The process of traveling to and settling in a new area.

mine: (myn) *n.* A hole in the earth where people dig out metals, salt, and other minerals.

minority: (muh-NOHR-uh-tee) *n.* A group of persons numbering less than half of the total.

missionary: (MISH-uh-ner-ee) *n.* Someone sent to another country to do religious work.

mock: (mok) *v.* To make fun of; ridicule; to treat with scorn.

moderate: (MAHD-uhr-it) *adj.* About in the middle; not too hot or cold; temperate.

moderation: (mahd-uh-RAY-shun) *n.* Avoiding extremes

modern: (MAHD-urn) *adj.* Having to do with the present time; recent or current time.

monarchy: (MAHN-ahrk-ee) *n.* Rule by one person—a king, queen, or other monarch.

moral: (MOHR-ul) *adj.* Designed to teach good and evil in terms of human behavior.

mourn: (mohrn) *v.* To feel sadness.

mud brick: (mud brik) *n.* A brick made out of mud and dried in the hot sun.

mystery: (MIS-tur-ee) *n.* Something that is unexplained, secret, or unknown.

mystical: (MIS-ti-kul) *adj.* Having spiritual meaning or symbolism.

myth: (mith) *n.* A traditional, ancient story that deals with supernatural beings, ancestors, or heroes that serves as a way for people to explain the world.

mythology: (mi-THAWL-uh-jee) *n.* A collection of myths.

N

natural disaster: (NACH-ur-ul di-ZAS-tur) *n.* Widespread destruction not caused by humans.

naval: (NAY-vul) *adj.* Relating to ships or shipping.

negotiate: (ni-GOH-see-ayt) *v.* To trade one thing for another.

network: (NET-wurk) *n.* Anything that looks like or functions like a net; a group of systems that is connected.

noble: (NOH-bul) *n.* A member of the highest rank in a society; nobles were usually wealthy landowners.

notorious: (noh-TOHR-ee-us) *adj.* Dishonorable; well known, but for evil rather than good.

O

oasis: (oh-AY-sis) *n.* A fertile area in the desert where underground water rises and travelers can get water and shade.

obelisk: (AHB-uh-lisk) *n.* A tall, slim stone pillar with a pyramid on the top.

opinion: (uh-PIN-yun) *n.* A belief or position that is not supported by positive knowledge or proof.

opponent: (uh-POH-nunt) *n.* One who goes against another or others in a battle, contest, controversy, or debate.

oration: (aw-RAY-shun) *n.* A formal speech, especially one given on a ceremonial occasion.

oratory: (AWR-uh-tawr-ee) *n.* Public speaking; from the Latin word *orare*, which means "to speak."

ore: (ohr) *n.* A mineral or group of minerals from which a valuable element, such as metal, can be taken out.

origin: (AWR-uh-jin) *n.* Beginning.

overlap: (oh-vur-LAP) *v.* To extend over and cover part of; to coincide partly.

overstatement: (oh-vur-STAYT-munt) *n.* An exaggeration.

P

paleontology: (pay-lee-awn-TAWL-uh-jee) *n.* The study of life forms from the past, especially prehistoric life forms, through the study of fossils.

paradise: (PAYR-uh-diys) *n.* Any place of ideal loveliness and plenty.

parallel: (PAYR-uh-lul) *adj.* Located side by side; areas that do not cross.

paralyzed: (PAYR-ul-izd) *adj.* Unable to move.

penalty: (PEN-ul-tee) *n.* Punishment for a crime.

perjury: (PUR-juh-ree) *n.* The act of lying under oath, usually in a court of law.

persecute: (PUR-suh-kyoot) *v.* To treat badly and unfairly.

perseverance: (pur-si-VIR-uns) *n.* Resolve; determination.

pessimistic: (pes-suh-MIS-tik) *adj.* Filled with negative thoughts.

piedmont: (PEED-mahnt) *n.* The area at the bottom of a mountain or highlands.

pillar: (PIL-ur) *n.* A column.

pioneer: (piy-uh-NEER) *n.* A person who is one of the first to do something or go somewhere; an innovator.

pirate: (PIY-rit) *n.* A person who steals at sea; a robber.

pith helmet: (pith HEL-mit) *n.* A sun hat made from dried pith, which is a substance found in the center of branches, stems, or plants.

plain: (playn) *n.* A large area of flat land.

plaster: (PLAS-tur) *v.* To apply a mixture of clay, sand, and water, usually to a wall.

plateau: (pla-TOH) *n.* A flat, elevated area of land.

plaza: (PLAZ-uh) *n.* A public square or open area.

pledge: (plej) *n.* A promise.

plumage: (PLOO-mij) *n.* A bird's feathers.

policy: (PAHL-i-see) *n.* Course of action.

polis: (POH-lis) *n.* An independent, small city which ruled over the surrounding countryside.

portable: (POHR-tuh-bul) *adj.* Capable of being carried; easily moved or carried.

posture: (POS-chur) *n.* The way a person stands, sits, or walks.

poverty: (PAHV-uhr-tee) *n.* The condition of being poor.

practical: (PRAK-ti-kul) *adj.* Useful.

precious: (PRESH-us) *adj.* Valuable; worth a great deal.

predictable: (pri-DIKT-uh-bul) *adj.* Something that is possible to know in advance.

prejudice: (PREJ-uh-dis) *n.* An opinion, usually unfavorable, formed before the facts are known.

prestige: (pre-STEEJ) *n.* Respect for a person or people resulting from past achievements and reputation.

primary: (PRIY-mer-ee) *adj.* Being first; basic or most important.

primary source: (PRIY-mer-ee sohrs) *n.* Artifacts, fossils; writings or pictures created by people who were involved in or saw the events they described.

principle: (PRIN-suh-pul) *n.* A basic truth, law, or assumption.

private: (PRIY-vit) *adj.* Personal; not available for public use.

profound: (proh-FAWND) *adj.* Very great; significant.

prophecy: (PRAHF-uh-see) *n.* A prediction of something that will happen in the future.

prophet: (PRAHF-it) *n.* A person who is believed to speak for a god or who brings a god's message to people.

prosperity: (prah-SPER-it-ee) *n.* Success; wealth.

protest: (proh-TEST) *v.* To complain or object.

provincial: (pruh-VIN-shul) *n.* Someone who lives in the provinces, which are areas outside the main city.

public: (PUB-lik) *adj.* For the use of everyone.

Punic: (PYOO-nik) *adj.* The Latin word for Phoenician; "Punic" refers to ancient Carthage and its people.

purify: (PYOOR-i-fiy) *v.* To clean; to get rid of impurities.

Q

quarrel: (KWOR-ul) *n.* Argument.

R

race: (rays) *n.* A group of people classified together because they have similar history, nationality, and/or physical characteristics.

racism: (RAY-sis-um) *n.* Feelings or actions of hatred toward a person or persons because of their race.

radiocarbon dating: (ray-dee-oh-KAHR-bun DAYT-ing) *n.* A scientific way to date plants and animals.

rage: (rayj) *n.* Intense anger.

rank: (rank) *n.* A group (of soldiers).

rapid: (RAP-id) *adj.* Very fast.

raw material: (raw muh-TEER-ee-ul) *n.* A resource from which something else can be made.

rebellion: (ri-BEL-yun) *n.* An organized attempt to openly resist authority; an uprising.

reign: (rayn) *n.* Rule.

reincarnation: (ri-in-kar-NAY-shun) *n.* The idea that a person's soul is reborn in another body—either animal or human.

reject: (ri-JEKT) *v.* To refuse to accept.

rejoice: (ri-JOIS) *v.* To feel happiness.

reliable: (ri-LIY-uh-bul) *adj.* Trustworthy.

relief: (ri-LEEF) *n.* Artwork that is created by projecting figures of forms from a flat surface.

remarkable: (ree-MAHRK-uh-bul) *adj.* Worthy of notice; amazing.

remiss: (ri-MISS) *adj.* Not pay attention to one's duty; negligent.

repent: (ri-PENT) *v.* To feel regret for past actions or wrongdoing.

restrain: (re-STRAYN) *v.* To hold back; contain.

retain: (ri-TAYN) *v.* To keep.

retreating: (ri-TREET-ing) *adj.* Going backward or withdrawing.

revered: (ri-VEERD) *adj.* Very highly thought of.

revolt: (ri-VOHLT) *n.* Rebellion; strong protest.

revolution: (rev-uh-LOO-shun) *n.* Any complete change of a system of government or other method or condition.

rhetoric: (RET-ur-ik) *n.* The ability to speak and/or write well in order to persuade others.

ridicule: (RID-uh-kyool) *v.* To laugh at; to mock.

ritual: (RICH-oo-ul) *n.* A ceremony that takes place the same way every time.

rival: (RIY-vul) *n.* A person who tries to equal or pass another person.

rivalry: (RIY-vul-ree) *n.* A competition.

river basin: (RIV-ur BAY-sin) *n.* An area of land that contains a river and all the streams that flow into it.

Roman Empire: (ROH-mun em-PIYR) *n.* The time in ancient Roman history after the Roman Republic when Roman emperors governed and controlled Rome and territory throughout the Mediterranean region (31 B.C. – A.D. 476).

Roman Republic: (ROH-mun ri-PUB-lik) *n.* The time in ancient Roman history when people elected leaders to govern (509 – 31 B.C.).

rotate: (roh-TAYT) *v.* To turn around on an axis or center.

rugged: (RUG-id) *adj.* Having a rough, irregular surface.

rumor: (ROO-mur) *n.* A story or piece of gossip that may or may not be true.

S

sacrifice: (SAK-ruh-fiys) *v.* To kill or give up for a higher purpose.

sarcophagus: (sar-KOF-uh-gus) *n.* A container (or coffin) carved or decorated with sculpture in which a dead body is placed.

satisfy: (SAT-is-fiy) *v.* To meet a need or expectation; to keep happy.

scandal: (SKAN-dul) *n.* A situation that brings disgrace or is considered shameful by a community.

school of thought: (SKOOL uv thawt) *n.* A group of people whose ideas have a common influence or unifying belief.

sculpture: (SKULP-chur) *n.* A figure or design that is carved in wood, chiseled out of stone, made out of clay, or cast in metal.

seaport: (SEE-pohrt) *n.* A harbor or town that has facilities for seagoing ships.

season: (SEE-zun) *n.* One of the four natural divisions of the year—spring, summer, fall, winter.

secondary source: (SEK-un-der-ee sohrs) *n.* Writings or pictures created later by people who were not involved in or who did not see the events they described.

sect: (sekt) *n.* a group of people forming a distinct unit or group within a larger group.

segregation: (seg-ruh-GAY-shun) *n.* Being set apart from the main group.

Semite: (SEM-iyt) *n.* One of the groups of people who lived in the eastern Mediterranean area; Semitic peoples include Jews and Arabs, and in ancient times, Babylonians, Assyrians, Phoenicians, and others.

Semitic: (suh-MIT-ik) *adj.* Refers to the language of nomadic groups of people, including the Hebrews, who traveled across the deserts of Mesopotamia.

senator: (SEN-uh-tur) *n.* A man who made laws and helped govern ancient Rome.

shepherd: (SHEP-urd) *n.* A person who takes care of and watches over a flock of sheep.

shirk: (shirk) *v.* To avoid or stay away from.

shrine: (shriyn) *n.* An altar, chapel, or other place where people express their religious beliefs.

Silk Road: (silk rohd) *n.* A land route that connected China with Europe.

silt: (silt) *n.* Fine dirt left behind by running water; typically rich in minerals necessary for farming.

slain: (slayn) *adj.* Killed.

smelt: (smelt) *v.* To use very high heat to combine different metals to make even stronger metals; many early civilizations smelted copper and tin to make bronze.

sole: (sohl) *adj.* The only one.

sovereign: (SAHV-ur-un) *n.* A king or queen; the ruler of an empire or country.

spectacular: (spek-TAK-yuh-lur) *adj.* Amazing, fantastic, dramatic.

squash: (skwahsh) *n.* A fleshy vegetable with a hard skin.

stable: (STAY-bul) *adj.* Not likely to fall apart or be thrown off balance.

stammer: (STAM-ur) *v.* To speak with pauses and repetitions.

standard: (STAN-durd) *n.* An agreed-upon measure of comparison.

standardize: (STAN-dur-diz) *v.* To make, cause, or adapt to fit a commonly used and accepted authority; to cause to be the same.

startled: (STAR-tuld) *adj.* Frightened.

steppe: (step) *n.* A plain with few or no trees.

stereotype: (STAYR-ee-uh-typ) *n.* A person, group, event, or issue considered to be typical; lacking any individuality.

strait: (strayt) *n.* A narrow channel joining two larger bodies of water.

stratigraphy: (struh-TIG-ruh-fee) *n.* The study of layers of material in the earth, especially their distribution and age.

strike: (stryk) *v.* To stop working as a group to get better pay and working conditions.

sturdy: (STUR-dee) *adj.* Strong.

submit: (sub-MIT) *v.* To give in; surrender.

summon: (SUM-un) *v.* To send for.

supremacy: (suh-PREM-uh-see) *n.* Having the greatest power.

surrender: (suh-REN-dur) *v.* To give up.

suspicious: (suh-SPISH-us) *adj.* Thinking that something is wrong, even though there is no proof.

T

technology: (tek-NAHL-oh-jee) *n.* The application of science for practical uses.

tectonic: (tek-TAHN-ik) *adj.* Having to do with a large piece of the earth's crust.

tend: (tend) *v.* To take care of or serve the needs of.

tension: (TEN-shun) *n.* A strained (tense) or barely controlled dislike between people or groups.

terrain: (TUH-rayn) *n.* The physical geography of an area or region; the characteristics of land (such as rocky, hilly, flat, mountainous).

theology: (thee-AWL-uh-jee) *n.* The study of religion.

theory: (THEER-ee) *n.* A set of assumptions or rules to explain something.

threat: (thret) *n.* Something or someone thought to be a possible danger.

thwart: (thwohrt) *v.* To prevent from taking place.

torch: (tohrch) *n.* A light that is produced by a burning flame.

transform: (trans-FOHRM) *v.* To make a great change in the appearance or character of something.

transition: (tran-ZISH-un) *n.* Changing from one form, state, activity, place, or time to another.

treaty: (TREE-tee) *n.* An agreement or settlement.

trench: (trench) *n.* A long, deep hole dug in the ground, usually with steep vertical sides.

tributary: (TRIB-yuh-tayr-ee) *n.* A small river (or stream) that flows into a larger river.

tribute: (TRIB-yoot) *n.* Gifts or payments to show loyalty, respect, or gratitude.

triumph: (TRIY-umpf) *v.* To be victorious; to win.

turbulent: (TUR-byuh-lent) *adj.* Chaotic; unstable; confused.

twin: (twin) *n.* Describing one of two persons or things that are very much alike.

tyrant: (TIY-runt) *n.* A ruler who governs without constitutional or other restrictions; the word *tyrant* has come to mean "a ruler who uses power in a harsh, cruel way."

U

underworld: (uhn-duhr-WURLD) *n.* According to Greek and Roman mythology, the world of the dead.

unembittered: (uhn-em-BIT-urd) *adj.* Not bitter or angry; accepting.

unequal: (uhn-EE-kwel) *adj.* Not the same as another in social position.

unexamined: (uhn-ig-ZAM-ind) *adj.* Not looking at or analyzing; lacking self-reflection.

union: (YOON-yun) *n.* An organization of workers.

unique: (YOO-neek) *adj.* Being the only one of its kind.

upper hand: (UP-ur hand) *n.* A position of control or advantage.

V

victorious: (vik-TOHR-ee-us) *adj.* Winning.

vigor: (VIG-ur) *n.* Energy, power, strength; from the Latin word *vigere*, which means "to be lively."

villa: (VIL-uh) *n.* A Roman country house, usually quite large.

violate: (VIY-uh-layt) *v.* To fail to keep; to break (a law or regulation, for example).

virtuous: (VUR-choo-us) *adj.* Having good moral character; being modest and pure.

W

weep: (weep) *v.* To cry.

welfare: (WEL-fayr) *n.* Benefit; happiness; well-being.

Western civilization: (WES-turn siv-uh-luh-ZAY-shun) *n.* Having to do with the culture and beliefs of people in Europe and areas settled by Europeans.

witness: (WIT-nus) *n.* A person who has seen or heard something.

wrath: (rath) *n.* Intense anger.

Z

zealot: (ZEL-ut) *n.* A person who is fanatically committed to something; a Zealot was a member of a Jewish group that resisted Roman rule.

Vowel Pronunciation Key

Symbol	Key Words
a	ant, man
ay	cake, May
ah	clock, arm
aw	salt, ball
e	neck, hair
ee	ear, key
i	chick, skin
iy	five, tiger
oh	coat, soda
oi	boy, coin
ohr	board, door
oo	blue, boot
ow	cow, owl
u	foot, wolf, bird, and the schwa sound used in final syllables followed by 'l,' 'r,' 's,' 'm,' 't,' or 'n,' for example, children (CHIL-drun)
uh	bug, uncle, and other schwa sounds, such as kangaroo (kang-guh-ROO)

Source: The vowel pronunciation key is derived from the American Heritage Dictionary of the English Language, 1981; Oxford American Dictionary: Heald Colleges Edition, 1982; and Webster's New World College Dictionary, Third Edition, 1990. Please note that the surrounding letters may affect the vowel sound slightly.

INDEX

Some entries include the Latin word passim, *which means "here and there and everywhere." This word indicates that the entry occurs frequently in the text.*

PHOTOGRAPHY AND ILLUSTRATION CREDITS
(t=top, b=bottom, c=center, l=left, r=right)

TEXT CREDITS

Simon and Schuster, 1981; from "Tim White: Conversations with History," Institute of International Studies, UC Berkeley, September 18, 2003, http://globetrotter.berkeley.edu/people3/White/white-con1.html. **1.5** From *The Atlas of World Archaeology*, edited by Paul G. Bahn, New York: Checkmark Books, 2000. **1.6** From *Dawn of Art: The Chauvet Cave: The Oldest Known Paintings in the World*, by Jean-Marie Chauvet, Eliette Brunel Deschamps, and Christian Hillaire, New York: Harry N. Abrams, 1996. **1.9** From *Gardner's Art through the Ages* (11th ed.), Vol. 1, by Fred S. Kleiner, Christin J. Mamiya, and Richard G. Tansey, Thomson Learning, 2001.

2.2 From the Code of Hammurabi, *Ancient Near Eastern Texts Relating to the Old Testament* (2nd ed.), edited by James Bennett Pritchard, Princeton: Princeton University Press, 1955. **2.3A** From "Table of the Phoenician Alphabet," http://phoenicia.org/tblalpha.html, 2005. **2.3B** From *Ancient Records of Assyria and Babylon*, by Daniel David Luckenbill, New York: Greenwood Press, 1968. **2.6** From Tablet VIII, the *Epic of Gilgamesh*, Baltimore: Penguin Books, 1965. **2.9** From *The Great Pyramid*, by Elizabeth Mann, New York: Mikaya Press, 1996. **2.10** From *The Oxford History of Ancient Egypt*, by Ian Shaw, Oxford: Oxford University Press, 2000. **2.14** From *Ancient Near Eastern Texts Relating to the Old Testament* (2nd ed.), edited by James Bennett Pritchard, Princeton, NJ: Princeton University Press, 1955. **2.15** From *The Ancient Egyptians: Life in the Nile Valley*, by Vivane Koenig and Veronique Ageorges, Brookfield, CT: Millbrook Press, 1992; from *Hatshepsut and Ancient Egypt*, by Miriam Greenblatt, Tarrytown, NY: Benchmark Books, 2000. **2.16** From *The Great Pyramid*, by Elizabeth Mann, New York: Mikaya Press, 1996; from "The Art of Ancient Egypt: A Web Resource," The Metropolitan Museum of Art, http://www.metmuseum.org/explore/newegypt/htm/a_index.htm, 2005. **2.17** From *The Egyptians* (3rd ed.), by Cyril Aldred, revised by Aidan Dodson, London: Thames & Hudson,

1998. **2.18** From *African Kingdoms of the Past: Egypt, Kush, Aksum*, by Kenny Mann, Parsippany, NJ: Dillon Press, 1997. **2.19** From *African Kingdoms of the Past: Egypt, Kush, Aksum*, by Kenny Mann, Parsippany, NJ: Dillon Press, 1997; from "The Meroitic Alphabet," Images from the Tune Collection, http://iac.cgu.edu//tunemeroitic.html, 2005.

3.7 From *The Penguin Encyclopedia of Ancient Civilizations*, edited by Arthur Cotterell, New York: Penguin Books, 1980; from *The Edicts of King Ashoka*, by Ven. S. Dhammika, Berkeley, CA: The Wheel Publication No. 386/387, 1994. **3.9** From *The Wonder That Was India* (3rd revised ed.), by A.L. Basham, New York: Taplinger Publishing Company, 1967; from *The Wonder That Was India*, by A.L. Basham, London: Sidgwick and Jackson, 1954.

4.1 From *Chronicle of the Chinese Emperors*, by Ann Paludan, London: Thames & Hudson, 1998; from *The Yellow River: A 5000 Year Journey through China*, by Kevin Sinclair, Los Angeles: The Knapp Press, 1987. **4.4** From *Confucian Analects*, translated by Ezra Pound, Bournemouth, England: Boscome Printing Co., 1933. **4.5** From *Dao De Jing: The Book of the Way*, translated by Moss Roberts, Berkeley, CA: University of California Press, 2001. **4.6** From *Chronicle of the Chinese Emperors*, by Ann Paludan, London: Thames & Hudson, 1998. **4.7** From *Chronicle of the Chinese Emperors*, by Ann Paludan, London: Thames & Hudson, 1998. **4.9** From *The Cambridge History of China*, Vol. 1, edited by Denis Twitchett and Michael Loewe, Cambridge: Cambridge University Press, 1986; from *A Brief History of Chinese and Japanese Civilizations* (2nd ed.), by Conrad Schirokauer, New York: Harcourt Brace Jovanovich, 1989. **4.10** From *Worlds of Bronze and Bamboo: Sima Qian's Conquest of History*, by Grant Hardy, New York: Columbia University Press, 1984.

5.1 From the *Holy Bible* (New International Version), Grand Rapids, MI: Zondervan, 1984. **5.2** From the *Holy Bible* (New International Version), Grand Rapids, MI:

Zondervan, 1984. **5.3** From the *Holy Bible* (New International Version), Grand Rapids, MI: Zondervan, 1984. **5.5** From *The Annals & The Histories*, by Cornelius Tacitus, edited by Moses Hadas, New York: Modern Library, 2003. **5.7** From *Aesop's Fables*, by Aesop, translated by George Fyler Townsend, Garden City, NY: Doubleday, 1968. **5.9** From *Iliad*, by Homer, translated by Richmond Lattimore, Chicago: University of Chicago Press, 1951. **5.11** From *Western Civilization: A Social and Cultural History (Vol. 1: Prehistory-1750)*, by Margaret L. King, Upper Saddle River, NJ: Prentice Hall, 2000. **5.12** From *Greek Lyrics* (2nd ed.), edited and translated by Richmond Lattimore, Chicago: University of Chicago Press, 1960; from *Western Civilization: A Social and Cultural History (Vol. 1: Prehistory-1750)*, by Margaret L. King, Upper Saddle River, NJ: Prentice Hall, 2000. **5.14** From *Persia and the Greeks: The Defense of the West, c. 546-478 B.C.* (2nd ed.), by Andrew Robert Burn, Stanford, CA: Stanford University Press, 1984; from *Persians*, by Aeschylus, edited by D. Grene and R. Lattimore, translated by S.G. Benardete, 1992; from *Civilization in the West* (4th ed.), Vol. 1, by Mark Kishlansky, Patrick Geary, and Patricia O'Brien, Addison-Wesley Educational Publishers, 2001; from *Western Civilization: A Social and Cultural History*, Vol. 1, by Margaret L. King, Upper Saddle River, NJ: Prentice Hall, 2000. **5.15** From *The Histories*, reprint edition, by Herodotus, translated by George Rawlinson, London: J.M. Dent, 1992. **5.16** From *Peloponnesian War*, by Thucydides, edited by Rex Warner, Baltimore, MD: Penguin Books, 1954. **5.18** From *Nicomachean Ethics*, by Aristotle, translated by Martin Ostwald, New York: Prentice Hall, 1962. **5.19** From *Plutarch's Lives*, translated by John Dryden and revised by Arthur Hugh Clough, New York: Modern Library, 1992. **5.20** From *Greek Religion*, by Walter Burkert, translated by John Raffan, Cambridge, MA: Harvard University Press, 1985; from *Combat Sports in the Ancient World: Competition, Violence, and Culture*, by Michael B. Poliakoff, New Haven, CT: Yale University Press, 1987. **5.25** From *Incidents of Travel in Central America, Chiapas, and Yucatan*, by John L. Stephens, New York: Harper, reprinted by Dover, 1962. **5.28** From *The Maya* (5th ed.), by Michael D. Coe, New York: Thames & Hudson, 1993. **5.31** From *Popul Vuh*, translated by Ralph Nelson, Boston: Houghton Mifflin, 1976.

6.2 From *A History of Western Society*, Vol. 1, by John P. McKay, Bennett D. Hill, and John Buckler, Boston: Houghton Mifflin, 1995. **6.3** From *The Rapes of Lucretia: A Myth and Its Transformations*, by Ian Donaldson, Oxford: Clarendon Press, 1982; from *Livy*, translated by B.O. Foster, New York: Heinemann, 1976; from *The Oxford Classical Dictionary* (3rd ed.), edited by Simon Hornblower and Antony Spawforth, New York: Oxford University Press, 1996; from *Goddesses, Whores, Wives, and Slaves: Women in Classical Antiquity*, by Sarah B. Pomeroy, New York: Schocken Books, 1975. **6.4** From *The History of Rome*, by Livy, translated by Aubrey de Selincourt, New York: Penguin Classics, 1991. **6.5** From the Law of the Twelve Tables, *Roman Civilization*, Vol. 1, by Naphtali Lewis and Meyer Reinhold, New York: Columbia University Press, 1951. **6.6** From *The Rise of the Roman Empire*, by Polybius, translated by Ian Scott-Kilvert, Harmondsworth, NY: Penguin, 1979. **6.8** From *Plutarch's Lives*, translated by John Dryden and revised by Arthur Hugh Clough, New York: Modern Library, 1979. **6.9** From *Plutarch's Lives*, translated by John Dryden and revised by Arthur Hugh Clough, New York: Modern Library, 1979. **6.10** From *Plutarch's Lives*, translated by John Dryden and revised by Arthur Hugh Clough, New York: Modern Library, 1979. **6.11** From *Plutarch's Lives*, translated by John Dryden and revised by Arthur Hugh Clough, New York: Modern Library, 1979. **6.12** From *Selected Works*, by Cicero, translated by Michael Grant, New York: Viking Press, 1960. **6.13** From *Horace The Complete Odes and Epodes*, translated by David West, Cambridge: Cambridge University Press, 2000; from *Plutarch's Lives*, translated by John Dryden and revised by Arthur Hugh Clough, New York: Modern Library, 1979; from *The Twelve*

Caesars, by Gaius Suetonius Tranquillus, translated by Robert Graves, Baltimore, MD: Penguin Books, 1957. **6.14** From *The Aeneid*, by Virgil, translated by David West, New York: Penguin Books, 1990. **6.16** From *The Complete Odes and Epodes*, by Horace, translated by David West, Oxford: Oxford University Press, 2000; from *The Aeneid*, by Virgil, translated by David West, New York: Penguin Classics, 1990; from *Metamorphoses*, by Ovid, translated by A.D. Melville, Oxford: Oxford University Press, 1998. **6.17** From *Roman History from Coins*, by Michael Grant, Cambridge: Cambridge University Press, 1958. **6.19** From *Merriam-Webster's Collegiate Dictionary* (10th ed.), Springfield, MA: Merriam-Webster, 2002; from *Cassell's Latin Dictionary*, edited by D.P. Simpson, New York: Cassell's, 1977; from *A Dictionary of Latin Words and Phrases*, edited by James Morwood, Oxford: Oxford University Press, 1998; from *Latin Phrases & Quotations* (revised ed.), by Richard A. Branyon, New York: Hippocrene Books, 1997; from *Veni, Vidi, Vici: Conquer Your Enemies, Impress Your Friends with Everyday Latin*, by Eugene Ehrlich, New York: HarperPerennial, 1995. **6.20** From *The Twelve Caesars*, by Gaius Suetonius Tranquillus, translated by Robert Graves, Baltimore, MD: Penguin Books, 1957. **6.22** From *Daily Life in Ancient Rome*, by Florence Dupont, Oxford: Blackwell Publishers, 1989. **6.23** From *Roman Civilization: The Republic and the Augustan Age, Selected Readings* (3rd ed.), Vol. 1, by Naphtali Lewis and Meyer Reinhold, New York: Columbia University Press, 1990; from *Daily Life in Ancient Rome*, by Florence Dupont, Oxford: Blackwell Publishers, 1989. **6.24** From *Roman Civilization: The Republic and the Augustan Age, Selected Readings* (3rd ed.), Vol. 1, by Naphtali Lewis and Meyer Reinhold, New York: Columbia University Press, 1990; from *Daily Life in Ancient Rome*, by Florence Dupont, Oxford: Blackwell Publishers, 1989; from *Livy*, translated by B.O. Foster, New York: Heinemann, 1976. **6.25** From the *Holy Bible* (New International Version), Grand Rapids, MI: Zondervan, 1984. **6.26** From the *Holy Bible* (New International Version), Grand Rapids, MI: Zondervan, 1984. **6.27** From the *Holy Bible* (New International Version), Grand Rapids, MI: Zondervan, 1984.
6.29 From *A History of Western Society*, Vol.1, by John P. McKay, Bennett D. Hill, and John Buckler, Boston: Houghton Mifflin, 1995.
6.30 From *Nero: The End of a Dynasty*, by Miriam Griffin, New Haven, CT: Yale University Press, 1985. **6.31** From *The Annals of Imperial Rome*, by Tacitus, translated by Alfred John Church and William Jackson Brodribb, The Franklin Library, 1982. **6.32** From *Meditations*, by Marcus Aurelius, translated by Maxwell Staniforth, New York: Penguin Books, 1964. **6.33** From *A History of Western Society*, Vol. 1, by John P. McKay, Bennett D. Hill, and John Buckler, Boston: Houghton Mifflin, 1995; from *Readings in European History*, edited by James Harvey Robinson, Boston: Ginn & Co., 1904; from *History of the Wars*, by Procopius, translated by H.B. Dewing, Harvard University Press & Wm. Heinemann, 1914, reprint ed., 1953-54.
6.35 From *Martin & Malcolm & America: A Dream or a Nightmare*, by James Cone, Maryknoll, NY: Orbis Books, 1991; from "I Have a Dream," a speech by Dr. Martin Luther King, Jr. in Washington, D.C., August 28, 1963, http://www.Nobelprize.org, 2005.
6.36 From *Cesar Chavez*, by Susan Zannos, Childs, MD: Mitchell Lane Publishers, Inc., 1999.

ACKNOWLEDGMENTS

We are thankful to many individuals who helped us realize our vision for this book. We owe a debt of gratitude especially to Rebecca Ratnam, editor, who guided our efforts and to Dr. Cheryl Riggs, who served as historical editor. We also want to express our appreciation to Philip Malcolm, graphic designer, and to the editorial team, including Kristin Belsher, Linda Mammano, Nina Chun, Cathy Sanchez, Danielle Arreola, and Ronaldo Benaraw. Our most heartfelt thanks are reserved for Patrice Gotsch for sharing her creativity, intelligence, hard work, and dedication. We hope our combined efforts have created an enjoyable, readable, and interesting educational resource for students.

Gregory Blanch & Roberta Stathis